The Changing Arctic and the European Union

# Nijhoff Law Specials

VOLUME 89

The titles published in this series are listed at *brill.com/nlsp*

# The Changing Arctic and the European Union

*A Book Based on the Report "Strategic Assessment of Development of the Arctic: Assessment Conducted for the European Union"*

*Edited by*

Adam Stępień
Timo Koivurova
Paula Kankaanpää

BRILL
NIJHOFF

LEIDEN | BOSTON

Cover illustration: A New and Accurate Map of the North Pole: E. Bowen, A Complete Atlas, or Distinct View of the Known World. London 1752. Collection of the Arctic Centre, University of Lapland, Finland.

This publication has been typeset in the multilingual "Brill" typeface. With over 5,100 characters covering Latin, IPA, Greek, and Cyrillic, this typeface is especially suitable for use in the humanities.
For more information, please see www.brill.com/brill-typeface.

ISSN 0924–4549
ISBN 978-90-04-30317-1 (paperback)
ISBN 978-90-04-30318-8 (e-book)



This book is printed on acid-free paper.

# Contents

# Editorial

The book is based on the reports prepared within the project "Strategic Environmental Impact Assessment of Development of the Arctic", a Preparatory Action funded by the European Commission, DG Environment (Service contract 191 105/2012/637465/SER/El):

- Stępień, Adam, Timo Koivurova and Paula Kankaanpää (Eds.) (2014). Strategic Assessment of Development of the Arctic: Assessment Conducted for the European Union, Preparatory Action, Strategic Environmental Impact Assessment of development of the Arctic. Arctic Centre, University of Lapland.
- Dahlbäck, Björn, Lize-Marié van der Watt, Kamil Jagodziński and Paula Kankaanpää (2014). European Arctic Initiatives Compendium. Preparatory Action, Strategic Environmental Impact Assessment of development of the Arctic. Arctic Centre, University of Lapland.
- Tedsen, Elizabeth, Arne Riedel, Katherine Weingartner, Roberto Azzolini, Frederic Guillon, Simona Longo, Corrado Leone, Outi Paadar, Anastasia Leonenko (2014). Gap Analysis Report. Preparatory Action, Strategic Environmental Impact Assessment of development of the Arctic. Arctic Centre, University of Lapland.
- Kankaanpää, Paula and Smieszek, Malgorzata (Eds.) (2014). Assessments in Policy-Making: Case Studies from the Arctic Council. Preparatory Action, Strategic Environmental Impact Assessment of development of the Arctic. Arctic Centre, University of Lapland.



The contents of the book as well as that of the reports on which it is based do not reflect the official opinion of the European Union. Responsibility for the information and views expressed therein lies entirely with the authors.

The network implementing the project: Arctic Centre, University of Lapland, Finland; Alfred Wegener Institute, Helmholtz Centre for Polar and Marine Research, Germany; Arctic Centre, University of Groningen, the Netherlands; Arctic Portal, Iceland; Committee on Polar Research, Polish Academy of Sciences; Ecologic Institute, Berlin – Washington, DC; Ecorys, the Netherlands; European Polar Board and European Science Foundation; Finnish Meteorological Institute; Fram Centre, Norway; GRID-Arendal, Norway; International Polar Foundation;

National Research Council of Italy; Pierre and Marie Curie University, France; Sámi Education Institute, Finland; Scott Polar Research Institute, University of Cambridge, United Kingdom; Swedish Polar Research Secretariat; Tromsø Centre for Remote Sensing, UiT The Arctic University of Norway; University of the Arctic Thematic Networks: Thule Institute of the University of Oulu, Finland.

All project partners participated in the production of original reports, but the opinions and statements in this book are those of the authors.

ARCTIC CENTRE

European Commission

ARCTIC

Strategic Environmental Impact
Assessment of development of the Arctic

Language editors: Zoë Chandler (Inkling Oy), Debra Justus, Maija Myllylä (Waria)

# Preface

This book constitutes an updated and expanded version of the report *Strategic Assessment of Development of the Arctic: An assessment conducted for the European Union* (SADA). The SADA is the final report of an assessment conducted within the "Strategic Environmental Impact Assessment of Development of the Arctic" project,[1] financed by the European Commission Directorate-General for the Environment, and carried out by a network of 19 leading Arctic universities, research and communication centres with extensive activities in and knowledge of the Arctic. The project was led by the Arctic Centre of the University of Lapland and tested the initiative of establishing the EU Arctic Information Centre.[2] The whole project network participated in the assessment process, drafting of the reports, and thus, contributed to the production of this book; however, the text should not be understood as a common statement endorsed by all institutions within the network. The responsibility for the publication and its content lies solely with the book authors and the opinions expressed therein do not reflect the official position of the European Commission nor that of other EU institutions.

The primary objective of the "Strategic Environmental Impact Assessment" project was to increase the awareness about the Arctic and its changing political, economic and environmental landscape, as well as to comprehend the influence of EU policies on the future of the Arctic region by participating in dialogues and information exchange between the EU and civil society. This was implemented by using assessment as a tool to put together information for the needs of decision-makers and for the benefit of a wider public. As a result, this work is a content-rich snapshot of the development of the Arctic, and at the same time an example how assessment methodologies can be used to better understand the changes occurring in the region.

The assessment process started in April 2013 with the design of methodology and selection of themes to be examined. Project partner experts produced thematic factsheets. These served as background papers for the consultation process that included thematic workshops and an online questionnaire. Stakeholders had a chance to comment on the draft report and their feedback has been implemented in the final stage of the assessment. The content of this publication is therefore a synthesis of stakeholder input and expert analysis.

---

1 See project website at www.arcticinfo.eu.

2 See the website of the Arctic Centre at http://www.arcticcentre.org/EN/ABOUT-US/EU-Arctic-Information-Centre. Accessed 20 February 2015.

The proposed ideas for the enhancement of EU Arctic policy have been developed on the basis of stakeholder input, although they should not be seen as a direct outcome of stakeholder consultations. The original report was finalised in May 2014.

For this publication, the updated text of the SADA report has been expanded by chapters summarizing findings of three other reports that constituted the project results: *European Arctic Initiatives Compendium*, *Gap Analysis Report* and *Assessments in Policy-making: Case Studies from the Arctic Council*.[3] The process leading to production of these reports was conducted between April 2013 and June 2015. These contributions complement the discussion in the thematic chapters and are a rich source of information for all interested in the European contribution to Arctic affairs and the role of assessments as tools in policy-making.

The book could be of use particularly to those less familiar with Arctic affairs and willing to broaden their understanding of the changes in the region or the role the European Union plays in shaping these developments. The consecutive chapters deliver a balanced and up-to-date overview of a broad spectrum of Arctic issues. Therefore, the publication may prove useful also for students or journalists.

The authors and the whole project network would like to express their utmost gratitude primarily to all those who participated in stakeholder workshops and in the online questionnaire. Their participation and contribution at various stages of the process was an indispensable element of the assessment. The authors are also grateful for the contribution provided by numerous researchers and experts, who are acknowledged in the respective chapters. We also express our gratitude to Filip Holiencin for his help with compiling the index. Last but certainly not least, gratitude is offered to the European Commission and particularly the staff of the DG Environment for their continued support to the work of the project team.

*Adam Stępień, Timo Koivurova and Paula Kankaanpää*

3 All original reports can be found at the project website www.arcticinfo.eu.

# List of Figures, Tables, Pictures and Textboxes

## Figures

## Tables



## Pictures

## Textboxes

# List of Acronyms

| | |
|---|---|
| AAC | Arctic Athabaskan Council |
| AACA | Adaptation Actions for a Changing Arctic |
| ABA | Arctic Biodiversity Assessment |
| AC | Arctic Council |
| ACCESS | Arctic Climate Change, Economy and Society (project) |
| ACIA | Arctic Climate Impact Assessment |
| AEC | Arctic Economic Council |
| AECO | Arctic Expedition Cruise Operators |
| AEPS | Arctic Environmental Protection Strategy |
| AHDR | Arctic Human Development Report |
| AIS | Automatic Identification System |
| AISG | Arctic Inter-Service Group |
| AMAP | Arctic Monitoring and Assessment Programme (AC working group) |
| ANISTIAMO | Addressing New Challenges in Satellite Based Maritime Surveillance and Arctic Monitoring |
| AoA | Assessment of Assessments |
| ARC | Arctic Research Centre |
| ARCTIS | Arctic Resources and Transportation Information System (Norway) |
| Arcum | Arctic Research Centre (Umeå University) |
| ARICE | Arctic Research Icebreaker Consortium for Europe |
| ARR | Arctic Resilience Report |
| ATQ | Autonomous Tariff Quota |
| AWI | Alfred Wegener Institute: Helmholtz Centre for Polar and Marine Research (Germany) |
| BAS | British Antarctic Survey |
| bcm | Billion Cubic Metres |
| BEAC | Barents Euro-Arctic Council |
| boe | Barrels of Oil Equivalent |
| BPAN | Barents Protected Areas Network |
| CAFF | Conservation of Arctic Flora and Fauna (AC working group) |
| CAP | Common Agricultural Policy (EU) |
| CBD | Convention on Biological Diversity |
| CBM | Community-based monitoring |
| CBSS | Council of the Baltic Sea States |
| CFP | Common Fisheries Policy (EU) |
| CHNL | Centre for High North Logistics (Norway) |
| COP | Conference of the Parties |

| | |
|---|---|
| CSR | Corporate Social Responsibility |
| DG | Directorate-General (European Commission or European Parliament) |
| DNV | Det Norske Veritas |
| DPSIR | Driving force–Pressures–State–Impact–Response framework |
| EBRD | European Bank for Reconstruction and Development |
| EC | European Community |
| ECA | Emissions Control Area (MARPOL) |
| ECDS | Environment Climate Data Sweden |
| ECRA | European Climate Research Alliance |
| EEA | European Economic Area |
| EEAgency | European Environment Agency |
| EEAA | European Economic Area Agreement |
| EEAS | European External Action Service |
| EEC | European Economic Community |
| EEZ | Exclusive Economic Zones |
| EFTA | European Free Trade Association |
| EGNOS | European Geostationary Navigation Overlay Service |
| EIA | Environmental Impact Assessment |
| EIB | European Investment Bank |
| EIP | European Innovation Partnership |
| EISCAT | European Incoherent Scatter Scientific Association |
| EMAS | Eco-management and Audit Scheme (EU) |
| EMSA | European Maritime Safety Agency |
| ENP | European Neighbourhood Policy |
| ENPI | European Neighbourhood and Partnership Instrument |
| EO | Earth Observation |
| EP | European Parliament |
| EPPR | Emergency Prevention, Preparedness and Response (AC working group) |
| ERDF | European Regional Development Fund |
| ERIC | European Research Infrastructure Consortium |
| ESA | European Space Agency |
| ETC | European Territorial Co-operation |
| ETS | Emissions Trading System (EU) |
| EU | European Union |
| EUAIC | EU Arctic Information Centre (initiative) |
| FAO | UN Food and Agriculture Organization |
| FMP | Fishery Management Plan |
| FOI | Swedish Defence Research Agency |
| FPIC | Free, Prior and Informed Consent |

| | |
|---|---|
| GAR | Gap Analysis Report |
| GDP | Gross Domestic Product |
| GEA | Global Environmental Assessments |
| GEOSS | Group on Earth Observation System of Systems |
| GHG | Greenhouse-gas |
| GLONASS | Global Navigation Satellite System (Russia) |
| GMES | Global Monitoring for Environment and Security |
| GNSS | Global Navigation Satellite System |
| GPS | Global Positioning System |
| GSA | European *GNSS* Supervisory Authority |
| HRIA | Human Rights Impact Assessment |
| IA | Impact Assessment |
| IACHR | Inter-American Commission on Human Rights |
| IASC | International Arctic Science Committee |
| IASOA | International Arctic Systems for Observing the Atmosphere |
| IASSA | International Arctic Social Science Association |
| ICC | Inuit Circumpolar Council |
| ICES | International Council for the Exploration of the Sea |
| ICOS | Integrated Carbon Observing System |
| ICT | Information and Communication Technology |
| IEA | International Energy Agency |
| IFI | International Financial Institution |
| IGO | Inter-governmental Organization |
| ILO | International Labour Organization |
| ILO169 | 1989 ILO Convention no 169 concerning Indigenous and Tribal Peoples in Independent Countries |
| IMO | International Maritime Organization |
| IMP | Integrated Maritime Policy (EU) |
| INSPIRE | Infrastructure for Spatial Information in Europe Directive |
| INTERREG | Interregional Co-operation Programmes |
| IOC | International Oil Companies |
| IPCC | Intergovernmental Panel on Climate Change |
| IPEV | Polar Institute Paul Emile Victor (France) |
| IPF | International Polar Foundation |
| IRF | Institute of Space Physics (Sweden) |
| IUU | Illegal, Unreported and Unregulated Fisheries/Fishing |
| IWC | International Whaling Commission |
| IWGIA | International Work Group for Indigenous Affairs |
| JRC | Joint Research Centre of the European Commission |
| KISS | Kangerlussuaq International Science Support |

| | |
|---|---|
| KTH | Royal Institute of Technology (Sweden) |
| LKAB | Luossavaara-Kiirunavaara AB |
| LME | Large Marine Ecosystems |
| LNG | Liquefied Natural Gas |
| LOS | Law of the Sea |
| MaReMa | Centre of Marine Resource Management |
| MARPOL | Convention on the Prevention of Pollution from Ships |
| MoU/MOU | Memorandum of Understanding |
| NAMMCO | North Atlantic Marine Mammal Commission |
| NCM | Nordic Council of Ministers |
| ND | Northern Dimension |
| NDBC | Northern Dimension Business Council |
| NDEP | Northern Dimension Partnership on Environment |
| NDI | Northern Dimension Institute |
| NDPC | Northern Dimension Partnership on Culture |
| NDPHS | Northern Dimension Partnership on Public Health and Social Well-being |
| NDPTL | Northern Dimension Partnership on Transport and Logistics |
| NEAFC | North East Atlantic Fisheries Commission |
| NEFCO | Nordic Environment Finance Corporation |
| NEP | Northeast Passage |
| NERC | Natural Environmental Research Council (UK) |
| NGLs | Natural Gas Liquids |
| NGO | Non-governmental Organization |
| NOAA | National Oceanic and Atmospheric Administration (US) |
| NOCs | National Oil Companies |
| NOCS | National Oceanography Centre Southampton (UK) |
| NOFIMA | The Norwegian Institute of Food, Fisheries and Aquaculture Research |
| NordMin | Nordic Network on Mining Expertise |
| Nordregio | Nordic Centre for Spatial Development |
| NPA | Northern Periphery and Arctic Programme 2014–2020 |
| NPFMC | North Pacific Fishery Management Council |
| NPP | Northern Periphery Programme 2007–2013 |
| NSIDC | National Snow and Ice Data Centre |
| NSPA | Northern Sparsely Populated Areas |
| NSR | Northern Sea Route |
| NWP | Northwest Passage |
| OGS | National Institute of Oceanography and Experimental Geophysics (Italy) |
| OSL | Otto Schmidt Laboratory for Polar and Marine Research (Germany) |

| | |
|---|---|
| OSPAR | Convention for the Protection of the Marine Environment of the North-East Atlantic |
| PAME | Protection of Arctic Marine Environment (AC working group) |
| PAN | Protected Area Network |
| PCB | polychlorinated biphenyl |
| PCW | Polar Communication and Weather (Canada) |
| POMOR | Master Program for Polar and Marine Research (Germany) |
| POPS | Persistent Organic Pollutants |
| PSSA | Particularly Sensitive Sea Area |
| PV | Polar View (ESA) |
| REDD+ | Efforts to reduce emissions from deforestation and forest degradation, and foster conservation, sustainable management of forests, and enhancement of forest carbon stocks |
| REE | Rare Earth Elements |
| REFIT | Regulatory Fitness and Performance Programme |
| RFMO | Regional Fisheries Management Organisation |
| ROSCOSMOS | Russian Federal Space Agency |
| SADA | Strategic Assessment of Development of the Arctic |
| SAON | Sustaining Arctic Observing Networks |
| SAR | Search and Rescue |
| SDWG | Sustainable Development Working Group (AC) |
| SEA | Strategic Environmental Assessment |
| SEIS | Shared Environmental Information System |
| SIA | Sustainability Impact Assessment |
| SIOS | Svalbard Integrated Observation System |
| SLCF | Short-Lived Climate Forcers |
| SLE | Sea level equivalent |
| SMHI | Swedish Meteorological and Hydrological Institute |
| SOLAS | Convention on the Safety of Life at Sea |
| STUK | Radiation and Nuclear Safety Authority (Finland) |
| SWD | Staff Working Document (European Commission) |
| SWIPA | Sea, Water, Ice and Permafrost in the Arctic |
| SYKE | Finnish Environment Institute |
| TAC | Total allowable catch |
| TEKES | Finnish Funding Agency for Innovation |
| TEN-T | Trans-European Transport Network |
| TEU | Treaty on the European Union |
| TFEU | Treaty on the Functioning of the European Union |
| UN | United Nations |
| UNCLOS | United Nations Convention on the Law of the Sea |

| | |
|---|---|
| UNDP | United Nations Development Programme |
| UNDRIP | United Nations Declaration of Rights of Indigenous Peoples |
| UNECE LRTAP | United Nations Economic Commission for Europe Convention on Long-Range Transboundary Air Pollution (Stockholm Convention together with POPs Protocol) |
| UNEP | United Nations Environmental Programme |
| UNESCO | United Nations Educational, Scientific and Cultural Organization |
| UNFCCC | United Nations Framework Convention on Climate Change |
| UNIS | University Centre in Svalbard |
| US | United States |
| USC | United Shipbuilding Corporation (Russia) |
| USGS | United States Geological Survey |
| VTT | Technical Research Centre of Finland |
| WFD | Water Framework Directive |
| WMO | World Meteorological Organization |
| WRH | Association of World Reindeer Herders |
| WWF | Worldwide Fund for Nature |

# List of Contributors

## Editors

*Adam Stępień*
Researcher, Arctic Centre, University of Lapland, Po. Box. 122, 96101 Rovaniemi, Finland, +358 404844298, adam.stepien@ulapland.fi

*Timo Koivurova*
Research Professor, Director, Northern Institute for Environmental and Minority Law, Arctic Centre, University of Lapland, Finland, timo.koivurova@ulapland.fi

*Paula Kankaanpää*
Professor, Director, Arctic Centre, University of Lapland, Finland, paula.m.kankaanpaa@ymparisto.fi

## Lead Authors

*Sigmar Arnarsson*
UiT The Arctic University of Norway, sigmar.arnarsson@gmail.com

*Kim van Dam*
Arctic Centre, University of Groningen, the Netherlands, k.i.m.van.dam@rug.nl

*Debra Justus*
LOCEAN, Université Pierre et Marie Curie, Paris, France, justusdebra@hotmail.com

*Kirsi Latola*
Thule Institute, University of Oulu, Finland; University of the Arctic Thematic Networks, kirsi.latola@oulu.fi

*Michał Łuszczuk*
Committee on Polar Research of the Polish Academy of Sciences; Maria Curie-Skłodowska University, Lublin, Poland, mluszczuk@gmail.com

*Arne Riedel*
Ecologic Institute, Berlin – Washington, DC, arne.riedel@ecologic.eu

*Gunnar Sander*
UiT – The Arctic University of Norway and Fram Centre, Norway, gunnar.sander@uit.no

*Annette Scheepstra*
Arctic Centre, University of Groningen, the Netherlands, a.j.m.scheepstra@rug.nl

*Małgorzata Śmieszek*
Arctic Centre, University of Lapland, malgorzata.smieszek@ulapland.fi

*Mikko Strahlendorff*
Finnish Meteorological Institute, mikko.strahlendorff@fmi.fi

## Contributors

*Karolina Banul*
Arctic Centre, University of Lapland, Finland; Barents Institute, UiT Arctic University of Norway

*Björn Dahlbäck*
Swedish Polar Research Secretariat

*Sébastien Duyck*
Arctic Centre, University of Lapland, Finland

*Jean-Claude Gascard*
LOCEAN, Université Pierre et Marie Curie, Paris, France

*Federica Gerber*
Ecorys, the Netherlands

*Johan Gille*
Ecorys, the Netherlands

*Kamil Jagodziński*
Arctic Centre, University of Lapland, Finland

*Mikko Jokinen*
Natural Resource Institute Finland, Economics and Society

*Chris Klok*
IMARES, the Netherlands

*Anastasia Leonenko*
Tromsø Centre for Remote Technologies, UiT The Arctic University of Norway

*Pamela Lesser*
Arctic Centre, University of Lapland, Finland

*Simo Sarkki*
Thule Institute, University of Oulu, Finland

*Marie-Theres von Schickfus*
Ecorys, the Netherlands/Ifo Institute, Ifo Center for Energy, Climate and Exhaustible Resources, Germany

*Elizabeth Tedsen*
Ecologic Institute, Berlin – Washington, DC

*Jennie Thomas*
Sorbonne Universités, UPMC Univ. Paris 06; Université Versailles St-Quentin; CNRS/INSU, LATMOS-IPSL, Paris, France

*Lize-Marié van der Watt*
Swedish Polar Research Secretariat; Arctic Centre at the Umeå University, Sweden

INTRODUCTION

# Understanding Arctic Change through Assessments and Stakeholder Engagement

*Adam Stępień, Paula Kankaanpää and Timo Koivurova**

## Abstract

The introductory chapter opens with a background overview of the change occurring in the Arctic and the international attention to the Arctic regions which is a result of that transformation. The discussion proceeds with the methodology and process of the *Strategic Assessment of Development of the Arctic* report, on which this book is largely based. The assessment analyzed changes in the Arctic, with focus on the European Arctic, identified trends and drivers of changes, as well as considered the presence of the European Union in the region. Particular attention is given to the methodology for stakeholder consultations and the overall role of the stakeholder engagement in the assessment process.

## 1 Introduction

The Arctic environmental, economic and social landscape is complex and diverse. EU institutional and regulatory frameworks are no less complicated and even confusing for many actors from outside of the EU. This book presents the results of over year and a half of work within the project "Strategic Environmental Impact Assessment of Development of the Arctic", implemented by a network of 19 European research and communication institutions and funded by the European Commission. The volume aims to provide a balanced and up-to-date overview of trends and changes occurring in the Arctic, with the focus on the European part of the region. Moreover, it is hoped that – by building and adding to earlier analyses[1] – the book will help the reader to

* The editors own acknowledgment to all members of the EU Arctic Information Centre initiative network (seewww.arcticinfo.eu), who participated in the design of the methodology for the assessment.

1 Cavalieri, S. et al. (Ecologic Institute and others) (2010). EU Arctic Footprint and Policy Assessment Report. European Commission: DG Environment, arcticfootprint.eu. Accessed

 | DOI 10.1163/9789004303188_002

better comprehend the multifaceted role of the EU in the region and to understand the broad array of EU-Arctic interlinkages. The core of this volume comprises contributions constituting updated and slightly expanded chapters of the *Strategic Assessment of Development of the Arctic* report (SADA).

Naturally, all topics and questions could not be addressed. The authors focused on issues currently at the centre of Arctic debate as well as those not well covered in earlier studies. All components of the project were implemented through various modes of stakeholder engagement. This applies in particular to the assessment of development of the Arctic and the analysis of information and knowledge gaps.

The chapter opens with the bird's view at the Arctic transformation. Then, a brief overview of the objective, scope and methodology of the assessment work are given. In addition, a more general discussion on the effectiveness of assessments and their potential as tools for decision-making can be found in the chapter by Śmieszek *et al.* The introduction closes with the presentation of the outline of this book.

## 2 Arctic in the Global Spotlight

Around 2007, notions of climate change doom, the scramble for Arctic resources, potential inter-state conflicts, resource bonanza and new ocean highways had become commonplace in discussion about the Arctic.[2] However, after a few years of the "Arctic boom, Arctic doom"[3] narrative, a more in-depth and balanced understanding of the Arctic reality has started to emerge. Some scholars even refer to a notion of "Arctic bust". This book constitutes a contribution to this shift in discourse about the Arctic, as the discussion gradually focuses on designing realistic responses to concrete challenges. And these are plenty. The changes in sea-ice, terrestrial snow and ice cover, thawing permafrost, and shifts in ecosystems amount to profound transformation of region's landscape. The economic activities, even if

25 January 2015; Koivurova, T., Kokko, K., Duyck, S., Sellheim, N. & Stepien, A. (2010). EU competencies affecting the Arctic, EP/EXPO/B/AFET/FWC/2009-01/LOT2/04, European Parliament, Directorate-General for External Policies of the Union.

2 Koivurova, T. (2011). 'The Actions of the Arctic States Respecting the Continental Shelf: A Reflective Essay' (2011) 42 Ocean Development & Intl L 211.

3 To quote a title of an insightful book by Barry Zellen, see Zellen, B.S. (2009). *Arctic Doom, Arctic Boom: The Geopolitics of Climate Change in the Arctic*, Praeger Security International.

not as expansive as originally predicted, entail grievous risks and bring change to Arctic communities.

Many human communities already feel the impacts of a changing Arctic climate through coastal erosion or disruptions in infrastructure. In addition to the impacts within the Arctic, the changing Arctic climate has major implications for the rest of the globe, such as through climate feedback mechanisms, including sea ice and snow albedo, sea level rise, release of methane from thawing permafrost and impacts on global migratory species.

The circumpolar North does not constitute a homogenous region, even though it is often described as such or treated as a single environmental and socioeconomic space in numerous policy documents. The Arctic is composed of sub-regions very different from each other, even though all parts of the Arctic share typically cold climate conditions, reflected in the environment and Arctic cultures, as well as certain similar socio-economic challenges. Thus, in this book often the authors employ a phrase "Arctic regions" in contrast to a single "Arctic region".

The Arctic, as defined by the 2004 *Arctic Human Development Report* (AHDR)[4] (which is a definition applied generally also in this volume), is home to approximately four million inhabitants out of whom around 10% are indigenous peoples.[5] Arctic societies represent a multiplicity of cultures and livelihoods. Mixed economies – combining formal and informal economic activities, cash and traditional forms of livelihood – are widespread throughout the region, both among indigenous and non-indigenous populations. Arctic regions share common challenges of peripherality, low population density, large distances and tensions between urban development and thinning-out of the northern countryside. Modern industries in the Arctic (extractive industries as well as tourism or transport) are also dependent on the environment and climate conditions. Social changes are manifested through urbanization, modernization, or changes in lifestyle. Conflicts occur between various users of the Arctic landscape.

Environmentally, socially and economically, Arctic environment and societies, while undergoing rapid changes, are seen as being at the same time robust and resilient as well as highly vulnerable and fragile. Current socio-economic developments impact on the indigenous and non-indigenous populations and their cultures, economies, politics, as well as the positioning of Arctic peoples and communities within global economic and political systems. The Arctic

4 Arctic Human Development Report (AHDR), 2004, Stefansson Arctic Institute, Arctic Council.

5 See the latest data in Arctic Human Development Report: Regional Processes and Global Linkages, Nordic Council of Ministers, TemaNord 2014:567, doi:10.6027/TN2014-567.

Council's recent and on-going work – such as *Snow, Water, Ice and Permafrost in the Arctic Report* (SWIPA), *Arctic Resilience Report, Adaptation Actions for a Changing Arctic* (AACA), and *Arctic Social Indicators* – is a testament to the broad spectrum of critical issues and challenges in the region.

While climate change is a critical issue throughout the circumpolar North and it is certainly what attracts international attention to the Arctic, it is not the only driver of change. Economic globalization, the influence of world markets on Arctic extractive industries, evolution of regulatory frameworks as well as social and cultural changes are profoundly transforming the region. This is particularly visible in the case of large-scale developments, which often are the focus of discussions on the future of the Arctic. As is shown in the chapter by Łuszczuk *et al.,* the effects of climate change might facilitate transportation of Arctic offshore hydrocarbons, but it is market forces, political choices, environmental and social concerns and the particular business decisions that will prove decisive for the commencement or continuation of activities. Many chapters in this book give account of the multiplicity and complexity of forces driving changes in the region. Their accurate comprehension is essential for proper design of actions and policies that affect the Arctic.

Research and policy-making in the Arctic are increasingly integrating economic, environmental, social and political dimensions. Integration is promoted in the development of standards, drafting of legislation as well as in multidisciplinary research projects. Therefore, a truly holistic assessment of and approach to various issues in the region is needed. Authors of this book hope that it contributes to acquiring and promoting such a more holistic overview. The following chapters in this book, as their first objective, attempt to identify main trends in the region and their drivers, as well as show the implications of the changes for the environment and Arctic societies. The next chapter explains how this assessment work has been done, emphasising in particular collecting and building on the input from stakeholders.

Such discussion needs also to take into account the complex structures of Arctic governance. Arctic is certainly not an institutional and regulatory desert. Numerous international conventions, agreements and soft-law documents (such as declarations or recommendations) apply to the Arctic. This is particularly true in the areas of the law of the sea, maritime affairs and environmental norms. National, sub-regional and local decision-making are in most cases decisive for the fate of various developments, especially those of terrestrial nature. Arctic regional cooperation – in particular the Arctic Council (AC) – endeavours to fit in-between those levels of governance by providing scientific assessments, recommendations, inputs for international processes, and recently even facilitating negotiations on binding agreements. It must be kept in mind that the Arctic Council – formed in 1996 as a continuation of the Arctic Environmental Protection Strategy – is not a decision-making body but rather an institution capable of shaping common understanding of developments in the region and providing policy guidance. The Arctic Council is not an international organization but an intergovernmental forum of eight Arctic states with participation of six indigenous organizations. The equal participation in discussion, although not decision-making, of the latter category of participants is a distinct and greatly celebrated feature of the Arctic Council. Apart from the Arctic Council other forums and initiatives exist in the region, perhaps the most well-known and relevant in the context of this book being the Barents Euro-Arctic Council (BEAC). In its sister Regional Council local level of governance is represented, which constitutes another interesting and fairly innovative feature of regional cooperation in the North. Various structures of Arctic governance and cooperation have over the last decades attempted, with much success, to shield themselves from international tensions, including those between Arctic states. However, the ongoing conflict in Ukraine and the Russian annexation of Crimea may present a new critical challenge for Arctic cooperation.

## 3 *Strategic Assessment of Development of the Arctic:* Objective and Scope

The general objective of the *Strategic Assessment of Development of the Arctic* (SADA) report was "to assess the impacts of development in the Arctic and of European Union policies affecting the Arctic on the political, economic, and environmental landscape of the EU and the Arctic region". This objective had three working dimensions:

- To provide an overview of changes, developments and trends occurring in the Arctic, including the implications of these changes for the EU.
- To examine the role and influence of EU policies and actions in the Arctic.
- To involve stakeholders in discussion on the EU-Arctic relationship and incorporate stakeholder input into the assessment by using professional, well-designed methodology.

Unlike typical strategic impact assessments, the SADA could not assess a proposed policy and alternative policy options, although a number of issues taken up in this book are listed in the policy documents produced by the EU institutions. The list of EU aims regarding the Arctic region in the 2012 Communication is very general and cannot be seen as constituting a practical action plan.[6] Neither was it an objective of the project to discuss in detail the overall impacts of existing and possible economic developments taking place in the Arctic. The primary aim was rather to provide an overview, based partly on input from stakeholders, of changes occurring in the Arctic and the relationship between the EU and the Arctic in relation to these changes. The report attempts to integrate all dimensions of Arctic change. A more intangible objective of the SADA was to enhance knowledge of the EU among Arctic actors and of the Arctic within the EU by providing balanced, concise and up-to-date information.

The consecutive chapters cover the European Arctic, understood as a region extending from Greenland to northwest Russia (Figure 0.1), with a focus on areas where EU policies have the greatest leverage (Northern Fennoscandia and the European Economic Area). The account of a pan-Arctic perspective is taken where it is relevant for EU policy-making or in order to provide background of the examined developments. The Arctic region is considered according to the boundaries drawn by the AHDR.[7]

The assessment themes were chosen on the basis of a scoping workshop (conducted among the project network in February 2013 in Rovaniemi, Finland), a review of recent Arctic assessments and debates, as well as initial outreach to stakeholders. Several issues are discussed across the report chapters, including indigenous peoples' issues, biodiversity, research and Arctic governance. Some important topics, such as persistent organic pollutants, are not elaborated here as they have been discussed comprehensively in recent reports.[8] Eventually, seven themes focused on change have been chosen for assessment:

- Climate Change in the Arctic
- Changes in Arctic Maritime Transport
- Changing Nature of Arctic Fisheries
- Developing Oil and Gas Resources in Arctic Waters
- Mining in the European Arctic

---

6 Developing a European Union Policy towards the Arctic Region: progress since 2008 and next steps. Joint Communication of the European Commission and the High Representative of the European Union for Foreign Affairs and Security Policy to the European Parliament and the Council. Brussels, 26.6.2012. JOIN(2012) 19 final.

7 As originally defined in the Arctic Human Development Report (AHDR), 2004, Stefansson Arctic Institute, Arctic Council, see also the new report, in Larsen, J.N., & Fondahl, G. (Eds.), (2014). Arctic Human Development Report: Regional Processes and Global Linkages, Nordic Council of Ministers, TemaNord 2014:567, doi:10.6027/TN2014-567.

8 *E.g.* Cavalieri, S. et al., (2010), *op.cit.*

FIGURE 0.1 *European Arctic as defined in the Strategic Assessment of Development of the Arctic study*

SOURCE: STELLA PAULI, ARCTIC PORTAL 2014

- Activities Affecting Land Use in the European Arctic
- Social and Cultural Changes in the European Arctic

## 4 Methodology and Process: Supporting EU Policy-making

For each of the seven themes an overview of current trends in the Arctic including main drivers, environmental, social, political and economic impacts was provided, including a modest outlook to 2030.[9] Further, EU policies relevant for identified Arctic trends and the implications of Arctic changes for the EU were analysed. Basing on the input from stakeholders, critical factors for EU decision-making and recommendations were identified. The process has been also designed to contribute to forging a lasting partnership between Arctic stakeholders, EU policy-makers and Arctic experts.

One of the aims of the SADA was to assist the EU in its stated goal of being an active, knowledgeable and responsible Arctic actor. Various dimensions of EU policy-making could be distinguished in that regard. First, the process of formulating an overarching Arctic policy. Second, numerous actions devised specifically with Arctic in mind, such as the funding of Arctic research. Third and by far the broadest dimension are policies that are designed for the general EU constituency, but have specific implications for the Arctic. Against that background, the authors identified five categories of Arctic-relevant EU policies/actions:

- Those directly relevant for the EU Arctic (Finland and Sweden) and the European Economic Area (EEA, including Norway and Iceland, where significant parts of EU regulatory frameworks apply), including cohesion and co-operation programmes.
- Indirect impacts via policies and actions shaping the EU's environmental and economic footprint in the region.
- Co-operation programmes in Greenland and northwest Russia.
- EU-funded research.
- EU influence on Arctic-relevant international developments (*e.g.* United Nations Framework Convention on Climate Change, Convention on Biological Diversity and the Arctic Council).

9 The assessment did not propose scenarios for Arctic developments. Nevertheless, as drivers and critical factors for decision-making have been identified, operational tools to consider Arctic futures are provided, with an emphasis on uncertainties.

The focus in the SADA was on the policies and actions of the EU and not its individual member states, although often these cannot be clearly separated. Importantly, as discussed in the preceding chapter, the majority of EU policies and actions affecting the Arctic are not designed specifically with the Arctic in mind, or if Arctic issues are considered, they constitute only a minor element within a multiplicity of policy considerations.

The SADA was built on two interlinked parallel processes: (i) internal expert-led assessment and (ii) stakeholder consultations (Figure 0.2). Thus, the study combined expert knowledge with stakeholders' input.

First, SADA experts provided an overview of Arctic trends and developments, including their key drivers and important implications. Based on this overview, implications of Arctic changes for the EU were identified (by pinpointing the EU's interests and related policy areas affected by Arctic changes). Moreover, EU policies that affect or are relevant for Arctic changes were flagged.

The information collected in the first phase of the assessment was presented in factsheets, which served as background papers for stakeholder consultations. These were conducted through workshops (focused on interaction between stakeholders) and online questionnaires (collecting individual perspectives). Eventually, the authors combined expert analysis with stakeholder input to develop a draft report, which was then submitted to stakeholders for further feedback.

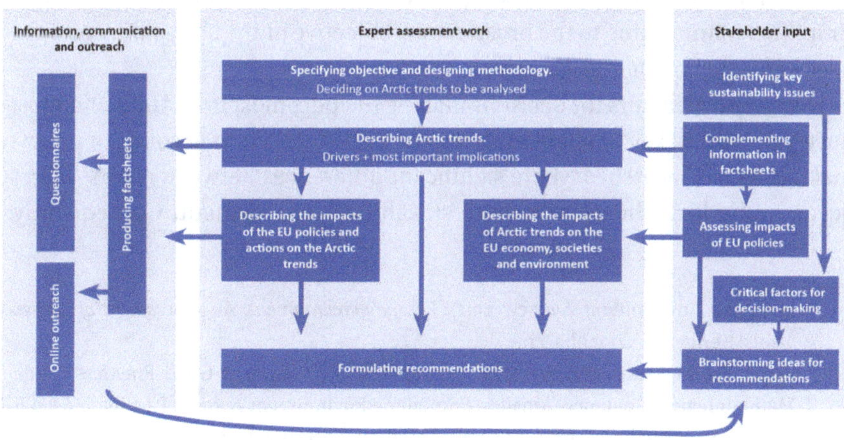


FIGURE 0.2 *Strategic Assessment of Development of the Arctic process*
SOURCE: ADAM STĘPIEŃ, ARCTIC CENTRE; AND ARCTIC PORTAL

### 4.1 *Arctic Trends and Their Implications*

The overview of Arctic trends and their implications as well as an understanding of the role of EU policies in shaping/responding to them was based on the significantly simplified *DPSIR* framework (driving force, pressures, state, impact and response). The framework, developed by the European Environment Agency (EEAgency), presents causal linkages between drivers and the pressures they exert on the environment/society, and the state of the environment/society under these stresses.[10] Instead of a pressure and a static notion of state in DPSIR, the SADA assessment team adopted a dynamic approach (trends and developments). The assessment takes into account the diversity of the Arctic, characteristics of particular regions and the diverse values or viewpoints of different groups.

*Trends* are understood as changes occurring in the region in the recent past, currently and expected in the near future, as well as their general direction and pace. Discussing "Arctic trends" is a major, although seen as useful, simplification, as they are in fact a bundle of various, temporarily and spatially diverse changes. The concept of a *driver* has been applied in SADA more broadly than in DPSIR (where it primarily signifies human needs), and is understood as all elements that cause or shape certain activities, synonymous with driving factors, shaping elements or conditions. *Impacts* or *implications* are understood as effects of changes on the environment, society, economy, culture and politics.

### 4.2 *Critical Factors for Decision-making*

Each chapter originating from SADA report includes a list of three to four critical factors for decision-making. The assessment team applied the concept of "critical factors for decision-making" – developed by Maria Partidário[11] – in a simplified manner, due to the broad scope/objective of the assessment and the needs of stakeholder engagement.

Here, critical factors for decision-making include: most important and most uncertain issues, key challenges that need to be taken into account in policymaking, as well as issues where significant differences between actors' values occur, and which therefore require stakeholder engagement. Consequently,

10 European Environment Agency (2011). *Europe's environment: An Assessment of Assessments*. EEAgency, Copenhagen.

11 Partidário, M.d.R., (2007). Strategic Environmental Assessment Good Practices Guide. Methodological Guidance. Amador: Portuguese Environment Agency; Partidário, M. d R. (2008). "Strategic-based model for SEA based on Critical Factors for Decision Making". Paper presented at the 28th Annual Conference of the International Association for Impact Assessment, Perth, 3–10 May 2008.

critical factors refer to a broad array of issues, including drivers, values, significant impacts (*e.g.* biodiversity or employment), or main aspects or tools of governance (such as spatial planning).

Identification of critical factors and conversation with stakeholders served several purposes. Internally within the assessment process, the authors had obtained a list of topics on which they needed to focus in the final stage of assessment work. The discussions on critical factors revealed also stakeholder opinions and values – information of key importance for report authors. From the point of view of policy-makers, critical factors help to create a basis for future development of scenarios and alternatives for EU policies and decisions relevant for the Arctic. Moreover, when policies referring to broad European constituency are considered, the critical factors allow for easier identification of issues that must be taken into account with regard to the Arctic implications of such policies.

### 4.3 *Suggesting the Ways Forward for the EU Policy-making*

The original SADA report contains a list of recommendations for the EU policy-makers. In this volume, the overview of these is presented in the concluding section of each chapter, with emphasis on what could be the way forward for the EU Arctic decision-making. Recommendations in the SADA aimed to suggest policy areas and actions that authors see as important for the EU policy-makers to consider. The recommendations have been developed by the experts, building on the ideas proposed by stakeholders in the thematic workshops and the online questionnaire, as well as on the analysis of Arctic trends and relevant EU policies. Therefore, these propositions should not be seen as coming directly from stakeholders. Both the specific content and order of recommendations in each chapter is the choice of the authors. It should be emphasized that the recommendations were not drafted and agreed as a common position of the whole project network.

The proposed ideas had been analysed in the light of EU competences, in terms of their feasibility and realism, and alignment with the current guiding principles of the EU Arctic policy (knowledge, responsibility, engagement).

## 5 Stakeholder Engagement

The interaction with Arctic stakeholders constituted a key feature of the assessment work and is a foundation for the findings presented in this book.

Broader stakeholder engagement, extending outside of the science-policy nexus, is currently a clear trend in assessment work and constitutes a basis for assessments' relevance, salience, and credibility (see chapter by Śmieszek *et al.* in this volume for discussion on these properties). Scholars underline that "establishing trust and credibility with stakeholders requires sustained interaction as well as demonstrated openness to incorporating stakeholders as full partners in the assessment effort".[12] Decision-makers are more eager to appreciate the assessment in which they participated. Public involvement is also a particularly effective way to integrate environmental, cultural, social and economic considerations, as a diversity of values and perspectives is brought into the view of assessment authors.[13]

Benefits from broader stakeholder engagement are twofold. For the immediate assessment outcome, engagement contributes to opening of an assessment to different types of knowledge and information coming from outside of science. Second, in the long-term perspective – and primarily in connection with assessment process itself – stakeholder participation builds trust and shared knowledge base, as well as enhances general awareness of existence of multiple perspectives on issues in question. Participation in assessments can be also seen as capacity-building and empowering process, *inter alia*, by equipping participants with new knowledge.[14]

Stakeholders comprise both those internal (those conducting, commissioning the assessment or using its results within policy-making) and external to the assessment process (those possibly affected by policy developments or decisions influenced by the results of assessment work).[15] According to UN Environmental Programme,[16] stakeholders include:

---

12 Lemos, M.C., & Morehouse, B.J. (2005). The co-production of science and policy in integrated climate assessments. Global Environmental Change, 15(1), 57–68. doi:10.1016/j.gloenvcha.2004.09.004.

13 National Research Council (2007). Analysis of Global Change Assessments: Lessons Learned. Washington, DC: The National Academies Press. http://www.nap.edu/catalog.php?record_id=118686o-61. Accessed 20 November 2014, pp. 60–61.

14 Arctic Environmental Protection Strategy. (1997). Guidelines for Environmental Impact Assessment (EIA) in the Arctic. Finland: Sustainable Development and Utilization. Finnish Ministry of the Environment. http://arcticcentre.ulapland.fi/aria/procedures/eiaguide.pdf. Accessed 20 November 2014; National Research Council (2007); Therivel, R. (2010). Strategic Environmental Assessment in Action. London: Earthscan.

15 Abaza, H., Bisset, R., & Sadler, B. (2004). Environmental impact assessment and strategic environmental assessment: towards an integrated approach, United Nations Environment Programme.

16 United Nations Environment Programme (UNEP) (2009). Integrated Assessment: Mainstreaming Sustainability into Policymaking. A Guidance Manual. UNEP, http://www.unep.ch/etb/publications/AIguidance2009/UNEPIAfinal.pdf. Accessed 20 September 2014.

- primary stakeholders – those likely to be positively or negatively affected;
- secondary stakeholders – intermediaries in the policy-making process and its implementation – those who have critical interests, knowledge and expertise;
- key stakeholders – those able to significantly influence the policy-making processes.

There is no single correct methodology for stakeholder involvement. Methods and tools for engaging stakeholders and conducting consultations depend on the type and purpose of an assessment, issues under consideration, expected inputs, social, cultural, political and institutional context, as well as available human and financial resources of the team conducting an assessment. In general, stakeholder engagement should be:

- effective: allowing stakeholders to voice their concerns and views as well as providing those asking questions with the input and information they need in decision-making;
- efficient: the costs of consultations are proportional to the input received;
- meaningful: not only provide the public with detailed and comprehensive information, but also create an opportunity to influence decisions;
- transparent and characterized by openness: enhancing acceptability, accountability and credibility of decision-making, as well as building understanding and trust between stakeholders, decision-makers and experts.[17]

Consequently, consultations limited to a basic 'informative' level (*e.g.*, hearings) are seen by many authors as ineffective. The comments are few, unhelpful, untargeted, either too specific or too general. Tangible inputs are usually based on more "targeted and intensive" consultation methodology. The specific techniques and tools include public hearings, workshops, focus groups, questionnaires, calls for statements, anthropological methods (*e.g.* visits and interviews), online tools or the establishment of stakeholder advisory committees.[18]

Engagement of stakeholders, especially those external to the assessment, may require proactive reach-out and capacity-building. Acquiring meaningful input from groups and organizations that have limited human and financial capacities is challenging. That is the case especially with marginalized and

17 Arctic Environmental Protection Strategy (1997), *op.cit.*; National Research Council (2007), *op.cit.*; Partidário (2007), *op.cit.*; Therivel (2010), *op.cit*; UNEP (2009), *op.cit.*

18 European Comission (2009). Impact Assessment Guidelines, http://ec.europa.eu/smart-regulation/impact/commission_guidelines/docs/iag_2009_en.pdf. Accessed 20 November 2014; Therivel (2010).

vulnerable groups (*e.g.*, women, youth, indigenous peoples, disabled persons, the poor), who are often the ones affected the most by environmental, economic or social changes which are assessed or policy developments that the assessment is about to trigger or advise.[19]

The United Nations Environmental Programme[20] identified numerous elements necessary for an effective consultation process, including consulting all relevant groups, sufficient publicity, adapting chosen tools to target groups and local conditions, allowing sufficient time for participation, and the acknowledgment of inputs and transparency of results. At the same time, consultations should never be seen as a substitute for an analysis of an issue and organizers should not be overly influenced by one stakeholder group.

Stakeholder engagement certainly makes the assessment complex and resource-intensive. A key difficulty connected with stakeholder engagement is balancing between acquiring meaningful involvement of stakeholders (including especially decision-makers) and allowing for stakeholders' influence over the process which skews the scientific outcomes. Another balancing act needs to be performed between the ideally as-broad-as-possible stakeholder involvement and the capacity of assessment team to incorporate stakeholder input. It is also important to avoid the entire process becoming too complex, inefficient and costly. Many smaller organizations with limited human and financial resources at their disposal may experience "participation overload" or "consultation fatigue".[21] Often, the stakeholder engagement has to be adjusted to the existing capacities, or capacity-building actions need to be taken.[22]

### 5.1 *Stakeholder Engagement in the* SADA

The consultation process was one of the most important elements of the SADA, creating a space for dialogue and contributing to long-term participatory

19 National Research Council (2007), *op.cit.*, pp. 118–120.

20 UNEP (2009), *op.cit.*, p. 25; see also Abaza et al. (2004), *op.cit.*, p. 75.

21 Abaza et al. (2004), *op.cit.*, pp. 71–72; Gauthier, M., Simard, L., & Waaub, J.-P. (2011). Public participation in strategic environmental assessment (SEA): Critical review and the Quebec (Canada) approach. Environmental Impact Assessment Review, 31(1), 48–60. doi:10.1016/j.eiar.2010.01.006, p. 51; Knigge, M., & Leipprand, A. (2003). Public Participation in Sustainability Impact Assessments. In Paper for the workshop "Sustainability Impact Assessment of Trade Agreements and New Approaches to Governance", Centre for Philosophy of Law, University of Louvain. Retrieved from http://www.ecologic-events.de/sustra/en/documents/ParticipationSIAsKniggeLeipprand.PDF. Accessed 10 October 2014.

22 Farrell, A.E., Jäger, J., & VanDeveer, S.D. (2006). Overview: Understanding Design Choices. In A.E. Farrell & J. Jäger (Eds.), Assessments of Regional and Global Environmental Risks. Designing Processes for the Effective Use of Science in Decisionmaking (pp. 1–24). Washington, DC: RFF Press.

partnerships. Stakeholders (in workshops and via an online questionnaire) scrutinised the approach of experts and were a crucial source of information. They provided guidance on the further focus of assessment work and proposed initial ideas for recommendations. The team followed the principles of expert humility (receptiveness to criticism and acknowledging limitations of expert knowledge), openness (to other viewpoints), critical approach (to information coming from different sources), and long-term engagement.

As a means of communication with stakeholders, a series of background papers (factsheets) were written in lay terms and based on existing studies.[23] The chapters in the report and in this book build from those factsheets. Several consultation tools and methods were used: hearings and workshops (in Rovaniemi in October 2013 and Tromsø in January 2014), online questionnaire, interactive website, feedback process (allowing participants to comment on the consecutive stages of the report drafting process), as well as direct outreach with key informants by the report authors.

Consultation meetings[24] in Rovaniemi and Tromsø consisted of plenary sessions and content-focused workshops. During the general meetings, an overview of the project was presented and experts gave presentations to stimulate discussion on important trends and issues. A total of nine workshops addressed seven assessment themes. More than 1100 individual invitations were sent and about 200 participants attended the consultation meetings (including 30 members of the project network in each meeting), 120 of whom actively participated in the workshops.

The workshops proved a good way to communicate between the Arctic stakeholders and experts conducting the study. Participants gave generally positive feedback on both the format and the content of the consultation meetings and appreciated having the chance to express their own views and hear the opinions of other stakeholders.

Stakeholders in general agreed that common drivers for many Arctic developments are global demand for resources and the main *natural physical driver* – climate change. Broad public participation, especially of the local Arctic communities, has been identified in several workshops as a need, critical factor and a corresponding area for recommendations for EU policy-making. The importance of supporting research, education and technological development was also emphasised very extensively across the themes. Entrepreneurship and

---

23 Factsheets can be found at the project website at http://arcticinfo.eu/en/the-u-arctic-impact-assessment-factsheets. Accessed 20 February 2015.

24 The stakeholder meetings in Rovaniemi and Tromsø was co-organized by GRID-Arendal (www.grida.no) and the overview of the meetings have been drafted by Tina Schoolmeester from GRID-Arendal.

international co-operation (in particular with Russia) proved to rate highly, too, as did good governance and the need for clear regulations. It was also pointed out that the EU should be more actively involved in international negotiations (*e.g.* Polar Code, climate change negotiations). Respecting the local Arctic communities and ensuring that revenues from resources in the Arctic reach the local communities were also recurrent issues. Safety, security and preparedness measures were deemed particularly important for offshore business development (shipping and oil and gas) due to the harsh and remote environment. Health and environmental concerns were among the frequently highlighted issues.

The online questionnaire in general followed similar steps to those used in the workshops, but it aimed to provide concrete, individual inputs. Respondents were able to freely choose the questions they were interested in answering. The questionnaire gathered 260 individual responses, around half of which were fairly substantial or extensive.

Often, the greatest criticism regarding the content of the factsheets was expressed by the representatives of the industry, clearly showing the need to engage practitioners in assessment work. Each comment from the stakeholders was considered and addressed as extensively as possible, taking into account stakeholders' background.

Stakeholders highlighted the importance of communication, participation and dialogue, in light of a number of misrepresentations of particular topics or of industries within the society. There is interest among the respondents in what the EU could do regarding various issues in the Arctic, but correspondingly little knowledge of the Union's competences, policies and regulatory framework. Differences of opinion between various groups are evident.

The detailed reports from the consultation meetings and on the results of the online questionnaire can be found in Annex 1 to the SADA report at the project website.[25]

## 6 The Origins of the Assessment and Its Methodology: The EU Arctic Information Centre Initiative

The reports on which this book builds were a result of a project dedicated, *inter alia,* to assessing feasibility of the initiative to establish the EU Arctic

25 http://www.arcticinfo.eu/images/pdf/sada_chapters/Chapter_Annexes.pdf. Accessed 20 February 2015.

Information Centre (EUAIC). While at the moment of publishing of this volume, the European Commission is still considering the results of the project, it is useful to provide some information on the EUAIC concept.

The proposed EUAIC has been devised as an innovative structure that enhances effective use of scientific information and practitioners' knowledge in public and private decision making in the Arctic. The EUAIC is designed to operate as a so called "boundary organization" between different knowledge groups and it aims at offering information products. Through its services it would guarantee improved awareness and understanding of the Arctic in the EU, and the EU in the Arctic.

Rapid economic development and environmental changes in the Arctic result in a considerable increase in demand among various stakeholders for information about the region. Recent studies show that awareness of the Arctic is modest, and at the same time information is urgently requested by EU institutions, EU member states, the private sector, scientists and other stakeholders operating and interested in the Arctic.

Despite the EU's investments in research and development programmes addressing the Arctic, and regardless of the Arctic excellence institutions funded by European states at the national level, the produced information is dispersed among various projects and organizations. The lack of overall institutional memory about results and completed projects means that this information is not readily accessible for effective use by stakeholders who need it for their decisions and actions. Additionally, the produced information is often too technical and thus these stakeholders do not consider it to be useful and applicable.

Scientific information alone cannot give comprehensive answers about Arctic development. There is also a need for deep understanding of the values and knowledge possessed by the people who have long experience of living, working in the Arctic. In order to come up with influential strategies, plans and decisions, or for social licensing of new investments, it is crucial to build bridges between scientists, policymakers and the private sector by facilitating multidimensional dialogues to gain access to the full spectrum of information and to increase trust between these knowledge groups.

The EUAIC has been proposed as a collaborative structure of European Arctic excellence institutes that have expertise, skills and contacts on Arctic issues and which are committed to filling the recognized information gap between the EU and the Arctic.

The EUAIC could improve (1) access, (2) dialogues and (3) dissemination of relevant and updated Arctic information and knowledge within and outside the EU. It would support the formulation and continuation of the EU's Arctic policy and help to guarantee its coherence. The EUAIC can provide a number of services to support improved knowledge about the Arctic such as:

- producing briefing papers, factsheets and knowledge brokering;
- documentation of the discussion in the form of reports useful for decision making;
- clearing house on the EU's Arctic initiatives;
- impact assessments to compile scientific and stakeholders' knowledge;
- serving the European Commission in its various Arctic needs.

The EUAIC would have its hub, the central office, in the European Arctic in Rovaniemi at the Arctic Centre of the University of Lapland. Locating a core activity in the European Arctic demonstrates that the EU is truly an Arctic actor. The idea of the EUAIC does not overlap or compete with any other existing Arctic organization.

## 7 The Outline of This Book

The book opens with a chapter discussing the history of the EU policy-making for the Arctic, the anxiety of Arctic actors regarding EU's interest, and the contradictions inherent to the process of formulating overarching EU policy stance on the Arctic (Stępień and Koivurova). It follows with thematic chapters on climate change (Strahlendorff *et al.*), maritime transport (Sander *et al.*), fisheries (Arnarsson and Justus), offshore oil and gas exploitation (Łuszczuk *et al.*), mining (van Dam *et al.*), activities affecting Arctic land use (Latola *et al.*) and socio-cultural changes (Stepien *et al.*). The three latter chapters focus exclusively on the European Arctic. Each of the thematic chapters discusses current trends, their drivers, environmental, economic and social implications of the changes at hand, and proposes moderate outlook towards the future. Against this background, the influence of the changes unfolding (or potentially unfolding) in the Arctic on the EU's environment, society and economy is traced. The thematic chapters also present the imprint of various EU policies and actions on developments in the region. Basing on the input from Arctic stakeholders, the critical factors for EU decision making as well as propositions for future EU action are identified. The discussion on the thematic areas is complemented by the overview of present and past Arctic initiatives conducted or initiated by European actors – the EU, Member States, private and public entities in the areas of research, policy or development (van der Watt *et al.*). This rich collection of information is augmented by the analysis of gaps, especially regarding information – and knowledge-production, where the EU institutions or other actors could engage. Eventually, the chapter by Śmieszek *et al.* discusses the role of assessments in policy-making, as well as the key properties of effective assessments, *i.e.* relevance, salience and credibility. Assessments are one of the key instruments in the policy-shaping within Arctic regional governance, as well as for the EU's presence in the Arctic. The chapter also allows positioning of the "Strategic Environmental Impact Assessment of development of the Arctic" project within the framework of Arctic governance, including the prominent role stakeholder engagement played in the effort. The final chapter presents the key general findings and messages of the SADA report both regarding Arctic developments and the future pathways for the EU policy-making.

CHAPTER 1

# The Making of a Coherent Arctic Policy for the European Union: Anxieties, Contradictions and Possible Future Pathways

*Adam Stępień and Timo Koivurova**

## Abstract

This chapter investigates what a coherent, united, integrated and concretized EU Arctic policy may entail and how it relates to regional actors' anxiety regarding the EU's Arctic policy formulation. It is argued that this anxiety has had a critical influence on the EU Arctic policy and may be even seen as a "blessing in disguise", contributing to the learning process taking place within the EU institutions. The question of what a coherent EU policy may entail is discussed against the background of the history of EU policy-making and examining the potential reasons for the Arctic actors' concerns, including the rejection of EU's environmental leadership, concern regarding the coordination role the European Commission may play in the Arctic Council, as well as the alleged lack of appropriate knowledge and sensitivity. The internal (consistence – lack of contradictory objectives), institutional (coherence between EU institutions) and vertical (between the EU and its member states) dimensions of coherence are discussed. The EU's overarching policy towards the Arctic is seen as complementary to the actions of the EU member states. There is a tension between the emphasis on the circumpolar versus European Arctic issues, between maritime and terrestrial, internal and external dimensions. There is also a contradiction between the EU environmental values, developmental goals, as well as the eagerness to adjust to the narratives prevalent in the EU Arctic and the need to respond to internal pressures. The chapter concludes with the appreciation of both EU's role in the region and the learning process taking place within the EU institutions regarding the Arctic. However, the authors also identify prevalent challenges that the EU policymakers are likely to face also in the future. Among the possible ways forward are: an emphasis on the issues crucial for the European Arctic, the focus on supporting Arctic research, developing mechanisms for dialogue, as well as the ongoing assessment of the impact of EU policies in the region. EU policy makers should consider Arctic

* The authors would like to acknowledge Małgorzata Śmieszek and Paula Kankaanpää for valuable comments, suggestions and support. The revised version of this chapter has been submitted as an article to the Yearbook of Polar Law, Vol. 7 (Brill/Nijhoff).

 | DOI 10.1163/9789004303188_003

policy-making institutional setting with a less dominant role of the European External Action Service and the DG Maritime Affairs and Fisheries.

## 1 Introduction

In 2014, the European Parliament called for the formulation of a "united EU policy on the Arctic" and a "coherent strategy and concretized action plan on the EU's engagement in the Arctic",[1] while the Council of the European Union requested the European Commission to work towards "further development of an integrated and coherent Arctic Policy".[2] This chapter investigates what such a coherent, united, integrated and concretized approach may entail and how it relates to the anxiety among many regional actors over the interest of the EU in the Arctic.

While the chapters that follow focus on specific thematic areas and examine a broad array of EU policies and actions that are of relevance for the Arctic, here the focus is on the overall EU Arctic policy-making. The analysis follows neither chronological nor sectoral approach but rather tackles four interrelated issues: the origins of EU institutions' interest in the Arctic, the resistance of Arctic actors to the EU's active presence in the region, the question of coherence of EU Arctic policy, and the contradictions that constitute a challenge in the formulation of the EU's coherent overarching stance.

First, the manifold EU-Arctic interlinks are reiterated and the origins of the EU policy-making for the region discussed. Further, the policy-making and a learning process within the EU is juxtaposed with anxiety among Arctic actors regarding more serious and conscious engagement of the EU in Arctic affairs. It is argued that it was the resistance the EU encountered in the Arctic that was chiefly responsible for fuelling the learning process within the EU. Against such background, the need for and the possible shape of EU Arctic policy/strategy are discussed, with particular emphasis on the contradictions inherent to the EU Arctic policy-making. The chapter concludes with the appreciation of both EU's role in the region and the learning process taking place within the EU institutions regarding the Arctic. However, the authors also reiterate the challenges that the EU policy-makers are bound to face in the future owing to the very nature of the EU-Arctic nexus.

1 European Parliament (2014). Joint Motion for a Resolution on the EU strategy for the Arctic (2013/2595(RSP)), http://www.europarl.europa.eu/sides/getDoc.do?pubRef=-//EP//TEXT+MOTION+P7-RC-2014-0229+0+DOC+XML+V0//EN. Accessed 15 March 2014, para. 2.

2 Council of the European Union (12 May 2014), Council conclusions on developing a European Union Policy towards the Arctic Region, Foreign Affairs Council meeting, Brussels, para. 15.

## 2 The EU's Presence in the Arctic and the Origins of the EU's Arctic Policy-making

The Arctic region came to the spotlight of the public, media and policy-makers less than a decade ago, following a series of events such as the 2007 Arctic sea ice minimum, Russian flag planting at the seabed of Arctic Ocean,[3] and the publication by the US Geological Survey of estimates of Arctic hydrocarbons reserves in 2008.[4] Notions of climate change doom, resource bonanza, potential inter-state conflicts over resources and territorial sovereignty, and new ocean highways had become commonplace. The "Arctic boom"[5] was supposed to be just around the corner. As a result, numerous actors developed interest in the region, including international organizations, major international players such as China, private sector and non-governmental organizations. The EU did not remain silent on the issue. To the contrary, it drafted policy documents as one of the first "Arctic external actors".

Located close to the Arctic, Europe has always had economic and environmental influence on the region (the following chapters in this book have as one of their aims to provide overview of various dimensions of this influence). However, EU institutions came to be interested in formulating an overarching approach to the region only when the Arctic had become an international hot topic. Arguably, the time for developing an Arctic policy was ripe, as the European institutions had finalized many years of work on the EU's Integrated Maritime Policy,[6] the EU was a major funder of research projects within the International Polar Year 2007–2009, and the Union was a key player in the climate negotiations process.[7] The Arctic had come to be seen as one of the crucial regions for climate science and politics, so at least some attention from the EU was to be expected. Moreover, over a decade earlier the EU had become a regulator in the region following Finland's and Sweden's accession and the conclusion of the European Economic Area (EEA) Agreement, resulting in

3 Koivurova, T. (2011). 'The Actions of the Arctic States Respecting the Continental Shelf: A Reflective Essay' (2011) 42 Ocean Development & Intl L 211.

4 USGS (United States Geological Survey), (2008). Circum-Arctic Resources Appraisal: Estimates of Undiscovered Oil and Gas North of the Arctic Circle, Fact Sheet 2008–3049, USGS, Boulder, United States.

5 Zellen, B.S. (2009). *Arctic Doom, Arctic Boom: The Geopolitics of Climate Change in the Arctic*, Praeger Security International.

6 Koivurova, T. (2012). "Integrated Maritime Policy of the European Union: Challenges, Successes, and Lessons to Learn", 40 *Coastal Management* 2, 161–171.

7 The process, which was then thought to culminate with the 2009 UNFCCC Conference of Parties in Copenhagen.

much of *acquis communitaire* (the body of law accumulated within the EU) being applicable for Iceland and Norway. As a result, five out of eight members of the Arctic Council were EU/EEA states. In addition, seven out of 12 observers to the Arctic Council are EU member states (since 2013). In fact, the EU can hardly be described as an "external actor".

Discussions on the role of the European Union in the Arctic often emphasise the fact that the EU has no Arctic Ocean shoreline. Indeed, Greenland, which acceded to the European Economic Community (EEC, the EU's predecessor) as a part of Denmark in 1973, withdrew from the EEC in 1985 after obtaining Home Rule and holding a referendum. However, that is only one dimension of the EU's presence. As mentioned earlier, the EU influences the region via factors such as its resource demand, emissions of pollution reaching Arctic regions and funding dedicated for Arctic research.

Today's EU has many competences to act in various policy spheres, which also extend to the Arctic.[8] In lay terms, EU competences mean that the Union can legislate and enact directives/regulations or develop policy in certain areas. To decide in which policy areas the EU has what kind of competence is an act with clear consequences. First of all, the competence can be exclusive to the EU, meaning that the member states do not have competence to legislate and develop policy in this field (*e.g.* conservation of marine biological resources under the common fisheries policy). The competence can also be shared between member states and the EU (*e.g.* environmental policies), and that is why in many policy areas it is both the EU and the member states that become parties to international treaties. In some cases, the competence still falls under the member states, but the EU is allowed to implement complementary actions (*e.g.* in tourism).

Most of these EU policies – in one way or another – influence all regions where the EU is present as an economic, environmental, political or funding actor. This is true also for the Arctic, even if a particular policy was designed with the general European constituency rather than the Arctic in mind. The 2010 EU Arctic Footprint and Policy Assessment Report[9] showed, for example, that PCB-153 (a congener of polychlorinated biphenyls – common persistent organic pollutants) emissions from Europe constitute 57% of all emissions reaching the Arctic. Furthermore, due to its geographical proximity, the EU's share of mercury emissions in the Arctic is about 24%, even though the EU

8 Koivurova, T. et al. (2012). "The present and future competence of the European Union in the Arctic", *Polar Record* 48(4), 361–371.

9 Cavalieri S. et al., (2010). EU Arctic Footprint and Policy Assessment Report, Ecologic Institute. http://arctic-footprint.eu/. Accessed 20 November 2013.

contributes only 5.5% to global mercury emissions. In 2013, the EU contributed 11% to global carbon dioxide emissions.[10] The EU accounts for 39% of fish imports from Arctic countries, and 24% of final demand for products from the Arctic oil and gas industry. 27% of Arctic tourists are Europeans.[11] As Alyson Bailes rightly concluded, the EU's "stake in the High North does not stand or fall just on calculation of geo-strategic presence",[12] and the geographical access to the Arctic Ocean.

The EU is present most visibly in the European Arctic. A part of the territories of the EU (Finland and Sweden) and EEA (Iceland and Norway) member states belong to the Arctic region.[13] The EU is also involved in developments in northwest Russia via its regional and cross-border funding (*e.g.* Kolarctic programme[14]) and various financing instruments, including the Initiative for Democracy and Human Rights. The EU has a special relationship with Greenland based on the 1985 Greenland Treaty, which includes Fisheries Agreement, a Partnership Agreement, and Greenland's status within the Overseas Countries and Territories Association.[15]

Accession of Finland and Sweden to the EU in 1995 resulted, owing to Finnish initiative, in the emergence of the Northern Dimension as a policy bringing together and coordinating numerous EU funding mechanisms in the North and in particular as a way to strengthen the regional cooperation with Russia. After a period of soul-searching, the Northern Dimension was developed into a common policy of the EU, Iceland, Norway and Russia. The policy

---

10 Olivier, J.G.J. et al. (2014). Trends in global $CO_2$ emissions: 2014, PBL Netherlands Environmental Assessment Agency and the Institute for Environment and Sustainability (IES) of the European Commission's Joint Research Centre (JRC) Report, http://www.pbl.nl/sites/default/files/cms/publicaties/PBL_2014_Trends_in_global_CO2_emisions_2014_1490_0.pdf, Accessed 25 January 2015.

11 Cavalieri *et al.* (2010), *op.cit.*

12 Bailes, A. (2009). "Potential Roles of NATO and the EU in High Northern Security", *Yearbook of Polar Law* 2, 201–224, 220.

13 As defined by the Arctic Human Development Report or Arctic Council's Arctic Monitoring and Assessment Programme. See, Larsen, J.N., & Fondahl G. (Eds.), (2014). Arctic Human Development Report: Regional Processes and Global Linkages, Nordic Council of Ministers, TemaNord 2014:567, doi:10.6027/TN2014-567.

14 See the website of the Kolarctic ENPI (2007–2013) Programme at http://www.kolarcticenpi.info/en. Accessed 20 February 2015.

15 Although Denmark is an EU member state, the Kingdom of Denmark is comprised of three territories: Denmark and the self-governing Faroe Islands and Greenland. Thus, the government of Denmark, itself member of the EU, represents the Faroe Islands and Greenland as non-EU territories in a number of policy areas, primarily related to foreign policy.

has had a clear focus on the Baltic/Barents area. However, between 2002 and 2013, the idea of the so-called "Arctic Window" had been discussed as a potential offshoot of the Northern Dimension directing the dialogue towards Arctic issues. It was even considered by some scholars as a first conscious policy engagement by the EU institutions referring to the Arctic.[16] If so, it was certainly not a particularly conspicuous statement of interest.

Given the multiplicity of elements comprising the "EU-Arctic nexus", the post-2007 Arctic policy-making within European institutions can hardly be seen as a consequence of recognizing the EU's impact on the Arctic as a policy agent. Nor was the EU's Arctic policy a product of realizing the profound importance of Arctic changes for Europe. Already in 2004, the European Environment Agency (EEAgency) published a report "Arctic environment: European perspectives – Why should Europe care?",[17] highlighting the crucial role of the Arctic in the future of Europe. If the EEAgency analysis had been published during the era of "Arctic hype" after 2007, it is likely that it would have been considered ground-breaking rather than largely ignored. There was little interest from the side of the EU institutions in taking part in the work of the Arctic Council, the main intergovernmental forum for discussing Arctic issues. This is surprising considering Council's increasing – starting from the early 2000s – focus on climate change, one of the key themes of the EU's international activity. The European Commission had been a member of the Barents Euro-Arctic Council since the forum was established, but its involvement was fairly limited. Eventually, global attention to the Arctic and the interest from other major global actors turned out to be a necessary trigger to make the EU institutions to pay attention.

## 3 The On-going Process of Formulating the EU Arctic Policy: Institutions and Learning Process

Numerous EU institutional actors are involved in the elaboration of a policy framework bringing together a variety of EU actions relevant for the Arctic.[18]

16 Archer, C. (2010). "An EU-Arctic Policy", UACES Conference Bruges, 6–8 September 2010 [Conference Working Paper], http://uaces.org/documents/papers/1001/archer.pdf. Accessed 15 December 2014.

17 European Environment Agency (2004). "Arctic environment: European perspectives – Why should Europe care?", http://climate-adapt.eea.europa.eu/viewaceitem?aceitem_id=3210. Accessed 10 February 2015.

18 Notwithstanding the process of formulating strategic policy for the Arctic, when the EU adopts specific legislation that is Arctic-relevant, its institutions act within the legislative procedures based on the EU founding treaties (Treaty on the European Union and the

Starting from 2007, the process had been initiated in connection with the EU's Integrated Maritime Policy (IMP, with the European Commission's DG Maritime Affairs and Fisheries in a key role) as well as the rising interest in Arctic affairs within the European Parliament.

During the pivotal for the IMP year 2006, the work on the IMP did not include Arctic dimension apart from brief mentioning the region in the context of climate change.[19] That has changed in the Fall 2007, following the burst of international interest in the region.[20] The representatives of the Parliament had already earlier participated in the Conferences of Parliamentarians of the Arctic Region. The first European Commission Communication on the European Union and the Arctic Region,[21] published in 2008, brought numerous and thus far autonomous EU activities under the umbrella of an "Arctic policy".[22] The objectives of the EU Arctic policy, approved by the Council of the European Union in 2009,[23] were defined as: "[p]rotecting and preserving the Arctic in unison with its population; [p]romoting sustainable use of resources; [and c]ontributing to enhanced Arctic multilateral governance."

The actual formulation of Arctic policy, where a number of the Commission's DGs have been involved, has been led by the DG External Relations (DG RELEX), which established the Arctic Inter-Service Group bringing together officers from various directorates-general. Following the Lisbon Treaty, the newly formed European External Action Service (EEAS) has come to the fore and lead the process. DG Maritime Affairs and Fisheries kept the technical coordinating function.[24] The European Parliament has had a prominent role in this process by way of its resolutions and the activities of its members, as the

Treaty on the Functioning of the European Union), which means in most cases a co-decision procedure of the European Parliament and the Council of the European Union.

19 See, e.g., European Commission (2006), Background paper no. 7 on climate change. Europa.eu. Accessed 25 March 2015.

20 Wegge, N. (2012). "The EU and the Arctic: European foreign policy in the making", *Arctic Review on Law and Politics* 3(1), 6–29.

21 European Commission (2008), 'The European Union and the Arctic Region', Communication COM(2008) 763 final.

22 The Communication was foreshadowed in the IMP "Blue Book" from October 2007, see European Commission (10 October 2007). "An Integrated Maritime Policy for the European Union", Communication, COM(2007) 574 final, para. 4.4.

23 Council of the European Union. (2009). Council conclusions on Arctic issues. 2985th Foreign Affairs Council meeting, Brussels, 8 December 2009.

24 See *e.g.*, Pelaudeix C. & Rodon, T. (2013). "The European Union Arctic Policy and National Interests of France and Germany: Internal or External Policy Coherence at Stake", *The Northern Review* 37, 57–85.

Parliament provides political incentives for policy developments. The Council of the European Union (the Council) would be the key formal decision-maker in terms of adopting a coherent strategic framework for the Arctic. The Council has taken a stance on Arctic policy in its 2009 and 2014 Conclusions, encouraging the Commission and High Representative to work further towards a formulation of the EU Arctic policy.[25]

The first EU Arctic policy statements met with a certain degree of anxiety among some Arctic actors – we will discuss this anxiety more in the next section. First, the EU's High Representative for Foreign and Security Policy and the European Commission expressed their concern, identifying Arctic developments as possibly affecting EU's security interests.[26] The security language fitted well to the prevailing discourse on the Arctic at the time, but was not greatly appreciated by the Arctic states, at least when it was used by actors considered external to the region.[27] Further, the European Parliament adopted a Resolution, now remembered perhaps mostly owing to its proposition for a treaty for the Arctic with a controversial reference to the Antarctic Treaty as an inspiration.[28] Even though the European Parliament's Resolution did not

---

25 Council of the European Union. (2009). Council conclusions on Arctic issues. (2985th Foreign Affairs Council meeting, Brussels, 8 December 2009); Council of the European Union (12 May 2014). Council conclusions on developing a European Union Policy towards the Arctic Region, Foreign Affairs Council meeting, Brussels.

26 The High Representative and the European Commission expressed their concern: "The rapid melting of the polar ice caps, in particular, the Arctic, is opening up new waterways and international trade routes. In addition, the increased accessibility of the enormous hydrocarbon resources in the Arctic region is changing the geo-strategic dynamics of the region with potential consequences for international stability and European security interests. The resulting new strategic interests are illustrated by the recent planting of the Russian flag under the North Pole. There is an increasing need to address the growing debate over territorial claims and access to new trade routes by different countries which challenge Europe's ability to effectively secure its trade and resource interests in the region and may put pressure on its relations with key partners". See: Climate Change and International Security: Paper from the High Representative and the European Commission to the European Council S113/08, 14 March 2008, *http://www.consilium.europa.eu/ueDocs/cms_Data/docs/pressdata/EN/reports/99387.pdf*. Accessed 5 March 2014.

27 Śmieszek, M. (2013). "The European Union in the Northern Latitudes", in: Boening, A., Kremer, J.-F., Van Loon, A. (eds.), *Global Power Europe – Vol. 2 Policies, Actions and Influence of the EU's External Relations*, Springer Verlag.

28 The European Parliament advocates in a 2008 resolution, "Suggests that the Commission should be prepared to pursue the opening of international negotiations designed to lead to the adoption of an international treaty for the protection of the Arctic, having as its inspiration the Antarctic Treaty, as supplemented by the Madrid Protocol signed in 1991,

represent the official standpoint of the EU, new concerns arose regarding the EU's possible actions as an active participant in Arctic affairs. Also later on, the Parliament proved to be a particularly problematic from the point of view of how the EU was perceived by Arctic actors, described even as an "elephant in the glass shop".[29] The calls for a moratorium on Arctic oil and gas exploitation[30] during a debate concerning EU's offshore oil and gas safety directive,[31] while not even leaving the stage of Parliament's committee, resonated particularly badly with Arctic states.[32] In 2013, some voices in the Parliament pressured the EU to support the prohibition of international trade in products originating from polar bears under the Convention on International Trade in Endangered Species, while the Commission was attempting (successfully) to find a middle-ground solution.[33] In 2011, a study on Svalbard treaty,[34] even though produced privately by Diana Wallis (earlier a vice-president of the European Parliament), added to the increasing suspicion among Norwegian policy-makers,[35] especially after 2011 Resolution of the European Parliament also mentioned Svalbard

but respecting the fundamental difference represented by the populated nature of the Arctic and the consequent rights and needs of the peoples and nations of the Arctic region; believes, however, that as a minimum starting point such a treaty could at least cover the unpopulated and unclaimed area at the centre of the Arctic Ocean". European Parliament resolution of 9 October 2008 on Arctic governance.

29 Pelaudeix and Rodon (2013), *op.cit.*

30 EurActiv (10 October 2012). "Lawmakers turn down EU Arctic drilling moratorium", http://www.euractiv.com/climate-environment/hopes-eu-arctic-drilling-morator-news-515306. Accessed 21 March 2015.

31 Eventually adopted as Directive 2013/30/EU of 12 June 2013 on safety of offshore oil and gas operations.

32 Nielsen, T. (3 October 2012). "Norway: 'EU has no jurisdiction in the Arctic'", Barents-Observer, http://barentsobserver.com/en/energy/norway-eu-has-no-jurisdiction-arctic-03-10. Accessed 20 February 2015.

33 Pelaudeix and Rodon (2013), *op.cit.* Moving polar bear from Appendix 2 to Appendix 1, which would prohibit the international trade, was proposed by the USA and supported by Russia while strongly opposed by Canada as well as the Inuit. Despite the pressures from European environmental groups and in contrast with the seal ban case, the EU had proposed to strengthen the measures available under Appendix 2, a solution which was eventually adopted to a great extent. See, Airoldi, A. (2014), The European Union and the Arctic: Developments and perspectives 2010–2014. TemaNord 2014:565, Nordic Council of Ministers.

34 Wallis, D. & Arnold, S. (2011). "The Spitsbergen Treaty: Multilateral Governance in the Arctic", *Arctic Papers* 1, http://dianawallis.org.uk/en/document/spitsbergen-treaty-booklet.pdf. Accessed 20 February 2015.

35 Østhagen, A. (2013). "The European Union – An Arctic Actor?", *Journal of Military and Strategic Studies* 15(2), 71–92.

as one of the issues to be resolved.[36] Norwegian partners could not understand why the EU would be particularly interested in the Svalbard Treaty, especially in the context of already existing disputes regarding its applicability to the exclusive economic zone and continental shelf surrounding the archipelago.[37] Markedly, the Parliament's Resolution from March 2014 does not even mention Svalbard.[38]

The 2008 Communication by the European Commission,[39] while clearly using more cautious and sensitive language than that of the 2008 Parliament's Resolution, emphasised the need for improvement of the Arctic governance framework,[40] a statement received not too well among some Arctic actors. Moreover, Maria Damanaki, before 2014 the Commissioner responsible for the Maritime Affairs and Fisheries and one of the European senior officials speaking for the Union regarding Arctic affairs, numerous times defined the Arctic as an area of the "common concern"[41] or "common responsibility".[42] Her predecessor, Joe Borg, has even used the term "common heritage".[43] The phrases in the context of the sudden international interest in Arctic developments and similar statements from, for instance, Chinese officials,[44] triggered little positive

36 European Parliament (2011). Resolution of 20 January 2011 on a sustainable EU policy for the High North, A7 0377/2010, P7_TA(2011)0024.

37 See, *e.g.*, Churchill, R. & G. Ulfstein (3 October 2011). The Disputed Maritime Zones Around Svalbard (October 3, 2011). Changes In The Artic Environment And The Law Of The Sea, Panel IX, Martinus Nijhoff Publishers, 2010, SSRN: http://ssrn.com/abstract=1937583. Accessed 20 February 2015.

38 European Parliament (2014), *op.cit.*

39 European Commission (2008), 'The European Union and the Arctic Region', Communication COM (2008) 763 final.

40 The 2008 Commission Communication reads: "The main problems relating to Arctic governance include the fragmentation of the legal framework, the lack of effective instruments, the absence of an overall policy-setting process and gaps in participation, implementation and geographic scope."

41 Damanaki, M. (2012). "The European Union and the Arctic Region", Speech at the Conference "Arctic Futures: A global partnership for the Arctic?", Brussels, 4 October 2012, ec.europa.eu. Accessed 20 March 2015.

42 Damanaki, M. (2010). "Arctic footsteps in Brussels", Speech at the 9th Conference of Parliamentarians of the Arctic Region European Parliament, Brussels, 13 September 2010, SPEECH/422, ec.europa.eu. Accessed 20 March 2015. See also, Østhagen (2013), 83.

43 Borg, J. (2009), "The European Union's strategy of sustainable management for the Arctic", Speech at Arctic Frontiers Conference, Tromsø, Norway, 19 January 2009. ec.europa.eu. Accessed 20 March 2015.

44 See, *e.g.*, Campbell, C. (2012, April 13). "China and the Arctic: Objectives and Obstacles", US-China Economic and Security Review Commission Staff Research Report. USCC;

excitement among Arctic states officials. To no surprise, the use of such language was eventually discontinued. In general, it may be said that the initial EU responses to the changes in Arctic governance fairly rapidly became more nuanced, which was visible already in the Council of the European Union 2009 Conclusions.[45]

The 2012 Joint Communication of the European Commission and High Representative for the EU Foreign and Security Policy, building on the objectives identified in the 2008 Communication,[46] underlined the notions of knowledge (connected with a further focus on Arctic research), responsibility (understanding the EU's environmental and social impact and acting responsibly in shaping EU footprint and Arctic developments) and engagement (cooperation with various Arctic partners).[47] As Adele Airoldi stated in her latest analysis of the EU Arctic policy,[48] these "three abstract catchwords [...] do not quite translate into a clearer vision nor in a better defined and developed programme than in 2008." Many measures or actions listed in the Communication continue to be "statements of fact rather than commitments to action, which appear to be in great part a continuation or intensification of existing activities at EU, bilateral or multilateral level". Similar criticism – assessing EU Arctic policy as fragmented and cluttered or even a "laundry list" – has been expressed by other analysts.[49]

---

Rosenthal, E. (2012, September 18), "Race is On as Uce Reveals Arctic Treasures", *New York Times*, http://www.nytimes.com/2012/09/19/science/earth/arctic-resources-exposed-by-warming-set-off-competition.html. Accessed 20 September 2014.

45 Council of the European Union. (2009). Council conclusions on Arctic issues. 2985th Foreign Affairs Council meeting, Brussels, 8 December 2009.

46 The objectives of the EU Arctic policy were identified in the 2008 Communication and approved by the Council in 2009 as: "Protecting and preserving the Arctic in unison with its population; Promoting sustainable use of resources; Contributing to enhanced Arctic multilateral governance".

47 European Commission and High Representative (2012), "Developing a European Union Policy..."

48 Airoldi, A. (2014), The European Union and the Arctic: Developments and perspectives 2010–2014. TemaNord 2014:565, Nordic Council of Ministers.

49 Østhagen (2013), *op.cit.*; Kobza, P. (2015). "Civilian Power Europe in the Arctic: How Far Can the European Union Go North?". EU Diplomacy Paper 01/2015, Department of EU International Relations and Diplomacy Studies, Brugge and Natolin: Collage of Europe; Keil, K. & Raspotnik, A. (5 July 2012). Further Steps Towards a Comprehensive EU Arctic Policy: Is the EU Getting There? The Arctic Institute. http://www.thearcticinstitute.org/2012/07/further-steps-towards-comprehensive-eu.html. Accessed 10 February 2014; Keil, K. (14 December 2011). EU Arctic Policy: Caught between Energy Security and Climate

If the policy is understood as a long-term action that is equipped in new, identified goals, based on some common need and includes at least some new measures, institutions or financing,[50] then the EU Arctic activities as reflected in 2008, 2012 and 2014 documents hardly amount to a "policy". However, co-drafted by the High Representative and the European External Action Service, the 2012 Communication can be seen as a document largely directed towards outside the EU institutions. Rather than only providing the direction and consistency for the multifaceted EU activities, it appears to be designed for the benefit of Arctic actors as well as the EU public. For that purpose, the 2012 Communication attempted to justify EU Arctic engagement or underlined the indispensable role the EU funding and contributions play in Arctic knowledge-production and regional development. The Communication also ensured Arctic actors that the EU's involvement would adjust to and support existing and future – developed under the lead of Arctic states – Arctic governance frameworks.

The greatest progress in adjusting EU institutional voice to the views prevalent in the Arctic regions is perhaps the 2011 Resolution of the European Parliament, which focused on the EU's role in ensuring the sustainable development of the region, affirmed the EU's Arctic interests, and stressed a need for a co-ordinated EU policy.[51] An even more balanced approach is also evident in the most recent European Parliament Resolution from March 2014.[52] Members of the Parliament clearly wanted to reconcile the environmental focus of the EU's Arctic agenda and the developmental discourse. The latter appears currently dominant among many Arctic actors including regional voices coming from the EU Arctic (*i.e.* the northernmost regions of Finland and Sweden). Ambitious environmental goals include, for instance, precautionary approach regarding fisheries and the call for the protection of the central Arctic Ocean. At the same time, the Parliament acknowledged the existing situation in the region and showed greater sensitivity regarding problematic issues (seal ban or hydrocarbon extraction). The Parliament emphasised the role of the EU in the European Arctic, and the need to focus on the activities in the northernmost part of Europe and "bear in mind the interests of [...] the European Arctic states and regions when utilizing, amending or developing EU programmes or policies that do or can affect the Arctic". In turn, the Council in its Conclusions from May 2014 dedicated much attention to relations with Greenland and to

Change. The Arctic Institute. http://www.thearcticinstitute.org/2011/12/4598-eu-arctic-policy-caught-between.html. Accessed 10 February 2014.

50 See Kobza (2015), *op.cit.*

51 European Parliament (2011), *op.cit.*

52 European Parliament. (2014), *op.cit.*

the maritime transport, including – to no surprise considering the timing of the document – the ongoing work in the International Maritime Organization (IMO) on the Polar Code. The Council also underlined the importance of the proper understanding by the EU institutions of Arctic reality for the process of formulating Arctic policy. The Commission and the EEAS have been requested to prepare a new communication on the Arctic by the end of 2015.[53]

In addition to the Parliament, Commission, the EEAS and the Council, there are other EU actors who have a role in discussions taking place in Brussels. The European Economic and Social Committee has taken stance on Arctic issues.[54] Northern Finnish, Norwegian and Swedish regions formed a coalition – Northern Sparsely Populated Areas[55] – to advocate their specific interests in the EU decision-making processes. Moreover, also the EEA institutions – EEA Consultative Committee[56] and Joint Parliamentary Committee[57] – made in 2013 statements on Arctic affairs, emphasising, *inter alia*, the role of the Arctic Council in the regional governance, supporting the EU's bid for observer status in the Council, celebrating the alignment of EU's objectives in the region with those of Iceland and Norway, and calling for strengthened EU participation in the BEAC.

At the same time, the EU has been implementing actions designed to enhance its contribution and engagement with local actors. A good example of such attempts to engage Arctic partners is the "Strategic Environmental Impact Assessment of development of the Arctic" project[58] – of which this book is a result – dedicated to assessing changes in the Arctic and the place of the EU within this changing landscape. That included strong interaction with Arctic stakeholders resulting in the formulation of a number of recommendations.

---

53 Council of the European Union (12 May 2014), Council conclusions on developing a European Union Policy towards the Arctic Region, Foreign Affairs Council meeting, Brussels.

54 European Economic and Social Committee (17 April 2013), "Opinion of the European Economic and Social Committee on EU Arctic Policy to address globally emerging interests in the region – a view of civil society", Rapporteur: Mr Hamro-Drotz, REX/371.

55 Northern Sparsely Populated Areas network website at http://www.nspa-network.eu/. Accessed 20 February 2015.

56 EEA Consultative Committee, Resolution and Report on the opportunities and challenges in a changing Arctic region, Brussels, 10 October 2013, Ref. 1126150.

57 EEA Joint Parliamentary Committee, Resolution on Arctic Policy, 41st Meeting, 28–29 October 2013, Vaduz, Liechtenstein, Ref. 1126335.

58 See project website at www.arcticinfo.eu.

Another instance of EU activity towards enhancing stakeholder involvement in the Arctic was facilitating the creation and providing funding for the Arctic NGO Forum, which for some years brought together representatives of – primarily environmental – non-governmental organizations with interest in Arctic affairs.[59]

A more long-term process was to a great extent connected to the overspill of the EU ban on seal products introduced in 2009.[60] The EU engaged in structured interaction with Arctic indigenous peoples (see more in the chapter by Stępień *et al.* in this volume). The European Commission organised altogether four meetings in the format of "Arctic Dialogue" between 2010 and 2014. The downside of these events was that the participation of the indigenous representatives was rather incidental and lacking continuity. They consisted to a great extent of the presentation of various EU projects relevant for Arctic indigenous peoples, somewhat reflecting the "shopping list" format typical for EU Arctic policy documents. However, these shortcomings have been gradually addressed in the 2013 and 2014 meetings. The EU representatives also try to involve the Sámi on a more systematic basis, including on-going discussions on establishing some form of Sámi presence in Brussels.[61]

In 2014, in order to streamline and facilitate the effectiveness of its funding dedicated to Arctic issues, the Commission organized extensive consultations.[62] Furthermore, a network of European polar research institutions under Horizon 2020 programme (EU-Polarnet[63]) has been established to enhance coordination of polar research in Europe. It is also to facilitate the development of a European Polar Research Programme together with stakeholders, users of scientific knowledge and global scientific networks.

---

59 Arctic NGO Forum website, http://arcticngoforum.org/. Accessed 20 February 2015.

60 Regulation (EC) No 1007/2009 of 16 September 2009 on trade in seal products.

61 European Commission, 'Summary of 'Arctic Dialogue' Workshop – 9 March 2010 – Brussels' MARE.C1/EH/ZB/2010; Personal communication with the European Commission DG Mare officer, Brussels, May 2013; Observations from Arctic Dialogue meeting in October 2013, Brussels; Personal communication with a Sámi and Inuit leaders attending the October 2013 meeting, October–December 2013.

62 European Commission, Public consultation on streamlining EU funding in the European Arctic, http://ec.europa.eu/dgs/maritimeaffairs_fisheries/consultations/arctic-eu-funding/doc/consultation-paper_en.pdf. Accessed 14 February 2015.

63 European Polar Research Cooperation under Horizon 2020. European Polar Board, EU Proposal on European Research Cooperation, http://www.europeanpolarboard.org/activities/scientific-initiatives/eu-proposal-on-polar-research-cooperation-eu-polarnet/. Accessed 15 February 2015.

## 4 Northern Anxiety Regarding the EU's Presence

Despite the multidimensional presence in the Arctic discussed above and quickly commenced learning process, the EU found it challenging to be acknowledged as an Arctic actor by the key regional players. Often that is attributed solely to the issue of the EU ban on seal products and the anger it caused in Canada and among the Inuit. However, we argue that this is not the whole story. Other, more general reasons for the resistance from the side of Arctic actors could be given. This includes the unease connected with the EU value-based rhetoric, rejection of the EU's actorness in international affairs, as well as concerns regarding the possibility of the European Commission attempting to coordinate EU member states' activities in the Arctic Council. Furthermore, the tension between upholding EU values and adjusting to the developmental narratives dominant in some corners of Arctic affairs may be here visible.

Perhaps the most striking example of the anxiety connected with EU involvement is a gradually changing approach of Norway to EU's involvement in the Arctic. Early in the 2000s, Norway was not only advocating but strongly, and largely ineffectively, encouraging the European Commission to become more involved in Arctic affairs and Arctic governance.[64] This has started to change in the wake of global interest in the region, following the unwary statements from EU institutions regarding Arctic governance, dispute over mackerel (see chapter by Arnarsson and Justus in this volume) and perhaps found its culmination in the Norwegian outrage[65] concerning the adoption of the EU directive on the safety of offshore oil and gas activities.[66] The directive, under environmental law, was designed as relevant also for the EEA /EFTA states, but Norway decisively rejected its application as a part of the EEA framework (see chapter by Łuszczuk *et al.* in this volume). The latter issue sheds light on the complexity of Iceland's and Norway's relationship with the EU in the Arctic context. The main economic issues that led to the rejection of the EU membership by Norway in 1994 referendum[67] and terminating the negotiations process by Iceland in March 2015 were extraction of

64 Wegge (2012), *op.cit.*; Østhagen (2013), *op.cit.*

65 Nielsen (2012), *op.cit.*

66 Directive 2013/30/EU of 12 June 2013 on safety of offshore oil and gas operations.

67 Norwegians rejected EU/EEC accession twice, in 1972 and 1994, while Iceland has applied for EU membership in 2009 following severe economic crisis but its bid was officially withdrawn by the Icelandic government in March 2015, after the *de facto* suspension of negotiations in 2013.

hydrocarbons and fisheries.[68] These vital resources were crucial in the choice Norway and Iceland made to remain outside of the EU[69] and are therefore clearly excluded from the EEA Agreement. Now, fisheries and hydrocarbons are among the main drivers of the EU's interest in the region, as is clear from the EU Arctic policy documents; and thus, some degree of tension is inevitable.

The question of EU observer status in the Arctic Council is the clearest manifestation of the Arctic actors' anxiety. The status is often seen as a symbolic acknowledgment by the Arctic states of actor's legitimate Arctic interests. As one of the key funders of Arctic research, the EU would probably have found the "Arctic club" more welcoming if it had become interested in obtaining observer status earlier on. However, the decision to submit the EU's application to the Arctic Council was made in 2008, when the Arctic had entered the global agenda of high politics and when the introduction of the ban on seal products was being debated by the EU institutions. The decision on EU's application, together with those submitted by other applicants, was postponed both in 2009 and 2011. In the meantime, the Arctic Council developed a set of criteria for observers, so-called Nuuk Observer Rules,[70] including some that referred indirectly to the EU's situation and its ban on seal products.[71] Eventually, at the Arctic Council's Kiruna Ministerial Meeting in May 2013, China, India, Japan, and other state applicants were accepted as observers, but the position of the EU[72] – through a phrasing constituting the apogee of

68 Thorhalsson, B. (2015). "The Outsiders: Norway and Iceland", Howard Grøn C., Nedergaard, P., Wive, A. (2015). *The Nordic Countries and the European Union: Still the other European community*. Routledge, pp. 32–50.

69 Markedly, in the 1994 Finnish, Swedish and Norwegian referendums the voters in northern Nordic regions were among those least favourable to the EU accession. One of the reasons could be the concern – not untypical for peripheral regions – that the decision-making processes, in which they are already marginalized within the national context, would be removed even further, to Brussels-based institutions, on which the sparsely populated regions may have even less influence. See Ingebritsen, Ch. (1998), *The Nordic States and European Unity*. Itaqa: Cornell University Press.

70 Graczyk, P. & Koivurova T. (2014). "A New Era in the Arctic Council's External Relations? Broader Consequences of the Nuuk Observer Rules for Arctic Governance", 50 *Polar Record* 225.

71 "Respect the values, interests, culture and traditions of Arctic indigenous peoples and other Arctic inhabitants.", (Senior Arctic Officials (SAO) Report to Ministers (Nuuk, Greenland, May 2011), 50–51).

72 The EU is considered for observership in the Arctic Council as an inter-governmental organization. However, there is formally no difference in the position of state and other observers.

diplomatic illegibility[73] – has become rather obscure. The Arctic Council "received the application of the EU for observer status affirmatively", with a formal decision on the observer status awaiting "final decision on implementation", but with the EU being invited to observe Arctic Council proceedings on an equal basis to other observers. As a result, the EU acts in practice as any other observer and has come to be called an "observer-in-principle". In fact, the representatives of the European Commission have had substantial contribution in areas such as short-lived climate pollutants or maritime transport, both before and after the Kiruna Ministerial Meeting.

Kiruna Ministerial Meeting, however, was not the end of this story. In autumn 2014, the EU reached a partial agreement with Canada on the seal ban issue in the course of finalizing the Canada-EU Comprehensive Economic and Trade Agreement (CETA). In the Joint Statement[74] both sides agreed on cooperating towards establishing a viable certification system and the promotion within the European market of seal products originating from indigenous hunt.[75] Moreover, the EU, at the time of completing this chapter, is working on amending the seal regulation[76] in order to comply with earlier World Trade Organization (dispute settlement panel) ruling and improve the modalities for the exception given to products of Inuit traditional hunt. Ideally, the EU could be thus well on its way to acquiring formal observer status. However, the tense relations between the EU and Russia connected with the 2014–2015 crisis in Ukraine have further postponed the "final implementation" of Kiruna decision during the Iqaluit Ministerial Meeting in April 2015.[77]

73 "The Arctic Council receives the application of the EU for observer status affirmatively, but defers a final decision on implementation until the Council ministers are agreed by consensus that the concerns of Council members, addressed by the President of the European Commission in his letter of 8 May are resolved, with the understanding that the EU may observe Council proceedings until such time as the Council acts on the letter's proposal." Arctic Council (15 May 2013). Kiruna Declaration. 8th Ministerial Meeting of the Arctic Council.

74 European Commission, DG Trade, Comprehensive Economic and Trade Agreement, European Commission website at http://ec.europa.eu/trade/policy/in-focus/ceta/. Accessed 15 February 2015.

75 European Commission, Joint Statement by Canada and the European Union on Access to the European Union of Seal Products from Indigenous Communities of Canada, C(2014) 5881 final, Brussels, 18 August 2014 (Annex to Commission Decision).

76 European Commission (2015). Proposal for a Regulation of the European Parliament and of the Council amending Regulation (EC) No 1007/2009 on trade in seal products. COM(2015) 45 final, 2015/0028 (COD).

77 The decisions in the Arctic Council are made by consensus.

The question arises what have been the reasons for Arctic actors' anxiety. The most obvious and most often raised concrete problem is the ban on placing seal products on the EU market.[78] The ban caused outrage, especially in Canada, among commercial sealers and indigenous peoples (despite an exemption for products originating from subsistence hunting).[79] Furthermore, in addition to the comments on Arctic treaty and insufficient governance frameworks, the EU institutions emphasised the freedom of navigation and the access of scientists to Arctic areas.[80] While these statements can be seen as generally in line with the customary law of the sea or the provisions of UN Convention on the Law of the Sea (UNCLOS),[81] they may be easily read in the context of disputes on the status of straits and waters in Northeast Passage and Northern Sea Route,[82] or in the light of restrictions on the access of foreign researchers in Arctic states' exclusive economic zones. In more general terms, there was a perception that the EU dedicated much space to things that are not as pressing as the tangible challenges experienced by Arctic regions affected by climate change and globalization.[83] As a result, the EU's competence to deal with Arctic affairs was seen by some actors as questionable, with Canadian foreign affairs minister

78 Regulation (EC) No 1007/2009 16 September 2009 on trade in seal products. The European Economic Community earlier, in 1983, adopted a ban on importation of products coming from seal cubs.

79 Sellheim, N. (2013). "The Neglected Tradition? – The Genesis of the EU Seal Products Trade Ban and Commercial Sealing", *Yearbook of Polar Law* 5, 417–450; Cambou, D. (2013). "The Impact of the Ban on Seal Products on the Rights of Indigenous Peoples: A European Issue", *Yearbook of Polar Law* 5, 389–415.

80 European Commission (2008). 'The European Union and the Arctic Region', Communication COM(2008)763final (the Communication (para. 3.3.) reads: "Member States and the Community should defend the principle of freedom of navigation and the right of innocent passage in the newly opened routes and areas"); European Parliament (2011). Resolution of 20 January 2011 on a sustainable EU policy for the high North, A7-0377/2010, P7_TA(2011)0024. The Resolution (para.61) reads: "it is vital that international teams of scientists be given full access to carry out research in this particularly sensitive area of our planet [*i.e.* Arctic]".

81 UNCLOS remains the key legal instrument governing the maritime Arctic. UN Convention on the Law of the Sea, Montego Bay, 10 December 1982, entry into force 16 November 1994, 1833 UNTS 3; 21 ILM 1261 (1982), arts. 87, 238–240. 246–253 (re. right to conduct scientific research).

82 Byers, M. (2013). *International Law and the Arctic*, Cambridge: Cambridge University Press.

83 See, *e.g.*, Weber, B. (2011, March 24). "European Parliament pushy, ill-informed on Arctic, Canadian diplomats say", The Canadian Press, http://www.winnipegfreepress.com/. Accessed 15 October 2014; Østhagen (2013), *op.cit.*

Lawrence Cannon openly stating in 2009 that the EU lacks "required sensitivity to be able to acknowledge the Arctic Council" and thus be accepted as an Arctic actor.[84] However, these concrete issues are – in the view of the authors[85] – just a part of the story and refer primarily to the question of Arctic Council observership. There are also more profound problems underlying EU-Arctic relations.

The EU's international identity has been often defined as a "normative power".[86] In this view, the EU is a "value-based community" aiming to internationally promote the "protection of human rights, extensions of democratic governance [and good governance more generally] and safeguarding the natural environment". It therefore positions itself as a "promoter and exporter of the values to which it claims commitment".[87] The article 3(5) of the Treaty of the European Union lists the basic EU values to be advanced internationally:

> In its relations with the wider world, the Union shall uphold and promote its values and interests and contribute to the protection of its citizens. It shall contribute to peace, security, the sustainable development of the Earth, solidarity and mutual respect among peoples, free and fair trade, eradication of poverty and the protection of human rights, in particular the rights of the child, as well as to the strict observance and the development of international law [...].[88]

In the Arctic context, in particular sustainable development, development of international law and good governance can be seen as the most relevant "EU values". That is visible particularly well in the first Arctic Communication from the European Commission in 2008[89] and is reiterated with softer

84 CBC News (24 April 2009). "Canada against EU entry to Arctic Council because of seal trade ban", http://www.cbc.ca/news/canada/north/canada-against-eu-entry-to-arctic-council-because-of-seal-trade-ban-1.806188. Accessed 20 February 2015. See also Østhagen (2013), *op.cit.*, 81–82.

85 Based partly on the stakeholder consultation process leading to the *Strategic Assessment of development of the Arctic* report, www.arcticinfo.eu/sada. Accessed 20 March 2015.

86 Manners, I. (2002). "Normative power Europe: a contradiction in terms?", *Journal of Common Market Studies* 40(2), 235–58; Østhagen (2013), *op.cit.*

87 Bretherton, Ch. & Vogler, J. (2006). *The European Union as a Global Actor*, London and New York: Routledge, 42–44.

88 Treaty on the European Union (Consolidated Version) *Official Journal* C83 (30 March 2010), art. 3(5)

89 European Commission (2008). "The European Union and the Arctic Region", *op.cit.*

language in the series of documents from various EU institutions that followed, especially in the 2012 Communication.[90]

The emphasis on environmental issues is consistent with the EU's self-ascribed role of "global environmental leader", who disseminates to other regions and to international system its own practices and in fact "externaliz[es] its environmental policies".[91]

At least in the 1990s and early 2000s, many regions and actors appeared willing – perhaps superficially and with hopes for access to EU funding[92] – to accept the EU's normative power, including in environmental affairs. However, in the Arctic the EU encountered not only an established international regional cooperation system but also powerful and self-confident actors, for whom the notion of the EU value-based leadership was unwelcome. Thus, while in other settings, the EU has been in a position to "export" its influence as a leading partner and dominant actor, that is not the case in the North.[93] The very notion of instructing the Arctic states regarding governance arrangements or proposing support in furthering environmental protection and sustainability in the region could discourage even the environmental champions among Arctic states. The European Commission from the beginning appeared to understand the difference between the Arctic and other regions or fields for which policies were developed, such as the Black Sea Synergy process[94] or the area of development cooperation, but the perception among the Arctic actors was fairly reserved.

While all Arctic states' policy statements highlight the vulnerability of the Arctic environment and the need for environmental protection, the developmental and economic agenda has received an especially prominent place in Arctic strategic considerations.[95] All policy documents of course ensure that

90 European Commission and High Representative (2012), Developing a European Union Policy towards the Arctic Region: progress since 2008 and next steps. Joint Communication of the European Commission and the High Representative of the European Union for Foreign Affairs and Security Policy to the European Parliament and the Council. Brussels, 26.6.2012. JOIN(2012) 19 final.

91 Bretherton and Vogler (2006), *op.cit.*, pp. 89–90.

92 See, *e.g.*, the discussion on the EU's attempts to make a normative influence in the Mediterranean, e.g.: Jones, A. (2011). "Making Regions for EU Action: The EU and Mediterranean", in Bialasiewicz, L. (ed.), Europe in the World: EU Geopolitics and the Making of European Space, Farnham: Ashgate.

93 Wegge (2012), *op.cit.*; Kobza (2015), *op.cit.*

94 European External Action Service, "Black Sea Synergy", EEAS website, http://eeas.europa.eu/blacksea/index_en.htm. Accessed 19 March 2015.

95 Bailes, A.J.K. & Heininen, L. (2012). *Strategy Papers on the Arctic or High Arctic: A Comparative Study and Analysis,* Centre for Small State Studies, Institute of International Affairs, University of Iceland.

any and all economic development is to be done "in a sustainable way". Thus, there is – superficially – a point of convergence between EU values and Arctic states' priorities. However, the Arctic states clearly want to carry out northern development on their own terms, as well as define – and redefine – what *sustainability* means in that context. A case in point is the way how the EU has been cut off from the initial stage of discussions among the Arctic Ocean coastal states regarding governance of future Arctic fisheries,[96] despite its strong position in North Atlantic fisheries and significant relevant outputs generated by the EU-funded research. Eventually, outside of the imagined reality of statements and declarations reiterating the words *environment* and *sustainability*, not all Arctic actors in fact share the EU's strong, principle-based environmental values.

The USA and Russia have been perceived as states with ambiguous relationship with environmental priorities, but other Arctic states a decade ago could be seen as clear partners for the EU's environmental norm entrepreneurship.[97] The Nordic nations are considered – perhaps not always accurately – as not only being among the most environmentally-minded states, but as being among the main drivers of making the EU a leader in setting environmental standards domestically and within the international environmental politics.[98] In the early 2000s, Canada would be among key EU allies in the international promotion of environmental principles. At that time, it appeared to be even fairly sympathetic to EU's Arctic presence.[99] However, that has changed with the consecutive Stephen Harper governments, exemplified clearly by Canadian Arctic Council chairmanship programme, which put particularly strong focus on economic development, with the word "sustainable" used primarily regarding "sustainable communities".[100] Consequently, even within the Arctic Council there is certain tension between the focus on large circumpolar (*i.e.* in fact global) environmental issues and the attention to the problems of immediate relevance for Arctic communities. That is for instance visible in shifting

96 For the discussion on the process, see Wegge, N. (2014). "The Emerging Politics of the Arctic Ocean. Future Management of the Living Marine Resources", *Marine Policy*, DOI: http://dx.doi.org/10.1016/j.marpol.2014.09.015.

97 Marta Finnemore M. & Sikkink, K. (1998). "International Norm Dynamics and Political Change", *International Organizations* 52(4), 891–892.

98 Bretherton and Vogler (2006), *op.cit.*, pp. 89–90.

99 Pelaudeix and Rodon (2013), *op.cit.*

100 Government of Canada, Canada's Arctic Council Chairmanship 2013-2015, http://www.arctic-council.org/index.php/en/document-archive/category/425-main-documents-from-kiruna-ministerial-meeting?download=1763:canadian-chairmanship-program-2013-2015-english. Accessed 20 February 2015.

priorities between chairmanships.[101] The presence of the EU with its clear global environmental agenda could be seen – perhaps unjustifiably – as potentially exacerbating existing tensions.

On the other hand, it could be argued that even if the Arctic region is a different space than Eastern Europe, Black Sea, Mediterranean or the field of development cooperation, the EU institutions cannot simply ignore the key values enshrined in the EU founding treaties. They cannot either disregard the strong voice of the European public opinion, non-governmental organizations, as well as some member states[102] or members of the European Parliament calling on the EU to promote these values also in the Arctic. That is bound to create a tension between internal pressures and the narratives currently dominant in Arctic cooperation.

Furthermore, there has been concern among Arctic actors that the European Commission may exercise pressure on or coordinate activities of the EU states participating in the Arctic Council (as members and observers).[103] In general, each EU member state is expected to abide by the *principle of loyalty*. The principle means, in broad strokes, that the member state is not supposed to act internationally in a manner undermining the effective implementation of EU law, objectives of the Union or adopted common positions.[104] It is unclear how the proceedings of an intergovernmental forum that does not make any binding decisions, such as the Arctic Council, could be affected in practical terms

101 See, *e.g.*, Exner-Pirot, H. (3 October 2014). "Arctic Council at a Crossroads: Still and Again", blog entry "Eye on the Arctic", RCI, http://www.rcinet.ca/eye-on-the-arctic/2014/10/03/the-arctic-council-at-a-crossroads-still-and-again/. Accessed 20 March 2015.

102 This is visible perhaps most prominently in the German Arctic policy, see Ministry of Foreign Affairs (FR Germany), "Guidelines of the German Arctic Policy: Assume responsibility, seize opportunities", Śmieszek, M., & P. Kankaanpää (2014)."Observer States' Commitments to the Arctic Council: The Arctic Policy Documents of the United Kingdom and Germany as Case Study", *The Yearbook of Polar Law* 6, 375–397.

103 *E.g.*, Klepsvik, K. (Special Advisor for Polar Affairs, Ministry of Foreign Affairs, Norway), as reported in: Maurer, A. et al. (December 2012). *The EU as an Arctic Actor? Interests and Governance Challenges,* Report on the 3rd Annual Geopolitics in the High North – GeoNor – Conference and joint GeoNor workshop, Berlin, 22-24 Mary 2012, Stiftung Wissenschaft und Politik.

104 See, Klamert, M. (2014). *The Principle of Loyalty in EU Law,* Oxford University Press, pp. 183–206. The article 4.3. of the Treaty on the European Union reads, *inter alia*: "The Member States shall facilitate the achievement of the Union's tasks and refrain from any measure which could jeopardise the attainment of the Union's objectives." (Consolidated versions of the Treaty on European Union and the Treaty on the Functioning of the European Union. Official Journal C83, 30 March 2010).

by the principle of loyalty. Moreover, as argued later, the EU overall policy towards the Arctic has primarily supplementary rather than coordinating role, notwithstanding and in contrast with decision-making in various specific regulatory areas relevant for the Arctic.[105]

The problems the EU has been facing in relations with Arctic actors could be considered a "blessing in disguise". It is to great extent this "Arctic resistance" that fuelled the EU learning process and encouraged the EU, for instance, to assess its environmental and economic footprint, use more balanced language or create space for dialogue with the Arctic indigenous peoples. Where does this learning process lead?

## 5 Developing a Coherent and Integrated EU Strategy for the Arctic?

The EU overarching policy for the Arctic has been so far a series of umbrella documents operating with general objectives and listing actions mostly being a continuation of existing activities. If a coherent and integrated EU strategy is to be developed, a number of question can be raised. What is the purpose of such a policy? What would be its content apart from the existing inventories of EU activities? If the concerns of Arctic actors were for the EU a "blessing in disguise", would a more coherent and integrated policy be a next step in the learning process or would it rather cause even more anxiety in the North? Thus, could and should the EU Arctic policy be formulated as a coherent and

105 There is still a certain degree of theoretical (particularly from those holding realist views of international relations) and political discomfort with accepting the EU as an international actor. That is reflected in ongoing challenges related to the EU's membership in international organizations, such as the International Maritime Organization. Furthermore, Russia, while engaging with the EU in respect to various funding programmes and establishing an ambitious partnership agreement, in many cases prefers to enter into dialogue with EU Members States and circumvent EU institutions, and seemed to be sceptical regarding the EU's policy interest in the Arctic. Andreatta, F. (2011). "The European Union's International Relations: A Theoretical View", in: Hill, Ch. & Smith, M. (eds.) International Relations and the European Union, Oxford: Oxford University Press, pp. 21–43; Hoffmeister, F. (2007). "Outsider or frontrunner? Recent developments under international and European law on the status of the European Union in international organizations and treaty bodies," Common Market Law Review 44(1), 41–68; van Leeuwen J. & Kern, K. (2013). "The External Dimension of European Union Marine Governance: Institutional Interplay between the EU and the International Maritime Organization", Global Environmental Politics 13(1), 69–87; Barents Observer (19 May 2009). "Russia: Arctic is no EU affair," BarentsObserver, http://barentsobserver.com/en/node/18866. Accessed 20 February 2015. See also Østhagen (2013), *op.cit.*, 78.

integrated strategy, and what does a coherent strategy mean? Therefore, the EU needs to find a balance between the contradictions inherent to the nexus of the complex EU and diverse Arctic. Likely, striking such a balance would be more an on-going process rather than a fixed choice.

The need for the EU to formulate an Arctic strategy is not self-evident, even if the EU's position as an actor relevant in the Arctic is nowadays rarely questioned. Some scholars have had doubts whether there is a need for any EU Arctic policy.[106] It is possible to imagine that various EU institutions, agencies, and Commission's directorates-general rather than struggling to formulate convincing abstract policy documents, simply put greater focus on Arctic dimension in their respective agendas and engage more in Arctic activities without being guided by umbrella policy documents. The coordination value of policy statements that bring together already existing actions, sum up achievements and provide a set of rather abstract objectives and priorities can be indeed impugned. However, there are explicit benefits of an Arctic strategy, policy documents and even very general policy objectives. First, the work on policy documents creates pressure often necessary for the intensification of work. Second, statements communicate values to other actors and may attempt to assure them of EU intentions and its positive contributions in the region. As described above, that had not worked well in the first years of the EU's Arctic policy-making. Third, even starting the debate on conflicting policy objectives allows the realization of existing contradictions. Fourth, the expected economic developments appear to be connected with many uncertainties and removed further in time than initially envisaged (see concluding chapter by Stępień *et al.* in this volume), conceivably resulting in waning of the currently still great attention to the Arctic. Strategic approach allows for a more sustained and long-term engagement. This is of key importance in the case of a policy area, which is rather marginal in the landscape of policy-making within the Union devising regulations for half a billion of citizens, recovering from economic crisis, and struggling to respond to a number of conflicts close to its borders. It is not clear how much interest in the Arctic there actually is within the EU institutions considering the long time it took the Commission and the EEAS to draft the 2012 Communication.[107] Eventually, the EU had little choice but to highlight its presence and interest in the Arctic,[108] as the region moved to the centre of global attention. This was done for the benefit of both international players as well as the EU's internal constituency, some member states and the public

106 Maurer et al. (2012), *op.cit.*

107 See, *e.g.*, Maurer et al. (2012), *op.cit.*; Keil (2012), *op.cit.*

108 Østhagen (2013), *op.cit.*

suddenly interested in the Arctic. The EU simply had to take a stance, it had to "do something about the Arctic".[109]

Nevertheless, it is still far from certain what shape – if any definite shape – the EU Arctic policy could (or should) assume: whether it continues to be a progression of consecutive umbrella documents by the Parliament, Commission and Council,[110] bringing together numerous otherwise unrelated EU policies and actions; or would it take shape of a regional strategy somewhat similar to those developed for the Baltic Sea, Black Sea or the Mediterranean. The latter possibility – although certainly not at the level of comprehensiveness characteristic, for instance, of the Baltic Sea strategy – seems to be closer to the notions pertinent in the 2014 Resolution of the European Parliament, which:

> Reiterates its call for a *united EU policy* on the Arctic, as well as a *coherent strategy and a concretised action plan* on the EU's engagement on the Arctic, with a focus on socioeconomic and environmental issues; believes that this strategic choice is integral in ensuring legitimacy and local support for the EU's Arctic engagement (emphasis added).[111]

Already the term "strategy" is problematic, even though there seems to be little tangible difference between policy and strategy within the EU policy-making culture.[112] Two EU member states – the UK and Germany – consciously avoided calling their policy documents strategies, partly in order not to cause concern among Arctic actors.[113] The anxiety connected with the word "strategy" derives from the notion that actors external to the region may perceive the Arctic as a "strategic region", where such southern actors act in a "strategic" manner in order to take part in shaping Arctic developments. Consequently, only Arctic states (and perhaps actors such as Arctic indigenous peoples) could be considered legitimate to formulate an Arctic strategy.

Further, the Council of the EU in its May 2014 Conclusions requested the European Commission and the High Representative to "present proposals for

---

109 Maurer et al. (2012), *op.cit.*

110 For instance, the comprehensive 2012 Communication of the Commission and High Representative is apparently not even internally perceived as an Arctic policy statement. See, Airoldi (2014), *op.cit.*

111 European Parliament. (2014). Joint Motion for a Resolution on the EU Strategy for the Arctic (2013/2595(RSP)), http://www.europarl.europa.eu/sides/getDoc.do?pubRef=-//EP//TEXT+MOTION+P7-RC-2014-0229+0+DOC+XML+V0//EN. Accessed 15 March 2014.

112 Kobza (2015), *op.cit.*

113 Śmieszek and Kankaanpää (2015), *op.cit.*

the further development of an *integrated and coherent* Arctic Policy by December 2015" (emphasis added). It will be interesting to see how the Commission and High Commissioner understand the integration and coherence, as neither the Council nor the Parliament provide sufficient clues as to what is meant by "coherent" in the Arctic context.

The coherence has a number of dimensions: the scope (how much and what issues are being integrated), the internal dimension (to what extent the objectives can be contradictory), horizontal dimension (between the actions of EU institutions), and the vertical dimension (coherence between the EU and its member states). Vertical coherence may mean harmonization and closer coordination or, in a weaker form, the EU's supplementary role.

The Arctic is a very different space than any region for which the EU has so far developed a strategic approach. The issues to be addressed, including the economic and human scales as well as the scope of the EU presence in the Baltic, Mediterranean or Black Sea regions, make for limited usefulness of the experiences of the earlier EU regional strategic processes.[114] Even the policy towards the Mediterranean region – where the international dimension is far more visible than, for instance, in the case of the Baltic region – is hardly comparable to that of the Arctic.[115]

One dimension of coherence is connected with the geographical scope of the EU Arctic policy. Geographical and "thematic" focus in the context of EU policy-making are closely interrelated. Arctic regions are very diverse in social, environmental and regulatory terms, and the EU's influence on specific issues and parts of the Arctic varies greatly. The EU may place emphasis on the Circumpolar Arctic in general or on the European Arctic comprised of the Arctic territories of EU member states, EEA/EFTA states, as well as regions linked with the EU particularly strongly via funding schemes and cooperation frameworks, that is Greenland and northwest Russia. The distinction is not academic, as the set of priority issues for both spaces is different. The former primarily includes maritime issues, international shipping, exploitation of offshore hydrocarbons and major international developments within IMO or climate

114 Koivurova, T., Stepien, A. & Kankaanpää, P. (2014). "Geography matters: The European Union and the Arctic Ocean", in: E.M. Vazquez Gomez and C. Cinelli (eds.), *Regional Strategies to Maritime Security: A comparative perspective*, Valencia: tirant lo bllanch, pp. 63–78. See also, see also Østhagen (2013), *op.cit.*

115 European Commission, DG Maritime Affairs and Fisheries, "Maritime sea basin", at the European Commission website at http://ec.europa.eu/maritimeaffairs/policy/sea_basins/mediterranean_sea/index_en.htm. Accessed 20 February 2015.

change regime. The latter, in contrast, has a very strong terrestrial dimension, with an apparent focus on sustainable development, livelihoods, concrete environmental protection and resources such as minerals, forestry or landscape rather than hydrocarbons. The EU's strong focus on circumpolar dimension of its Arctic policy is encouraged by locating Arctic policy in the EEAS and DG Maritime Affairs and Fisheries, which yields clear emphasis on the Arctic as a maritime and external policy space. The EU's global environmental agenda also draws attention to circumpolar problems. It must be also remembered that it was the work on the Integrated Maritime Policy that brought EU institutions' attention to primarily to marine affairs in the Arctic context. While the EU Arctic policy has undergone gradual evolution over the last decade, the initial momentum towards giving primary attention to maritime and environmental considerations has been affecting EU policy-making ever since its IMP-based inception in 2007.

From one point of view, the circumpolar and maritime focus could be even seen as surprising as it is in the sphere of foreign affairs that the EU institutions received the weakest mandate from the member states.[116] Moreover, the presence in the European part of the Arctic is reflected in the EU being in a very different position towards the region than actors such as China, Japan or India, to the extent that it is difficult to call it an "external actor".

Arguably, the "Circumpolar Arctic – European Arctic" contradiction can be resolved. The issues grouped under these two labels are interconnected. The resolution, however, requires clearer distinction between various policy areas, defining the presence of the EU within different Arctic spaces as well as formulating a more focused sets of priorities. The concluding chapter in this volume (Stępień *et al.*) proposes that the European Arctic should receive greater attention in the EU policy-making.[117] The earlier (before 2007) EU presence in the European Arctic was fragmented and not framed as "Arctic", but rather related separately to the EEA, the special relationship with Greenland, relations with Russia (including via Barents region), Northern Dimension or the Baltic cooperation. Now, the EU's actions in the European Arctic have already been placed in the Arctic context. This bears similarity to the trend visible in the strategies of the Arctic Eight, who build their standing in Arctic affairs through development

116 Østhagen (2013), *op.cit.*

117 And this approach seems to be at least partly shared by some scholars, see, Østhagen (2013), *op.cit.*; Raspotnik, A. & Østhagen, A. (17 March 2014). "To Svalbard and Beyond – The European Parliament is Back on its Arctic Track", The Arctic Institute: Centre for Circumpolar Security Studies [Commentary], http://www.thearcticinstitute.org/2014/03/to-svalbard-and-beyond-european.html. Accessed 20 February 2015.

of their Arctic regions and then link these internal efforts with enhancing international cooperation and strengthening the political regime for the whole Arctic.[118] There seems to be an increasing understanding of the need for greater attention to the EU's own Arctic backyard, as visible in the shift taking place between the 2008 to 2012 Communication.[119] The 2008 document constituted an external policy document with certain internal aspects (energy savings, use of renewables, focus on the Sámi in the dialogue with indigenous peoples, land transport, highlighting the EU's regional and cross-border programmes), while in the 2012 communication (with the accompanying Joint Staff Working Document[120]) numerous "EU-domestic"[121] elements became a part of the apparent definition of the EU Arctic policy (in particular, regional funding in the northernmost areas of the EU,[122] trans-European transport networks, extraction of raw minerals within the EU, research projects focused on the European Arctic, tourism developments in Lapland, as well as the EEA regulatory framework). The shift is manifested particularly clearly in the 2014 documents from the European Parliament[123] and the Council.[124] The 2014 statements resonate with the pressure of the European Arctic actors. These actors had felt that the EU Arctic policy deals with more abstract international questions pertaining to the central Arctic Ocean and seems to be preoccupied with gaining an observer status in the Arctic Council, while the issues in the European Arctic on which the EU has very tangible influence are largely overlooked or used solely as the justification for the EU's Arctic actorness.[125] It is indeed surprising how the EU policy-makers at the beginning of their Arctic adventure could assume that the EU Arctic policy could be maintained solely as an element of

118 See, *e.g.*, Bailes and Heininen (2012), *op.cit.*

119 European Commission (2008), *op.cit.*; European Commission and High Representative (2012), *op.cit.*

120 European Commission and High Representative (2012). Joint Staff Working Document "Inventory of Activities in the framework of developing a European Union Arctic Policy", SWD(2012) 182 final, Brussels, 26.6.2012.

121 The distinction between domestic and foreign and external and internal in the context of the EU is in any case often blurry.

122 Including purely internal European Regional Development Fund financing in Finland and Sweden. In fact, majority of EUR 1,14 bln mentioned under the title "Investing in sustainable development in the North" was spent in the EU northernmost regions.

123 European Parliament. (2014), *op.cit.*

124 Council of the European Union (12 May 2014).

125 As visible from the discussions during stakeholder consultations in the framework of the "Strategic Environmental Impact Assessment of development of the Arctic" assessment process. Stępień et al. (2014), *op.cit.*

Union's foreign policy when there are numerous actors considering themselves as Arctic within the EU and EEA (the Sámi, regional authorities in Northern Europe, Finnish and Swedish administrations and agencies, non-governmental and business actors in Lapland). These actors were from the inception of the EU's Arctic policy likely to utilize EU Arctic policy-making process to advance their own interests, safeguard or even enhance EU funding for the northernmost regions of Europe as well as bring attention to specific implications of EU policies in the region and highlighting Arctic-specific considerations in the general policy-making processes taking place at the EU level. Consequently, also the earlier analyses of the EU Arctic policy-making process considered it as an exclusively external/foreign policy, drawing a distinction between the policy-making process and the actual presence of the EU in the Arctic.[126] Few analysts, like Kathryn Keil, highlighted the "contradicting demands towards the EU regarding its external and internal role".[127]

The policy which is internally coherent has to reconcile divergent objectives and interests, in the Arctic particularly vivid in the tension between the drive towards economic development and the aim to protect fragile Arctic environment. For the EU, this is visible in the interplay of its climate targets, work towards effective international climate regime, and the need to secure and diversify hydrocarbon imports. As discussed earlier, the EU has to navigate between the developmental discourses currently prevalent among Arctic states and the values-driven internal pressures.[128] A similar tension occurs within the EU Arctic between the aim to increase internal EU production of minerals, the protection of valuable habitats, and commitment to indigenous rights and livelihoods (see chapters by van Dam *et al.* and Latola *et al.* in this volume). The Arctic policy is here intertwined with the developments and tensions taking place within the EU. The new focus on economic development, reindustrialization and jobs and growth – as clearly manifested in the programme of the Jean-Claude Juncker's collage of Commissioners[129] – has been criticized by various European actors, particularly NGOs. There is a perception, that the EU is gradually compromising its environmental leadership,

---

126 Wegge (2012), *op.cit.*; Østhagen (2013), *op.cit.*

127 Keil (2012), *op.cit.*

128 Keil (2012), *op.cit.*; see also Offerdal, K. (2010). "Arctic Energy in EU Policy: Arbitrary Interest in the Norwegian High North", *Arctic* 63(1), 30–42.

129 Juncker, J.-C. (15 July 2014). A New Start for Europe: My Agenda for Jobs, Growth, Fairness and Democratic Change. Policy Guidelines for the new European Commission, http://ec.europa.eu/priorities/docs/pg_en.pdf#page=5. Accessed 20 February 2015.

particularly regarding climate policies.[130] Thus, the work on Arctic questions within the EU becomes a part of intra-EU tensions between the established EU environmental values and the post-crisis emphasis on growth, reindustrialization and economic security.

Another issue is the horizontal coherence between the EU institutions. It remains difficult to perceive the EU – especially for those unfamiliar with the complexity of the EU's internal structure – as a unified actor in relation to the Arctic. The Commission, the Parliament and the Council continue issuing their own statements, each equipped in slightly different emphasis or set of priorities. That results in sending mixed signals both to Arctic partners and to the EU's own public.[131] Arguably, although the positions expressed by the EU institutions have grown closer to each other over the years,[132] it is hard to expect the Parliament to refrain from expressing a more outspoken or even at times controversial stances. While that of course undermines the horizontal coherence, in a long term the Parliament's pressure holds a potential to tilt the balance of internal policy coherence towards environmental values. There remains a question whether various actions undertaken by EU institutions are (horizontally) coherent. For instance, numerous Arctic stakeholder engagement processes discussed above – 'Strategic Environmental Impact Assessment of Development of the Arctic' commissioned by the DG Environment, the operation of the Arctic NGO Forum supported also by DG Environment, the DG Mare consultations on streamlining Arctic funding and the work with stakeholders within the EU-Polarnet process leading to the European Polar Research Programme, supervised by the DG Research – are fairly close in terms of content and the group of involved stakeholders. However, these processes appear almost completely disconnected structurally and in terms of the obtained outputs. Compartmentalization among various EU services – even within the European Commission – remains a problem despite the establishment of coordination mechanisms, particularly the Arctic Inter-service Group.

The vertical dimension refers to the relationship between the EU Arctic policy and the actions of EU member states: three Arctic states as well as major countries such as France, Germany and the UK.[133] The Nordic states seemed to

130 See, *e.g.*, Herrero A. & Knaepen, H. (September 2014). "Run-up to 2015: A moment of truth for EU external climate action?", Briefing Note no. 67, European Centre for Development Policy Management, http://ecdpm.org/wp-content/uploads/BN67-Run-up-2015-moment-truth-for-EU-external-climate-action.pdf. Accessed 20 March 2015.

131 Śmieszek (2013), *op.cit.*

132 Pelaudeix and Rodon (2013), *op.cit.*

133 Maurer et al. (2012), *op.cit.*; Pelaudeix and Rodon (2013), *op.cit.*

be surprisingly reluctant towards very active external EU Arctic policy. However, they clearly encourage the EU's supportive role and the process of sensitizing of the EU institutions regarding Arctic realities.[134] And indeed, the reading of the EU Arctic policy documents suggests that so far the EU Arctic policy has been focused on coordinating EU's actions taken at the "community level" and not harmonizing the actions of EU member states.[135] The EU has assumed a supplementary role. In the last years the EU dedicated resources to surveying the activities of European states and other actors in order to avoid the duplication of efforts and identifying the gaps that could be filled. That was a focus in "Strategic Environmental Impact Assessment of development of the Arctic", which developed a *Compendium of European Arctic Initiatives*[136] (see chapter by van der Watt *et al.* in this volume). It is also the role of the EU-PolarNet project,[137] where, in addition to surveying existing research efforts, the EU provided funding for autonomous network of scientific institutions to develop ways of coordinating research infrastructures, rather than attempting such coordination itself, which would lie outside of the EU's competences.

It remains to be seen whether any elements of the process of Europeanization[138] of Arctic policies of EU member states occurs. This is at best

134 Kobza (2015), *op.cit.*

135 Østhagen (2013), *op.cit.* That undermines the concerns of Arctic states that the European Commission in the Arctic Council would attempt to coordinate positions of Council members and observers who are EU member states.

136 Dahlbäck, B., van der Watt, L.-M., Jagodziński, K. & Kankaanpää, P. (2014). European Arctic Initiatives Compendium. Preparatory Action, Strategic Environmental Impact Assessment of development of the Arctic. Arctic Centre, University of Lapland, http://www.arcticinfo.eu/en/. Accessed 20 February 2015.

137 European Polar Board, EU Proposal on European Research Cooperation, http://www.europeanpolarboard.org/activities/scientific-initiatives/eu-proposal-on-polar-research-cooperation-eu-polarnet/. Accessed 15 February 2015.

138 "Europeanization" has been defined by Robert Ladrech as an "incremental process reorienting the direction and shape of politics to the degree that EC [European Community] political and economic dynamics become part of the organizational logic of national politics and policy making", and could have a number of dimensions: (1) governmental and administrative adaptation of practices of policy making in politics, administration and law; (2) projection of national interests through the EU policy-making level; (3) socialization of elites into pan-European values, worldviews and processes; (4) modernization process (re. less developed European states). See, Wong, R. (2011). "The Europeanization of Foreign Policy", in: Ch. Hill & Smith, M. (eds.), *International Relations and the European Union,* Second edition, Oxford: Oxford University Press, pp. 149–170. Quote from Ladrech, R. (1994). "Europeanization of Domestic Politics and Institutions: The Case of France", *Journal of Common Market Studies* 32(1), 69–88, as quoted in Wong (2011).

doubtful in the case of three EU Arctic states as well as Iceland and Norway, as the Arctic has become a part of these states' national and foreign policy identity. However, it could be argued that EU activities have potential to trigger and sustain in a longer term the interest of member states in Arctic affairs.[139] The EU can be also seen as one of the channels to realize nationally-defined values, aims and interests.[140] Such a function of the EU Arctic policy could constitute an element or a dimension of a rather soft type of "Europeanization" of member states' Arctic or Arctic-relevant policies. This is perhaps most visible in the case of Finland.

Among Arctic states, Finland appears to be a country the most interested in bringing the EU's input to the Arctic table. That is in line with the history of Finnish policy initiatives, starting from the Northern Dimension, one of primary goals of which was to bring Brussels's attention to Europe's north-east periphery and strengthen its regional cooperation with Russia. Similarly, the EU Arctic policy is seen as a means to draw EU's attention to the North. This is visible in particular in Finland's 2010 Arctic strategy, which underlines that "it is important that the EU has recognized the importance of the Arctic Region".[141] Seemingly, Finnish policy-makers also hoped that the increased attention to Arctic issues would be reflected in sustained funding for sustainable development in the North and for Arctic research.[142] Answering a question whether any adjustment of policy goals occurs for Arctic policies of EU member states would be a subject for another study.[143]

Through the lens of the vertical, horizontal and thematic coherence, is it then at all possible or beneficial to develop an "integrated and coherent" Arctic policy for the EU? And if so, what would be the shape or scope of such integration?

One possible way forward in developing Arctic policy is to place emphasis on the process by which Arctic-relevant decisions are made rather than the content of the policy (*i.e.* action plan – understood as a temporally-nested list of specific actions). That entails, *inter alia*: establishing information and

---

139 *Ibid.*

140 As may be read from the analysis of European Arctic states Arctic policies, see, *e.g.*, Bailes and Heininen (2012), *op.cit.*

141 Prime Minister's Office (Finland) (2010). "Finland's Strategy for the Arctic Region", 8/2010, Prime Minister's Office Publications. This is also, albeit less clearly, reiterated in Finland's 2013 statement, see Prime Minister's Office (Finland) (2013). "Finland's Strategy for the Arctic Region 2013.Government Resolution on 23 August 2013", 16/2013, Prime Minister's Office Publications.

142 Maurer et al. (2012).

143 See, Śmieszek and Kankaanpää (2015), *op.cit.*; Pelaudeix and Rodon (2013), *op.cit.*

communication channels, meaningful long-term engagement with Arctic stakeholders, procedures for assessing impacts of EU policies and actions on Arctic regions and communities, as well as modes of continued (as opposed to incidental) and content-oriented involvement in Arctic governance structures, particularly regarding the Arctic Council working groups.[144]

One aspect that needs to be considered in this light is an institutional set-up of Arctic issues that balances foreign and internal, maritime and terrestrial, Northern European and Circumpolar, as well as environmental and developmental contradictions within the EU Arctic policy. It is unclear how that could be achieved. Arctic Inter-service Group meets regularly to facilitate coordination and the preparation of policy documents produced by the Commission. It is composed of officials dealing with Arctic issues from various directorates-general (environment, research, transport, regional policy, maritime affairs and fisheries) and agencies (EEAgency, European Maritime Safety Agency), led by EEAS and coordinated by DG Maritime affairs and fisheries. So far the leadership of the EEAS and DG Mare resulted in the focus on circumpolar, maritime and external dimensions. The new construction of the European Commission with vice-presidents responsible for cross-cutting issues could offer an opportunity for institutional solution facilitating such a balance. Similarly, bringing in Juncker's Commission the environment and maritime affairs portfolios in the hand of one commissioner offers possibility for strengthening terrestrial dimension of Arctic policy.

Eventually, many if not most aspects of EU's Arctic presence that could be further strengthened by the development of regional strategy have incremental value notwithstanding their importance for the position of the EU in the Arctic, including primarily research, facilitating sustainable development of the European Arctic, enhancing international governance, as well as engaging in dialogue with Arctic actors, particularly with Russia. These issues may be considered pillars on which coherent approach is built.

## 6 Conclusion

The process of conscious formulation of EU policy towards the Arctic was triggered primarily by the sudden international interest in northern affairs. The

---

144 Arctic Council working groups are the space where observers in the Council can provide the most tangible contribution. See Graczyk, P. (2011), "Observers in the Arctic Council – Evolution and Prospects", 3 *The Yearbook of Polar Law* 575; Graczyk and Koivurova (2014), *op.cit.*

early responses by European institutions, informed by prevalent dramatic narratives, triggered unease among many Arctic actors. Ever since, however, the approach of EU institutions to the Arctic has become more nuanced and cautious over the fairly short time that the EU has been formulating its Arctic policy, manifested in the 2012 Joint Communication.[145] Compared with the 2008 Commission Communication, the 2012 Joint Communication is no longer critical of Arctic governance and expresses the EU's willingness to responsibly engage to meet the challenges the Arctic region faces with its prime actors, namely the region's nation-states and indigenous peoples. Indeed, as Østhagen justifiably noticed, the EU institutions have become "more attuned to the sensitiveness of Arctic states"[146] as the EU finds itself in an international environment where it is not a leader or dominant partner and where it cannot simply externalize its own values and disseminate European practices.

It could be even stated that the problems the EU has encountered in gaining recognition as a legitimate actor in the Arctic, became for the EU Arctic policy a "blessing in disguise". European institutions had to make effort in order to prove EU's Arctic credibility. The learning process visible in the evolution of EU Arctic policy documents constitutes the main aspect of that effort.

However, the increased sensitiveness of the European Union to the narratives and positions of Arctic states may not always interplay well with the pressures from inside the EU, particularly from the environmental NGOs and from interest groups represented chiefly in or through the European Parliament. Since 2008, the European Commission has attempted to reconcile the – as high as possible – degree of EU fit to Arctic international regime with its prevalent narratives and EU environmental values and internal pressures towards greater and bolder involvement. The upcoming new Communication requested by the Council to be delivered by the end of 2015 will surely constitute next but not the final chapter of this story. The upcoming US[147] and Finnish chairmanships in the Arctic Council, likely coming back to greater emphasis on environmental protection as well as slower pace of expected economic developments (see concluding chapter by Stępień *et al.* in this volume), give also hope for some change in the prevailing developmental narrative in the Arctic.

145 See, *e.g.*, Østhagen (2013), *op.cit.*

146 *Ibid.*

147 See, *e.g.*, American Geosciences Institute (23 October 2014),"State Department announces priorities for Arctic Council chairmanship", http://www.americangeosciences.org/policy/state-department-announces-priorities-arctic-council-chairmanship. Accessed 20 March 2015.

The more typical tensions between the environmental protection on one hand and economic development or energy and trade security interests on the other – visible despite repeating the word "sustainable" 27 times[148] – are but one of contradictions troubling EU Arctic policy affecting its internal coherence. The choice between the emphasis on the issues relevant for the European Arctic and the circumpolar reach of EU Arctic policy is as important. The current trend – supported by a greater role of actors from the European North – seems to be towards increasing focus on the European Arctic. That means also greater attention to terrestrial and internal issues, as opposed to maritime and external focus of the 2008 Communication. No one expects the EU to abandon its global agenda and to refrain from linking its Arctic policy to the EU's role in the international climate change regime. Nor the EU is to defer from participation in developing international regulations aimed at limiting the risks connected with Arctic shipping. However, the attention to the European Arctic could certainly become one of the cornerstones of EU actions in the Arctic.[149] In the long term, the EU's actions in the European Arctic are likely to translate into broader acknowledgment of the EU's actorness in the region – actorness which goes beyond granting the EU an observer status in the Arctic Council. Institutional set-up within the EU, including possible less dominant role of EU services dedicated to external and maritime dimensions may be an important element of striking a balance between these contradictions and tensions.

It could be argued that, analysing EU's influence and competences, the emphasis in EU policy could have been from the beginning on areas where the EU has the greatest influence. It must be, however, remembered that the origins of the EU attention to the Arctic was the global outburst of interest in the North, connected with dramatic security, environmental, economic and political narratives. A gradually more nuanced language of EU documents does not mean that these narratives ceased to play a role. That is not necessarily a downside, as it allows upholding EU environmental and governance values despite the anxiety expressed by Arctic states, and keeps the Arctic as a part of the EU's global environmental agenda. The emphasis on the European Arctic without abandoning the circumpolar environmental goals may constitute the balance the European institutions struggle to strike.

It is still unclear what shape the future Arctic policy will take. The temptations of copying experiences from the Baltic, Mediterranean, Black Sea or North Sea are unlikely to be realized. The very notion of coherent and integrated EU Arctic

148 As is the case with the 2012 Joint Communication, see European Commission and High Representative (2012).

149 Note that the authors of this chapter live and work in the European Arctic.

strategy is vague at best. With the aforementioned contradictions, specific setting of the EU towards the Arctic and overwhelming differences between Arctic regions, "coherence" may turn into either artificial and often even unnecessary adjustments in current EU actions in the region or may settle at the current level of abstract, hardly helpful slogans of "knowledge, responsibility, engagement".

Over the years, the stances expressed by the different EU institutions have come closer to each other, strengthening the horizontal coherence. The voices coming from the European Parliament are likely to take Arctic actors by surprise also in the future. Contrary to the often repeated criticism that is not necessarily a disadvantage in the long-term. The Parliament may serve as an important voice reminding the EU of its founding values and raising bolder environmental goals.[150] This is providing the actors in the European Parliament are properly informed regarding Arctic developments and aware of regional sensitivities so that Antarctic Treaty-type of gaffes are not repeated.

In terms of vertical coherence, the EU policy – as expressed in the documents from the Commission and High Representative – has clearly focused on the EU's own activities and has positioned them largely as supplementary to those of member states. As a result, any more substantial coordination of Arctic policies between the Union and its member states is incidental at best. The EU is bound to focus primarily on surveying various initiatives concerning the Arctic and identifying gaps where the EU actions can play a complementary role.

Ultimately, the EU Arctic policy format and content, after eight years of stronger interest from the EU institutions in the region, there are few who would question the role the EU plays in the Arctic. It is not policy documents and vague statements that constitute the contribution of the EU to the sustainable development of the Arctic and regional governance, but its paramount contribution to Arctic research, regional development and the ongoing dialogue with Arctic partners – whether such dialogue is framed as Arctic or not. That still includes upholding dialogue with Russia, as the Arctic may be one of few themes where relatively normal relations may continue in the light of

150 Visible for instance in the raising the question of the environmental management in the central Arctic Ocean in the 2014 Resolution or conducting recently a study on indigenous peoples' rights and extractive industries, see Burger, J. (September 2014). "Indigenous Peoples, Extractive Industries and Human Rights", In-depth Analysis, European Parliament Directorate-General for External Policies of the Union, EXPO/B/DROI/2013/23, PE 534.980.

overall West-Russia tensions connected with the conflict in Ukraine.[151] All these aspects have their own intrinsic, independent of "Arctic policy" value and hold as major inputs into global and regional developments notwithstanding the excitement the publication of consecutive policy documents triggers among analysts.

Environmental, economic and regulatory footprint or the EU's participation in international negotiations relevant for the Arctic are all clear elements of the EU's role. It is due to this undeniably significant role played by the EU, that the EU institutions may consider focusing in their Arctic policy-making on processes and mechanisms in which the EU engages the Arctic and streamlines Arctic concerns into its general decision-making. This would entail emphasising procedural rather than outcome coherence. The key actions are, therefore, the development of the spaces for dialogue, like the "Arctic (EU-Indigenous) Dialogue" format, as well as the assessment of impacts the EU policies and regulations have on the Arctic. That has to be done with consideration for the diversity of the Arctic regions and the differences in the relationship the EU has with each of them. In the long term, this may constitute the greatest added value of the EU Arctic policy-making process: for the EU institutions, for EU Arctic constituency as well as for the Arctic actors.

---

151 There is currently much discussion on the extent of immunity of Arctic cooperation to external tensions. See, *e.g.*, Käpylä, J. & Mikkola, H. (April 2015), "On Arctic Exceptionalism: Critical Reflections in the Light of the Arctic Sunrise Case and the Crisis in Ukraine", FIIA Working Papers 85, Finnish Institute for International Affairs.

CHAPTER 2

# Climate Change in the Arctic

*Mikko Strahlendorff, Sébastien Duyck, Johan Gille, Timo Koivurova, Anastasia Leonenko, Marie-Theres von Schickfus, Adam Stępień and Jennie Thomas**

## Abstract

Due to climate change, the Arctic is the most rapidly changing region on Earth. There is clear evidence that change has already occurred due to emissions of greenhouse gases and aerosols from human activities, which affect the fundamentals of the Arctic ecosystems and the lives of the Northerners. Over the second half of the 20th century, warming in the Arctic led to increased loss of snow cover in spring and summer and simultaneously increased snowfall during boreal autumn and winter. Arctic sea-ice change has been linked to changes in mid-latitude weather patterns that increase the probability of extreme weather events. The warming trend also appears to result in increased precipitation in northern Europe. The sea level rise is another major concern.

The EU can influence Arctic climate change by limiting its own emissions, including short-lived climate forcers, and championing an effective and broad global climate agreement. The EU has made progress in curbing GHG emissions, partly through policy measures in energy, transport and efficiency improvements, and has set targets for further gains in the period to 2030. The EU, as a key actor in the UNFCCC negotiations, can highlight the Arctic within international processes and support any potential initiatives coming from the Arctic Council. The EU is in a good position to support adaptation in the European Arctic.

The EU is encouraged to increase its efforts and contributions to enhance sustained observation activities in the Arctic in order to improve monitoring of climate change and effects in the region. Current ground- or satellite-based earth observation systems do not fulfil monitoring needs and communication includes bottlenecks. Both for decision-making in the near term and for long-term guidance for Arctic adaptation and sustainable development, climate indicators specific to the Arctic should be identified and corresponding data obtained.

* The authors would like to thank the stakeholders participating in the workshop and online questionnaire. Moreover, they would like to acknowledge Jouni Pulliainen, Ari Laaksonen, Heikki Lihavainen, Adriaan Perrels, Hilppa Gregow (Finnish Meteorological Institute), Agneta Fransson (Norwegian Polar Institute) and Kathy Law (CNRS/INSU, LATMOS-IPSL, France) for their comments, suggestions and input.

 | DOI 10.1163/9789004303188_004

## 1 Introduction

This chapter considers climate change in the Arctic from a European perspective. The Arctic is the region where most rapid changes occur due to climate change. There is clear evidence that change has already occurred due to emissions of greenhouse gases and aerosols from human activities, which affect the fundamentals of the ecosystems of the Arctic and the lives of its inhabitants. The Arctic is a particularly fragile region where strong feedback linkages accelerate changes at a faster pace than in other regions – an effect called "Arctic amplification". Shifts in Arctic ecosystem dynamics have global consequences.

Today, significant changes in Arctic landscapes and marine environments have been monitored. Climatic changes are affecting the Arctic cryosphere, hydrology, habitats and species. In northern Fennoscandia, the changes in snow cover are particularly important for biodiversity, livelihoods and economy. Changes in temperature, sea ice cover, snow cover and water regimes are linked to the loss of important habitats for Arctic species, as well as shifts in species composition due to landscape transformations, which in turn impact on people's livelihoods (Figure 2.1).

Uncertainties regarding various driving mechanisms, evolution and specific impacts of Arctic climate change remain. More long-term observations are

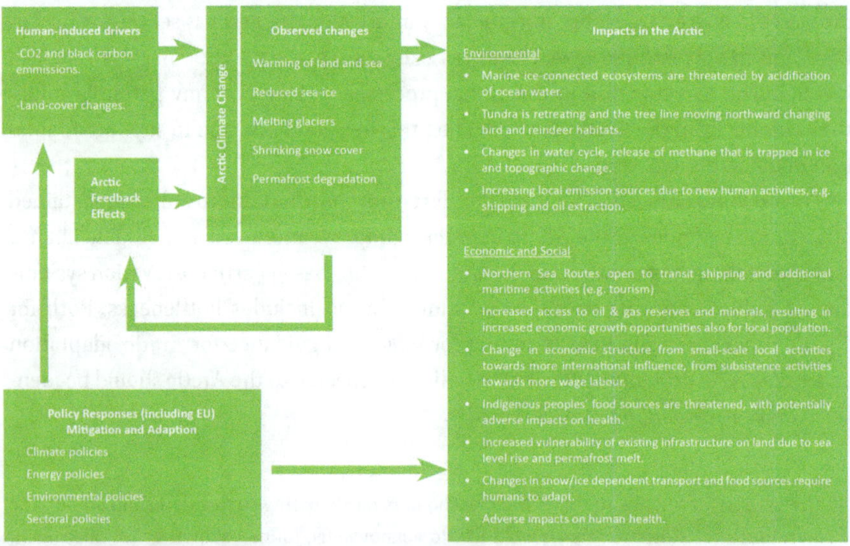


FIGURE 2.1 *Climate change in the Arctic: drivers and impacts*
SOURCE: MIKKO STRAHLENDORFF, FINNISH METEOROLOGICAL INSTITUE; AND ARCTIC PORTAL

needed to improve climate-related predictions in the Arctic. Because of limitations in representing the cryosphere, climate model predictions for the Arctic have a lower confidence level than for other regions. Thus, existing climate prediction models still need to be improved. Nevertheless, the outlook for change in the Arctic is alarming and must be taken into account despite prevalent uncertainties and limitations in the current models.

This chapter looks at potential impacts in the Arctic based on the most recent Intergovernmental Panel on Climate Change (IPCC) reports and region-specific information coming from the Arctic Monitoring and Assessment Programme (AMAP), assessments such as *Sea, Water, Ice and Permafrost in the Arctic* (SWIPA) and the 2004 *Arctic Climate Impact Assessment* (ACIA). The IPCC reviews and assesses the recent available scientific, technical and socioeconomic information relevant for the understanding of human-induced climate change and issues its reviews every four to six years. The IPCC's most recent assessments – which together comprise its *Fifth Assessment Report* – have been released in the period from September 2013 to November 2014. The *IPCC Physical Science Basis* report was the first to be released and the climate change trends and impacts discussed in this chapter are largely based on its findings.[1]

## 2 Trends and 2030 Outlook

Globally the most significant increase in temperature is in the Arctic. Models foresee an almost threefold increase in warming compared to the global average (see Textbox 2.1). Climate prediction models agree that the most pronounced warming (between 4 degrees Celsius (°C) and 10 °C) would likely occur over land surfaces, particularly during the boreal winter. The Arctic amplification effect results in projected temperature anomalies of more than 10 °C in the Arctic region.

### 2.1 *Arctic Sea Ice Cover is Rapidly Shrinking*

The summer extent of sea ice has declined notably in recent years (Figure 2.2). The difference in the extent of sea ice in September 2012 compared with the median over the last three decades is striking (Figure 2.3). In addition, the ice that remains has less multi-year ice, which means it is weaker and thinner.

1 IPCC (2013), *Climate Change 2013: The Physical Science Basis. Contribution of Working Group I to the Fifth Assessment Report of the Intergovernmental Panel on Climate Change* [*Stocker, T.F., Qin, D., Plattner, G.-K., Tignor, M., Allen, S.K., Boschung, J., Nauels, A., Xia, Y., Bex, V. & Midgley, P.M. (eds.)*].

TEXTBOX 2.1 *Why does the arctic warm faster than lower latitudes? – arctic feedbacks*[2]

- As snow and ice melt, darker land and ocean surfaces catch more solar energy and the additional trapped energy directly increases the warming of the atmosphere.
- The Arctic atmosphere is shallower than in lower latitudes (thus, the same amount of absorbed energy warms the atmosphere more) and less effective in transporting energy away.
- Black carbon (soot) increases energy absorption both in the atmosphere and on snow and ice cover.

The outlook is that the extent of the sea ice will continue to decline and that there will be less multi-year ice. If the current trends in global warming hold, the Arctic Ocean could be nearly ice-free in late summer by the mid-2030s.[3]

## 2.2 *Melting Ice Is Raising Sea Levels*

Since 1993, the world average sea level has been rising by 3.2 millimetres (mm) per year, compared with the 1901–2010 average of 1.7 mm per year. As this rise is not uniform, an area in the western North Pacific has risen by even more than 10 mm per year. The melting of glaciers in the Arctic accounts for almost 80% of total ice loss in the last decade. In addition globally warming water is expanding, giving similar rise to sea level as glaciers melting.

Glaciers in Greenland are losing ice mass at a pace over six times greater than in the previous decade (2002–2012 average in comparison to 1992–2002) (Figure 2.4). Moreover, the speed at which the melting occurs has accelerated. Glacier melt predictions involve considerable uncertainties, but the IPCC estimates that melting ice and thermal expansion would result in a sea-level rise of about 15 centimetres in 2030 compared to 2000 levels.

## 2.3 *Snow Cover Is Shrinking Faster than the Sea Ice Extent*

Both the duration and spring/summer extent of snow cover are diminishing. Snow observations in recent years show a more rapid change than in sea ice. Over the period 1967–2012, the extent of the northern hemisphere snow cover

2 ACIA (2004). Impacts of the warming Arctic. Arctic Climate Impact Assessment. Arctic Council.
3 Wang, M. & Overland, J. (2012). A sea ice free summer Arctic within 30 years: An update from CMIP 5 models, Geophysical research letters.

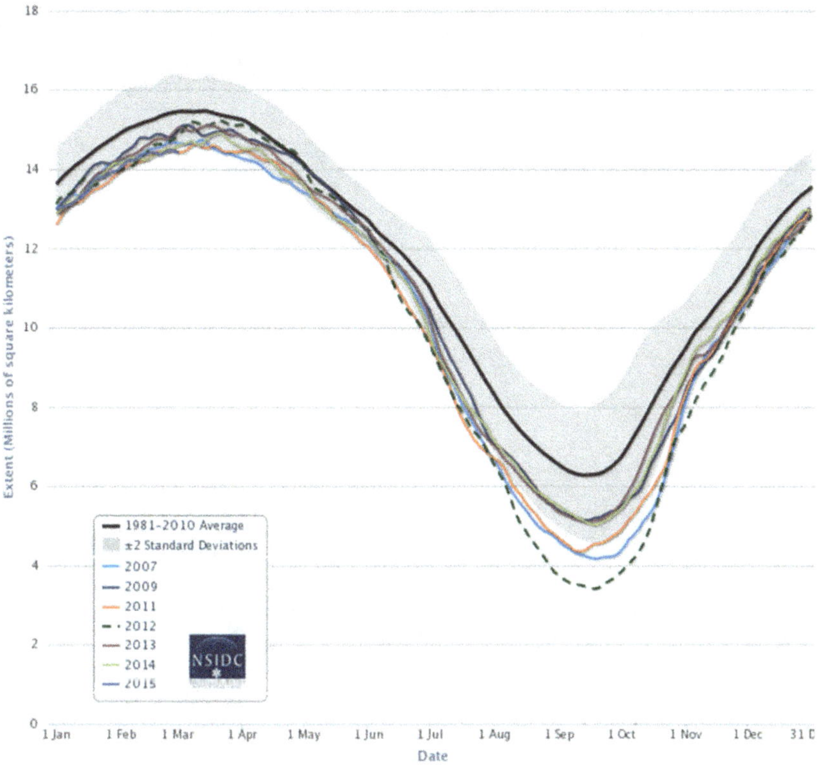


FIGURE 2.2 *Arctic sea ice extent, 2007–2015*
Note: Area of ocean with at least 15% sea ice. The green concatenated line is record low extent in 2012. The dark grey shows the average for 1979–2000; light grey shading represents standard deviations
SOURCE: US NATIONAL SNOW AND ICE DATA CENTER, 2015, MODIFIED

decreased most in June, by 53%. Models indicate a future where winters will likely have more precipitation in the European Arctic, while summers show only modest increases. Hence, the Arctic could see a shorter period of snow cover, while having more snow during winter. In this case, snow cover in the summer would continue to shrink.

## 3 Drivers

The main drivers of Arctic climate change are the same as the drivers of global climate change. The complex interactions governing our atmosphere are

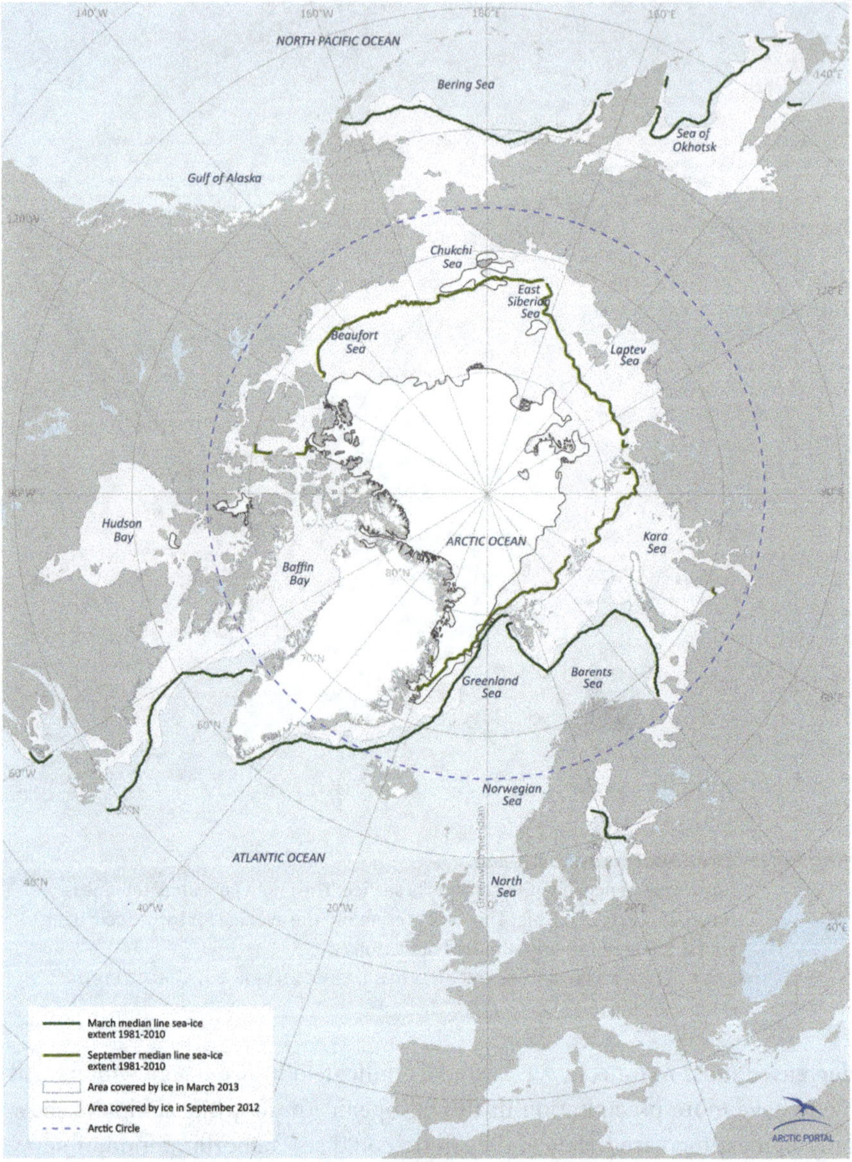


FIGURE 2.3 *Arctic sea ice extent, September 2012, and median September sea ice extent, 1981–2010*
Note: Sea ice extent on 16 September 2012 is shown in dark cyan (all-time minimum). The extent was larger in 2013 (the smallest sea ice extent occurs annually in mid-September). Median September extent for 1981–2010 is shown with an orange contour
SOURCE: ARCTIC PORTAL, BASED ON DATA FROM US NATIONAL SNOW AND ICE DATA CENTER, 2012

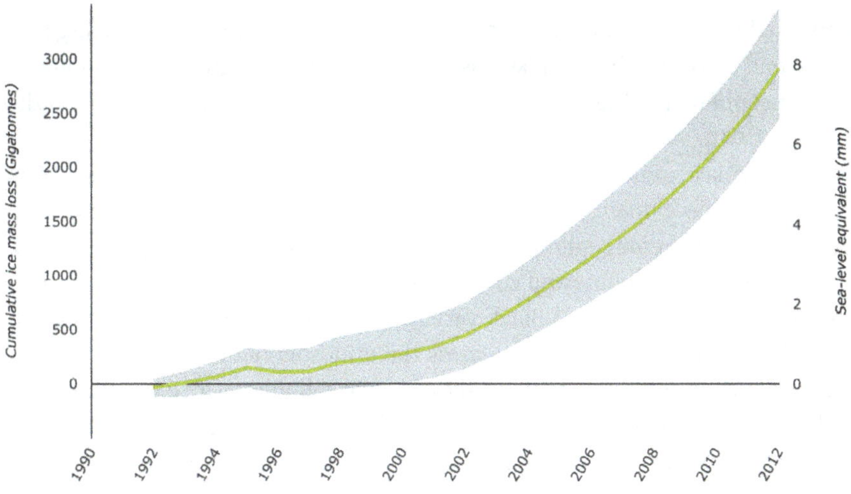


FIGURE 2.4 *Greenland: cumulative ice mass loss and sea level equivalent* (*SLE*)
Note: Derived as annual averages from 18 recent studies
SOURCE: INTERGOVERNMENTAL PANEL ON CLIMATE CHANGE 2013

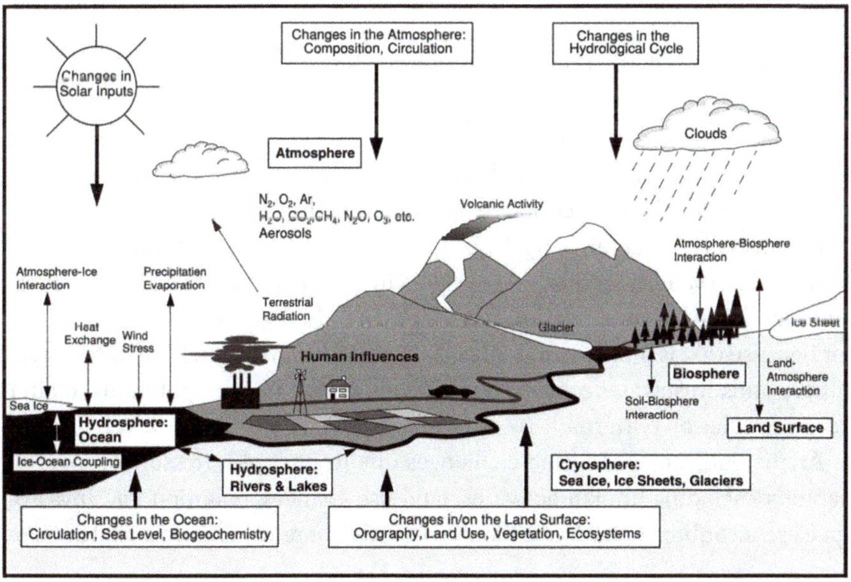


FIGURE 2.5 *Earth climate system and main forcing mechanisms on our atmosphere*
SOURCE: INTERGOVERNMENTAL PANEL ON CLIMATE CHANGE, THIRD ASSESSMENT REPORT, 2002. REPRODUCED FROM WWW.WINDOWS2UNIVERSE.ORG. ACCESSED 20 FEBRUARY 2015

simplified in Figure 2.5. Human activities cause emissions of greenhouse gases (GHG) and aerosols. These emissions increase the natural greenhouse effect of the atmosphere, forcing it to warm and thereby changing many other conditions on Earth.

Aerosols have more complicated processes than long-lived greenhouse gases that impact the climate, such as by changing the location and properties of clouds or by darkening snow or ice surfaces. Aerosols, including soot (black carbon particles), sulphate and co-emitted substances are estimated to contribute to Arctic amplification.[4] Black carbon on snow/ice absorbs more sunlight than clean snow. Soot in the air warms the atmosphere directly and sulphate cools it. Short-lived climate forcers (SLCFs or SLCPollutants), including methane and ozone, also have complicated feedback effects and, taking into consideration changing anthropogenic emissions, SLCFs might either accelerate or mitigate the warming.

The Arctic has a specific amplification mechanism associated with the changing Arctic sea ice extent. Warmer air and water enhance the melting of Arctic sea ice in summer. Ice reflects most sunlight back, but the open ocean absorbs the sunlight energy, resulting in additional warming.

## 4 Climate Change Impacts in the Arctic

Today's global-scale climate prediction models lack the precision and complexity for detailed regional and local impact analysis. Nonetheless, predicted changes can be related to concrete challenges for life in the Arctic.

Oceans absorb some $CO_2$ from the atmosphere in natural processes. Additional $CO_2$ in the atmosphere results in ocean acidification. In the Arctic and high latitudes, acidification is stronger than in regions closer to the equator because $CO_2$ is more soluble in cold water. In addition, melting of the cryosphere adds freshwater to the Arctic Ocean, which has the potential to alter ocean circulation patterns.

Arctic biodiversity is facing challenges due to multiple stressors on natural habitats, including human activities, land-use changes, pollution and invasive species. According to the Arctic Biodiversity Assessment, human-caused climate

4 Shindell, D. & Faluvegi, G. (2009). Climate response to regional radiative forcing during the twentieth century, *Nature Geoscience*, 2, 294 – 300; AMAP (Arctic Monitoring and Assessment Programme) (2011). The Impact of Black Carbon on Arctic Climate. Quinn, P.K., Stohl, A., Arneth, A., Berntsen, T., Burkhart, J.F., Christensen, J., Flanner, M., Kupiainen, K., Lihavainen, H., Shepherd, M., Shevchenko, V., Skov, H. & Vestreng, V.

change is by far the most serious threat.[5] Northward range expansion of many species is already occurring and further shifts are predicted. The overall reduction of the geographical extent of terrestrial Arctic habitats is expected. Warmer temperatures and more precipitation may result in increased plant growth and expansion of animal populations, but in the long term the changes might destroy large tracts of specifically Arctic ecosystems and populations. Habitat changes include earlier and more variable snow melt, increased frequency of winter thaw-freeze events and ice crust formation, disappearance of perennial snow beds, coastal erosion and flooding of low coasts, as well as more frequent and severe extreme events. The risk is particularly high for rare species and for freshwater ecosystems, although the changes are expected to be non-linear.

Ocean acidification is one of the most concrete habitat changes for marine flora and fauna: some populations of traditional species are already growing at a slower rate and invading species are spreading.[6] The substantial loss in multiyear sea ice threatens the biology in and under the ice. Effects along the whole food chain are not yet clearly visible, but marine wildlife is already migrating and habitat changes will be more extreme in the future.

Reduced sea ice, ocean acidification and changes in landscape increase the vulnerability of Arctic inhabitants, especially indigenous peoples and their cultures.[7] Traditional food sources may decline, leading to disruption in hunting and food-sharing practices. Changes in ice, snow cover and permafrost can make traditional transport and hunting routes more dangerous or inaccessible. Changing landscapes can disrupt forage availability, migration routes of reindeer, as well as community infrastructure, water supply and connectivity with population centres. Traditional harvesting and other nature based activities as well as landscapes endowed with cultural and spiritual values are intimately connected with Arctic cultures and identities, both indigenous and non-indigenous, with implications for well-being. Vulnerability and adaptive capacity as properties of human societies are not straightforward concepts. Climate change vulnerability varies with time and is dependent on complex social, economic and cultural structures and interactions.[8]

5 CAFF (2013). Arctic Biodiversity Assessment. Synthesis. Conservation of Arctic Flora and Fauna. Arctic Council, pp. 89–101.

6 AMAP (2013). AMAP Arctic Ocean Acidification Assessment: Summary for Policy-makers. Arctic Monitoring and Assessment Program. Arctic Council.

7 ACIA (2004). Arctic Climate Impact Assessment, Impacts of a Warming Arctic: Arctic Climate Impact Assessment.

8 Stepien, A., Koivurova, T., Gremsperger A. & Niemi, H. (2014). Arctic Indigenous Peoples and the Challenge of Climate Change, in Tedsen, E., Cavalieri, S. & Kraemer, R., Arctic Marine Governance: Opportunities for Transatlantic Cooperation. Dordrecht: Springer. Also the concept of well-being

The climate change impacts that have already been experienced in the European Arctic, especially in Northern Fennoscandia, are connected primarily to changing weather patterns and snow conditions. These may affect winter tourism – the main economic activity for many local communities – and may also complicate reindeer herding due to scarcity of winter pastures, as well as increase flood risk (Picture 2.1). There are also concerns regarding human health due to more active vector-borne diseases. Issues of concern outside the EU Arctic are the thawing of the permafrost and coastal erosion. Conversely, climate change is often perceived as an opportunity for economic and social development, with better conditions for agriculture depending on location, lower costs of infrastructure maintenance, higher attractiveness of winter tourism and greater economic opportunities for more resource exports along Arctic sea routes.[9]

Reduced sea ice can increase access for harvesting marine resources (*e.g.* fish or oil and gas), although that itself may not constitute the main trigger for the occurrence of actual activities, as other factors need to be taken into account. Expanding human activities in fragile Arctic ecosystems may lead to more pollution. For instance, increased maritime traffic leads to bigger emissions of black carbon and other pollutants that can negatively impact Arctic air and water quality and amplify climate change (see other chapters, particularly by Sander *et al.*, in this volume).[10]

## 5 Governance

As a global problem, climate change needs to be tackled together by the world community. In 1992, United Nations Framework Convention on Climate Change (UNFCCC) laid down general obligations to reduce greenhouse gas emissions and to adapt to consequences of climate change. Currently it has 196 parties (including the EU).

---

may have multiple meanings, including cultural, social and economic, not necessarily directly connected to income.

9 See, *e.g.,* Mettiäinen, I. (2013). Climate Change Turn in the Regional Development Strategies of an Arctic Region, Case Finnish Lapland, *Yearbook of Polar Law*, 5, 143 – 183; Tennberg, M. (ed.) (2012). Governing the Uncertain. Adaptation and Climate in Russia and Finland. Dordrecht: Springer; Evengård, B. & Sauerborn R. (2009). Climate change influences infectious diseases both in the Arctic and the tropics: joining the dots, *Global Health Action* 2.

10 See Intergovernmental Panel on Climate Change (IPCC) (2014). Climate Change 2014: Impacts, Adaptation and Vulnerability. Summary for Policy-makers. Fifth Assessment Report. See http://ipcc-wg2.gov/AR5/images/uploads/IPCC_WG2AR5_SPM_Approved.pdf. Accessed 31 March 2014.

PICTURE 2.1 *Ice road and skiing trails on Kemijoki river in Rovaniemi, Finland*
Ice and winter roads are an element of the transport network. Due to mild winters and changes in hydropower systems, it has not been possible to establish ice roads in some locations in Lapland during the past decade
PHOTO BY ILONA METTIÄINEN, ARCTIC CENTRE, UNIVERSITY OF LAPLAND

The treaty, which only establishes general GHG emissions commitments for industrialised countries, provides a framework for negotiating further instruments, such as additional legally briding agreements, defining additional obligations for its parties, including setting binding limits on greenhouse gases. The Kyoto Protocol, concluded in 1997, established legally binding obligations for developed countries to reduce their greenhouse gas emissions. Not all developed states adopted the Protocol and others have since withdrawn from it.

As part of the 2010 Cancun Agreements, 91 countries representing nearly 80% of global greenhouse gas emissions have adopted and submitted targets for international registration or pledged other actions for reductions (see Textbox 2.2). These pledges are not legally binding, but they may be considered politically binding. Most importantly, they fall short of what is necessary to deliver the 2 degree Celsius goal according to UNEP.[11]

11 UNEP (2012), The Emissions Gap Report 2012. United Nations Environment Program (UNEP), Nairobi.

**TEXTBOX 2.2** *Governments agree on a target of 2 degrees celsius and 450 ppm* $CO_2$

At the 2010 UNFCCC Conference of Parties, governments agreed that the average global temperature increase, compared with pre-industrial levels, must be held below 2 °C. Therefore, GHG emissions must be reduced (Cancun Agreements), because an increase of 0.8 °C has already occurred and scientific reports anticipate that this target will be overshot rapidly under business as usual assumptions.

There is broad international acceptance that stabilising the atmospheric concentration of greenhouse gases at below 450 parts per million (ppm) of carbon-dioxide equivalent gives a 50% chance to curb global warming below 2 °C. This threshold is drawing close. Carbon dioxide levels reached 400 ppm in May 2013, having jumped by 2.7 ppm in 2012 – the second-highest rise since record-keeping began.

In 2012, 38 countries, representing 13% of global GHG emissions, extended the Kyoto Protocol to 2020, taking on binding targets. Major GHG emitters either do not have binding emission reduction targets, such as China, or are outside of the Kyoto Protocol, such as the United States, the second-largest emitter. Canada has also withdrawn from the Protocol, while Russia, Japan and New Zealand have refused a post-2012 Kyoto target.

A new phase in the international climate change negotiations resulted from the COP in 2011. The focus is on the negotiation of "a protocol, another legal instrument or an agreed outcome with legal force under the UNFCCC applicable to all Parties," to be negotiated by December 2015 and to enter into force by 2020. It would be the first global climate agreement applicable to all countries, establishing binding reduction targets for both developed and emerging economies.

The Inuit, under the auspices of the Inuit Circumpolar Council, initiated legal proceedings against the United States (in the Inter-American Commission on Human Rights [IACHR]) on the basis of climate change having adverse effect on the human rights of the Inuit. The petition was unsuccessful in legal terms but highlighted the plight of Arctic indigenous peoples. More recently, the Arctic Athabaskan Council initiated proceedings against Canada for its failure to address black carbon pollution, that is increasing warming and melting in the Arctic.

Climate change is also being addressed at the regional, Arctic level. Since countries in the Arctic can directly influence some effects by reducing the sources of short-lived climate forcers, they agreed recently within the Arctic Council to pursue actions to establish national black carbon emission inventories.

*Vulnerability and Adaptation to Climate Change in the Arctic* has been the main climate change adaptation programme under the auspices of the Arctic Council. Ongoing work is carried out via the Adaptation Actions for a Changing Arctic project. The aim is to enhance the capacity of decision-makers to manage climate risks via an information portal and through improved predictions of multivariate impacts.

Local and regional authorities in the European Arctic are taking measures to address climate adaptation in the development of strategies where both relevant risks and opportunities are considered.[12] In Russia, even though the mainstream discourse on climate change diverges from that prevalent in the West, the Barents regions are also taking up strategic work with regard to climate change.[13]

## 6 How Climate Change in the Arctic May Affect the European Union

Climate change is evident in the Arctic areas of EU member states and the impacts are felt all over the world. The Arctic, as an important part of the global climate system, plays a crucial role in how Europe is affected by climate change. European weather will become harder to predict as the Arctic melting progresses.

The European Environment Agency (EEAgency) highlighted the main impacts of climate change in Europe,[14] including: increased mean temperature and longer heat waves, increase in precipitation in northern and northwestern Europe and decrease in southern Europe, warmer rivers and lakes, changes in river flows depending on the region, earlier spring and later autumn, and changes in conditions for agriculture. The contribution of climate change to the costs of damage caused by natural disasters is expected to increase in the future. Specific impacts vary to a great extent across the continent.

The melting of the Greenland ice sheet is a significant cause of the rise in the sea level. The impact will affect coastal areas in central and southern

12 Mettiäinen (2013), *op. cit.*

13 Forbes, B. & Stammler, F. (2009). Arctic climate change discourse: the contrasting politics of research agendas in the West and Russia, 2 Polar Research, 28–42.

14 See, *e.g.* European Environment Agency (2012). Climate change, impacts and vulnerability in Europe 2012. EEAgency Report No 12/2012.

Europe.[15] The Netherlands is already commercialising adaptation measures against coastal flooding.

Arctic amplification has implications for weather over Europe.[16] A warmer Arctic already led to increased loss of snow cover in spring and summer over the second half of the last century. In contrast, the snow cover in the boreal autumn and winter increased over the 20th century, since a warmer atmosphere produces greater snowfall in autumn (especially in October). This trend seems to be accelerating.[17]

Arctic sea ice change has also been linked to changes in mid-latitude weather patterns that increase the probability of persistent extreme weather events, such as droughts, floods and heat waves in summer and cold snaps in winter.[18] Loss of Arctic sea ice appears to result in increased precipitation in northern Europe.[19] The very low extent of sea ice in summer and autumn enhances the probability of a colder following winter in Europe. Considering that climate modelling in the Arctic is not as reliable compared to lower latitudes, the same presumably applies to Arctic weather prediction modelling. Weather predictions over Europe will probably be more challenging in the coming decades as European weather is related to Arctic conditions.

Decreased winter sea ice coverage, accompanied by a higher surface temperature over the Arctic Ocean, results in a less maritime, more continental climate in Europe. Anomalously low sea ice coverage in the Barents and Kara Seas in winter increases variability in European winter temperatures.

The Arctic environment will be under stress from rapid changes. This will also affect EU territory, thus exerting pressure on EU regulatory frameworks. The most imminent area is biodiversity, as many Arctic species will be threatened in Europe. Arctic species today enjoy large areas of habitat that support a range of ecological processes and interactions.[20] However, climate change, industrial development, pollution, local disturbances and invasive alien species are affecting the Arctic, and their impacts are increasing. Nature conservation goals (like stopping biodiversity loss) may be hard to achieve.

---

15 *Ibid.*

16 Francis, J.A. & Vavrus S.J. (2012). Evidence linking Arctic amplification to extreme weather in mid-latitudes. *Geophysical Research Letters*, 39. L06801, doi:10.1029/2012GL051000.

17 IPCC (2013).

18 Tang, Q., Zhang, X. & Francis, J.A. (2014). Extreme summer weather in northern mid-latitudes linked to a vanishing cryosphere. *Nature Climate Change*, 4, 45–50, doi:10.1038/nclimate2065.

19 Screen, J.A. (2013). Influence of Arctic sea ice on European summer precipitation. *Environmental Research Letters* 8(4), doi:10.1088/1748-9326/8/4/044015.

20 CAFF (Conservation of Arctic Flora and Fauna)(2013). Arctic Biodiversity Assessment: Report for Policy Makers. CAFF, Akureyri, Iceland.

EU policy areas likely affected by Arctic change include transport, energy, fisheries, climate change and the environment. Therefore, it would be useful to prepare the next Multiannual Financial Framework of the EU (2021–2027) with the relevant predicted climate impacts in mind.

## 7 EU Policies Relevant for Arctic Climate Change

The EU has the most significant influence on Arctic climate change via its transport, energy, trade and climate policies, and particularly in its role in helping to shape a global climate regime. A significant portion of the black carbon reaching the Arctic originates in Europe. The EU accounts for about 11% of global GHG emissions (2013).[21]

The EU's share of global emissions has been declining (Figure 2.6). In part this reflects positive results from mitigation and efficiency gains, as well as shifts in economic structure with less manufacturing and more services as well as the economic slowdown since 2008. It is also due to the increase in GHG emissions from large emerging economies such as China and India, whose production supplies European markets.

The most visible components of the EU's climate change-related policies have been its 20-20-20 targets – 20% cut in GHG emissions, 20% share of renewables in energy consumption and 20% increase in energy efficiency – by 2020. The EU is well on the way to meeting the emissions goal, with a 27% reduction expected by 2020.

New climate and energy goals for 2030 were launched in January 2014. The target is to reduce domestic GHG emissions by 40% from the 1990 levels (and towards the target of an 80% cut by 2050) and increase the share of renewables to at least 27% by 2030.[22] The role of energy efficiency in the 2030 framework will be further considered in a review of the Energy Efficiency Directive[23] due to be concluded in the coming years. In the context of the UNFCCC and

---

21 Olivier, J.G.J. et al. (2014). Trends in global $CO_2$ emissions: 2014, PBL Netherlands Environmental Assessment Agency and the Institute for Environment and Sustainability (IES) of the European Commission's Joint Research Centre (JRC) Report, http://www.pbl.nl/sites/default/files/cms/publicaties/PBL_2014_Trends_in_global_CO2_emissions_2014_1490_0.pdf, Accessed 25 January 2015; European Environment Agency.

22 European Commission (2013). 2030 climate and energy goals for a competitive, secure and low-carbon EU economy. *europa.eu,* Accessed 10 January 2014.

23 Directive 2012/27/EU of the European Parliament and of the Council of 25 October 2012 on energy efficiency, amending Directives 2009/125/EC and 2010/30/EU and repealing Directives 2004/8/EC and 2006/32/EC (Text with EEA relevance).

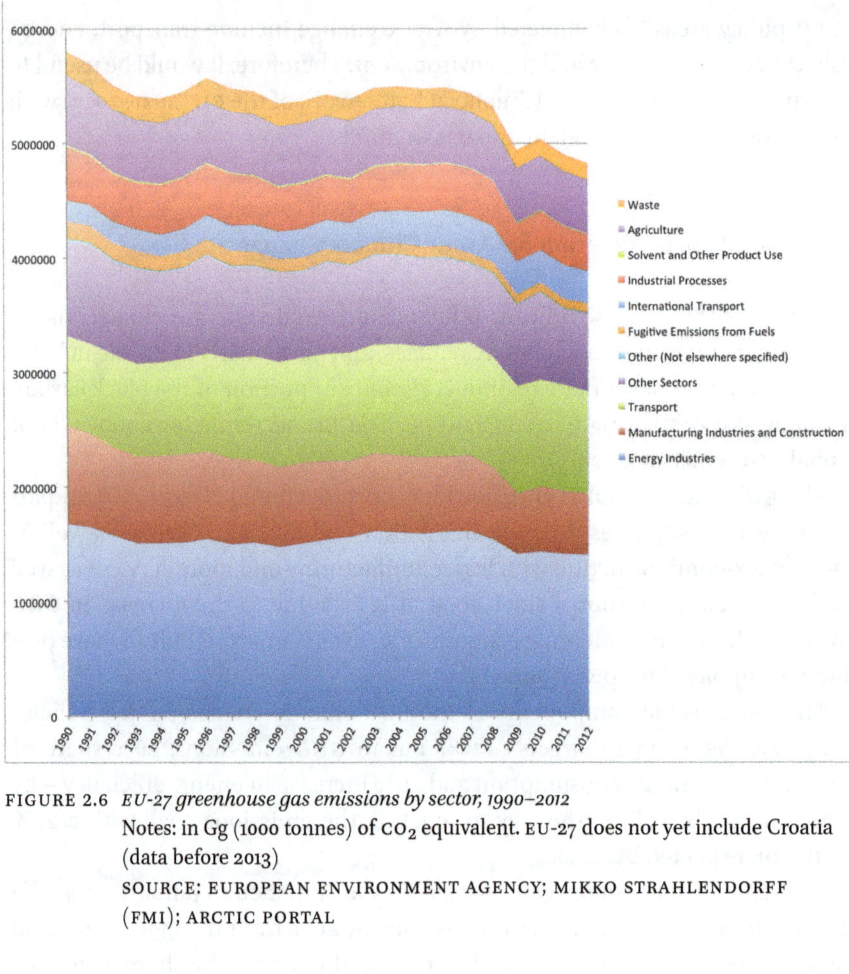


FIGURE 2.6 *EU-27 greenhouse gas emissions by sector, 1990–2012*
Notes: in Gg (1000 tonnes) of $CO_2$ equivalent. EU-27 does not yet include Croatia (data before 2013)
SOURCE: EUROPEAN ENVIRONMENT AGENCY; MIKKO STRAHLENDORFF (FMI); ARCTIC PORTAL

international negotiations, the EU has a joint reduction target, which is internally shared among member states.

EU policies in many areas affect energy production, the largest contributor to $CO_2$ emissions. In the transport sector, curbing emissions remains challenging, even though the EU has fuel-economy standards, supports public and rail transport and has made attempts to introduce a carbon tax for aviation. The EU established the world's first GHG emissions trading system (EU ETS). It covers about 45% of EU GHG emissions and is a key instrument to reach the emission reduction targets. However, the carbon price in the EU ETS declined by more than 80% from 2008 to 2013, partly due to the economic slowdown. To make the EU ETS more robust and effective in promoting low-carbon investment at least cost to society, the Commission proposes to establish a market stability reserve at the beginning of the next ETS trading period in 2021. The reserve would both address the emission allowances surplus that has built up in recent years and improve the system's resilience to major shocks by automatically adjusting the supply of allowances to be auctioned.[24]

The EU Clean Air policy package adopted in December 2013 includes short-lived climate forcers (including black carbon). The EU is also active in addressing black carbon emissions from ships within the International Maritime Organization. The European Commission is a leading partner in the UNEP-led Climate and Clean Air Coalition.[25]

The EU is increasingly active in climate adaptation within Europe, including its northernmost regions, on the basis of the 2013 Climate Adaptation Strategy package. Adaptation is to be taken into account, with Arctic regions perceived as particularly vulnerable, across various EU policies: transport, health, migration, cohesion, agriculture, disaster insurance, fisheries, maritime and coastal issues. The EU climate adaptation platform, CLIMATE-Adapt, is intended to support informed decision-making at all governance levels and to include a toolset for adaptation planning. However, so far no case studies from the Arctic have been included in the platform.[26] The EU adaptation strategy also encourages member states to prepare national adaptation strategies. Swedish and Finnish strategies have already been adopted. In addition, EU funding programmes have supported development of regional and local climate change strategies (*e.g.* European Regional Development Fund in Finnish Lapland).

Various initiatives supported by the European Commission serve exchanging information and experience regarding climate change adaptation in Europe. One example is the initiative "Mayors Adapt" launched in 2014, which focuses on adaptation measures.[27] Apart from Oulu and Reykjavik, Arctic cities are not involved in this network. While participation is dependent on the will of particular local authorities, including representation of a region as special in relation to climate change impacts as the Arctic should be encouraged as it, would, *inter alia*, be beneficial for having early experience of adaptation in action.

The EU will provide EUR 12 billion for space technologies in the 2014–2020 financial framework, including the Copernicus and Galileo programmes. Copernicus, the EU's Earth Observation Programme, will significantly

24 European Commission website at http://ec.europa.eu/clima/policies/2030/index_en.htm. Accessed 5 March 2014.

25 The Climate and Clear Air Coalition to Reduce Short-Lived Climate Pollutants website, http://www.ccacoalition.org/. Accessed 26 January 2015.

26 Climate-ADAPT website, http://climate-adapt.eea.europa.eu/sat/. Accessed 26 January 2015.

27 Mayors Adapt Initiative website, http://mayors-adapt.eu/. Accessed 18 August 2015.

contribute to the regular monitoring of the atmosphere, oceans and land surfaces, and will provide information in support of a broad range of environmental and security applications and decisions.[28] The data provided will also enable progress in improving maritime security, climate change adaptation and providing support in emergency and crisis situations. Copernicus services have Arctic information included, but not in a holistic crosscutting way. There is still potential to establish an EU Arctic Monitoring Centre within the Copernicus programme.

Good quality Arctic reanalysis[29]– that combines satellite (areal) and ground station point measurements in a multi-parameter data set in 3D – would help to improve climate predictions in the Arctic. Such analysis for the Arctic should be facilitated following the launch of the Copernicus programme's climate change service (due to start in 2015).[30] Full quality in reanalysis can mainly be achieved by comparing to other reanalyses, so conducting several is necessary. For example, Ohio State University in the United States is currently completing the first Arctic reanalysis that covers the period 2000–2012.

## 8 Critical Factors for EU Decision-making

Stakeholder consultations included strong representation from researchers, among a variety of many other interests. The following issues were raised as particularly relevant and challenging when considering actions related to Arctic climate change.

### *Energy*

The topic encompasses global energy production as well as hydrocarbon exploitation in Arctic territories. Combustion of carbon fuels is the primary contributor to human-induced $CO_2$ emissions worldwide. While climate change is opening access to unexploited resources in the Arctic, their potential development would expand the global fuel supply and exacerbate the climate

28 European Commission. Press Release: EP adopts European Earth Observation programme Copernicus, 12 March 2014. http://europa.eu/rapid/press-release_IP-14-257_en.htm. Accessed 18 March 2014.

29 Reanalysis is a scientific method for developing a comprehensive record of how weather and climate are changing over time using observations and numerical models. (See http://reanalyses.org/. Accessed 20 February 2015).

30 European Union (2014). Regulation of the European Parliament and of the Council establishing the Copernicus Programme and repealing Regulation (EU) N° 911/2010.

change effects. Investments in Arctic hydrocarbon extraction would lock in emissions for decades to come. The contradictions around Arctic reserves of fossil fuels have become a focus of many environmental NGO s, some of which advocate a ban on Arctic exploration and development activities. Other parties consider these reserves to be a key driver of new economic activities in the Arctic, helping to address the region's varied challenges and problems.

### *Holistic Governance Frameworks for Economic and Climate Sustainability*

To find a balance between economic, environmental and social interests and still to pursue sustainable development, it is necessary to connect all types of governance and economic frameworks. Ideally this contributes to sustainable development (low-carbon green economy, land/marine spatial planning, ecosystem-based management). In order to move closer to holistic governance, such frameworks need to include all three dimensions of sustainability, following the outcomes of Rio + 20.[31] The structure of governance plays a key role in addressing the challenge of climate change, in terms of both mitigation and adaptation.

### *Monitoring of Arctic Change*

Arctic observations have many operators with different requirements, but few ground stations for achieving good spatial coverage. Satellites give good spatial coverage except over the pole, but the resulting data represents an areal average rather than point measurements (like stations). Combining both sets is desirable to produce consistent data sets for understanding the whole situation. Particularly climate change modelling requires data with both full coverage and station precision.

Reanalysis is an approach that uses numerical models to calculate from all available observations (ground stations and satellite areal coverage) a consistent state of all variables of the atmosphere and its boundaries over land, ocean, lakes and ice surfaces. For the Arctic, past records like this are strongly needed. Many current climate change models have difficulties with reproducing the past sea ice correctly, which results in higher uncertainty. Currently it is wise to use trends from recent observations rather than rely solely on model predictions.

Monitoring the Arctic is a challenge and would need more ground stations, satellite systems flying over the pole and broadband communications.

31 RIO + 20 conference outcome (2010). The Future We Want: Outcome document adopted at Rio + 20.

### *Communication*

Communication is important to better understand the role of the Arctic in climate change, to grasp the challenges it poses to society and to broaden participation in climate action. In the EU context, one of the key issues is linking Arctic change to feedback impacts in Europe. Europeans need to pay attention to Arctic changes, as these affect their own lives as well.

## 9 Conclusions: Ways Forward for the EU

The Arctic is the region where most rapid changes occur due to climate change. There is clear evidence that change has already occurred due to emissions of greenhouse gases and aerosols from human activities, which affect the fundamentals of the Arctic ecosystems and the lives of the Northerners. For the European Arctic, changes in snow cover are likely to be more significant than sea ice loss. Over the second half of the 20th century, warming in the Arctic led to increased loss of snow cover in spring and summer. Arctic sea-ice change has been linked to changes in mid-latitude weather patterns that increase the probability of extreme weather events. The warming trend also appears to result in increased precipitation in northern Europe. However, forecasting Arctic weather remains challenging as observations in the Arctic are sparse. The resulting changes have already had notable impacts on biodiversity and livelihoods. More profound implications for Arctic economies and societies are expected in the future.

The EU aims to build flexible legislation frameworks that can adapt to new information. In association with the member states, the EU needs to establish an effective policy monitoring system to produce this guiding information. The framework model for this is already accepted in the EU and many monitoring activities have been launched to enable policy evaluation, but the monitoring and information production are not developed yet – at least not for the Arctic.[32]

Science-based policy-making and continuous performance evaluation of policy actions should become a common practice. This requires availability of accurate and updated data as well as proper communication of the current state of knowledge so that the information and its implications are understood and can be used by decision-makers. Current monitoring is not sufficient for this; it is necessary to both extend and sustain observations in the Arctic. In addition, the chain from observations to decision-making needs to

32 European Commission (2014). Regulatory Fitness and Performance Programme (REFIT).

be organised in an effective manner. Several key areas for improvements have been identified:

- Sustain support for monitoring infrastructure (*i.e.* stations, networks, data platforms, etc.).
- Station operations need to evolve from research campaigns to continuous measuring.
- Extend the observation station networks on sea ice and in the sea.
- Prioritise Arctic user requirements for earth observation (EO) satellite missions.

Co-ordination and communication of EU Arctic research needs to be improved. This implies increasing support for actions that enable Arctic information to more effectively inform and influence EU policy-making.

***Support Sustaining Systematic Observation Activities***

As a member of Sustaining Arctic Observing Networks (SAON), the EU should effectively support SAON's actions. So far, SAON has had limited success as tasks are performed on a voluntary basis, usually within projects with little funding. Arctic countries have not yet pooled any meaningful resources for sustaining observation infrastructure in the Arctic, so offering a European top-up could encourage them to do more.

EU research infrastructure development can add to the Arctic Observing System: examples include soon-to-be established legal entities such as the European Research Infrastructure Consortia (ERIC), like:

- Euro-Argo for marine profiling floats.[33]
- Integrated Carbon Observing System for carbon flux stations.[34]
- EuroFleets for co-ordinating marine research vessel sharing.[35]
- Svalbard Integrated Observation System (SIOS) for connecting and sharing infrastructure around Spitsbergen.[36]

EuroFleets2 has secured project funding through 2017. SIOS is currently in its preparatory phase. Other research infrastructure initiatives (INTERACT, PanEurasian EXperiment) make significant contributions to Arctic monitoring, but the ERIC groups have made the greatest progress in stepping up their

33 See Euro-Argo: http://www.euro-argo.eu/. Accessed 13 February 2014.

34 See ICOS: http://www.icos-infrastructure.eu/. Accessed 13 February 2014.

35 See Eurofleets: http://www.eurofleets.eu/. Accessed 13 February 2014.

36 See SIOS: http://www.sios-svalbard.org/. Accessed 13 February 2014.

operations from pure research campaigns to continuous operational observations. The cryosphere is poorly addressed on the current ESFRI (European Strategy Forum for Research Infrastructures) roadmap, although it would have the potential to warrant specific actions.

To have a stronger impact, a research infrastructure project should prepare a more robust planning and implementation mechanism for Arctic observation activities. This action could effectively be arranged with Horizon 2020 infrastructure funding, but it would need to include partners from all Arctic countries to produce a full Arctic Observing System. For example, continuous observations on the ice and in the sea should be extended and sustained. This project could also set up continuous information production processes for EU Arctic policy needs.

As current satellite-based EO systems are not fulfilling user needs for communication and monitoring, the EU should take remedial measures. EO is crucial for Arctic monitoring, as the ground-based station networks are sparse and lined up on the edges of the Arctic area. Current development of the third-generation geostationary (GEO) satellites will provide an image of the whole earth every 15 minutes, from 60° south to 60° north at 0.5–2.0 km spatial resolution, which is standard in modern state-of-the-art meteorology. However, the spatial resolution degrades above 60° due to the earth's curvature, leaving the Polar Regions without coverage.[37] On polar orbiting satellites most Arctic-specific data is gathered as a secondary target as the prime targets are over populated areas.[38]

Both for decision-making in the next few years and for long-term guidance for Arctic adaptation and sustainable development, climate indicators should be identified and corresponding data obtained. The indicators should be derived for both recent monitoring and predicted futures. This is a clear goal in the Copernicus climate change service plans and should be a priority reflecting the strong nature of change in the Arctic.

### *Support Regional and Local Adaptation*

Apart from facilitating more sustained and better monitoring, the second Arctic-specific domain for EU action is supporting adaptation in the European

37 See Polar Communication and Weather Mission: http://www.asc-csa.gc.ca/eng/satellites/pcw/. Accessed 18 March 2014.

38 There are plans for Canadian and Russian satellites in highly elliptical orbits that would have a major impact on monitoring in the Arctic. Unfortunately neither the Canadian Polar Communication & Weather (PCW) mission nor the Russian ARKTIKA missions are close to launch, as their funding remains uncertain. By 2030, a multilateral Joint Arctic Weather Satellite system could be envisaged. Such a system would provide near real-time weather and ice data for ensuring safe maritime transport and other human activities in the Arctic.

Arctic. As the rate of warming in the Arctic is two to three times faster than the global average, the European Arctic is among the first parts of the EU where widespread climate change adaptation is needed. The EU should promote regional adaptation, including appropriate early planning and reliable risk analysis, in order to decrease the possible costs of adaptation.

National-level adaptation plans are common practice for EU member states, while regional and local plans are only starting to emerge. The EU should strengthen its efforts to build local capacities and facilitate local and regional strategic planning and actions. Local governance levels face challenges in applying current climate change data. Current prediction information is generally too broad in terms of spatial and temporal resolution. Downscaling and extracting target data should be improved. Many elements of adaptive actions need expert guidance for reaching optimal efficiency.

Tracking local adaptation plans would be useful to the EU both for ensuring that decisions are based on knowledge and for identifying information gaps. Analysis of the first adaptation activities should discover effective means for making efficient decisions. For example, the Arctic Council is currently implementing the *Adaptation Actions for a Changing Arctic* project, which the EU could support. Scientific dialogue with local authorities, inhabitants and indigenous peoples is needed. Arctic adaptation-related education in schools and universities would lead to wider public dissemination of information.

Flora and fauna are affected by ecosystem changes triggered by climate change. This requires effective EU policy responses, including the need to adjust conservation policies to the paradigm of "habitats in change" and to support the monitoring and reporting of species on a more frequent and detailed basis.

Efforts should be made that various EU initiatives relevant for climate adaptation include representation from the Arctic regions, as these areas face – in the European context – special climate challenges and circumstances, and these are manifested in the earliest stage.

### *Contributing to Highlighting the Arctic in International Co-operation and Acting via Own Energy Policy*

Eventually, the primary areas of EU activities remain for the coming years in progressive participation in UNFCCC process and acting through the EU's own energy policies. The stakeholders agreed that the EU should promote a precautionary approach regarding Arctic climate change. The EU should work together with Arctic countries to address Arctic concerns within the UNFCCC process. Practically, the EU could call for the Arctic perspective to be taken up in the UNFCCC process by inviting information related to determine "dangerous climate change" thresholds in the region and highlight such information in the context of the ongoing review of the global long-term goal.

The EU could reiterate its willingness, as an Arctic Council *observer in principle* (see chapter by Stępień and Koivurova in this volume), to "support the work of the Arctic Council, including through partnerships with member states and Permanent Participants bringing Arctic concerns to global decision making bodies" (in accordance to the Arctic Council Observer Manual).[39] Moreover, the EU should ensure that the outcomes of EU-funded Arctic research are fed into the UNFCCC process. In more ambitious terms, "Arctic interests" within the UNFCCC could be facilitated by the Arctic Council becoming an observer at the UNFCCC. If such a proposal comes from the Arctic states, the EU could play a supportive role.

The EU's own actions need to accelerate progress to a competitive low-carbon future. This includes increasing support to alternative energy sources and showing leadership in technology innovation and uptake to make energy use more efficient. The Arctic could be the showcase for intelligent carbon neutral solutions that are not dependent on resource extraction.

Concluding, the EU can influence Arctic climate change by limiting its own emissions, including short-lived climate forcers, and championing an effective and broad global climate agreement. The EU has made progress in curbing GHG emissions, partly through policy measures in energy, transport and efficiency improvements, and has set targets for further gains until 2030. The EU, as a key actor in the UNFCCC negotiations, can highlight the Arctic within international processes and support potential initiatives coming from the Arctic Council. Eventually, the EU is in a good position to support adaptation in the region and the EU can significantly improve Arctic monitoring supporting all its potential actions.

39 Arctic Council, Arctic Council Observer Manual for Subsidiary Bodies, www.arctic-council.org. Accessed 10 March 2014.

CHAPTER 3

# Changes in Arctic Maritime Transport

*Gunnar Sander, Johan Gille, Adam Stępień, Timo Koivurova, Jennie Thomas, Jean-Claude Gascard and Debra Justus**

## Abstract

Arctic shipping is dominated by internal and destinational traffic. This is likely to remain the case for the coming decades. Extraction of Arctic resources is a major driver. Future traffic volumes and patterns are uncertain and depend on the future developments in key sectors such as mining, oil and gas, fisheries, forestry and cruise tourism.

Trans-Arctic shipping is slowly emerging, but there are major constraints for rapid expansion. Sea-ice causes risks, additional costs, lower predictability and only seasonal opportunities that make Arctic routes less attractive particularly for the large volume of container ships operating on fixed schedules. There are also severe shortages in supporting infrastructure. Arctic sea routes must be safe, reliable and more profitable than alternative routes and modes of transport before they can become commercially attractive.

Harsh natural conditions and lack of adequate infrastructure pose substantial risks for safety of operations. There are also major environmental concerns about accidental oil spills, pollution from regular operations, introduction of alien species, emissions to air and disturbance of wildlife.

Europe may benefit from Arctic shipping through access to new resources, growing trade and economic benefits to ship owners and maritime industries. Developments in the Arctic will probably be uneven both geographically and socially unless there are mechanisms ensuring distribution of benefits in place.

The European Union can have a role in improving the international governance of Arctic shipping, supporting the development of critical maritime infrastructure – for instance, through its surveillance and communication systems – and contribute to the production of knowledge needed for safer and environmentally responsible maritime activities. Effective measures reducing risks and negative impacts should be introduced

* The authors would like to thank Stig Dalsøren (CICERO, University of Oslo), Kathy Law (CNRS/INSU, LATMOS-IPSL), Anastasia Leonenko (UiT), Lawson Brigham (University of Alaska) and Marie-Theres von Schickfus (Ecorys; Ifo Institute) for input, discussions and reviews. We are also grateful to the stakeholders who sent us written comments to the fact-sheet, and to those who participated at a workshop in Tromsø January 2014.

 | DOI 10.1163/9789004303188_005

before the traffic increases to levels that pose unacceptable risks for accidents and environmental degradation. This should be a prerequisite for harvesting the gains that may follow the activities.

## 1 Introduction

The recent melting of the sea-ice and several highly publicised ship voyages in the Arctic have sparked great interest in Arctic maritime transport. This chapter provides an overview of current traffic development, its drivers and future prospects, impacts, governance and relevance to the European Union.

## 2 Where are the Ships Sailing?

There are two main sea routes in the Arctic Ocean today. The Northeast Passage (NEP) follows the coasts of Norway, Russia and Alaska. The major part of its Russian section is called the Northern Sea Route (NSR). The other traditional route is the Northwest Passage (NWP), which runs along the northern coast of North America. The Central Arctic Ocean Route in international waters is a trans-Arctic transport corridor that may become navigable as the sea ice further retreats (Figure 3.1).

Maritime transport along these routes can be:

- *Internal to the Arctic* for shipping between ports in the Arctic region, or for activities in the ocean area such as cruise tourism, research and transport related to fisheries, offshore oil and gas, etc.
- *Destinational* for all types of ships sailing to and from the Arctic.
- *Trans-Arctic* for traffic that uses the Arctic as a transport corridor between the Pacific and Atlantic Oceans.

For the sake of simplicity, internal and destinational traffic are discussed jointly, with an emphasis on freight transport.

Today the NEP/NSR is the most attractive option for navigation due to the more favourable ice conditions and infrastructure available, including nuclear-powered icebreakers. The Russian government has high ambitions for the NSR both as a means of developing its northern regions and as an international trade route. In the NWP, the narrow sounds are more frequently clogged by sea-ice, the infrastructure for shipping is scant and there is no clear political commitment to develop the route. This chapter therefore focuses on the NEP/NSR.

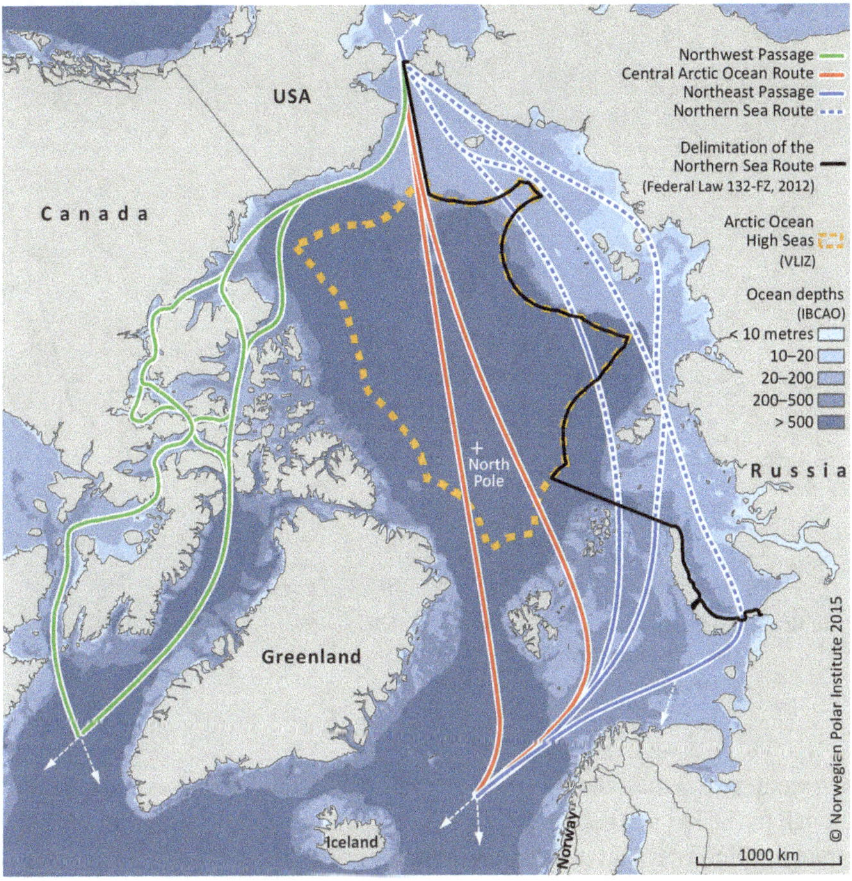


FIGURE 3.1 *Arctic maritime transport routes*
SOURCE: G. SANDER/A. SKOGLUND, NORWEGIAN POLAR INSTITUTE, 2015

## 3 What Changes Are Observed?

### 3.1 *Growth in Both Destinational and Internal Traffic in the Arctic*

The NSR was developed as a part of the Soviet industrialisation of Siberia and was linked to an internal transport system that included inland waterways and the Trans-Siberian railway. After initial exploration, it opened for regular traffic in 1935. Transport activity peaked in 1987 and plummeted after the dissolution of the Soviet Union and introduction of market economy. Both economic activities and population in the Russian north declined. Russia opened the route for foreign-flagged ships from 1991.[1]

1 For an account of the Soviet maritime history in the north, see Fairhall, D. (2010). *Cold Front. Conflict Ahead in Arctic Waters*. London/New York: I.B. Tauris.

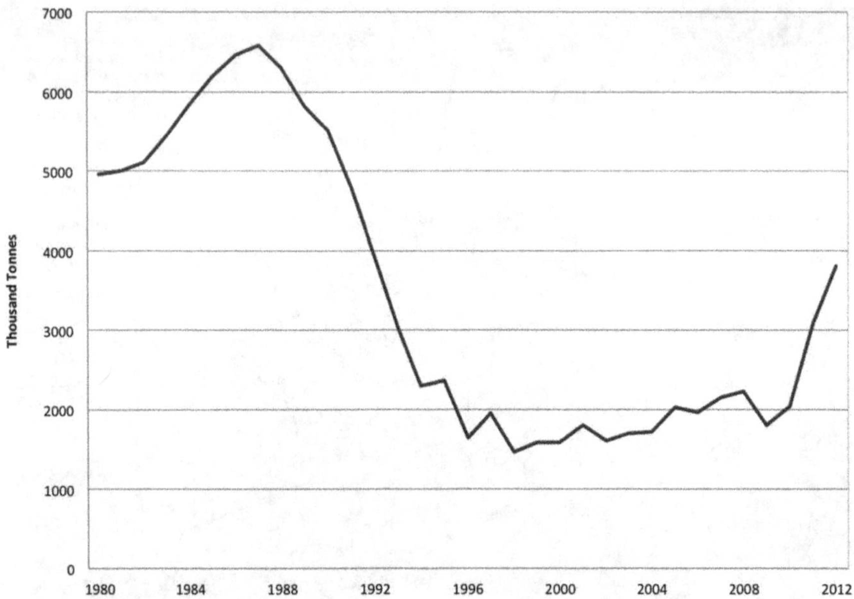


FIGURE 3.2 *Total annual cargo volumes on the Northern Sea Route. Data include intra, destinational and transit traffic*
SOURCE: NSR INFORMATION OFFICE, 2013

In recent years, the volume of cargo transported along the NSR has risen, though traffic has not reached the levels seen in the Soviet era (Figure 3.2). An emerging pattern is that Russian raw materials such as gas condensate and iron ore from the northwest are being exported eastwards directly to Asia.

Activity in the NWP is linked to re-supply of remote communities, Canadian Coast Guard and research activity and support for some resource development operations. Most of the growth in traffic comes from non-commercial crafts such as yachts and Canadian government ships, not freight vessels.

## 3.2 *Trans-Arctic Shipping is Emerging*

The number of ships using the NEP as a transport corridor between Europe and Asia is on the upswing, though the numbers are still small and varying (Table 3.1). In the NWP, the first bulk carrier transited the whole route in 2013.[2] Compared with the 17–18 000 ships that pass through the Suez Canal each year, Arctic

2 There is a detailed record of 135 transits of the whole NWP according to a strict definition of transits in Headland, R.K. (2010). "Ten decades of transits of the Northwest Passage", *Polar Geography* 33 (1–2): 1–13. The list is dominated by icebreakers and yachts and seem to support press statements that the Maersk ship Nordic Odeon that sailed the NWP on its way from Vancouver to Pori in Finland in 2013 was the first transit with a bulk carrier.

TABLE 3.1 *Number of Arctic transit voyages by freight carriers, 2009–2014*

| | 2009 | 2010 | 2011 | 2012 | 2013 | 2014 |
|---|---|---|---|---|---|---|
| Transits of NSR | 4 | 5 | 33 | 44 | 40 | 31 |
| Transits of NEP | 2 | 1 | 10 | 4 | 18 | n/d |

Note that the numbers for NEP transits are lower than for NSR since NEP is a longer voyage (ref Figure 3.1). Numbers on NSR transits deviate from the Russian numbers for some years since voyages that per definition are internal or destinational have been excluded here, even though some of these traverse long sections of the NSR. Neither are three passenger ships included in the 2014 data. It is not possible to calculate transits of NEP for 2014 because information about port of origin and destination is no longer in the published statistics

SOURCES: MIDGARD M, *ET AL.* (2009–2011); NSR INFORMATION OFFICE (2012, 2013, 2014).

shipping today holds minor global significance. Yet, recent developments represent a major shift in the Arctic that signals future development and requires attention and action prior to the expected build-up of activities.

### 3.3 *Uneven Regional Developments of Cruise Tourism*

Worldwide, the number of passengers carried by cruise ships has grown about 7% per year since 1990, and continued growth is expected.[3] However, the passenger volumes in the Arctic vary from region to region, with Svalbard and Greenland having the highest number of cruise tourists (Figure 3.3). Cruise ships have become larger; the biggest vessels in Svalbard can carry 3 300 passengers. At the other end of the spectrum, the region is frequented by smaller expedition cruises using vessels carrying anywhere from 5 to 300 passengers. In Svalbard, this segment accounts for approximately 20–25% of the total number of cruise passengers. In Franz Josef Land and Canada, the cruise market is significantly smaller and dominated by small vessels.

## 4 What is Shaping Change in Arctic Maritime Transport?

Commercial ship operations in the Arctic will expand if they are safe, reliable and profitable. A number of framing conditions and drivers determine whether

3 Cruise Market Watch, *www.cruisemarketwatch.com.* Accessed 20 March 2015.

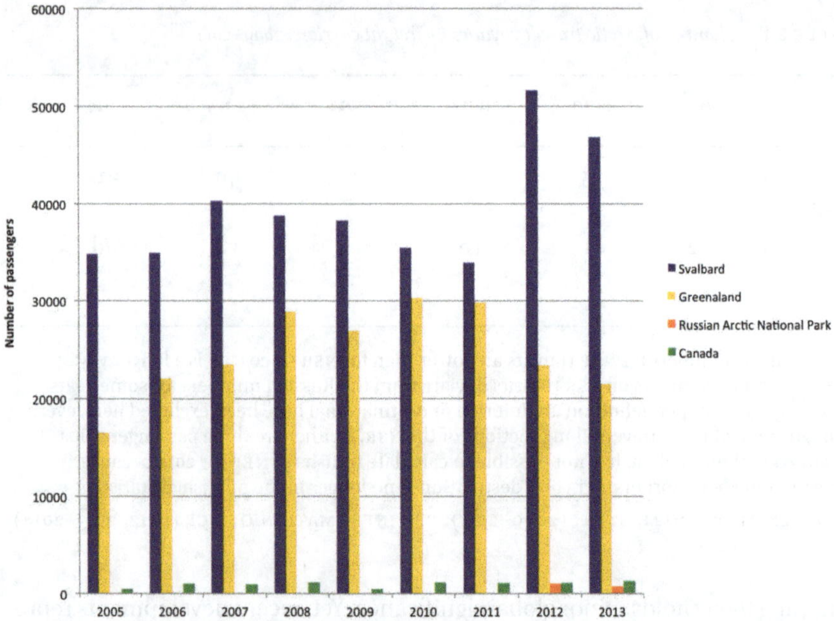


FIGURE 3.3 *Cruise tourism in some Arctic areas by number of passengers*
SOURCE: ASSOCIATION OF ARCTIC EXPEDITION CRUISE OPERATORS BASED ON DATA FROM: THE GOVERNOR IN SVALBARD, VISIT GREENLAND, NATIONAL PARK RUSSIAN ARCTIC AND NORREG

this can be achieved. Some of these are general for all voyages, some of them are specific for destinational or transit traffic, as summarised in Figure 3.4.

### 4.1 *Drivers for Destinational Shipping*

There is a general perception that the rich natural resources of the Arctic, particularly energy and minerals, are new sources for meeting growing global demand. However, the costs of exploiting Arctic resources are generally high. Market prices must compensate for this for production to become profitable. At least in the near term with low prices on oil, gas and many minerals, this may leave Arctic resources largely unexploited (see chapters by Łuszczuk et al. and van Dam et al. in this volume). Though there are few and uncertain estimates of future Arctic resource exploitation, it is commonly expected that resource exploitation will increase in a more distant future.

Turmoil in some resource-producing regions such as the Middle East increases the relative attractiveness of the Arctic as a secure source region. If the current tensions between the West and Russia over Ukraine continues

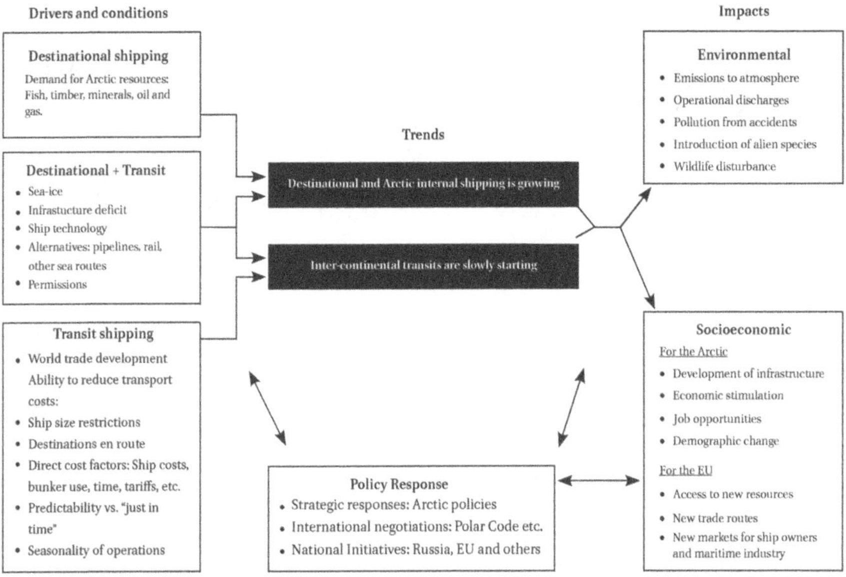


FIGURE 3.4 *Trends and shaping factors for Arctic shipping*
SOURCE: GUNNAR SANDER, NORWEGIAN POLAR INSTITUTE/UIT ARCTIC UNIVERSITY OF NORWAY; ARCTIC PORTAL

Russia seem to lose this comparative advantage to Europe, while other parts of the Arctic still may be considered stable. The point to be made in this context is that long-term security of supplies introduces a logic which differs from short term market considerations.

During exploration and production, there is a need to transport goods and equipment to the sites of operations, and to bring out the products. This is a typical pattern of nature resource related destinational traffic.

## 4.2 *Shaping Elements Common for Destinational and Transit Shipping*

### Melting Sea-ice

The extent of the summer sea-ice in the Arctic Ocean has decreased by about 40% on average since 1979, when satellite measurements started. The decrease in winter is only about 8% (Figure 3.5). Sea-ice has also become younger and thinner. There is large variation between years since the thinning makes the sea-ice more vulnerable to weather events.

In light of the current global warming trend, the Arctic Ocean is likely to become nearly ice-free in summer. It is uncertain when this will happen. The Intergovernmental Panel on Climate Change (IPCC) has estimated before mid-century for a scenario of comparatively high greenhouse-gas concentrations

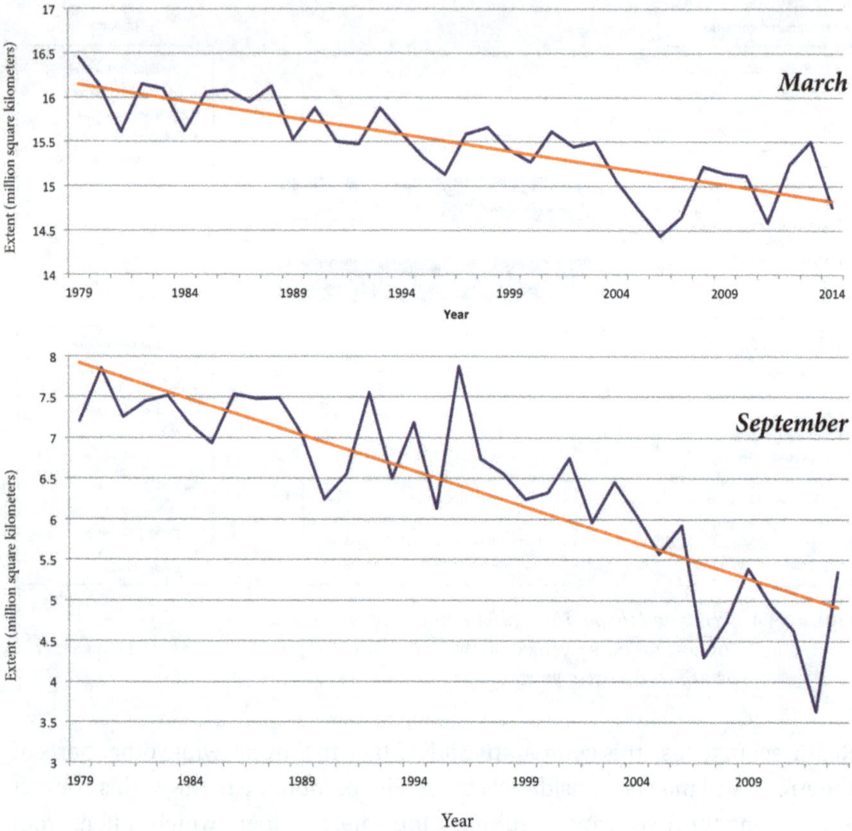


FIGURE 3.5 *Average monthly Arctic sea-ice extent in September and March 1979–2014*
SOURCE: NATIONAL SNOW AND ICE DATA CENTRE

(RCP 8.5), but states that it is not possible to make such projections with confidence for other scenarios.[4]

The planning of shipping operations in the Arctic is complicated by the large variations in sea-ice conditions between summer and winter as well as between years, and the uncertainty in predicting sea-ice on all time scales. For instance, in 2014 the sailing season in the NSR was delayed for weeks compared to previous years since sea-ice covered large sections of the route until late summer.

4 Intergovernmental Panel on Climate Change (2013). "Summary for Policymakers", in *Climate Change 2013: The Physical Science Basis. Contribution of Working Group I to the Fifth Assessment Report of the IPCC*, Stocker, T., Qin, D., Plattner, G., Tignor, M., Allen, S., Boschung, J., Nauels, A., Xia, Y., Bex, V. and Midgley, P. (eds.), Cambridge University Press, Cambridge, United Kingdom and New York, NY, United States.

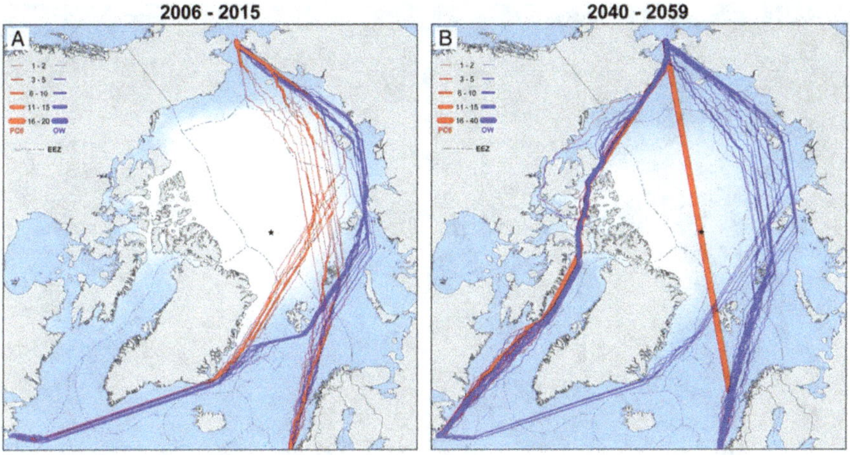


FIGURE 3.6 *Modelled routes physically accessible for ships sailing in September between the Bering Strait and St. Croix in Canada or Rotterdam in the Netherlands*
Current conditions are on the left, mid-century conditions under a modest climate scenario (rcp 4.5) on the right. Red routes are for moderately ice-strengthened ships, blue routes for ordinary vessels. The lines do not indicate traffic levels, just physical accessibility
SOURCE: SMITH, LAURENCE C. AND SCOTT R. STEPHENSON (2013), "NEW TRANS-ARCTIC SHIPPING ROUTES NAVIGABLE BY MID-CENTURY", PNAS EARLY EDITION, DOI: WWW.PNAS.ORG/CGI/DOI/10.1073/PNAS.1214212110

Reduction of summer sea-ice will expand the navigable area and extend the sailing season. Both the NWP and the Central Arctic Ocean route could become navigable under summer conditions by mid-century, or even earlier (Figure 3.6). Winter sea-ice will remain, but will gradually be replaced by first-year ice, which is thinner and easier to penetrate for a reinforced ship hull than multi-year ice. The occurrence of winter ice and drifting ice from glaciers means that ships will need to always be prepared for ice, even in summer. Icing of the ship surfaces in low temperatures is another ice-related challenge that may threaten the stability of a vessel and the operation of its equipment (Picture 3.1).

### Overcoming the Infrastructure Deficit

There are severe shortcomings in the Arctic marine infrastructure. Hydrographic surveys are needed to improve nautical charts. Improved safety of navigation also requires better navigational aids, communication systems, ship surveillance and reporting, as well as better meteorological and ice services. The current search and rescue services are not capable of serving the huge ocean areas

PICTURE 3.1 *Icing of vessels due to sea spray and humidity in the air is a serious challenge*
PHOTO BY WILLIAM MOWITT, NOAA

within acceptable response time and with the capacity needed in case of major events. Preparedness for emergencies also requires oil-spill combating equipment that works in ice-infested waters and designation of "places of refuge". Further, there is a need to improve services along the routes for bunkering, repair and maintenance and reception of ship's waste. In order to reach acceptable risk levels, substantial investments are needed. There is a significant dilemma if there is willingness to pay this price, and who shall bear the burden.

The Russian government wants to upgrade the services along the NSR, which decayed after the dissolution of the Soviet Union. Sea routes are being charted, investments are being made in ports, search and rescue centres have been designated and a programme for investments in new icebreakers has been approved.

### Permissions and Tariffs

There have been complaints from the shipping industry about inefficient administrative procedures for obtaining permission to sail along the NSR and the tariffs demanded. In order to make the route more attractive, Russia has changed its legislation and administration of the sea route including the tariff system and application procedures for foreign ships. Procedures for obtaining sailing permission are more streamlined, prior inspection of ships in a Russian port is no longer required and payment shall only cover the costs of services actually rendered. The new rules also provide for the use of ships without ice-class under favourable ice conditions.[5]

### Ship Technology

Ship technology for ice conditions has evolved, with advances in areas such as new propulsion systems, winterisation of equipment and workplaces, and concepts for oblique icebreakers. For example, Aker Arctic was a pioneer in developing double-acting vessels that can traverse ice that is up to 1.5 metres thick, and moves stern-first in ice and bow-first in open waters. Another example is the Sovcomflot liquefied natural gas (LNG) tankers operating in ice-covered waters (Picture 3.2). These technologies will be taken further in the tankers ordered by the Yamal LNG project. The prototype will be 299 meters long and can break up to 2.1 meters thick ice when navigating stern first. Further technology advances may increase Arctic accessibility and safety margins. Investments in new ice-class vessels with modern technology are necessary to accommodate more Arctic maritime transport.

5 Solski, J. (2013). "New developments in Russian regulation of navigation on the Northern Sea Route", *Arctic Review on Law and Politics* 1, 90–120.

PICTURE 3.2 *Sovcomflot (SCF) LNG tanker operating in the Sea of Okhotsk*
PHOTO: SOVCOMFLOT

### Availability of Competent Crew

Sailing in harsh Arctic waters puts the competence and endurance of marine crews to the test and increases the risks of fatigue, injuries and lower decision-making capacity. Today there is a shortage of qualified sailors. Special skills must be acquired through education and training. Requirements for training and certification of deck officers and masters will be included in the new Polar Code (see below).

### Interlinkages and Competition with Other Modes of Transport

Maritime freight transport competes with – and interacts with – other modes of transport. For transporting Arctic oil and gas, pipelines are the main alternative when volumes are large enough to justify the costs, supplemented by ships, which are more flexible and cheaper for smaller volumes. Railways, waterways and trunk pipelines are used internally in Russia for transport to the coast, where oil is loaded onto ships for export.[6] Similar chains of transport ending in ships are common in Arctic mining. Fish is transported with a variety of alternatives: ships, train, trucks and planes.

6 Bambulyak, A. & Frantzen, B., (2011). *Oil transport from the Russian part of the Barents Region. Status per January 2011.* The Norwegian Barents Secretariat and Akvaplan-niva, Norway.

The Trans-Siberian Railway and a few other rail connections are alternatives to shipments between Asia and Europe, particularly from inland areas. Trains offer faster connections for containers, but at higher costs, making railways an appealing alternative mainly for high-value commodities.[7]

## 4.3 *Shaping Elements for Transit Shipping*

### Volume and Direction of Global Trade Flows

Macroeconomic factors will shape the size and direction of trade flows globally and hence the demand for transport. The growth or stagnation of the world economy as a whole and for different economic sectors is important for transport demand. Transport patterns are further shaped by the regional distribution of economic activities, in particular the localization of production and consumption. Growth in economies in South America, Africa and Asia may for instance lead to increased south-south trade for which the Arctic route is of little relevance; the opposite will be the case if the North grows.[8] The international trade regime has so far stimulated global liberalization of trade and economic globalization. On the other hand, the global climate negotiations may address international transport more comprehensively in the future, possibly making global transport less attractive.

### Reducing Maritime Transport Costs

Cutting transport costs is a primary driver. The competitiveness of the Arctic routes is assessed against other modes of transport and other shipping routes, primarily the Suez Canal. Important factors include:

#### *Size and Draft Restrictions*

Larger ships reduce costs per unit of cargo transported. This is a drive for a shift towards increased vessel sizes. Today's Arctic sea routes accommodate only limited ship sizes as they follow the shallow continental shelf and must pass through narrow straits. Reduced sea-ice will gradually allow greater access to deep-water routes, however, with more unstable sea-ice conditions (ref. Picture 3.3 and Figure 3.6). This must be assessed against the competing routes. The Suez Canal was upgraded in 2015, first of all reducing waiting time. The canal may accomodate ships up to 240 000 DW tons and 66 feet draft. The ongoing upgrading of the Panama Canal will almost triple the number of containers that can be carried on the new Panmax ships.

7 Tavasszy, L., Minderhoud, M., Perrin, J. & Notteboom, T. (2011), "A strategic network choice model for global container flows: Specification estimation and application", *Journal of Transport Geography*, 19(6), 1163–1172.

8 A growth in the north is predicted in Smith, L.C. (2011). *The New North: The world in 2050*. Profile books, London, 256 p.

PICTURE 3.3 *Vladimir Tikhonov*
Vladimir Tikhonov (160 000 DW tons) is the largest vessel so far to traverse the NSR. It established a new sea lane outside the New Siberian Islands in 2011
PHOTO: SOVCOMFLOT

*Combining Multiple Hubs and Destinations en Route*

Operational patterns, particularly for container shipping, frequently rely on hub ports and intermediate stops to load/unload and redistribute cargo. These are dispersed along the traditional sea routes. Since there are no such services in the Arctic, even a full-year accessible Arctic route would face disadvantages compared to current shipping networks.

*Predictability*

Container ships in particular are part of integrated logistical chains where goods must arrive "just-in-time". Variable sea-ice and weather conditions and navigational challenges pose risks of delays in the Arctic. This will limit the attractiveness of Arctic routes until more reliable services can be established.

*Seasonality*

Thus far, the Arctic sailing season is limited to late summer. This makes the route less attractive for ships operating on fixed routes, as is the case with much of the container market, since they would have to change logistics twice a year as long as the Arctic winter is not navigable. Most ship owners so far have considered this an unattractive business proposition.[9] Those who may be able to take advantage of the opportunities offered by late summer Arctic routes are first of all operations where route flexibility is an option, for example spot market transports.

9 Lasserre, F. & Pelletier, S. (2011), "Polar super seaways? Maritime transport in the Arctic: an analysis of ship owners' intentions", *Journal of Transport Geography* 01/2011, 19(6): 1465–1473.

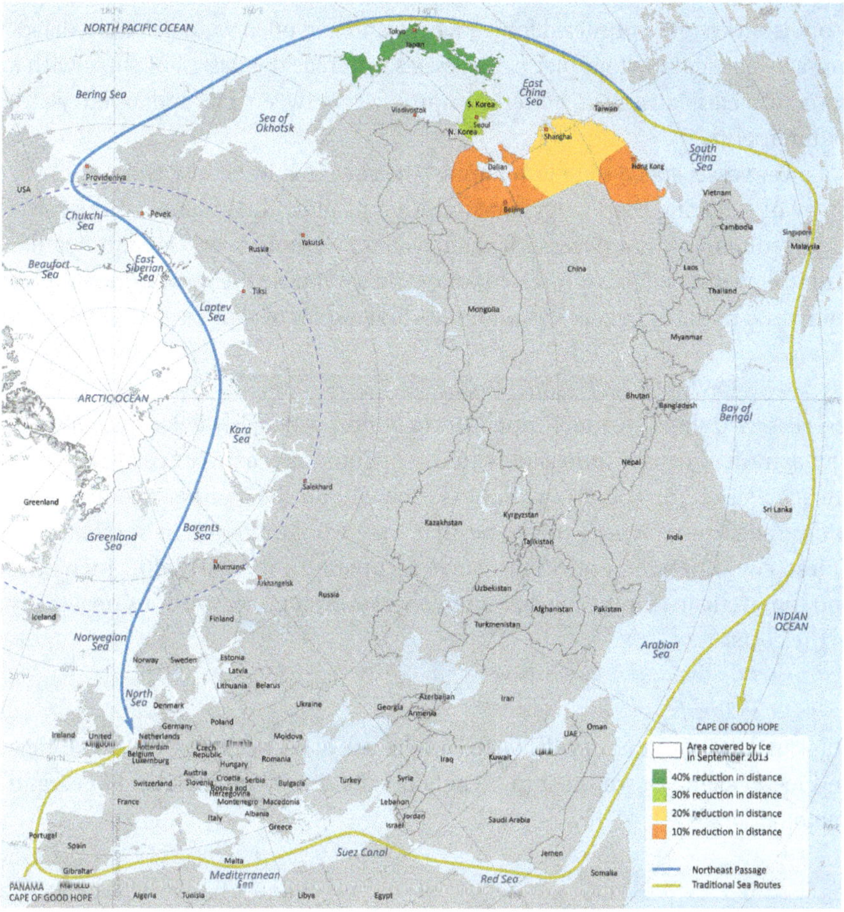


FIGURE 3.7 *Distance savings between Rotterdam and regions in East Asia by sailing the Northeast Passage instead of the Suez Canal. South of the coloured area, the Arctic route is longer*
SOURCE: ARCTIC PORTAL BASED ON DNV GL

### *Distance and Time*

For transits between ports in northern Asia and northern Europe, the distances through the Arctic are shorter than via the Suez Canal; further south, the Suez route is shorter and the Arctic becomes a detour (Figure 3.7). Speed is reduced when sailing in ice, so savings in distance may not deliver the same time savings. Sailing times in the Arctic also depend on weather conditions, approval procedures and waiting times for convoys or icebreakers.

### *Fuel Consumption*

Sailing shorter distances saves fuel. Breaking ice, however, requires extra energy. So does moving a heavy, ice-reinforced vessel with a hull and propulsion system optimised for ice when sailing in open water. This is a disadvantage, particularly for Polar class vessels, whereas the design of ships with a lower ice class strikes a better compromise between ice and open water requirements.

Lower vessel speed ("slow steaming") has become increasingly accepted as a way of reducing the energy consumption of individual vessels, though the same reduction is not necessarily achieved for a whole fleet. One implication is that slower speed in ice-infested waters may not pose the same disadvantage compared to the Suez route as under normal modes of sailing.

#### *Costs of Ice-Classified Vessels*

Ice-classified ships are more expensive to build, particularly Polar class vessels. The extra fuel consumption adds to the operational costs. Since vessels that are specialised for operations in heavy ice will not be competitive in worldwide trade, the outcome might be that they would only be in seasonal use unless combinations are found, such as operating in the Baltic in winter and the Arctic in summer. Suspending operations for a season adds negatively to the costs.

#### *Tariffs*

Ships using the NSR pay tariffs based on the use of services such as ice pilotage and icebreakers. However, ship owners must also pay tariffs in the Suez and Panama Canals.

## 5 Outlook to 2030

Many Arctic voyages are still trial shipments to test the viability of new routes and destinations, types of ships and technology, and safety schemes. The Arctic Marine Shipping Assessment in 2009 projected that the main increase in maritime transport in the next decade would be destinational rather than trans-Arctic.[10] This still seems to be a sound outlook. Within this broad picture, what types of shipping that will grow and when, where and to what extent, will depend on the activities in different industries: mining, offshore oil and gas, tourism and scientific research, among others (see outlooks in other chapters).

10 Arctic Council (2009). *Arctic Marine Shipping Assessment 2009 Report*. Protection of Arctic Marine Environment working group, Akureyri.

Future Arctic transit traffic crucially depends on its attractiveness to container ships, which account for the largest share of global marine shipments. The few models used to project Arctic transits involve a high degree of uncertainty, but generally indicate that the number of ships will be rather modest. For example, DNV has estimated that the number of transit voyages with container ships will amount to 480 in 2030 and 850 in 2050, representing about 8% and 10% of predicted container traffic between Europe and Asia for those years.[11] Thus, it seems more likely that Arctic transit shipping will be a niche activity supplementing the traditional routes than a new main route ousting them.

## 6 Impacts

### 6.1 *Environment*

#### Ship Emissions Affecting the Environment and Human Health

Ship emissions contain many gases and particles with multiple effects caused by their original components and subsequent chemical and physical reactions (Figure 3.8). Both nitrogen and sulphur components cause acidification that damages vegetation, freshwater fish and materials. Nitrogen also adds to the problem of excessive enrichment of nutrients in ecosystems, whereas surface ozone reduce crop yields. These gases and soot (which contains black carbon) have negative effects on health too. Several estimates have demonstrated that ship emissions significantly contribute to diseases and increased mortality globally.[12] However, in the sparsely populated Arctic, less people will be exposed than along many southerly sea routes.

#### Ship Emissions and Climate Change

Carbon dioxide ($CO_2$), nitrous oxides ($NO_x$) and methane ($CH_4$) are greenhouse gases that result from ship emissions and contribute to global warming. Soot has a warming effect both in the atmosphere and when it is deposited onto white snow and ice surfaces. On the other hand, other shipping emissions have a cooling effect (*e.g.* sulphur dioxide that forms aerosols). The net global

11 Det Norske Veritas (DNV), 2010: *Shipping across the Arctic Ocean. A feasible option in 2030–2050 as a result of global warming?* Research and Innovation, Position Paper 04 – 2010, DNV, Oslo.

12 Corbett, J., Winebrake, J., Green, E., Kasibhatla, P., Eyring, V. & Lauer, A. (2007). "Mortality from Ship Emissions: A Global Assessment", *Environ. Sci. Technol.*, 41, 8512–8518.

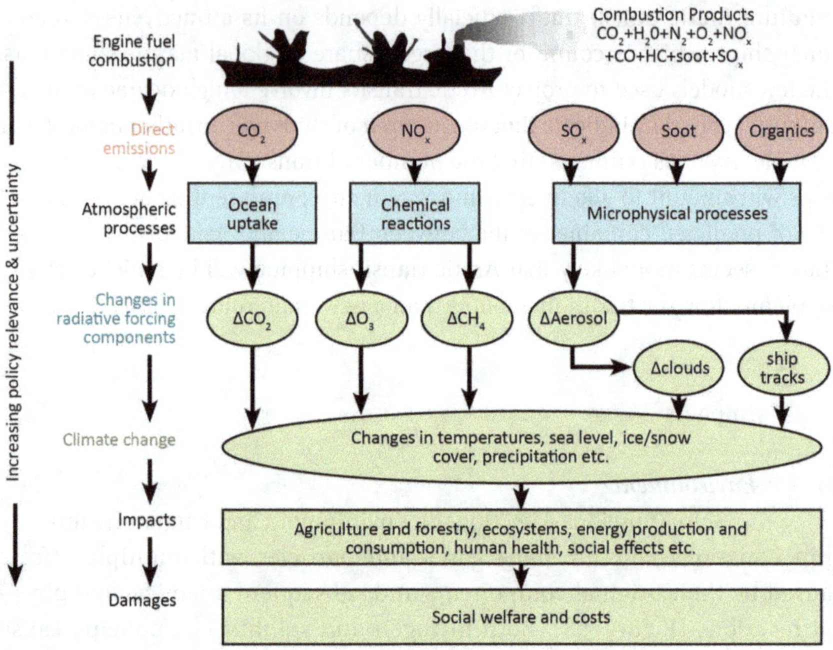


FIGURE 3.8 *Shipping emissions and climate change*
SOURCE: SECOND INTERNATIONAL MARITIME ORGANIZATION GHG STUDY[13]

effect of shipping emissions has been shown to be an initial cooling on timescales of decades to centuries and thereafter a warming due to accumulation of long-lived greenhouse gases, mainly $CO_2$.[14]

Calculating the net climate effect of growth in Arctic shipping is not easy and depends on the scenarios envisaged, the time horizon and location of emissions.[15] However, emissions of short-lived climate pollutants and particles in the Arctic have a stronger climate effect than at more southern latitudes

13 Buhaug, Ø., Corbett, J., Endresen, Ø., Eyring, V., Faber, J., Hanayama, S., Lee, D., Lee, D., Lindstad, H., Markowska, A., Mjelde, A., Nelissen, D., Nilsen, J., Pålsson, C., Winebrake, J., Wu, W. & Yoshida, K. (2009). *Second IMO GHG Study 2009*, International Maritime Organization, London, April 2009.

14 Eide, M., Dalsøren, S., Endresen, Ø., Samset, B., Myhre, G., Fuglestvedt, J. & Berntsen, T. (2013). "Reducing $CO_2$ from shipping – do non-$CO_2$ effects matter?", *Atmos. Chem. Phys.*, 13, 4183–4201.

15 Ødemark, K. *et al.* (2012). "Short-lived climate forcers from current shipping and petroleum activities in the Arctic", *Atmos. Chem. Phys.* 12, 1979–1993; Dalsøren, S.B., Samset, B.H., Myhre, G., Corbett, J.J., Minjares, R., Lack, D. & Fuglestvedt, J.S. (2013), "Environmental impacts of shipping in 2030 with a particular focus on the Arctic region", *Atmos. Chem. Phys.*, 13, 1941–1955.

and must always be included. Moving ships from the Suez Canal to shorter Arctic routes therefore may lead to an initial net warming for time-scales of one-and-a-half centuries. Thereafter, the effects of reducing the emissions of long-lived $CO_2$ will become dominant, resulting in a net cooling.[16]

#### Operational Discharges

The Convention on the Prevention of Pollution from Ships (MARPOL) restricts emissions from ships. Nevertheless, oil residues, garbage and sewage may be discharged legally when diluted and away from shore.

#### Pollution from Accidents

Common pollution resulting from an accident is the discharge of the ship's own fuel, bunker oil. The damage depends on whether the ship runs on heavy fuel oil or lighter fuels such as diesel. Accidents with tankers loaded with crude oil and other petroleum products may cause massive and devastating discharges, but fortunately occur rarely. Cleaning up oil spills in ice-covered waters is even less effective than in open waters, and the resources available are scarce. Ships' cargo may also contain other toxic or harmful substances that may leak out.

#### Introduced Alien Species

Ships are the most common vector for introducing alien marine species to other ecosystems, not only from ballast water tanks and hulls, but also from the cargo. Alien species may alter marine ecosystems and cause economic losses. Transports from the relatively species-rich Pacific to the Atlantic along the same latitudes and hence temperature gradients may pose a particular risk. Warming of the Arctic Ocean reduces the temperature barriers that have prevented species survival *en route*.[17]

#### Wildlife

Noise, collisions and the mere presence of humans may disturb Arctic wildlife, *e.g.* birds and whales at chokepoints and in sensitive areas.

### 6.2 *Economic and Social Impacts in the Arctic*

Upgrading of existing ports and construction of new ones as well as increased demand for supply services for ships like bunkering and repairs, will lead to

16 Fuglestvedt, J, Dalsøren, S.B., Samset, B.H., Berntsen, T., Myhre, G., Hodnebrog, Ø., Eide, M.S., & Bergh, T.F. (2014). "Climate Penalty for Shifting Shipping to the Arctic", *Environ. Sci. Technol.*, 48 (22): 3273–13279.

17 Ware, C., Kirkpatrick, J., Sundet, J., Jelmert, A., Berge, J., Coutts, A., Floerl, O., Pellissier, L., Wisz, M. & Alsos, I. (2014). "Climate change, non-indigenous species and shipping: assessing

direct, indirect and induced economic effects. However, this will also entail substantial costs. Investments in maritime transport infrastructure and many related services will require long-term government commitments, even if done in partnership with the private sector.

Increased accessibility and lower transport costs could increase goods availability and decrease prices in remote settlements. This would directly benefit local communities and raise welfare levels. Improved transport could also lower the costs of export and import, thereby facilitating more trade with other (non-Arctic) partners. Manufacturing centres in the region might see an improvement in their competitive position if transport costs were lower.

Whether or not the current inhabitants of the Arctic regions will benefit from employment growth, depends on the qualifications needed and the available skill base. As the current Arctic population is small and in several regions have a low level of education, the specific skills needed may not be present. Importing skilled labour from elsewhere is a common short-term solution for extractive industries, solved by commuting or workers settling with their families. Raising education levels among the local population or tailoring their skills to the new needs will take more time, but is vital for increasing local employment. The fact that the Arctic sea routes will remain seasonal for some time may mean that new jobs are seasonal too. This poses issues about seasonal labour migration and off-season economic activities.

More economic and social opportunities in Arctic port communities could stimulate migration from rural areas, causing shifts in local economies. This may have negative impacts both on rural areas (reduced population, possibly below levels that allow sustainable maintenance of public services like schools and healthcare) and in urban areas (lack of housing facilities, pressures on local infrastructure).

## 7 Governance

The United Nations Law of the Sea (LOS) Convention provides a fundamental framework for the governance of navigation including in the Arctic.[18] A coastal state has full rights to set the conditions for ships in its ports and internal

---

the risk of species introduction to a high-Arctic archipelago". *Diversity and Distributions*, 20, 10–19.

18 See *e.g.* VanderZwaag, D. *et al.* (2008). *Governance of Arctic Marine Shipping,* Marine & Environmental Law Institute, Dalhousie University, and Molenaar, E. (2009), "Arctic marine shipping: Overview of the international legal framework, gaps and options", *Journal of Transnational Law & Policy,* 18, 289–325.

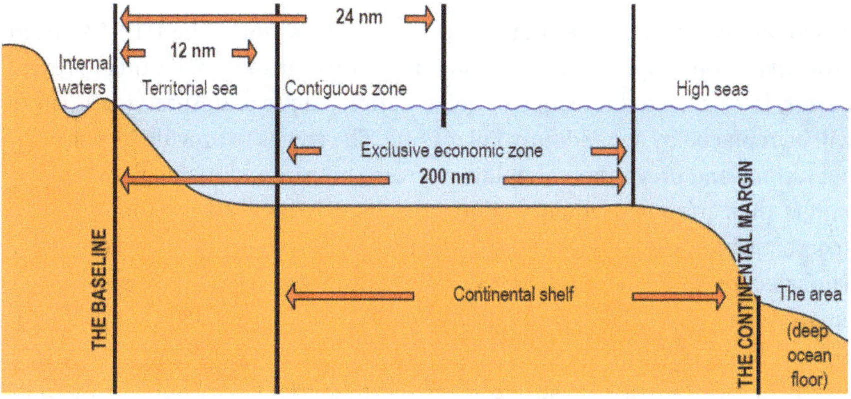


FIGURE 3.9 *Maritime zones*
The right to regulate navigation of ships varies between the maritime zones, as defined in the UN Convention on the Law of the Sea
SOURCE: G. SANDER/A. IGESUND, NORWEGIAN POLAR INSTITUTE

waters, but has less authority in its territorial sea where ships enjoy the right to innocent passage (Figure 3.9). In the exclusive economic zones (EEZ), navigation can mostly take place under the principle of freedom of navigation, as on the high seas. Under this sailing regime, the main rule is that only the flag state has authority over a vessel, with the duty to enforce customary laws and all international conventions to which it is a party.

When the EEZ is ice-covered, Article 234 of the LOS Convention makes an exception to this general division of responsibilities. Then coastal states have the right to adopt and enforce non-discriminatory laws and regulations for the prevention, reduction and control of marine pollution. Canada and Russia have developed the most comprehensive regulations based on this article, and their drawing of baselines whereby parts of their maritime areas are designated as internal waters.[19] Until ships can sail on the high seas along the Central Arctic Route (see Figure 3.1), Canadian and Russian rules to a large degree set the standards for ships operating in the high Arctic.

The International Maritime Organization (IMO) is the specialised United Nations agency responsible for important regulations related to maritime safety and environmentally sound and efficient shipping. The MARPOL Convention to prevent pollution from ships and the Convention on the Safety

19 See Brubaker, D. (2001). Straits in the Russian Arctic, *Ocean Development and International Law*, 32:263–287, Kraska, J. (2007). "The Law of the Sea Convention and the Northwest Passage", *International Journal of Marine and Coastal Law*, Vol 22, No 2, 257–282 and VanderZwaag, D. *et al.* (2008), *op.cit.*

of Life at Sea (SOLAS) are prominent results of its work. The IMO has been proactive in developing voluntary guidelines, first for ships operating in Arctic waters, later adjusted for ships in polar waters (Arctic and Antarctica). These will be replaced by a mandatory Polar Code. The goal is to provide for safe ship operations and prevention of pollution from ships by addressing risks in polar waters that are not adequately mitigated by existing IMO instruments. The SOLAS and MARPOL conventions therefore will have regional amendments. The safety requirements (SOLAS) were adopted in November 2014, whereas the environmental provisions (MARPOL) were adopted in May 2015. The entire Polar Code will enter into force in January 2017.

The Arctic Council has a strong record of undertaking scientific assessments, in some cases influencing subsequent policies by contributing to the framing of an issue or through direct policy recommendations. The Arctic Marine Shipping Assessment (AMSA) was a response to the melting of the Arctic Ocean sea-ice and the first pan-Arctic report on shipping.[20] It recommended a strategic framework for actions to enhance safe operations and protection of the environment. The Arctic ministers adopted it and the progress in implementation has been regularly monitored ever since.[21] Both the process in the IMO for the Polar Code and the adoption of the Search and rescue agreement and the Oil spills agreement, are implementation of recommendations from AMSA.[22]

For the global shipping industry, the preferred option is to have uniform Arctic standards rather than different national regulations. This could be achieved through the Polar Code, but also by means of a harmonised set of national standards from the Arctic coastal states, as recommended by AMSA. Uniform regulations can also be strengthened through the current port state agreements – the Paris and Tokyo Memoranda of Understanding (MoU) – or creating a new one for the Arctic region.[23]

20 Lasserre and Pelletier (2011), *op.cit.*

21 See the 2011 and 2013 reports documenting the status of implementation at http://www.pame.is/index.php/projects/arctic-marine-shipping/amsa. Ref also Stokke, O.S. (2012). "Regime interplay in Arctic shipping governance: explaining regional niche selection", *International Environmental Agreements: Politics, Law and Economics,* vol 13(1), pp 65–85 and Graczyk, P. & Koivurova, T. (in print), "The Arctic Council", in: Jensen, L. Ch. & Hønneland, G. (eds), *Handbook of the Politics of the Arctic,* Cheltenham: Edward Elgar.

22 Agreement on Cooperation on Aeronautical and Maritime Search and Rescue in the Arctic (signed in Nuuk on 12 May 2011, entered into force 19 January 2013) 50 I.L.M. 1119 (2011) (SAR Agreement); Agreement on Cooperation on Marine Oil Pollution, Preparedness and Response in the Arctic (signed in Kiruna on 15 May 2013), www.arctic-council.org/eppr accessed 2 December 2014 (Oil Spills Agreement).

23 Molenaar, E. (2007). "Port state jurisdiction: Towards comprehensive, mandatory and global coverage", *Ocean Development and International Law*, 38, 225–257.

## 8 How Changes in Arctic Maritime Transport May Affect the European Union

Changes in Arctic maritime transport may affect the economic, political and environmental interests of the EU and European businesses. Their implications and magnitude will depend on the pace and extent of the changes and may differ for destinational and transit shipping. Some potential effects are:

- Access to trade routes.
- Access to new sources of energy and other natural resources at relatively close distances and from politically stable countries. This is significant for the EU in order to enhance security of supply of raw materials and energy. The crisis in Ukraine means that the Russian part of the Arctic will be less attractive in this respect.
- Potential cost savings related to shorter shipping routes, contributing to lower logistics costs for the European economy.
- Greater demand for ice-class ships, icebreakers and related technology. This is a market in which European industries already have a significant position, primarily companies and shipyards in Finland. Estimates of the annual potential for this market amount to EUR 500 million.[24]
- European ship owners who want to operate in the Arctic may be expected to have a share of the market to be served as well as substantial shares of the required investments in ice-strengthened vessels.
- Within Europe, the availability of a trans-Arctic shipping route may affect competition between ports.

## 9 How the European Union Influences Arctic Maritime Transport

### 9.1 *European Union International Activities*

Competence in maritime transport is shared by the EU and its member states. Member states cannot act in a manner that is detrimental to EU competence or interests, or adversely affect the effective implementation of EU policies. In areas where the EU internally regulates maritime transport, the EU also acquires external competence. This means that member states cannot act internationally without taking into account established EU policies and common positions.

24 Ecorys (2012). *Green Growth Opportunities in the EU Shipbuilding Sector.* Final Report. Commissioned by the European Commission, DG Enterprise and Industry, http://ec.europa.eu/enterprise/sectors/maritime/files/green_growth_shipbuildingfinal_report_en.pdf, accessed 20 February 2014.

This is relevant for instance in the IMO, where the EU is not a member, but its member states are. Due to extensive EU regulations on shipping-related issues, the European Commission and the European Maritime Safety Agency (EMSA) co-ordinate with the member states in the IMO committees, for example with regard to the Polar Code. As the co-ordination involves 28 out of 170 members of the IMO and represents considerable tonnage, the EU has significant influence. It is thus a potentially strong mechanism for EU-influence to co-ordinate positions in the IMO and other international organisations that can set conditions relevant for Arctic shipping. The EU has clearly supported the development of a strong mandatory Polar Code, but at the same time attempted to balance the interests of ship operators with concerns for the environment and safety.[25]

Within the Arctic Council, the EU has been active in the Protection of the Arctic Marine Environment (PAME) Working Group, contributing substantial input to a number of topics particularly from the European Commission's DG Mobility and Transport. The EMSA and PAME are currently exploring possible areas of co-operation.

The EU has also developed an Integrated Maritime Policy that includes the Arctic Ocean. It is one of the sea basins for which a separate policy is being developed.[26]

### 9.2 *EU Regulations Affecting Flag State and Port State Measures*

Many ships traversing Arctic sea lanes are either owned by companies based in Europe or have European ports of departure or destination. The EU member states therefore can influence Arctic shipping via requirements on vessels flying their flags and through port state control. The EU affects this when setting common standards that the member states must follow.

The EU has developed a comprehensive regulatory framework regarding shipping safety and environmental standards, in particular in the aftermath of major accidents.[27] Relevant EU regulations include maritime safety and pollution prevention, ship inspection, improved flag state performance, liability of carriers and training of seafarers. Selected examples that may be relevant for the Arctic include:

---

25 See *e.g.* answer to the Member of European Parliament question (17 June 2010), Kallas on behalf of the Commission. E-2863/2010, OJ C 138 E, 07/05/2011, www.europarl.europa.eu/sides/getAllAnswers.do?reference=E-2010-2863&language=EN, accessed 20 February 2014.

26 See http://ec.europa.eu/maritimeaffairs/policy/sea_basins/index_en.htm, accessed 10 February 2015.

27 See: DG Transport, www.ec.europa.eu/transport/modes/maritime/safety/third_maritime_safety_package_en.htm, accessed 24 February 2014.

- The directive on vessel traffic monitoring and information system is one of few EU regulations referring directly to sea-ice. Member states are required to provide information on ice conditions, recommend routes and icebreaking services, and request certification documents commensurate with the ice conditions.[28]
- The directive on sulphur in marine fuels limits the maximum content according to MARPOL requirement.[29] Additional legislation affects maritime emissions that contribute to acidification, eutrophication and the formation of ground-level ozone.[30]
- The EU framework for port state control is mainly the 2009 directive, which builds on the Paris MoU.[31] The Paris MoU includes a new inspection regime for all ships calling at MoU ports seen as a whole instead of the previous goal of controlling 25% of ships calling at the ports of an individual state. The EMSA hosts an information system for selecting which ships should be inspected in Europe.[32]

## 9.3 *Supporting Improved Infrastructure and Services for Arctic Maritime Transport*

EU policy documents express interest in supporting Arctic-relevant maritime infrastructure. For instance, the Galileo satellite system will increase the accuracy of satellite-based positioning in the Arctic, thereby making Arctic navigation safer.[33] Galileo also has a dedicated search and rescue function that will locate ships in distress more efficiently.

The Copernicus earth observation programme has an operational service providing geo-spatial information worldwide in case of emergencies.[34] As

28 Directive 2002/59/EC, 27 June 2002 establishing a Community vessel traffic monitoring and information system, amended by Directive 2009/17/EC.

29 Directive 2012/33/EU, 21 November 2012 amending Council Directive 1999/32/EC regarding sulphur content of marine fuels.

30 Directive 2001/81/EC, 23 October 2001 on national emission ceilings for certain atmospheric pollutants, Official Journal L 309, 27.11.2001. The directive had required the Commission to prepare reports, *inter alia*, on ship emissions.

31 Directive 2009/16/EC of 23 April 2009 on port state control.

32 THETIS is a new targeting system for selecting ships for inspections set up by European Commission regulation. See also http://ec.europa.eu/transport/modes/maritime/safety/actions_en.htm, accessed 25 February 2014.

33 The first services are becoming available in 2014/2015, while the full system is expected to be operational in 2019.

34 Copernicus: http://www.copernicus.eu/. COPERNICUS was formerly known as Global Monitoring for Environment and Security, accessed 8 February 2015.

new satellites and services are launched, observation capabilities in the Arctic will increase and could provide a wide array of improved services like more accurate meteorological data, better ice forecasts, detection of oil spills and increased understanding of many climatic and environmental issues.

Surveillance is useful in tracking ships and has multiple applications in preventing collisions and monitoring whether ships discharge oil or engage in illegal fishing, for example. The EU has developed SafeSeaNet and CleanSeaNet[35] and given practical support to IMO initiatives such as Automatic Identification System (AIS) and Long-Range Identification and Tracking. Satellite-based AIS is necessary for the Arctic marine areas where terrestrial AIS cannot cover vast ocean areas.[36]

### 9.4 *Research*

EU-funded research projects[37] *inter alia* help to support the safety and environmental performance of Arctic shipping and improve the understanding of its driving forces and implications.

### 9.5 *Indirect Effects of EU Regulations and Policies*

The EU can have indirect effects on the volume and pattern of maritime transport in Arctic waters via other policies and actions. Examples include general transport policies, engagement in Arctic resource development and trade or consumer-related actions that affect the demand for Arctic resources.

## 10 Critical Factors for EU Decision-making

Stakeholders were asked during consultations in 2013–2014 about the most important factors for EU policy-making related to Arctic maritime transport. The responses show strong interest in issues that can be clustered into three areas that constitute key challenges. Some statements are shown in textbox 3.1.

35 See http://emsa.europa.eu/operations/cleanseanet.html and http://emsa.europa.eu/operations/safeseanet.html.

36 Polar View (2012). The contribution of space technologies to Arctic policy priorities. Report for the European Space Agency.

37 For a comprehensive list of projects see, Dahlbäck B., van der Watt, L.-M., Jagodziński, K. & Kankaanpää, P. (2014). European Arctic Initiatives Compendium. Preparatory Action, Strategic Environmental Impact Assessment of development of the Arctic. Arctic Centre, University of Lapland, http://www.arcticinfo.eu/en/. Accessed 20 February 2015.

TEXTBOX 3.1 *What stakeholders say about Arctic shipping*

"The Polar Code has no provisions related to heavy fuel oil use or carriage regulation, mandatory ballast water or hull fouling requirements (concerning invasive species introduction) or black carbon restrictions. These are three of the most pressing and important matters concerning Arctic shipping, and the Code is severely wanting in all three areas."
*Environmental NGO, US*

"There is a lack of sufficient infrastructure on communication, navigation and search and rescue, among others."
*Respondent from the shipping industry, Norway*

"The most significant policy issues are to develop uniform shipping regulation that will be applied equitably throughout the Arctic Ocean."
*Academic, US*

"The Arctic is a common natural heritage area, not the property of an individual country. It is the responsibility of the EU to take an active role in ensuring its protection to secure the ecosystem services that the Arctic provides."
*Environmental NGO, Russia*

### Minimising Risks in Arctic Shipping

The Arctic is a frontier region for shipping. Sea-ice and environmental conditions such as polar lows, temperatures and darkness are challenging. There is scant infrastructure to service maritime transport. Vast areas must be covered by search and rescue capacities and preparedness to cope with accidents and incidents. Seafarers with sufficient training are scarce. Discharges of oil and the introduction of alien species are environmental risks of particular concern. These additional risks must be overcome for Arctic shipping to become safe and secure.

### Insufficient Governance System

The governance of Arctic shipping should be improved. There was a clear recommendation from stakeholders to focus on international regulations, highlighting the Polar Code in particular. Concerns were expressed about whether its standards will be sufficient to safeguard the Arctic and whether the full suite of environmental issues will be addressed. Another concern was the need to ensure uniform regulations and harmonised standards ("level playing field").

Need for Supporting Research, Data Collection and Technology Improvements

Stakeholders emphasised many outstanding science questions that need to be addressed to underpin safe and efficient shipping and better governance. The key topics they identified are better mapping and understanding of environmental conditions, better predictions of ice and weather conditions, better knowledge about the impacts of Arctic shipping and how to address them, and technological developments to boost safety and reduce the environmental footprint of ships.

## 11 Conclusions: The Way Forward for the EU

In this section, we will expand on what could be the role for the EU in adressing the challenges associated with Arctic shipping.

Advantages and disadvantages seldom are distributed evenly. Actors in the EU mostly will harvest economic benefits from increased maritime transport in the Arctic. Significant factors include access to new resources, increased deliveries for the maritime industry and growing trade and potential cost savings in the transport sector. In the Arctic, the picture is more nuanced. Increased maritime transport may contribute to economic development, most notably when linked to exploitation of natural resources. The Russian ports of Varandey, Dudinka and the new one under construction in Sabetta are examples of industrial ports that serve particular industrial projects, exporting oil, nickel and LNG, respectively.[38] In comparison, economic effects from transit voyages that have no incentives to visit Arctic ports seem moderate and are linked to, for instance, developments of centres for search and rescue and other services for a distant fleet. Certain ports may develop into transportation hubs, like Murmansk, Kirkenes and Churchill, maybe Longyearbyen or ports in Iceland too. However, the majority of ports in Canada, Alaska, Russia and Greenland are mainly used for re-supply of small settlements, and improvements are highly dependent on government investments. Developments therefore may be uneven, both geographically and socially. The businesses involved, central governments and the regions where new developments take place may gain. The majority of Arctic inhabitants may not benefit unless they

38 Buixadé Farré, A., et al, (2014). "Commercial Arctic shipping through the Northeast Passage: routes, resources, governance, technology, and infrastructure", *Polar Geography*, DOI 10.1080/1088937X.2014.965769.

live where new opportunities arise and they are qualified for accompanying jobs. This calls for mechanisms that can ensure distribution of benefits.[39]

The distributional side of environmental disadvantages, on the other hand, is rather clear. Oil spills, discharges to the oceans, introduced alien species and disturbances to wildlife will affect the Arctic environment and its inhabitants directly, not the EU. That is mostly the case also for air pollutants, though shifts in transport routes to the Arctic may lead to increased global warming followed by cooling. In order to harvest the gains from activities in the distant Arctic region, a recommended strategy for the EU would be to try to prevent and ameliorate negative impacts in the Arctic.[40] This clearly points out addressing safety and environmental issues as far as shipping is concerned. Stimulating positive economic and social effects of shipping in the Arctic may be harder for the EU. This will mostly be determined by national policies in the Arctic states. However, none of the Arctic coastal states are members of the EU and bound by its policies.[41] Policy options for the EU therefore may be restricted to dialogue with local and indigenous Arctic peoples and governments, partnership agreements and use of the various funds for external action.

Based on the competences of the EU descried above and the advice from stakeholders, the *Strategic Assessment of Development of the Arctic* process[42] developed a number of recommendations for the EU.

### EU Contribution to Good Maritime Governance

The EU could use its influence in the IMO to show leadership in Arctic maritime transport. In the course of the SADA project, the Polar Code negotiations were by far the most important process. Stakeholders recommended the EU to develop unified positions in support of high safety standards and effective measures against pollution, both in IMO and other international forums.

39 Such mechanisms vary according to tradition and political system. This is clearly demonstrated by the differences between the case studies in Chapter 3 on social and economic effects in AMAP (2007): *Assessment 2007: Oil and Gas Activities in the Arctic – Effects and Potential Effects. Volume 1.* ISBN 13 978-82-7971-061-5. AMAP, Oslo.

40 This strategy is clearly in accordance with the general policies of the EU towards the Arctic, though formulated differently. See REF COM 2008: http://eur-lex.europa.eu/legal-content/EN/ALL/?uri=CELEX:52008DC0763and the update in COM 2012: http://ec.europa.eu/maritimeaffairs/policy/sea_basins/arctic_ocean/documents/join_2012_19_en.pdf. Accessed 20 March 2015.

41 Greenland has self-rule in the Kingdom of Denmark and only a collaborative agreement with the EU. Norway has strong links to the EU through the European Economic Area, but Svalbard is outside the geographical scope of the agreement.

42 See the project website and the assessment report at www.arcticinfo.eu/sada, as well as the introductory chapter to this book by Stępień et al.

The EU also was recommended to address issues that are not taken care of adequately in the Polar Code:

- Invasive species are an increasing risk to Arctic ecosystems as traffic grows and the Arctic Ocean becomes warmer. The global Ballast Water Convention needs additional ratifications to enter into force. The EU should urge all its member states to become parties and to implement it.[43] Urgent action is also needed on measures to prevent the introduction of invasive species via ship hulls.[44] Another option is to support regional measures in the Arctic, by means of either the early implementation of the convention in a similar way as for the European seas, or by co-ordinated measures based on port and coastal state jurisdiction.[45]
- The IMO addresses emissions from ships to air as a global issue through MARPOL annex VI, partly motivated by its Arctic impacts. However, the Arctic states and the EU should also consider a regional approach by establishing an IMO Emission Control Area within the Arctic Ocean. Short-lived climate forcers and particles emitted in the Arctic atmosphere have a stronger impact than elsewhere, which could justify a regional approach with stricter emission standards than the global ones.
- Measures pertaining to heavy fuel oil are currently discussed in PAME in the Arctic Council. The EU should follow these discussions and be active in finding solutions like substitution of fuels in order to reduce this risk to the marine environment.

The Polar Code and other IMO instruments will be important for ensuring a level playing field for all operators. The EU should also support recommendations from the Arctic Council with a view to harmonising Arctic coastal state regulations.[46] This will be an emerging issue after the adoption of the Polar

43 See IMO status of ratifications at: http://www.imo.org/About/Conventions/StatusOfConventions/Pages/Default.aspx

44 Ref IMO 2011: *2011 Guidelines for the control and management of ships' biofouling to minimize the transfer of aquatic species.* Resolution MEPC.207(62), http://www.imo.org/blast/blastDataHelper.asp?data_id=30766.

45 See: *Joint Notice to Shipping from the Contracting Parties of the Barcelona Convention,* OSPAR *and HELCOM on: General Guidance on the Voluntary Interim Application of the D1 Ballast Water Exchange Standard by Vessels Operating between the Mediterranean Sea and the North-East Atlantic and/or the Baltic Sea.* (Agreement 2012–2104). Such regional arrangements are encouraged by the Ballast Water Convention. However, these guidelines are voluntary, which seems to have limited their application.

46 Recommendation I C in Arctic Marine Shipping Assessment (*ibid*).

Code when particularly Canada and Russia must decide what to do with their national shipping regulations. The EU also could encourage the strengthening of Arctic regulations, both from IMO and from the Arctic coastal states, by supporting their inclusion in the Paris MoU.

The EU and the Arctic Council share the goal of basing their ocean policies on ecosystem-based management. Themes for collaboration could include exchange of experience in this field and marine spatial planning including marine protected areas. Designation of ecologically sensitive sea areas and marine protected areas for the Arctic are also brought up in OSPAR and the Convention on Biological Diversity, where the EU could support relevant developments.

Stakeholders also highlighted the need for fostering effective cross-border co-operation on Arctic maritime transport, particularly stepping up collaboration with Russia and Nordic countries.

### Minimising Risks by Developing Improved Maritime Infrastructure

Ship accidents in the Arctic may have severe consequences for humans, ships and the fragile environment. Prevention of accidents and incidents therefore should have the highest priority. At the same time, response capabilities for search and rescue, and oil spills must be improved. However, such systems cannot realistically be expected to deliver the same level of protection as in more densely trafficked seas. A ship's readiness in the Arctic therefore will depend largely on its own resources; ship operators must carefully assess the risks of operations and select the equipment and procedures necessary for avoiding problems and handling them on their own if they should occur. Large cruise ships are probably the most prominent example.

Reducing risks will require better maritime infrastructure. The Arctic coastal states are responsible for improvements in their ports and many services in their waters. They also have taken on major responsibilities for search and rescue operations in the entire Arctic marine area, including the high seas.[47] This responsibility entails a high financial burden. The European Commission has signalled its willingness to collaborate with the Arctic countries in this respect.[48] Possible mechanisms include bilateral collaboration, partnership agreements with Greenland and the Northern Dimension. Such EU contributions to improved infrastructure and services gained strong support from stakeholders involved in the SADA dialogue.

---

47 The Arctic Search and Rescue Agreement divides the responsibility between six coastal states.

48 European Commission and High Representative (2012). Developing a European Union Policy towards the Arctic Region, *op.cit.*

There will be a need for international collaboration on much of the maritime infrastructure. It is suggested that the EU and its member states may contribute with:

- The Galileo and Copernicus programmes. The challenge for the EU is to develop better services for the maritime community based on these satellite platforms and find ways of sharing the information with other systems.
- A common monitoring system for ships in the Arctic providing an overview of ships and cargo transport *en route* would improve safety. SafeSeaNet could be one model for such collaboration.
- Supporting wider operational networks of meteorological and oceanographic observations and communication of weather, ice and wave forecasts.
- Supporting the coastal states in their hydrographic mapping by using merchant vessels as observational platforms. Ships can also collect and share data on meteorology and ice, for instance.
- Supporting targeted technology innovation to advance ship design and operation to improve efficiency and safety, and to reduce emissions.
- Supporting training on Arctic conditions for seafarers within the EU.
- Working with industry to disseminate best practices in Arctic marine shipping and transport.
- Pooling of resources for search and rescue, and oil spill prevention, with European states and agreements in areas bordering the Arctic. CleanSeaNet is an example of a European system that could be used as a model.

### Better Knowledge through Research, Monitoring and Assessment

The EU and its member states have long-standing engagement in Arctic research. There is a need for a better understanding of the region's environmental conditions:

- Observational data should be shared in the scientific community and be made easily available for ships. The EU countries have practical solutions that could be useful for Arctic collaboration.[49] Research is needed to advance predictive capabilities and develop forecasting services.

---

49 One example is the European Environment Information and Observation Network (EIONET) of the European Environment Agency, https://www.eionet.europa.eu/. Accessed 20 March 2015.

- EU mapping and research could also contribute to identifying valuable and vulnerable areas as a basis for establishing marine protected areas.
- Improve knowledge about the Arctic-specific environmental impacts of shipping and what may be done to address them efficiently. Steps should be taken to determine which species are actually being carried by ships and how they survive en route. This information should then be used in risk assessments, supplemented by targeted baseline inventorying. Better technologies for cleaning hulls and ballast water under low temperatures are also needed. Further, impacts of ship emissions on the Arctic atmosphere need more attention. There is also a need to improve knowledge of the Arctic-specific impacts of discharges of oil and other harmful substances, and to develop better abatement technologies.

There are also needs for many technological developments. Stakeholders have suggested working with states and the maritime industry towards achieving zero-waste and zero-emissions targets. Shipping technologies could be improved on issues like hull design, energy efficiency, new fuels and winterisation. Ships should be supported with better systems for communication under high Arctic conditions, tracking and assistance in voyage planning.

Stakeholders agreed that there is a need to follow the drivers behind Arctic shipping, such as developments in extractive industries and competition with other sea routes. While this could be a task for strategic collection of information, it also involves research questions of understanding the importance of different drivers and using this information to predict future developments in Arctic marine transport.

## Final Remarks

Despite the negligible volume of Arctic shipping so far in a global context, the activity marks a significant change for the Arctic that entails new risks to safety and the environment. There have been responses in terms of developing more adequate governance and, to a certain degree, to address the infrastructure deficit. These efforts may be offset by increasing traffic volumes. The anticipated slow growth in activities creates a window of opportunity for continued work. New and effective measures to improve regulations and the maritime infrastructure must be taken *before* the traffic increases to levels that may pose unacceptable risks (see Picture 3.4). That should be a prerequisite for taking advantage of the economic gains that Arctic shipping may bring.

PICTURE 3.4 *Maksim Gorkij passengers waiting for the rescue on an ice floe. The cruise ship Maksim Gorkij hit an ice floe SW of Svalbard in perfect weather 19 June 1989 and sprang a leak. A Norwegian coast guard vessel happened to be just 4 hours away. When arriving, almost 400 passengers had been evacuated, some of them waiting for rescue on ice floes. Due to a series of fortunate circumstances, all 954 passengers, the crew and the ship were salvaged.*

PHOTO: ODD MYDLAND

CHAPTER 4

# Changing Nature of Arctic Fisheries

*Sigmar Arnarsson and Debra Justus**

## Abstract

Fishing is a vital economic activity in the Arctic. Fisheries are characterised by fluctuations that may be exacerbated by climate change. Aquaculture production is growing fast and becoming a crucial part of the economy in many Northern communities. The EU is a major consumer of Arctic fish and is keen to ensure good co-operation with Arctic states in the sustainable management of marine living resources. The EU influences Arctic fisheries via food safety standards, legislation related to the port state and flag state responsibilities of its members, and participation in international and regional regulatory frameworks.

## 1 Introduction

Fisheries and aquaculture make crucial contributions to the world's well-being and prosperity. In addition to serving as an important food source, the fisheries sector provides livelihoods and income, both directly and indirectly. According to the UN Food and Agriculture Organization (FAO), fish and fishery products are among the most traded food commodities worldwide. While the production of capture fisheries remains stable, aquaculture production is expanding.[1] Arctic fisheries represent more than 10% of the global marine fish catch by weight and 5.3% of the crustacean catch.[2] In the North Atlantic, Arctic fisheries represent about 4% of the global catch.[3] The marine Arctic, as defined by

* The authors would like to thank stakeholders who participated in the consultations and key contributors, particularly Arne Eide (UiT), Øystein Hermansen (Nofima), John Isaksen (Nofima) and Timo Koivurova (Arctic Center).

1 Food and Agriculture Organization of the United Nations (FAO) (2012). *The State of World Fisheries and Aquaculture 2012*.

2 Christiansen, J. & Reist, J.D. (2013). "Fishes." in Arctic Biodiversity Assessment. Status and Trends in Arctic Biodiversity, Akureyri, Iceland, Conservation of Arctic Flora and Fauna (CAFF), 2013.

3 Rudloff, B. (2010). *The EU as Fishing Actor in the Arctic: Stocktaking of Institutional Involvement and Existing Conflicts*, Working Paper FG 2, Stiftung Wissenschaft und Politik.

 | DOI 10.1163/9789004303188_006

the *Arctic Human Development Report* (AHDR) and the Conservation of Arctic Flora and Fauna (CAFF), extends south of the Faroe Islands, and includes all of Hudson Bay and Alaska.[4]

## 2 Arctic Fisheries Sector

Fisheries have been and still are a key industry and employer across the Arctic. In fact, the economies of some communities and countries are almost wholly reliant on the sector.[5] For instance, fisheries and related activities are the single most important component of the economy in Iceland, accounting for 27% of GDP in 2011.[6] In Norway, fish and fish farming accounted for 0.7% of GDP in 2010 with production of about 3.5 million tonnes of seafood, of which 25% was from aquaculture. The regional impact is significant as the majority of fisheries are located in northern Norway. On a regional basis, the fisheries sector around the Barents Sea is estimated to contribute about 8% of GDP in the Murmansk area and 0.3% in Russia. Fisheries generated more than 90% of export earnings in Greenland and the Faroe Islands, around 40% in Iceland and about 6% in Norway in 2010. In Canada, Russia and the United States, countries with larger and more diversified economies, fish account for less than 1% of export earnings. That said, the sector is an important source of employment and food in many rural communities in northern Canada, Arctic Russia and Alaska.[7]

## 3 Arctic Fisheries Ecosystems

Arctic fisheries are mostly located in the low and sub-Arctic – the marine ecosystems and the shelf areas off the coasts of Labrador, Greenland and Iceland, and the Bering and Barents Seas below the central Arctic Ocean (Figure 4.1).[8] These areas are part of the Arctic region in social, economic and political terms as defined by the AHDR and have also been identified as "Arctic gateways" – the seas that connect the Atlantic and Pacific Oceans with the Arctic Ocean and

---

4 Arctic Human Development Report (AHDR), 2004, Stefansson Arctic Institute.

5 Arctic Monitoring and Assessment Programme (AMAP), *AMAP Assessment 2013: Arctic Ocean Acidification*; Duhaime, AHDR (2004).

6 Sigfússon, Þ. & Gestsson, H. (2012). Iceland's Ocean Economy: The Economic Impact and Performance of the Ocean Cluster in Iceland in 2011. Iceland Ocean Cluster.

7 FAO, "Fisheries and Aquaculture Topics. Geographic Profiles."

8 Arctic Portal, Interactive Data Map.

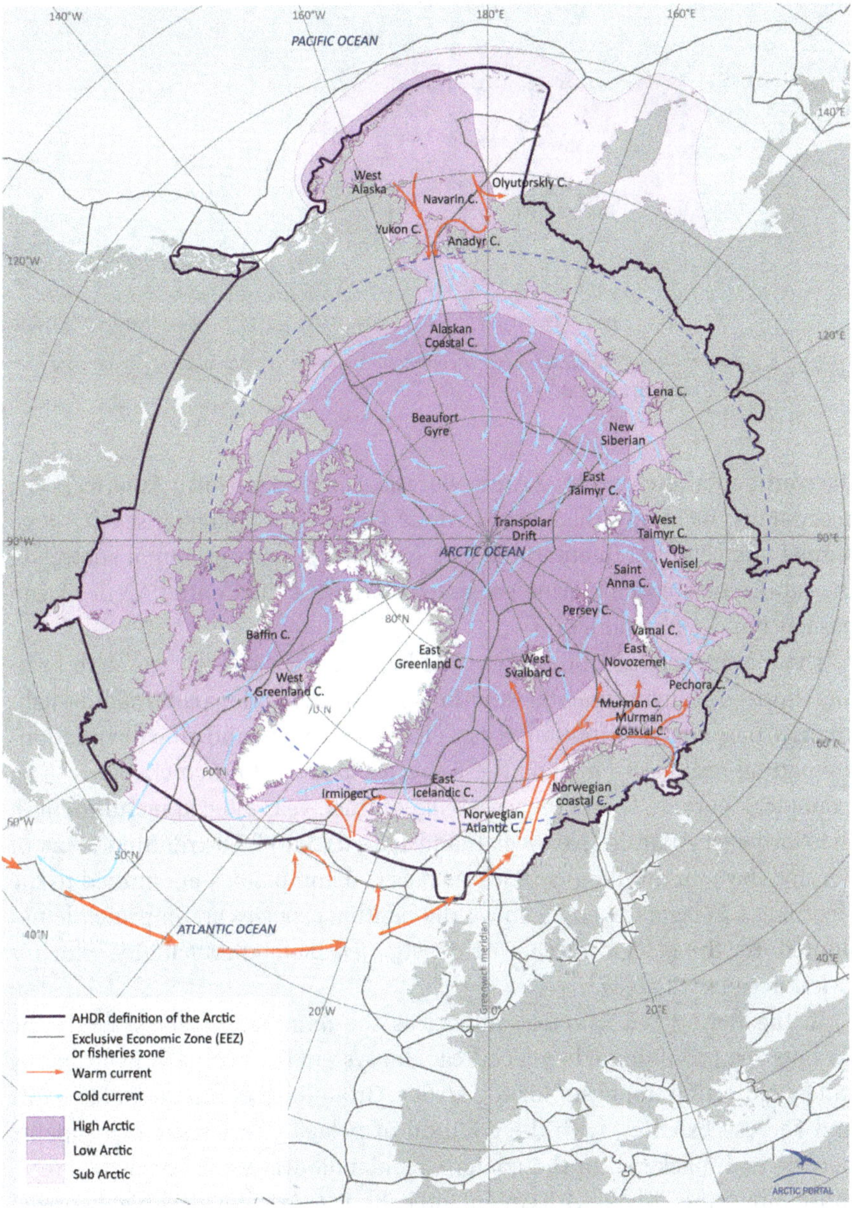


FIGURE 4.1 *Arctic characterisation: High, Low and Sub Arctic and ocean currents*
SOURCES: ARCTIC PORTAL: BASED ON ARCTIC HUMAN DEVELOPMENT REPORT; AMAP ASSESSMENT: ARCTIC OCEAN ACIDIFICATION, 2013

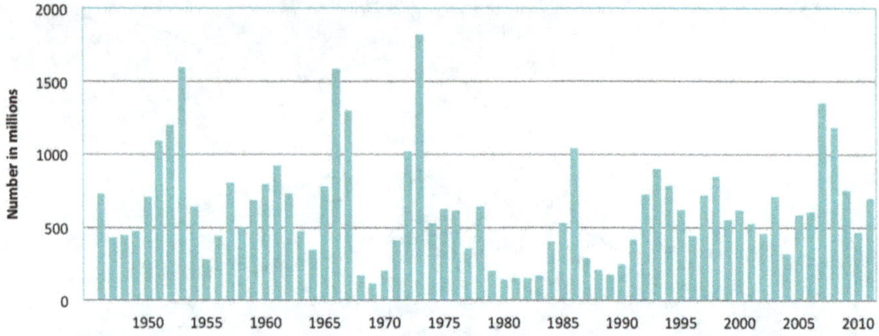


FIGURE 4.2 *Variability of Northeast Atlantic cod recruitment (three-year-old cod), 1946–2010*
SOURCE: ICES, 2012

the continental shelves along Arctic Eurasia, Siberia and North America.[9] The ecosystems, including the Central Arctic Ocean, are characterised by large annual and seasonal fluctuations. The seas above the continental shelves in the sub-Arctic are rich marine ecosystems, whereas the Central Arctic Ocean has low biological production.

The marine species in the Arctic are highly specialised to cope with long- and short-term environmental variations. Annual migration patterns and slight changes in spatial distributions[10] as well as recruitment and growth variations are natural responses enabling these species to adapt to such changes. As an example, Figure 4.2 shows the variability of three-year-old cod recruitment in the Northeast Atlantic (Norwegian and Barents Sea).[11] Distribution areas of benthic (bottom dwelling) species such as cod and pollock are limited to the shelf areas. Pelagic (dwelling above the benthos) species are in principle not limited. Yet the pelagic species are constrained by food availability, which is richer in the shelf areas.[12]

In the Bering Sea fisheries, pollock is the dominant species, while the Barents Sea is dominated by a cod-capelin system occasionally disturbed by inflow of herring from the Norwegian Sea. Groundfish dominate in Icelandic and Faroese fisheries, with the addition of pelagic species such as capelin, herring and mackerel. In the colder Greenlandic waters, crustaceans are of most importance, along with Greenland halibut. Cod is the most highly prized

9 Sigfússon and Gestsson (2012), *op. cit.*

10 Christiansen and Reist (ABA) (2013), *op. cit.*

11 International Council for the Exploration of the Seas (ICES) (2012), *Report of the Arctic Fisheries Working Group 2012*.

12 LME. (2013). Large Marine Ecosystems of the World. Retrieved March 6, 2014, from http://www.lme.noaa.gov/. Accessed 20 March 2015.

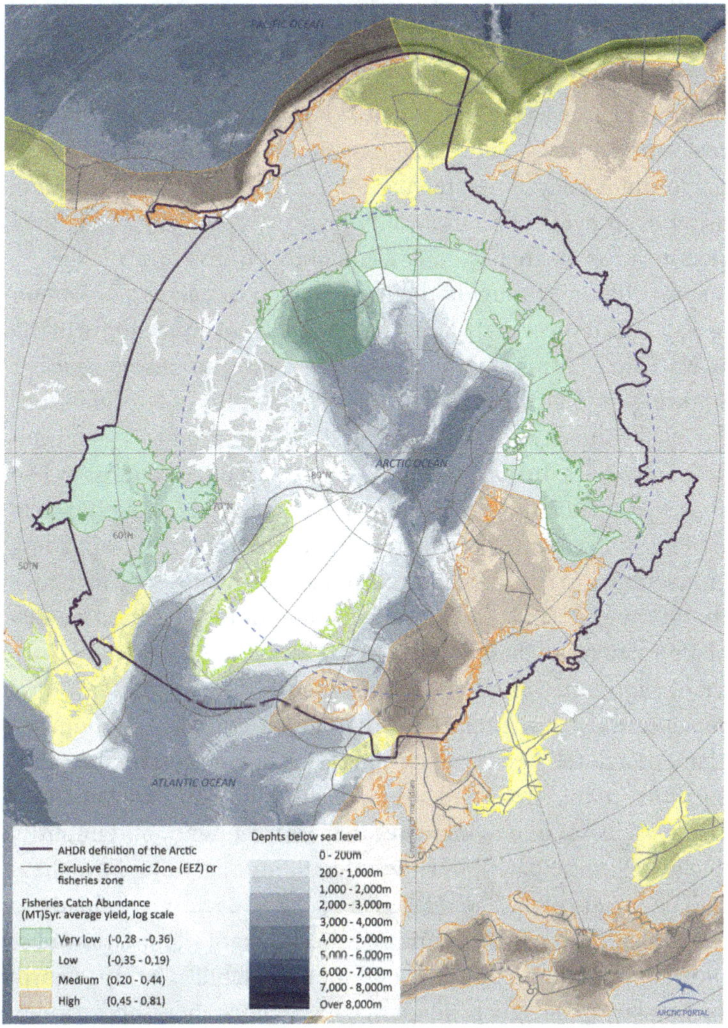


FIGURE 4.3 *Large Marine Ecosystems – catch abundance*
SOURCE: ARCTIC PORTAL, 2014, BASED ON NATIONAL OCEANIC AND ATMOSPHERIC ADMINISTRATION (NOAA), 2013

species for human consumption caught in the Arctic.[13] Fisheries' catch abundance and biological productivity are illustrated in Figure 4.3.

13 Christiansen and Reist (2013), *op. cit.*; Vilhjálmsson, H., Hoel, A., Agnarsson, S., Árnason, R., Carscadden, J., Eide, A. & Fluharthy, D. (2005). "Chapter 13: Fisheries and Aquaculture" in Arctic Climate Impact Assessment: Scientific Report, 691–780. Fairbanks, Alaska: Cambridge University Press.

## 4 Aquaculture

Aquaculture is a fast-growing food production sector, with an average annual growth rate of almost 9% over the last decade.[14] It is an economic activity that uses and transforms natural aquatic resources into commodities valued by society and in so doing may generate environmental impacts. Aquaculture, along with fisheries, provides important employment opportunities as they are often in remote areas where few other livelihood options are available.

The vast majority of aquaculture in the Arctic region is made up of salmon culture in Norway. This represents 93% of the total value of aquaculture in the Arctic region. Norway is also home to the second- and third-largest species, trout and cod, bringing the Norwegian share of Arctic (in AHDR definition) aquaculture to 98%. Aquaculture in Finland and Sweden produces small volumes of freshwater species. In 2012, the Faroe Islands produced almost 63 000 tonnes, which is significant for a small country. Iceland produces Arctic char, cod and salmon in small volumes, but there is increased interest in expanding production. Aquaculture in the Russian Arctic is also on the upswing with production in the Murmansk and Karelia regions amounting to about 34 000 tonnes and plans are to more than double that by 2020.[15]

Climate change-induced variations in water temperature are a key challenge for aquaculture as they impact on the overall aquatic environment, which is fundamental to the performance of farming operations. Models indicate that aquaculture in the Arctic will be enhanced by warming waters. Other direct effects such as losses due to increases in storm frequency and intensity can be relatively well anticipated, but the uncertainty regarding how these parameters will change is high. The resilience of the aquaculture industry to climate change is higher than that of capture fisheries thanks to the control of production, location, population density and food availability.[16] Impacts will depend on the industry's capacity to adapt to new circumstances, accessibility to new production areas, existing regulations and markets. Significant environmental changes may lead to spatial displacement of aquaculture production, thereby posing other challenges and opening up new opportunities. Increased temperatures could lead to more activity in peripheral areas, such as in Arctic Russia, but could also lead to increased disease risk and parasites related to

---

14 FAO (2012), *op. cit.*

15 Hermansen, Ø. & Troell, M. (2012). *Aquaculture in the Arctic*; Salmon Faroe Islands, "Salmon Production Hits Record High in 2012"; Staalesen, "Big Bounce for Arctic Aquaculture"; Vigfússon, Gestsson and Sigfússon, *Economic activity and performance 2012*.

16 This finding is based on recent analysis by the Arctic Climate Change, Economy and Society (ACCESS) project, www. access-eu.org.

higher temperatures in the southern periphery of aquaculture in the Arctic, along with lower growth rates for cold and temperate water species like salmon.

## 5 Fisheries Resource Management

All Arctic countries with significant fisheries have well-established resource management regimes with comprehensive systems for producing the knowledge base required for fisheries management, promulgation of relevant regulations and compliance measures. They are based on societal goals and objectives – usually sustainable use – through appropriate policies and regulatory instruments. The regimes vary with regard to the design of resource management policies, as harvest control rules differ (Table 4.1). Most regimes have imposed a discard ban or measures to hinder discarding and by-catch.

Most systems provide for a certain degree of flexibility in transferable quotas within the set total allowable catch (TAC). Challenges in fisheries management are to reduce the overcapacity of the fishing fleet, as this hinders the sustainable use of resources, and to establish broad consensus and legitimacy for the regimes in the light of conflicting biological, social, economic and cultural goals inherent in most fisheries.[17]

TABLE 4.1 *Fisheries management systems in the Arctic* (+ = *yes;* – = *no*)

| | Uniform system | Quota | Restricted # of licences | Transferrable | Community/ Co-operative quotas | Fishing licenses |
|---|---|---|---|---|---|---|
| US | +/– | +/– | + | +/– | +/– | +/– |
| Faroe Islands | + | + (Effort) | + | + | – | – |
| Greenland | – | + | + | +/– | – | +/– |
| Iceland | + | + | – | + | – | + |
| Canada | – | +/– | + | +/– | +/– | +/– |
| Norway | – | + | + | +/– | +/– | – |
| Russia | – | + | | | +/– | +/– |

SOURCE: VALTÝSSON, H.Þ., SÆVALDSSON, H. & BJÖRNSSON, J.I., (NOVEMBER 2014). FISKVEIÐISTJÓRNUNARKERFI Á NORÐURSLÓÐUM. SAMANTEKT UPPLÝSINGA [ARCTIC FISHERIES MANAGEMENT SYSTEMS]. VERKNÚMER: S11002SJA, RHA-RANNSÓKNA- OG ÞRÓUNARMIÐSTÖÐ HÁSKÓLANS Á AKUREYRI, HTTP://WWW.RHA.IS/STATIC/FILES/RANNSOKNIR/FISKVEIDISTJORNUNARKERFIN_SKYRSLA.PDF. ACCESSED 20 MARCH 2015.

17 Charles, A. (2001), *Sustainable Fishery Systems*, Oxford: Blackwell Science; Garcia, S.M. and A.A. Rosenberg (2010), "Food Security and Marine Capture Fisheries: Characteristics,

## 6 Governance

Governance of fisheries has local, national, regional and international dimensions. It is complex, covering long-term strategic planning as well as short-term operational management. Its scope ranges from local fisheries, such as inlets or fjords to whole ecosystems, such as the Barents Sea. Good governance and monitoring is vital for the optimal and sustained use of marine fisheries resources. In the case of aquaculture, effective governance – the sector's use of natural resources to ensure long-term sustainability and employ best husbandry practices – is essential for its continued growth.

TEXTBOX 4.1 *UN Fish Stocks Agreement*

The United Nations Fish Stocks Agreement, which came into force in 2001, aims to improve international and domestic management of straddling and highly migratory fish stocks. That is done through regional fisheries management organisations (RFMOs) and also includes conservation obligations for the waters within the exclusive economic zones for those stocks. The Arctic states are among the 166 countries that have become parties to this Agreement.

Various international frameworks for managing fisheries have been adopted. The most significant are the United Nations Convention on the Law of the Sea (UNCLOS), the Fish Stocks Agreement (see Textbox 4.1), the FAO Compliance Agreement, the FAO Code of Conduct for Responsible Fisheries and some UN General Assembly resolutions, such as on driftnets and destructive fishing practices.

UNCLOS enshrines the right of coastal nations to extend their exclusive economic zone (EEZ) up to 200 nautical miles and thus decide on how fishing is governed and how TAC is determined. Moreover, UNCLOS made the freedom to fish in high seas conditional on each state's willingness to co-operate with other states to ensure the conservation and good management of the fish stocks concerned (see Textbox 4.2).

The United States has enacted proactive regulation regarding Arctic fisheries. The North Pacific Fishery Management Council (NPFMC) plays a crucial role in federal regulation with regard to the maritime zones of the United

---

Trends, Drivers and Future Perspectives" Philosophical Transactions B, DOI: 10.1098/rstb.2010.0171; Vilhjálmsson *et al.* (ACIA) (2005).

States in the north Pacific. In 2009, the NPFMC approved a Fishery Management Plan for Fish Resources of the Arctic Management Area (Arctic FMP), which closes commercial fishing in US waters off the Arctic coast.[18]

TEXTBOX 4.2 *Conflicts*

A major challenge for a fisheries management regime is to adjust to possible changes in migration patterns of stocks. Changes in fish stock migration patterns in the past have disrupted established resource management arrangements and triggered conflicts between countries.[19] A recent example is the northwest expansion of mackerel, which has led to conflict between the EU, Faroe Islands, Iceland, Norway and most recently Greenland. The migration and feeding patterns of mackerel changed in recent years, shifting further northwest into Faroese, Greenlandic and Icelandic waters. Iceland started fishing mackerel and the Faroese increased their catch, which was objected to by the EU and Norway. Some mackerel fishing has been carried out in the Greenlandic EEZ and its volume is expected to increase. Negotiations have been ongoing and the Faroe Islands, EU and Norway have reached an agreement on the quota shares.[20] Greenland and Iceland have not agreed on shares, leaving the total distribution of the quota share unresolved. These coastal states are members of the North East Atlantic Fisheries Commission and have the obligation to co-operate on fisheries conservation and management, and to find solutions to conflicts.

The North East Atlantic Fisheries Commission (NEAFC) is the regional fisheries management organisation (RFMO) for the northeast Atlantic, one of the most abundant fishing areas in the world. The aim is to manage the high seas, and straddling and highly migratory fish stocks. The regulatory area of NEAFC is outside of the 200-mile EEZs (Figure 4.4). It is the only fisheries convention

18 Cavalieri *et al.*, (Ecologic Institute and others) (2010). *EU Arctic Footprint and Policy Assessment*: Molenaar, E. (2014), "Status and Reform of International Arctic Fisheries Law", in: E. Tedsen, S. Cavalieri, A. Kraemer (eds.), *Arctic Marine Governance: Opportunities for Transatlantic Cooperation*, Springer.

19 Vilhjálmsson *et al.* (ACIA) (2005), *op. cit.*

20 DG Maritime Affairs and Fisheries (European Commission) (2014, 21 November). "Coastal State consultations mackerel in the North-East Atlantic", DG Mare Press Release, http://ec.europa.eu/information_society/newsroom/cf/mare/itemdetail.cfm?item_id=19317. Accessed 20 January 2015.

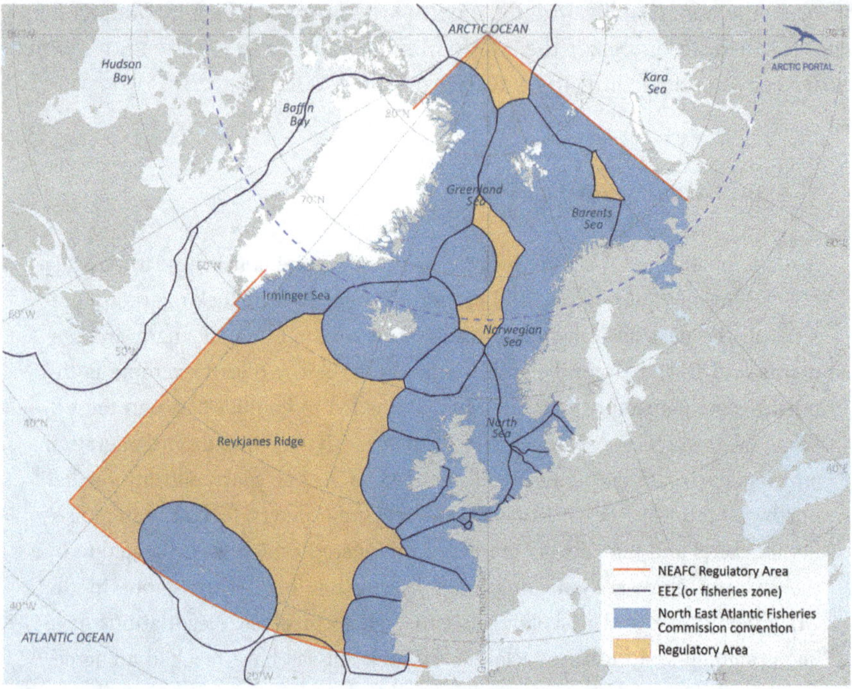


FIGURE 4.4 *North East Atlantic Fisheries Commission Convention (dark blue) and Regulatory Area (orange, international waters beyond* EEZ*s)*
SOURCE: ARCTIC PORTAL BASED ON NEAFC, WWW.NEAFC.ORG

that extends to the North Pole and covers about 8% of the high seas in the central Arctic Ocean (see also Textbox 4.3). Its aim is to ensure the long-term conservation and optimum use of the regional fishery resources to provide sustainable economic, environmental and social benefits. It adopts management measures for various fish stocks and control measures to ensure that they are properly implemented, along with other measures to protect the marine ecosystems. In addition, NEAFC is a venue for dispute settlement.[21]

The International Council for the Exploration of the Sea (ICES), the world's oldest inter-governmental science organisation, is the leading forum for the exchange of scientific information, stock assessment and management advice for the North Atlantic fisheries. ICES provides member states (as well as NEAFC) with advice based on an ecosystem management approach. This implies a higher focus on uncertainty than in the former single species management scheme. Harvest control rules have been developed for the fish stocks

21 Vilhjálmsson et al., ACIA (2005).

assessed by ICES, which incorporate an ecosystem perspective even though full knowledge of the dynamics of these systems is lacking.[22]

TEXTBOX 4.3 *Gap at the top*

That the centre of the Arctic Ocean was unregulated was hardly a concern when it was an ice-bound backwater. This is changing. In summer 2012, 40% of the central Arctic Ocean ice cover melted. Only 8% of the Central Arctic Ocean is within the area under fisheries regulation overseen by NEAFC.

Five national governments with coastline on the Arctic believe that the future establishment of a binding international agreement for the Central Arctic Ocean could be considered because enough of the polar ice cap now melts regularly.

There is consensus among officials from Norway, Denmark, Canada, United States and Russia to acknowledge the desirability to improve scientific understanding of the Arctic marine environment in part to determine whether fish stocks of commercial interest may in the future occur in the Central Arctic Ocean and assess their potential ecosystem impacts. There are currently no fisheries management regulations in place in this high seas area outside of national EEZ s. In July 2015, the five governments adopted a declaration where they agreed to authorize their vessels to fish in high seas only pursuant to RFMO arrangements, to establish a joint research programme and to engage with Arctic residents and other states towards implementing these interim measures.

Based on available scientific information, it is generally understood that commercial fishing in the high seas area of the Central Arctic Ocean is unlikely to occur in the near future, due to physical constraints such as depth, cold water and habitat loss for species currently present in the area. Nevertheless, even the possibility of future commercial fishing in the Central Arctic Ocean triggers the need for more research and better understanding.

## 7 Drivers

Commercial fisheries in Arctic regions are based on the use of relatively few fish species. The dynamics of many of the ecosystems are not well understood. The impacts of climate change on these ecosystems add to the already significant uncertainty.

22 ICES (2012), *op. cit.*

Physical changes are perhaps easier to predict, but significant uncertainties remain. Climate change shifts warmer Atlantic water into the Arctic region. But at the same time, the influx of Atlantic water may be reduced, moderating an overall warming effect. The picture is different in the Bering Sea, which may experience slightly more warming than the Barents Sea. With sea-ice cover also expected to decline, marginal fishing grounds will become more accessible. Invasive species may increase and compete for habitat with resident species.[23]

There is increasing worldwide demand for fish and fish products that provide important food supply. Over the last fifty years, the world fish food supply has outpaced global population growth. The sector also provides livelihoods and income. Fish and fishery products are among the most traded food commodities worldwide, with trade volumes and values reaching new highs in recent years. This trend is expected to continue. While capture fisheries production has remained stable over the last decades, aquaculture production has expanded to meet growing demand. It is not possible to accurately predict how climate change may affect supply and demand of fish products globally, given all the dynamic factors at play.[24]

Aquaculture production in the Arctic is different than that of capture fisheries because its location, population density and food availability are controlled. Variations in the physical environment, however, are essentially not controlled, although aquaculture production may be moved to alternative sites. Significant long-lasting shifts in environmental conditions may therefore lead to changes in the spatial distribution of aquaculture activities.[25]

Effects of climate change are evident in Arctic regions. However, it is not easy to predict how ongoing climate change will affect marine ecosystems and hence the fisheries. Some outlooks foresee greater abundance and limited northward shift of commercial Arctic fish stocks (*e.g. Arctic Climate Impact Assessment*).[26] Or it could be that climate-driven changes in other parts of the world will result in a shift in global fish supply markets with consequent implications for Arctic fisheries. The challenge for fisheries management remains the same: to use the natural resources in a sustainable manner according to the expressed objectives and due consideration of the inherent uncertainty. There is an indication that the choice of management regimes may have a greater impact on Arctic fisheries than the potential environmental changes caused by

23 Christiansen and Reist (ABA) (2013), *op. cit.*; Vilhjálmsson *et al.* (ACIA) (2005), *op. cit.*

24 FAO (2012), *op. cit.*

25 Hermansen and Troell (2012), *op. cit.*

26 Vilhjálmsson, *et al.* (ACIA) (2005), *op. cit.*

climate change.[27] A crucial factor for resource management under conditions of climate change is therefore the development of robust and precautionary approaches and institutions.[28]

## 8 Impacts of Fisheries

Fisheries impact ecosystems as they can alter species composition and abundance. Sudden stock changes can be related to fish harvesting. Unfavourable natural conditions can multiply the impact of such changes and result in a stock collapse. Fishing has cumulative effects on whole ecosystems and economic systems, as it provides income, food security and livelihood for people and communities (see Picture 4.1). Climate change and resource management will have unknown impacts on both. In the Arctic, communities are highly specialised in dealing with environmental changes due to the interdependence of their socio-economic systems and the biophysical environment. Changes in the marine environment affect the socio-economic systems and in some cases also vice versa.[29] In addition to reliance on unpredictable natural systems, the fishing communities also depend on unpredictable global markets, which can again affect the natural system.[30]

PICTURE 4.1 *Pelagic trawlers in Iceland*
PHOTO: SIGMAR ARNARSSON

27 Eide, A. (2007)., Economic Impacts of Global Warming.: The case of the Barents Sea Fisheries. *Natural Resource Modelling* 20(2), 199–221.

28 Vilhjálmsson *et al.* (ACIA) (2005), *op. cit.*

29 Perry, R.I. & Ommer, R. E (2010). "Introduction: Coping with Global Change in Marine Social-Ecological Systems," 34 Marine Policy 4: 739–741.

30 Daw, T., Adger, W.N., Brown, K., & Badjeck, M.-C. (2009). Climate change and capture fisheries: potential impacts, adaptation and mitigation. In Cochrane, K., C. De Young, Soto,

## 9 Outlook to 2030

The Arctic is vibrant and constantly changing. However, it does not appear likely that the changes in Arctic fisheries will be significant in the period to 2030 if the current management schemes are maintained with a precautionary approach as a guiding principle and consensus in distribution of catch quotas of highly migratory species. Minor temperature increases in sub-Arctic areas could lead to increased productivity and access to peripheral fishing grounds, while any major climatic change could have negative impacts.

With growing markets for fish, aquaculture production could expand further into peripheral areas. That may underpin high prices of fishmeal products and provide incentives to exploit fish that are lower in the food chain.

It is not evident that fisheries in the Arctic Ocean, beyond EEZs, will be significant in the coming years, due to physical, biological and economic constraints. Deep and cold water conditions in the Central Arctic Ocean pose a barrier to sub-Arctic species' northern migration. However, there are indications of major changes in long term perspective, especially with the opening of the Arctic gateways and mixture of habitats between Pacific and Atlantic fish stocks, adding to the future uncertainty.[31]

Increased utilisation of high Arctic species in the Arctic Ocean and surrounding waters, such as polar cod, is also unlikely since sea-ice reduction and warming will bring habitat loss. In addition, the capital-intensive nature of such fisheries and the fact that the majority of the catch would go into reduction, *e.g.* fishmeal, would probably render it economically unattractive. Aquaculture could create increased incentives in the long term.

## 10 Implications of Arctic Fisheries Developments for the European Union

Both fish consumption and dependence on imports are growing in the EU, which is one of the world's top three importers of fish and aquaculture

D. & Bahri. T. (eds). Climate change implications for fisheries and aquaculture: overview of current scientific knowledge. FAO Fisheries and Aquaculture Technical Paper. No. 530. Rome, FAO. pp. 107–150; Hovelsrud, G. *et al.* (2010), "Adaptation in Fisheries and Municipalities: Three Communities in Northern Norway," in: Hovelsrud, G. & Smit, B. (eds.), *Community Vulnerability and Adaptation in Arctic Regions*, Springer Netherlands.

31 Wisz, M., *et al.* (2015). "Arctic warming will promote Atlantic-Pacific fish interchange", *Nature Climate Change*, doi:10.1038/nclimate2500.

products. Two of its three biggest suppliers (exporters into the EU) are in the Arctic: Norway with 22% of the share and Iceland with 6%. It is further estimated that more than one-third of fish caught in the Arctic are sold on the European market. Across the EU, average annual fish consumption is more than 23 kg per person, compared with a global average of about 17 kg per person.[32]

The EU is keen to ensure good co-operation with Arctic states in the sustainable management of marine biological resources. Fisheries conservation is a priority, in addition to access and supply. Agreements based on the exchange of fishing opportunities dominate the EU's relations with its neighbours to the north, particularly Norway, Iceland and Greenland. The EU has a long history of mutually overlapping fisheries with these nations. Since the creation of the Common Fisheries Policy, the EU has negotiated the annual exchange of quotas on behalf of its member states, wherein the quotas are shared on the basis of relative stability. These agreements play a vital role in preserving the continuity of traditional fisheries following the establishment of 200-mile EEZ s. They enable each fleet to continue to fish in other parties' waters. Indeed, one of the main purposes of these annual negotiations is to enable mutual access to stocks that straddle territorial boundaries, and which shift back and forth between EU waters and those of northern partners according to the time of the year. These agreements are extremely important to a large section of the EU fleet, especially the agreement with Norway, which covers quotas worth more than EUR 2 billion.[33] The EU has also fisheries partnership with Greenland, which starting from 1985 is valid through consecutive protocol periods. In the 2013–2015 protocol, the EU's financial contribution amounts to nearly EUR 18 million per year for fishing rights and quotas in Greenlandic EEZ.[34] Clearly, good co-operation in international fisheries resource management is crucial for the EU's presence in the landscape of Arctic fisheries.

## 11 How Does the European Union Influence Arctic Fisheries?

The European Union influences the development of Arctic fisheries directly and indirectly through a wide variety of policies, practices, market mechanisms,

32 Cavalieri *et al.*, (2010), *op. cit.*; FAO (2012), *op. cit.*; Rudloff (2010), *op. cit.*

33 European Commission, "Northern Agreements" at the European Commission website europa.eu. Accessed 20 February 2015; Rudloff (2010), *op. cit.*

34 "Fisheries Partnership Agreement," *Government of Greenland*, 2015, at the Naalakkersuisut (Government of Greenland) website at http://naalakkersuisut.gl/. Accessed 20 February 2015.

collaborative engagements and research. For example, marine pollution originating in the EU and EU-flagged vessels fishing in Arctic waters can affect fish stocks. The EU may influence Arctic fisheries by way of its participation in RFMOs and international developments such as the FAO and NEAFC. Its support for scientific research in the Arctic to underpin improved fisheries management may have implications for Arctic fisheries.[35] The EU has significant influence through its role in resource management, the size of its market, and its trade and regulatory elements – which are highlighted briefly here.

### 11.1 *Regulatory Framework*

The European Union has extensive experience in setting regulatory standards for fishing with both environmental and socio-economic criteria at a supranational level through its Common Fisheries Policy (CFP), launched in 1970. Notably, however, no current EU members are coastal states to oceans in the Arctic, which constrains EU policy. The European Economic Area Agreement (EEA, which includes Iceland and Norway) does not cover CFP, although it includes trade in fisheries products and regulates state aid and competition in the sector. EU member states can still act in a wide range of other capacities, *e.g.* as flag states, port states, market states, or with respect to their natural and legal persons. In a flag state capacity, the EU and its members are able to exercise their rights and discharge their obligations with respect to the Arctic Ocean and adjacent areas, most notably freedom of the high seas, such as marine scientific research, freedoms in the maritime zones of Arctic Ocean coastal states; and obligations relating to the marine environment and living resources connected to these rights and freedoms.[36]

### 11.2 *Resource Management*

Fish move across borders and seas, and fishing fleets have done the same for centuries. Since the activities of each fishing fleet affect the opportunities of other fleets, the EU countries chose to manage their fisheries collaboratively through the CFP. The CFP may impact on the health of some of the fish stocks that extend into the Arctic, such as Atlantic mackerel and herring.

The EU has revamped the CFP to make it more efficient in ensuring the economic viability of European fleets, conserving fish stocks and providing good quality food to consumers. The major changes came into effect in 1 January

35 Cavalieri *et al.*, (2010), *op. cit.*

36 European Commission, "Fisheries," European Commission, http://ec.europa.eu/fisheries/index_en.htm. Accessed 20 February 2015.

2014 and include maximum sustainable yield, improved multi-annual planning, landing obligations that prohibit discards (gradually introduced from 2015 to 2019) and special funding for low impact, small-scale local fleets.[37] Substantial efforts have been made to integrate the objectives of its Marine Strategy Framework Directive within the new CFP as part of an ecosystem-based management approach.[38] Fisheries ecosystem plans have been developed for three major European marine regions (North Sea, north-western waters and south-western waters).[39]

The EU had been earlier criticized by North Atlantic actors for poor management of living marine resources under the former Common Fisheries Policy. Ideally, the new CFP could present an opportunity to strengthen the bargaining position of the EU and raise its reputation in respect to management of fisheries. That, however, depends to a great extent on implementation of new rules after 2015. This is of key importance for the possible contribution the EU could make to the discussion on the future management of fisheries in the Arctic Ocean, where it wishes to have its voice heard.

The EU supports the exploitation of Arctic fisheries resources at sustainable levels based on sound scientific advice, while respecting the rights of local coastal communities, as stated already in the Commission's first Arctic communication in 2008. The EU continues to advocate a precautionary approach whereby, prior to the exploitation of any new fishing opportunities, a regulatory framework for the conservation and management of fish stocks should be established for those parts of the Arctic high seas not yet covered by an international conservation and management system.[40] This is in line with the conclusions of officials from the coastal states surrounding the Central Arctic Ocean that it should be protected from unregulated fishing since there are no management regulations in place for high seas outside of national EEZs, except

37 Regulation (EU) No 1380/2013 of the European Parliament and of the Council of 11 December 2013 on the Common Fisheries Policy, Amending Council Regulations (EC) No 1954/2003 and (EC) No 1224/2009 and Repealing Council Regulations (EC) No 2371/2002 and (EC) No 639/2004 and Council Decision 2004/585/EC.

38 Directive 2008/56/EC of the European Parliament and of the Council of 17 June 2008 establishing a framework for community action in the field of marine environmental policy.

39 European Commission, "Fisheries."

40 European Commission and High Representative (2012), Developing a European Union Policy towards the Arctic Region: progress since 2008 and next steps. Joint Communication of the European Commission and the High Representative of the European Union for Foreign Affairs and Security Policy to the European Parliament and the Council. Brussels, 26.6.2012. JOIN(2012) 19 final.

for the regulatory area of NEAFC (see Textbox 4.3: Gap at the top). The need for joint management of high seas fish stocks has been raised by the European Commission at meetings of the North Atlantic Fisheries Ministers Conference. RFMOs could in principle extend their geographical scope for this purpose.

### 11.3 *Market Size and Proximity*

The European Union accounts for about 26% of global fish imports, making it the largest import market in the world, with a value of about EUR 36 billion in 2011. The EU's dependence on imports for fish consumption is growing. This is a result of the rising trend in consumption, but also illustrates the constraints within the EU on further expansion of supply. In this respect, the current reform of its CFP aims to rebuild its fish stocks, as well as boost aquaculture production. The results of the reform and the effects on supply and trade will only be felt in the medium-to-long term. Today the EU is an important market for Arctic fisheries, especially those in the North Atlantic. Faroese, Greenlandic, Icelandic and Norwegian fisheries in particular are highly dependent on exports to the EU.[41]

### 11.4 *Trading Fish in a Globalised World*

In the early days of the CFP, the EU decided on its own trade policy on fish. Since the launch of the General Agreement on Tariffs and Trade/World Trade Organization process, trade policy and tariffs are strongly influenced by international developments. The common organisation of the EU market includes measures to ensure a stable and predictable supply of fish as a vital raw material. A relevant tool is the autonomous tariff quotas (ATQs). The aim of ATQs is to enhance access for EU processors to fish from third countries by granting reduced tariff rates on the import of specific products for which domestic production is in deficit. These preferential tariffs are intended to provide balanced incentives, which give priority to EU production where it exists, while ensuring that the European processing industry is not unfairly penalised when it has to compete in the world market.[42]

### 11.5 *Combating Illegal Fishing*

EU rules to deter illegal, unreported and unregulated (IUU) fishing came into force in 2010 and include:

---

41 Hagstova Føroya, *Faroe Islands in Figures 2013*; Rudloff (2010), *op. cit.*; Statistics Greenland, *Greenland in Figures 2013*.

42 European Commission, "Fisheries."

- Only marine products validated as legal by the relevant flag state or exporting state can be imported to or exported from the EU.
- A black list has been established covering both IUU vessels and states that turn a blind eye to illegal fishing activities.
- EU operators who fish illegally anywhere in the world, under any flag, face substantial penalties proportionate to the economic value of their catch.[43]

There is an increasing need for international co-operation among fishing and seafood-importing countries to improve fisheries management of shared marine resources and to preserve the associated employment and other economic benefits of sustainable fisheries. In line with a commitment to prevent IUU fishing, the EU issued a catch certification scheme to ensure full traceability of all marine fishery products traded from and into the EU. The regulation also seeks to ensure that no EU citizens engage in IUU activities, no matter where they take place. In addition to the certification scheme, the regulation also addresses issues of port state control and mutual assistance. Moreover, it introduces an EU alert system to detect the most suspect cases of illegal practices, the vessels involved and any non co-operating third countries. Proper enforcement is supported by a harmonised system of proportionate and deterrent sanctions for serious infringements. An agreement between Norway and the EU is an example wherein Norway will issue a catch certificate for all Norwegian landings and exports to the EU.[44]

## 11.6 *Food Safety Standards*

EU legislation harmonises food safety control across the member states. A key aspect is that all food and feed business operators, from farmers and processors to retailers and caterers, have principal responsibility for ensuring that food placed on the EU market meets the required food safety standards. The regulations apply at every stage in the food chain, including primary production, *i.e.* fishing, aquaculture and farming, in line with a "farm to fork" approach to food safety.[45] Traceability is an important factor in implementing such standards.

43 European Commission, "Illegal Fishing (IUU)," at the European Commission website at http://ec.europa.eu/fisheries/cfp/illegal_fishing/index_en.htm. Accessed 20 February 2015.

44 Cavalieri *et al.*, (2010), *op. cit.*; European Commission, "Fisheries."

45 European Commission, EUROPA – Food Safety: From the Farm to the Fork.

## 12 Critical Factors for EU Decision-making

Three critical factors for EU decision-making were identified in stakeholder consultations.[46] The inter-linkages of the socio-economic system in relation to the biophysical marine environment are at the forefront of where human decisions and actions face the natural system and vice versa. Sustainable use of renewable resources such as fish is highly dependent on the drivers for their use and management.

### *Governance and Management*

More research is needed to address the uncertainties faced in fisheries management, along with increased co-operation, especially regarding quota setting and distribution. Increased co-operation would also help to control overfishing and fight IUU fisheries. In addition it can help mitigate conflicts with other economic activities, such as aquaculture, oil and gas extraction, shipping and tourism. Creating a more stable system through active co-operation could help establish better inflow of safe and sustainably caught seafood into the EU market.

### *Climate Change and Species Distribution and Composition*

Another issue is species distribution due to natural changes, whether climate-induced or not. Distribution change challenges current management agreements, rules and regulations, both now and in the future, and that could lead to the possibility of overfishing since there is no control over the fisheries. Distribution change could also lead to conflict with other economic sectors, such as oil and gas extraction and aquaculture, as fisheries and other sectors might become more spatially integrated.

### *Global Demand for Fish*

Fisheries in the Arctic are facing changes and uncertainties that might affect the sector in both the short and long term. Global demand for fish products is one of the main drivers of Arctic fisheries, as increasing demand provides a greater incentive for fishing. This affects the EU market as global demand influences market value.

46 See Annex 1.1. and 1.2 of the SADA report at http://www.arcticinfo.eu/images/pdf/sada_chapters/Chapter_Annexes.pdf. Accessed 20 February 2015.

## 13 Conclusion: The Way forward for the EU

Fishing is a vital economic activity in the Arctic. Fisheries are based on relatively few fish species located in rich marine ecosystems in the low and sub-Arctic and characterised by major fluctuations. Climate change increases the uncertainties faced by Arctic fisheries. Adjusting to possible changes in the migration patterns of stocks poses a major challenge.

Arctic countries have well-established resource management regimes, including production of knowledge required for management. However, the Central Arctic Ocean is only partly covered by RFMOs. Arctic coastal states are currently exploring possibilities for establishing some kind of binding agreement regarding fisheries management in the Arctic Ocean, likely in the form of interim measures in the short-term perspective, even though it seems unlikely that large-scale fisheries will be established in the area in the future. Aquaculture production is growing fast and becoming a crucial part of the economy in many Northern communities.

The EU is a major consumer of Arctic fish and is keen to ensure good co-operation with Arctic states in the sustainable management of marine living resources. The EU influences Arctic fisheries via food safety standards, legislation related to the port state and flag state responsibilities of its members, and participation in international and regional regulatory frameworks. Possible steps for the EU – elaborated basing on input from stakeholders in the SADA consultations – in facing challenges and issues in Arctic fisheries include improved management and quota setting, decreasing capacity, ensuring that IUU measures are effective and secure inflow of Arctic seafood into EU markets.

Improved management and quota setting is an important issue as it helps to create a sustainable system for Arctic fisheries and ensures equitable sharing and avoids overfishing. A well-managed system can help to mitigate climatic impacts. This includes participation in international agreements on quota setting and the development of a mechanism for setting fishing targets in a sustainable manner. The EU could help ensure that Arctic fisheries resources are sustainably managed through a common Arctic regional fisheries agreement in close co-operation with Arctic nations, especially in the north Atlantic. Effective co-operation, discussions and a formal venue could help to mitigate potential conflicts. Wide co-operation and information sharing in applicable areas could benefit Arctic fisheries research to underpin improved management approaches and practices. There is a need for more scientific research, including local and traditional knowledge, of issues relevant to future fisheries in the Arctic, especially the Central Arctic Ocean.

In addition, improved management could ensure the effectiveness of measures to combat illegal, unreported and unregulated fishing. The EU holds sway as a large market force to continue to combat IUU through best practice measures, such as port state control, document catches, catch certificates, traceability and promotion of sustainable use of fisheries resources. The EU could establish better port monitoring in co-operation with Arctic states and continue efforts to register fish catches. Combating IUU fisheries benefits all Arctic states and the EU by enhancing sustainability and stable markets. In principle, there should be no economic incentives to partake in IUU fisheries. Strengthened IUU measures would boost consumer confidence and give a more positive image to fisheries.

Measures should be taken to reduce fishing capacity. Abolishing distortionary subsidies, such as those that mask the true costs of operation, could be key as they cloud market signals and can lead to overcapacity. Capacity is already at a high level: more capacity could lead to unsustainable fisheries and spur IUU fishing. A profit-driven market should create ample incentives. This could be encouraged through an improved market-driven and co-operative management system. Distortionary subsidies should be eliminated in order to provide economic and social incentives in fisheries and management.[47] As the EU CFP is being reformed, the phasing out or elimination of subsidies could be implemented in the short term.

The EU's enormous seafood market is dependent on imports to meet demand and Arctic fisheries are dependent on this market. Conflicting issues can have negative consequences for both. Trade sanctions have already had drastic effects on the livelihoods of Arctic nations along with limiting the inflow of goods to the EU. Co-operation and open dialogue need to be effective to avoid such developments. Open communication and co-operation in trade could be implemented in the short term for long term benefits. While EU members are not Arctic coastal states, the scale of its market, where the EU has numerous policy and regulatory influence, provides it with significant opportunity to exercise an influence.

There has always been a close interaction between the Arctic and the European nations in the field of fisheries and that is likely to continue. With improved management, co-operation and consensus in distribution of catch quotas, the current picture of Arctic fisheries is likely to prevail in the near future, even in light of climatic change.

---

47 Garcia and Rosenberg (2010), *op. cit.*

CHAPTER 5

# Arctic Offshore Hydrocarbons and the European Union: More Constraints and Less Opportunities

*Michał Łuszczuk, Debra Justus, Jennie Thomas, Chris Klok and Federica Gerber*

## Abstract

While interest in Arctic offshore hydrocarbon exploitation has increased in recent years, actual developments have been slow to follow, with major differences across the Arctic region. Meeting the growing demand of EU citizens for energy in a safe and environmentally responsible manner is a key challenge. The EU has limited, but multi-faceted, functional competences that enable it to play a role in promoting high standards for resource development including through support for developing technologies specific for Arctic application, efforts to address climate change and relations with Arctic partners.

Funding and investment frameworks can facilitate high standards for regulators and industry to ensure that Arctic hydrocarbon developments are environmentally and socially responsible. It is recommended that the EU increase its support for research on the Arctic environment and relevant technology advances. Despite numerous challenges, the EU should continue and strengthen energy dialogues with non-EU Arctic partners within existing forums.

## 1 Introduction

Production of hydrocarbons in the Arctic region has many facets and is connected with many challenges. Most of the region's oil reserves are in Alaska while reserves in Russia are dominated by natural gas. Onshore resources have been produced for decades, while in terms of offshore extraction the Arctic is

* The chapter was drafted with support from Timo Koivurova (Arctic Centre), Adam Stępień (Arctic Centre), Johan Gille (Ecorys), Kathy Law (CNRS/INSU, LATMOS-IPSL) and Narangerel Davaasuren (IMARES).

 | DOI 10.1163/9789004303188_007

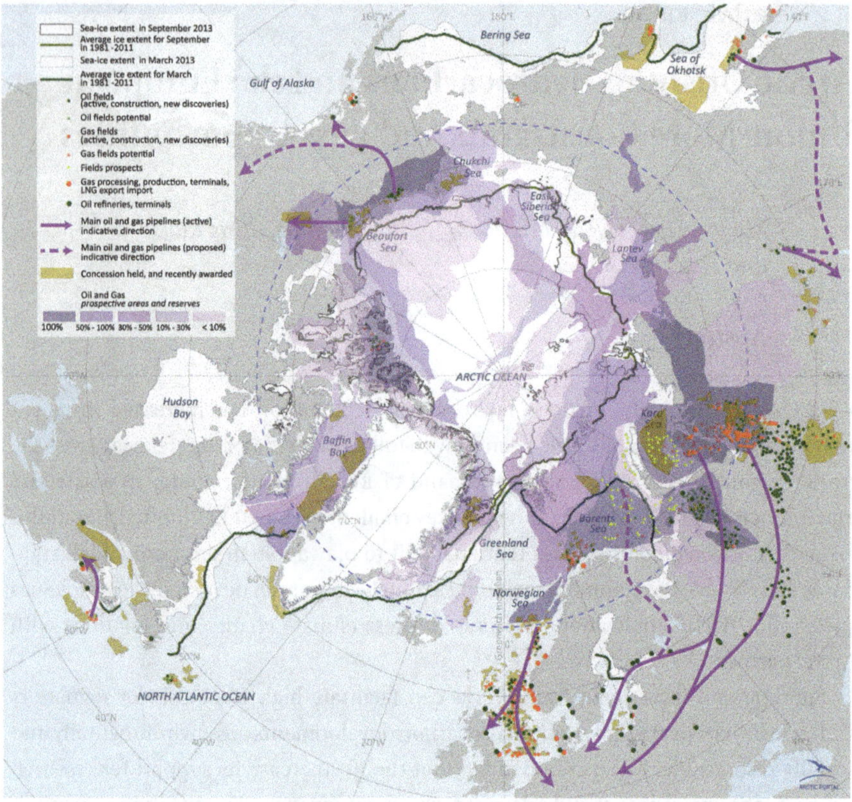


FIGURE 5.1 *Main oil and gas areas, mining sites and sea-ice extent in the Arctic*
SOURCE: ARCTIC PORTAL, BASED ON NORDREGIO; JOHANNA ROTO AND JOSÉ STERLING, 2011

largely a frontier region (Figure 5.1).[1] The common thread is that prospects for hydrocarbon exploitation in the Arctic are uncertain, particularly offshore.[2]

1 Crandall, R. & Thurston, D. *et al.* (2010). *Oil and Gas Activities in the Arctic*. In Arctic Council: Arctic Monitoring and Assessment Programme (AMAP), *Assessment 2007: Oil and Gas Activities in the Arctic – Effects and Potential Effects, vol.* 1; International Association of Oil & Gas Producers (2013). *Environmental management in Arctic oil and gas operations: Good practice guide*. International Association of Oil & Gas Producers. www.ogp.org.uk/pubs/449.pdf. Accessed 15 February 2014.

2 Koivurova, T. & Hossain, K. (2008). *Offshore Hydrocarbon: Current Policy Context in the Marine Arctic*. Arctic TRANSFORM. www.arctic-transform.org/download/OffHydBP.pdf. Accessed 10 March 2013. Johnston, P.F. (2010). Arctic Energy Resources and Global Energy Security. *Journal of Military and Strategic Studies*, 12(2), 13–32.

Some parts of the Arctic waters are becoming more accessible due to improved technologies and changes in sea-ice related to climate change.[3] Concurrently, expectations and interests in offshore hydrocarbons in the Arctic have increased in recent years. Largely untapped to date, the estimated offshore resource base is significant. Yet the technical and environmental aspects and high costs of operating in severe conditions present many challenges.[4] Investments in exploration and production are influenced by dynamic variables including global markets and prices, energy demand and policies concerned with economic development, energy security and environmental protection.[5] The timing and extent of Arctic hydrocarbon developments is not easy to predict.[6] Extraction may influence the Arctic environment, economies, geopolitics and societies. Arctic oil and gas exploitation also has implications for the economic, political and environmental landscape of the European Union (EU).

The main focus in this chapter is offshore oil and gas hydrocarbon exploitation in a broadly defined European part of the Arctic region. It looks at recent trends, their drivers and possible economic, environmental and social impacts with relevance to the EU. Further, it highlights EU policies and actions relevant for oil and gas developments in the Arctic. Drawing on previous research and input from the regional and non-regional stakeholders collected by the authors in 2013/2014, the chapter discusses constraints and opportunities for further engagement of the EU in developing energy resources in the European Arctic, which constitute critical issues for EU decision-making. It also suggests a set of recommendations for EU action.

## 2 Overview of Offshore Oil and Gas Trends – Lower Expectations and More Doubts

While there has been a surge in interest in exploiting Arctic hydrocarbon resources in recent years, actual developments have been slow to follow. Arctic

3 Harsem, Ø. *et al.* (2013). Oil exploration and sea-ice projections in the Arctic. *Polar Record,* DOI: www.dx.doi.org/10.1017/S0032247413000624.

4 Arctic Council, (2009). Sustainable Development Working Group Report on Arctic Energy. Arctic Portal. www.library.arcticportal.org/1531/1/SDWG_ArcticEnergyReport_2009.pdf. Accessed 21 April 2013.

5 Harsem, Ø., Eide, A. & Heen, K. (2011). Factors influencing future oil and gas prospects in the Arctic. Energy Policy. DOI: www.dx.doi.org/10.1016/j.enpol.2011.09.058.

6 Hong, N. (2012). The energy factor in the Arctic dispute: a pathway to conflict or cooperation? *Journal of World Energy Law and Business,* 5 (1), 13–26.

oil and natural gas have been explored and developed for decades – with onshore production dating back to the 1920s and offshore starting in the 1970s.[7] A decade ago, the Arctic accounted for about 25% of the world's natural gas and 10% of oil production.[8] Yet most of the estimated Arctic reserves remain untapped. Undiscovered resources could amount to 90 billion barrels of oil, up to 50 trillion cubic metres of natural gas and 44 billion barrels of natural gas liquids (NGLs), according to the U.S. Geological Survey (USGS).[9] That is about 13% of the world's undiscovered, technically recoverable oil and up to 30% of global gas reserves, and some 84% of it is offshore. Undiscovered natural gas is likely to be three times more abundant than oil in the Arctic and is largely concentrated in Russia (Figure 5.2).[10]

In recent years there has been increased business interest in the hydrocarbon potential of the Arctic even in the face of a complex mosaic of challenges and constraints.[11] According to some estimates, investments in the circumpolar north will amount to EUR 75 billion over the next decade.[12] Yet, so far, the

---

7 Ernst and Young, 2013, Arctic Oil and Gas, www.ey.com/Publication/vwLUAssets/Arctic_oil_and_gas/$FILE/Arctic_oil_and_gas.pdf More details at: Bishop, A. *et al.* (2010). Petroleum Potential of the Arctic: Challenges and Solutions. *Oilfield Review*, 22(4), 36–49; Arctic Council, (2009).

8 Lindholt, L. (2006). Arctic natural resources in a global perspective, in S. Glomsrød and I. Aslaksen (eds.), *The Economy of the North*. Oslo, Statistics Norway, p. 27. "From 1990–2004, Arctic oil production was dominated by west Russia (79%) followed by Alaska (18%), Norway (3%), and small amounts in the other regions. Gas production was also dominated by west Russia (96%) followed by Alaska (3%) and small amounts from the other regions. (…) Around one-half of cumulative Arctic production is oil (51%), with large regional differences: Canada (59% oil), Alaska (87%), east Russia (9%), west Russia (46%), and Norway (84%)." See: Peters, G.P. *et.al.* (2011). Future emissions from oil, gas, and shipping activities in the Arctic, *Atmos. Chem. Phys. Discuss.*, doi: 10.5194/acpd-11-4913-2011, p. 4917.

9 USGS (United States Geological Survey), (2008). Circum-Arctic Resources Appraisal: Estimates of Undiscovered Oil and Gas North of the Arctic Circle, Fact Sheet 2008–3049, USGS, Boulder, United States.

10 Another appraisal focused only on the Russian Arctic oil and gas potential suggests that collectively the Arctic regions constitute one of the world's largest petroleum super basins that could provide markets with energy resources corresponding to those of the Persian Gulf or West Siberian petroleum basins. Bishop, A. *et al.* (2010), p. 41.

11 Arctic Council (2009), *op.cit.*

12 Emersson, C. & Lahn, G. (2013). *Arctic opening: Opportunity and Risk in the High North*. Chatham House-Lloyd's Risk Insight Report. Potential Arctic hydrocarbon production is ultimately determined by a cumulative factor – profitability. Bishop, A. *et al.* (2010)., p. 41; Nakhle, C. & Shamsutdinova, I. (2012). Arctic Oil and Gas Resources: Evaluating Investment Opportunities. Oil, Gas and Energy Law Intelligence.

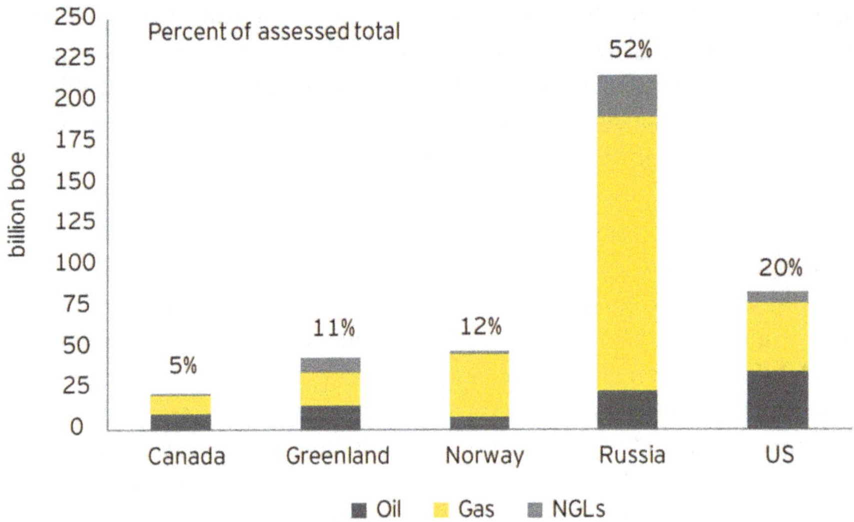


FIGURE 5.2 *Potential Arctic oil and gas resources. Total assessed resources: 412 billion barrels of oil equivalent (boe).* NGLS = *natural gas liquids*
SOURCE: ARCTIC GAS AND OIL, EY ARCTIC OIL AND GAS REPORT, MAY 2013 (BASED ON DATA FROM USGS AND THE US DEPARTMENT OF ENERGY)

intensity of recent discussions concerning hydrocarbon development in Arctic regions has not been matched by commensurate on-the-ground activities.[13]

Optimistic outlooks for further hydrocarbon development in the Arctic arose following the 2008 USGS estimates of resource potential. It is important to consider the complex multitude of areas, geology, economics, levels of development, governance, multiple interests, etc., that span the region rather than to view potential resource development as homogeneous across the circumpolar

13 Arctic Council (2009). In the report released by Marsh Risk Management it is claimed that "only 22 of the 174 fields discovered (in the Arctic) have produced hydrocarbons, with an average lag time of 13 years. Just 38 new fields are expected to come into production between 2012 and 2018." Marsh Risk Management Research (2013). *Managing Risk on the New Frontiers of Energy Exploration*, p. 4. Marsh. https://uk.marsh.com/Portals/18/Documents/MRMR%20New%20Frontiers%20of%20Energy%20Expl%202013_A4.pdf. Accessed 18 December 2013. "The actual ongoing and planned development in the Arctic offshore is then still quite limited in extent. It means that the Arctic's designation as a new energy province is built more on anticipated potentials than on significant proven reserves of oil and natural gas and other energy resources." Arctic Council, (2009); cf. Lindholt, L. & Glomsrød, S. (2012). *No big bonanza for the global petroleum industry*. Energy Economics, 34(5), 1465–1474.

Arctic.[14] It is also vital to view Arctic prospects in a worldwide context. The global oil market is dynamic, the best example being the unconventional hydrocarbon revolution in the United States in recent years, and the significant drop in world oil market prices in 2014 and early 2015.[15] It is also fundamental to assess possible developments in the context that the Arctic offshore is a frontier region with challenging conditions and fragile ecosystems.

A number of companies are pursuing Arctic exploration projects, including Shell in the Chukchi and Beaufort Seas; Cairn in offshore Greenland; Rosneft/ExxonMobil in the Kara Sea; and Rosneft/ENI in the Russian Barents Sea. However, the costs are high and the environmental risks substantial, both of which influence companies' plans and activities.

Recent developments in various parts of the region illustrate this trend.[16]

Fourteen test wells have been drilled in Baffin Bay, off Greenland's west coast, though no drilling has been conducted since 2011. A licencing round in 2012–2013 for fifteen blocks attracted some interest, but exploration activities are likely to remain on stand-by in the near term. Licences for four blocks have been granted also in the Greenland Sea area in Northeast Greenland. Oil and gas development in Greenland is not viewed as a near-term prospect.[17]

Two areas on Iceland's continental shelf have potential for commercial oil and gas development: Dreki (east and northeast) and Gammur (north). Three licences for Icelandic, Chinese and Norwegian companies were awarded in 2013–2014, paving the way for the first drilling off Iceland's coast.[18] "Arctic Services" – an initiative of more than 50 companies and institutions in Iceland's north – was launched in 2013 to provide improved service levels and infrastructure for oil and gas exploration.[19]

---

14 See: Østhagen, A. (2013). *Arctic oil and gas. The role of regions.* IFS Insights 2/2013, Oslo, Norwegian Institute for Defence Studies, p. 22.

15 International Energy Agency (IEA), 2013, *World Energy Outlook-2013*, IEA/OECD, Paris.

16 Cf. Ermida, G. (2014). Strategic decisions of international oil companies: Arctic versus other regions. *Energy Strategy Reviews*, 2(3–4), 265–272.

17 Kay, J. & Thorup. S. (2014). Oil and Gas in Greenland – Still on Ice? http://www.andrewskurth.com/media/pressroom/1726_14467_AK_Notes_Greenland_Nov2014.pdf. Accessed 15 December 2014. As Runi M. Hansen, Statoil country manager for Greenland and the Faroes explains: "Being in a frontier area, this licence (Avinngaq) is a long-term project for Statoil and the company will follow its stepwise approach, not going faster than technology allows (…)." Statoil News (2013). http://www.statoil.com/en/NewsAndMedia/News/2013/Pages/Dec20Greenland.aspx., Accessed 19 February 2014.

18 National Energy Authority, 2014.

19 IceNews (2014). http://www.icenews.is/2014/02/26/joint-initiative-in-iceland-offers-services-for-arctic-operations/. Accessed 26 February 2014.

The Norwegian Petroleum Directorate estimates that the undiscovered resources in the Barents Sea amount to 6 billion barrels of oil equivalent, most of it in the form of natural gas.[20] While Norway is a leading country in Arctic hydrocarbon production, the outlook for its oil and gas sector faces challenges in terms of rising operating costs; lower gas prices (depending on region); adjustments to the fiscal regime, which *inter alia* reduces the attractiveness of future projects that require new infrastructure; and availability of qualified workers.[21] Costs in Norway's petroleum sector have roughly doubled between 2005 and 2012, and a tax hike in 2013 put several projects at financial risk.[22]

New developments could help to revive Norway's output, which is at a 25-year low. Both oil and gas production in northern Norwegian fields dropped significantly in 2013. There are also delays in the construction of the floating production unit for the Goliat field (when in production, it will be the northernmost on the Norwegian shelf and the first in the Norwegian Barents sea), where oil production is planned to start in mid-2015.[23] Statoil has finalised its large scale 2013–2014 exploration program in the Barents Sea. Although the commercial results did not meet Statoil's expectations, the company collected a lot of data and knowledge about the petroleum potential in different areas of the Barents Sea and gained additional unique experiences when it comes to working in remote northern areas and solving logistical and operational challenges.[24]

Nevertheless, there remains considerable interest with 40 energy companies nominating 160 desired blocks in northern Norwegian waters for the 23rd licence round expected to be finalised in the first half of 2015.[25] The northernmost

20 The Arctic Journal. http://arcticjournal.com/oil-minerals/oil-discovered-barents-sea. Accessed 15 February 2014.

21 Stolen, H. *et al.* (2014). *Norway's rising oil costs hit Arctic output hopes*. Reuter. http://www.reuters.com/article/2014/01/16/oil-norway-delays-idUSL3N0KP4BB20140116. Accessed 18 February 2014.

22 *Ibid.*

23 Nilsen, T. (2015). While oil plunges, ENI floats out giant Barents Sea platform. BarentsObserver.com. http://barentsobserver.com/en/energy/2015/01/while-oil-plunges-eni-floats-out-giant-barents-sea-platform-07-01. Accessed 10 January 2015.

24 Pettersen, T. (2014). Statoil ends disappointing Arctic campaign. BarentsObserver.com. http://barentsobserver.com/en/energy/2014/11/statoil-ends-disappointing-arctic-campaign-10-11. Accessed 15 December 2014.

25 In the 22nd Norwegian Licence Round in 2013, 29 companies got licence rights in Arctic waters, for the first time including two Russian companies - Lukoil and Rosneft. Staalesen, A. (2014), see n. 26.

blocks are located 73°north (the furthest north to date[26]). Additionally, in 2014 there were a record number of applications for awards in predefined areas on the Norwegian shelf (including three blocks in the Barents Sea), as the authorities received applications from 47 companies.[27]

About 75% of Russia's estimated offshore hydrocarbon resources are located in Arctic regions, accounting for 22–27% of global offshore resources.[28] Major international oil and gas companies have shown interest in Russia's expansion into the Arctic offshore for the last decade or so.[29] However, due to the political tensions between the West and Russia concerning the latter's role in the geopolitical situation in Ukraine in 2014 which led to EU, US and Canadian sanctions that restrict the export of certain technology such as that for oil and gas exploitation, the current prospects for the resumption of co-operation appear to be very limited in the near term.

Russia's Ministry of Energy estimates that only 5% of its oil production and 10% of gas will come from the Arctic shelf by 2035.[30] This reflects that there is no current shortage of supply possibilities in Russia before moving into the more expensive resource areas in the Arctic over the longer term.[31] It also

26 Staalesen, A. (2014). *Drilling further north, farther east.* BarentsObserver.com. http://barentsobserver.com/en/energy/2014/02/drilling-further-north-farther-east-18-02. Accessed 18 February 2014.

27 Norwegian Petroleum Directorate. (2014). *Recod number of applications in APA 2014.* http://www.npd.no/en/Topics/Production-licences/Theme-articles/Licensing-rounds/APA-2014/Record-number-of-applications-in-APA-2014/. Accessed 18.12.2014.

28 Kobzev, A. (2012). Oil exploration in Russia beyond 2025. *Performance Journal, 4*(2), *pp. 54–61. EY Performance.* http://performance.ey.com/wp-content/uploads/downloads/2012/02/Performance-4.2-January-2012-Journal-v13-oil-russia.pdf. Accessed 15 February 2013.

29 Henderson, J. (2012). *Joint Ventures in the Russian Offshore – Positive News but only for the Long Term.* Oxford Institute for Energy Studies. http://www.oxfordenergy.org/wpcms/wp-content/uploads/2012/05/Joint-Ventures-in-the-Russian-Offshore-%E2%80%93-Positive-News-but-only-for-the-Long-Term-.pdf. Accessed 28 January 2014; Locatelli, C., Rossiaud, S. & Loskot-Strachota A. (2012). *POLINARES working paper n. 45 Case 1: Russia, institutionalism and the effect on oil and gas investments.* Polinares. http://www.polinares.eu/docs/d3-1/polinares_wp3_case1.pdf. Accessed 18 October 2013.

30 Arctic-info. http://www.arctic-info.ru/News/Page/dola-nefti-s-arkticeskogo-sel_fa-k-2035-gody-sostavit-do-5-?id=7090. Accessed 26 February 2014.

31 It should be also mentioned that after having lain idle in the Pechora Sea since August 2011, the "Prirazlomnaya" platform in late December 2013 started pumping oil in Russia's first oil producing offshore field in the Arctic. Staalesen, A. (2014). Delayed Arctic breakthrough. BarentsObserver.com. http://barentsobserver.com/en/energy/2014/01/delayed-arctic-breakthrough-02-01. Accessed 15 February 2014.

reflects shifts in global markets such as the impacts of unconventional resources lowering prices and putting the economic viability of liquefied natural gas (LNG) projects like Shtokman in Russia under scrutiny. The supply outlook in the near term – drawn up before the Ukrainian crisis – suggested modest growth in Russian domestic demand and weak growth in exports to Europe significantly influenced by the constraints on the pace of securing a meaningful position in Asia-Pacific markets.[32] In the current political landscape (as of first-quarter 2015) and the very difficult economic situation in Russia, this scenario does not seem to be valid anymore and sketching a new one would be very challenging in the light of prevalent uncertainty.

## 3 Primary Drivers of Arctic Oil and Gas Exploitation

Arctic resource development is unique, complex, high cost and high risk. Key determinants can be considered in four clusters that illustrate opportunities and constraints.[33]

1) *Scope and pace of climate change in the Arctic*

- Changes in sea-ice cover.
- Expanding access and transport routes.
- More difficult weather conditions.
- Increased coastal erosion.
- New and additional pollution sources contributing to climate change, *e.g.* ozone, black carbon, aerosols.

2) *Economic conditions and global markets*

- State of national and regional economies.
- Economic potential of hydrocarbon development.
- Dynamic global energy supply and demand landscape, intensifying interactions between different fuels, technologies, markets and prices.[34]

32 IEA (2013), *op.cit.*

33 Harsem, Eide and Heen (2011), *op.cit.*

34 Two major shifts in global energy markets in the last decade have impacts on the prospects and timing of Arctic offshore oil and gas developments. The first is the rise in energy demand in emerging Asian economies that now accounts for more than half of global demand. The second includes market shifts in response to unconventional resource production in North

3) *Advances in offshore technology and maritime transport*

- Improved technology for offshore oil and gas exploration, and development to reduce environmental impacts and enhance safety.
- Infrastructure for production and transport.
- Co-operative approaches and technical capacity to address pollution, oil spill and rescue operations.[35]

4) *Policy developments*

- Government policies and granting new licences.
- International governance frameworks, regional and national oil and gas regulations.
- Global and regional climate change agreements.
- Stakeholder influence.

## 4 Overview of the Implications of Arctic Offshore Exploitation

Experience with exploration and extraction of hydrocarbons has shown that they have considerable effects on the vulnerable Arctic environment, as well as regional economy and society, including traditional livelihoods of indigenous people.[36,37] Impacts usually vary depending on the spatial scale of a given offshore development, type of specific activity, stage of development and the required technology and infrastructure.[38] Generalised impacts associated with hydrocarbon development in the Arctic include:

America and global LNG markets leading to a significant drop in natural gas prices in North America while energy prices remained high in Europe. Solanko, L. & Vilmi, L. (2013). *The transformation of global energy markets*, BOFIT Online 2013 No. 6, http://www.suomenpankki.fi/bofit_en/tutkimus/tutkimusjulkaisut/online/Documents/2013/bon0613.pdf. Accessed 10 January 2014.

35 Martin, A.S. (2012). *Deeper and Colder. The Impacts and Risks of Deepwater and Arctic Hydrocarbon Development.* Sustainalytics. http://www.sustainalytics.com/sites/default/files/unconventional-oil-and-gas-arctic-drilling_0.pdf. Accessed 22 October 2013.

36 Koivurova and Hossain (2008), *op.cit.*

37 International Centre for Reindeer Husbandry, (2009). *Reindeer Husbandry and Barents 2030: Impacts of Future Petroleum Development on Reindeer Husbandry in the Barents Region*, GRIDA. http://www.grida.no/files/publications/reindeer-husbandry-barents_lores.pdf. Accessed 15 March 2012.

38 Arctic Council (2010), *op.cit.*

*Environmental*

- Physical impacts on marine and terrestrial ecosystems, including air pollution and noise.
- Risk of long-lasting negative impacts from catastrophic events, *e.g.* oil spills.
- Effects on terrestrial and marine biodiversity and habitats: directly on species confronted with pollution and disturbance; indirect effects of pollution that disrupt food chains.
- Production and consumption of additional hydrocarbon resources adding to greenhouse-gas emissions.
- Increased concentration of climate forcers, *e.g.* ozone, black carbon.
- Damage to important ecosystem services of value to humans, *e.g.* fisheries.

*Social*

- Demographic trends, *e.g.* influx of workers, migration patterns.
- Increased economic and employment opportunities.
- Social relations and health.
- Education and training patterns, *e.g.* new opportunities.
- Increased urbanisation.
- Cultural and economic factors, *e.g.* indigenous livelihoods, traditional practices, contact with nature.

*Economic*

- Macroeconomic effects, *e.g.* projected increase in national and regional GDP.
- Microeconomic effects, *e.g.* expected increase in economic opportunities, incomes, growth of businesses, increased employment and stimulation of overall economic activity.
- Multiplier effect and improved services.
- Increased public revenues from royalties and other payments or production sharing approaches to fund services and support sovereign wealth funds.
- Risks to traditional livelihoods.

*Governance/political*

- New geopolitical roles and economic potential.
- New regional and global relations, *e.g.* energy security.
- Further development of environmental and economic governance for regulation, fiscal regimes, resource management, *e.g.* development of oil spill preparedness and response regimes.

- Strengthen comprehensive and long-term monitoring and research capabilities.
- Improved stakeholder engagement stemming from regulatory and NGO pressures.

It is important to keep in mind that the impacts and consequences:

- cannot be considered in isolation from one another as they are usually closely interlinked;
- are unevenly distributed, *e.g.* physical disturbance of the environment from offshore oil and gas activities and onshore infrastructure has a larger impact on people in the specific areas compared to those more distant, whereas financial benefits can extend far beyond the region;
- some impacts may lead to dissimilar outcomes depending on the particular situation or location;
- impacts must be considered in terms of long-term effects on the environment and society.

While climate change is presented as increasing access to offshore oil and gas deposits in the Arctic in the long term, the burning of fossil fuels and resulting greenhouse-gas emissions are largely responsible for human-induced climate change. Two-thirds of all proven fossil fuel reserves must stay in the ground if the world is to avoid dangerous climate change (above 2 °C), according to the International Energy Agency (IEA).[39] Building infrastructure for hydrocarbon development in the Arctic is expensive and once in place there is a strong incentive to make the most of such investments during their economic lifespan. This presents a dilemma as climate change triggers Arctic opening options that can exacerbate further climate change.

There are many concerns about the environmental impact of resource developments both onshore and offshore in the Arctic.[40] On the other hand, investment and development of hydrocarbon resources can have positive social and economic effects in remote communities. Responsible, knowledge-based governance is key to effectively and successfully responding to the challenges and opportunities presented by further development of Arctic oil and gas resources.[41]

39 International Energy Agency (2012). *World Energy Outlook – 2012*, IEA/OECD, Paris.

40 Oil spills were indicated as the number one uncertainty regarding offshore oil and gas developments in the Arctic in the EU Arctic Impact Assessment online stakeholder questionnaire.

41 Hasle, J.R., Kjellén, U. & Haugerud, O. (2009). Decision on oil and gas exploration in an Arctic area: Case study from the Norwegian Barents Sea. *Safety Science*. DOI: http://www.dx.doi.org.sciencedirect.han.bg.umcs.edu.pl/10.1016/j.ssci.2008.10.019.

TEXTBOX 5.1 *Economic and social benefits: Snøhvit case*

The first offshore gas development in the Barents Sea is a milestone in developing the hydrocarbon province (Picture 5.1). About 2 500 people were employed in the five-year construction phase. Operation, maintenance and support services now provide about 400 jobs and 75% of the employees have been recruited from north Norway. Nearly EUR 380 million of the overall deliveries to the field came from companies registered in north Norway. Assessments show that the development of Snøhvit reversed declining population and employment trends in the Hammerfest area. New companies were established in the area, housing construction expanded and municipal revenues increased substantially. Significant investments have been made in upgrading schools and infrastructure and in developing cultural facilities.[42]

PICTURE 5.1 *LNG plant in Melkøya island in Hammerfest, Norway*
THE PLANT LIQUEFIES NATURAL GAS EXTRACTED FROM OFFSHORE SNØHVIT FIELD
PHOTO: GETTYIMAGES

It should be emphasised that the resilience of Arctic ecosystems to withstand adverse events, such as incidents during offshore activities, is weak. While particular risk events – such as an oil spill – are not necessarily more likely in the Arctic than in other environments, the potential environmental consequences

42 Government of Norway (2011). *The High North: Visions and Strategies.* Meld.St. 7 (2011–2012), Report to the Storting (The Parliament of Norway).

and costs of clean-up may be significantly greater. These risks have significant implications for governments, businesses and the insurance industry.[43] Given that most Arctic hydrocarbon reserves are located offshore, it is of particular concern that there is little knowledge concerning the suitability of existing methods for oil clean-up in ice-covered waters or in areas of broken sea-ice.[44]

The International Association of Oil and Gas Producers launched a four-year, USD 20 million research programme in 2013 to address issues specific to Arctic oil and gas exploitation, including spill trajectory modelling and remote sensing, and oil recovery techniques in sea-ice areas.[45]

## 5 Governance and Best Practice for Arctic Offshore Oil and Gas Extraction

Effective governance, regulations, international standards and best practices are crucial factors to reduce the risks of negative environmental and socio-economic effects of oil and gas activities.[46] Many international conventions and agreements relevant to hydrocarbon extraction are applicable in the Arctic (Table 5.1). They address the following key areas:

- Nature conservation and environmental protection, including environmental impact assessments.
- Rights of indigenous peoples.
- Oil spill preparedness, response and co-operation for ships and offshore facilities.
- Occupational safety and health requirements.
- Marine pollution from ships.
- Liability and compensation for damage from pollution incidents.

43 Sydnes, A.K. & Sydnes, M. (2013). Norwegian–Russian co-operation on oil-spill response in the Barents Sea. *Marine Policy*. DOI: http://www.dx.doi.org/10.1016/j.marpol.2012.12.001.

44 Potter, S. *et al.* (2012). *Spill Response in the Arctic Offshore*. American Petroleum Institute and the Joint Industry Programme on Oil Spill Recovery in Ice. http://.api.org/~/media/Files/EHS/Clean_Water/Oil_Spill_Prevention/Spill-Response-in-the-Arctic-Offshore.pdf .Accessed 27 February 2014.

45 Arctic Oil Spill Response Technology Joint Industry Programme (JIP): http://www.arcticresponsetechnology.org. Accessed 20 January 2014.

46 Koivurova and Hossain (2008), *op.cit.*; Barry-Pheby, E.A. (2014). The international law and governance of the Arctic's offshore oil industry: Inert or altered? OGEL 1 (2014) Special: Offshore Petroleum Exploration and Production: Challenges and Responses, https://www.academia.edu/5632614/Ov12-1-article03. Accessed 20 February 2014.

TABLE 5.1 *Selected international instruments relevant to Arctic offshore oil and gas activities*

| Conventions, agreements, standards and guidelines | Year |
|---|---|
| United Nations Convention on the Law of the Sea | 1982 |
| International Convention for the Prevention of Pollution from Ships (MARPOL) | 1973/78 |
| International Convention for the Safety of Life at Sea (SOLAS) | 1974 |
| Agreement on Co-operation on Marine Oil Pollution, Preparedness and Response in the Arctic | 2013 |
| The Convention for the Protection of the Marine Environment of the Northeast Atlantic (OSPAR) | 1992 |
| International Convention on Oil Pollution Preparedness, Response and Co-operation (OPRC) | 1990 |
| Protection of the Marine Environment (PAME) Arctic Offshore Oil and Gas Guidelines | 2009 |
| PAME Guidelines for Transfer of Refined Oil and Oil Products in Arctic Waters | 2004 |
| International standards for safe exploration, production and transportation of oil and gas, *e.g.* ISO 19906 – Petroleum and natural gas industries – Arctic offshore structures. | 2010 |

- Minimum standards for the construction and operation of ships; training and certification of seafarers.
- Rules to prevent collisions at sea relevant to the transport of oil.

A study of the current international framework at global level related to offshore oil exploitation highlights both its fragmented and incomplete nature.[47] To some extent, the lack of adequate international and regional governance contributes to a shortage of current, comprehensive and effective enforcement of rules covering the Arctic marine area.[48] Part of the solution could be to

47 Rochette, J. (2012). *Towards an international regulation of offshore oil exploitation.* IDDRI. Accessed 17 June 2013; Humrich, C. (2013). Fragmented International Governance of Arctic Offshore Oil: Governance Challenges and Institutional Improvement. *Global Environmental Politics*, 13(3), 79–99.

48 Ebinger, Ch.K., Banks J. & Schackmann, A. (2014). *Offshore Oil and Gas Governance in the Arctic: A Leadership Role for the U.S.* http://www.brookings.edu/~/media/research/files/

combine governance norms – both national and international – with the corporate social responsibility standards of operating companies.[49]

TEXTBOX 5.2 *Health, safety and environmental protection industry standards*

Recognised technical standards are used worldwide by the oil and gas industry. Accumulated experience over many years and from all parts of the world influence the standards through systematic updating and issuance of new standards. The standards represent best international practices for achieving an acceptable level of safety. Yet, updating standards is a time-consuming process requiring consensus from many parties.

Existing regulations and technical standards generally have not been developed to address the Arctic's harsh offshore conditions. Existing technical standards need to be supplemented for the Arctic challenges with:

- Definition of societal and company safety objectives.
- Risk assessment from concept to execution, operation and decommissioning.
- Acquisition and analysis of site-specific environmental data and loads.
- Definition of additional or modified functional requirements.
- Adaptation for site-specific and project-specific conditions.

*Adapted from Barents 2020, Det Norske Veritas, 2012.*

There are major differences between regulatory regimes, standards and governance capacity across the Arctic states.[50] The challenges of Arctic development call for co-ordinated responses where viable and common standards are possible, along with an ecosystem-based approach, transparency and best practices. The Arctic Council continues its efforts to facilitate fundamental regional solutions that could become a framework supporting sustainable

reports/2014/03/offshore%20oil%20gas%20governance%20arctic/offshore%20oil%20and%20gas%20governance%20web.pdf. Accessed 20.12.2014.

49 Koivurova, T. (2013). Resource exploitation in the Arctic: incorrect diagnoses, misinterpretations and wrong solutions – how to avoid these? *Baltic Rim Economies*, Special Issue On The Future Of The Arctic, Issue No. 2.

50 Dagg, J. *et al.* (2011). *Comparing the Offshore Drilling Regulatory Regimes of the Canadian Arctic, the U.S., the U.K., Greenland and Norway.* Pembina Institute. http://www.pubs.pembina.org/reports/comparing-offshore-oil-and-gas-regulations-final.pdf. Accessed 20 December 2013.

development and uphold the public trust. The Arctic coastal states have signed two agreements with particular relevance to oil and gas development. The 2011 Search and Rescue Agreement, a legally binding instrument that is now in force, establishes a framework for co-ordination of international maritime and aeronautical coverage, and response across an area of about 34 million km$^2$.[51] In May 2013, the Arctic states concluded a legally binding Agreement on Co-operation on Marine Oil Pollution Preparedness and Response in the Arctic to improve oil spill management.[52]

## 6 How Oil and Gas Development in the Arctic May Affect the European Union

The European Union is a major energy market with a variety of producers and consumers. In 2012, the EU's oil and gas imports amounted to more than EUR 400 billion or approximately 3.1% of the EU GDP.[53] EU policies relevant to, *inter alia*, economy and trade, energy and the environment alongside national policies of its member states make for a complex policy landscape.[54] For example, the growing demand for transport fuels, largely based on oil, versus EU policy approaches to reduce greenhouse gas and other emissions, and to curb the use of fossil fuels. The EU energy market is increasingly relying on imports to meet energy demand.

EU energy imports increased from less than 40% of energy consumption in the 1980s to 53,4% in 2012. In that year, the highest dependency rates were for

51 Agreement on Cooperation on Aeronautical and Maritime Search and Rescue in the Arctic. See: Kao, S., Pearre, N.S. & Firestone, J. (2012). Adoption of the Arctic search and rescue agreement: A shift of the Arctic regime toward a hard law basis? *Marine Policy*. DOI: http://www.dx.doi.org.sciencedirect.han.bg.umcs.edu.pl/10.1016/j.marpol.2011.12.001; Łuszczuk, M. (2014). The Regional Significance of the Arctic Search and Rescue Agreement. *Rocznik Bezpieczeństwa Międzynarodowego*, 18(1), 38–50.

52 Boyd, A. (2013). Binding oil spill agreement signed. BarentsObserver.com. http://www.barentsobserver.com/en/arctic/2013/05/binding-oil-spill-agreement-signed-15-05. Accessed 15 June 2013.

53 European Commission (2014). *A policy framework for climate and energy in the period from 2020 to 2030*. p. 2.

54 Cavalieri, S. *et al.* (2010). *EU Arctic Footprint and Policy Assessment. Final Report.* Berlin: Ecologic Institute. http://arctic-footprint.eu/sites/default/files/AFPA_Final_Report.pdf. Accessed 20 June 2013; Airoldi, A. (2008). The European Union and the Arctic: Policies and actions. Nordic Council of Ministers. http://www.norden.org/fi/julkaisut/julkaisut/2008-729. Accessed 15 June 2013; Airoldi, A. (2010). EU and the Arctic. Main developments 2008–2010. Nordic Council of Ministers. http://www.norden.org/fi/julkaisut/julkaisut/2010-763. Accessed 15 June 2013.

crude oil and NGL (87,8%) and natural gas (65,8%). Russia is the main supplier, accounting for 34% of the EU's crude oil imports in 2012. Almost 63% of EU imports of natural gas in 2012 came from Russia and Norway.[55] The IEA projects a big increase: net gas imports into the EU will rise from 302 billion cubic metres (bcm) in 2011 to 525 bcm in 2035, with the share of imports in total consumption jumping from 63% to 85%. EU policy aims to improve energy security, while delivering a low-carbon and competitive energy system, through common action, integrated markets, import diversification, sustainable development of indigenous energy sources, investment in the necessary infrastructure, end-use energy savings and supporting research and innovation.[56]

Meeting the growing demand of EU citizens for energy in a safe and environmentally responsible manner is a key challenge for EU institutions.[57] The Arctic region has the potential to play an important role. As security of supply becomes a concern when a high proportion of imports are concentrated among relatively few partners, the EU may look to the Arctic as a potential source of hydrocarbons. Due to the importance of a stable and sufficient supply of energy for the EU societies and economies, the European Commission released an EU energy security strategy in May 2014. This plan, based on an in-depth study of member states' energy dependence, generally suggests reducing EU external dependency on particular suppliers by diversifying its energy sources, suppliers and routes as well as negotiating effectively with current major energy partners. In particular, the strategy proposes a reinforced partnership with Norway through the development and further expansion of gas supply infrastructure and limiting the dependence of the EU refining industry on Russian oil.[58] An increased focus on EU energy security in the near term will have an effect on energy trade relationships with Russia and Norway,

---

55 European Commission (2014), EU energy in figures. Statistical Pocektbook 2014. http://ec.europa.eu/energy/sites/ener/files/documents/2014_pocketbook.pdf. Accessed 11 March 2015.

56 *Ibid.*, p. 4.

57 See the Joint Research Centre Institute for Energy and Transport, which supports the development and implementation of offshore safety legislation analysing past accidents in order to identify the existing conditions related to sharing of information, transparency and lessons learned. It contains also useful statistical information on the frequency and severity of accidents. Christou, M. & Konstantinidou, M. (2012). *Safety of offshore oil and gas operations: Lessons from past accident analysis. Ensuring EU hydrocarbon supply through better control of major hazards.* European Commission JRC IET.

58 European Commission (2014). *European Energy Security Strategy* [COM/2014/0330].

and will constitute a factor in developing their oil and gas activities in the Arctic area.[59,60]

The development of hydrocarbons in the Arctic influences a broad scope of policy fields within the EU. Selected issues, which are highly correlated, are shown in Table 5.2.

TABLE 5.2 *Arctic oil and gas development: Significance for the EU*

| **Changes in EU Energy Demand and Supply Patterns** | **Challenges and Opportunities for EU Economy** | **Environment and Sustainable Development** |
|---|---|---|
| Shifts in regional and global energy markets.<br>– Russia, Norway (interdependency)<br>– US unconventional resources boom (shale gas and tight oil) | Investment opportunities in Arctic.<br>Opportunities for the EU industries. | Effects on the EU energy, economic, geopolitical and climate change policies.<br>Environmental risks, e.g. air pollution, oil spills. |
| Changes in energy consumption patterns.<br>– More use of low-carbon energy.<br>– Accelerated deployment of renewables.<br>– Energy efficiency improvements. | Further development of the EU energy market.<br>Research and technology.<br>Scientific investigations. | EU support for monitoring systems.<br>Change in the EU environment and climate footprint. |

## 7 Outlook to 2030

Continued interest in the opportunities to exploit oil and gas resources in the Arctic, particularly the "lower Arctic," are expected to be driven by growing global demand, shifting market conditions, increased physical access and geopolitics.

59 Boussena, S. & Locatelli, C. (2013). Energy institutional and organisational changes in EU and Russia: Revisiting gas relations. *Energy Policy*. DOI: http://dx.doi.org/10.1016/j.enpol.2012.11.052; Harsem, Ø. & Claes, D. (2013). The interdependence of European – Russian energy relations. *Energy Policy*. DOI: http://dx.doi.org/10.1016/j.enpol.2013.04.035.

60 European Commission (2011). *Energy Roadmap 2050* [COM/2011/885].

Effective governance and infrastructure, including search and rescue, are required framework conditions. A step-wise approach is expected as resources are defined through exploration techniques, experience is gained in the extreme conditions, environmental and social protections are put in place, and companies assess their investment strategies.

It is likely that the Arctic states will be able to delineate and delimit their continental shelves in the foreseeable future in an orderly manner, on the basis of the law of the sea and UN Convention on the Law of the Sea. In the context of expected gradual improvement of the governance framework for Arctic resource exploitation, this may enable gradual development of resources in these areas.

Hydrocarbon development in the Arctic will depend on technological and economic feasibility, as well as environmental protection and social acceptance, even if new technologies will help to reduce current risks. Stricter regulations for safety standards for development, transport and shipping activities, and more attention to local benefits, social and corporate responsibility are also expected. More worldwide attention to the environmental aspects of potential development is anticipated. The importance of Arctic oil and gas resources for European countries will be important, although not vital.

## 8 Relevant EU Policies and their Role in Arctic Development

The EU has numerous, albeit limited, functional competencies that enable it to play an important role in supporting effective co-operation and to help meet the challenges that confront the Arctic region. It has earned broad recognition for its strong international efforts to address climate change, expand renewable energy sources, promote energy efficiency and support polar research in order to contribute to addressing global challenges. The EU's most important Arctic energy partners are Russia and Norway. The EU conducts regular energy dialogues with both partners. Because the EU's dependence on energy imports is expected to continue to grow, these dialogues will become increasingly important for the EU in influencing the environmental footprint of its energy consumption.[61],[62]

About 24% of Arctic oil and gas output went to the EU-27 in recent years.[63] Market influence and co-operation with Arctic partners such as through

61 See: Roadmap EU-Russia Energy Cooperation until 2050, March 2013, p. 10 and p. 17.

62 European Parliament and Council, (2010). *Regulations concerning measures to safeguard security of gas supply and repealing Council Directive 2004/67/EC.*

63 Cavalieri, S. *et al.* (2010), *op.cit.*

the European Economic Area (EEA) Agreement enable the EU to influence hydrocarbon exploration and development.[64] Existing EU policies, particularly related to energy and the environment, affect oil and gas developments in the Arctic in direct and indirect ways.[65] Selected mechanisms are highlighted below.

- *Directive on Safety of Offshore Oil and Gas Operations*,[66] adopted in June 2013, calls for special attention to ensure environmental protection taking into account the risk of major accidents and the need for effective responses. The directive contains provisions for licensing, monitoring, reporting and risk management for oil and gas extraction in EU waters. It also encourages member states to require companies registered in these member states to report[67] on major accidents occurring also outside of the EU waters. This may be relevant for operations in the Arctic waters. The EU considers the directive to be applicable to the EEA, but this position has been challenged by Norway (as of 2015). The new legislation encourages EU members of the Arctic Council to actively promote the highest environmental safety standards, such as through the creation of international instruments on prevention, preparedness and response to Arctic marine oil pollution (currently in the process of development in the Arctic Council). The directive obliges the Commission to promote high safety standards for hydrocarbon operations taking place across the world, in relevant global and regional fora, including those relating to Arctic waters as well as to facilitate exchange of information with countries adjacent to EU waters.
- *EU Offshore Oil and Gas Authorities Group*, established in 2012, is a forum for national authorities and the EU to exchange experiences and expertise relevant to major accident prevention and response for offshore oil and gas operations within EU waters and beyond its borders, where appropriate.[68]

---

64 The EEA Joint Parliamentary Committee, (2013). *Resolution on Arctic Policy*. Adopted during 41st Meeting 28–29 October 2013, Vaduz, Liechtenstein.

65 Koivurova, T. *et al.* (2010). *EU Competencies Affecting the Arctic*. Report completed for the European Parliament. www.europarl.europa.eu/activities/committees/studies/download.do?language=sv&file=33381. Accessed 23 March 2013; Cf. Neumann, A. (2012). European Interests as Regards Resource Exploitation in the Arctic: How Sustainable Are European Efforts in This Regard? *The Yearbook of Polar Law*, 619–645.

66 Directive 2013/30/EU of 12 June 2013 on safety of offshore oil and gas operations.

67 Such information would be collected also at the EU level.

68 European Commission (2012). *Decision of 19 January 2012 on setting up of the European Union Offshore Oil and Gas Authorities Group* (2012/C 18/07).

- *Environmental Impact Assessments* (EIA) framework provides minimum standards for assessments based on several directives. Energy installations and related infrastructure subject to EIA s include oil refineries, road construction, extraction of petroleum and natural gas, and petroleum storage facilities. The EIA Directive is EEA relevant.[69]
- *Fuel Quality Directive*[70] seeks to reduce life-cycle emissions from transport fuels by 10% by 2020. Petroleum products must meet quality requirements concerning sulphur and lead content.
- *Measures to safeguard security of natural gas supply*.[71] This Directive establishes a common framework within which member states define general, transparent and non-discriminatory security of supply policies compatible with the requirements of a competitive internal gas market; it also clarifies the general roles and responsibilities of the different market players and implements specific non-discriminatory procedures to safeguard security of gas supply.
- *Limits on air pollutants* from large combustion facilities[72] aims to reduce acidification, ground level ozone and particles by controlling emissions of pollutants (sulphur dioxide, nitrogen oxides and dust) from large combustion plants, *e.g.* power stations, petroleum refineries, other industrial processes running on solid, liquid or gaseous fuels.
- *Renewable Energy Directive*[73] sets a goal of renewable energy comprising 20% of total EU energy consumption by 2020 and is EEA relevant.
- *Energy Efficiency Action Plan*[74] aims to increase total energy savings by 20% in 2020.
- Research projects and facilities that increase knowledge of the Arctic and are very important for oil and gas developments include CryoSat-2, an

69 Council Directive (2011). On the assessment of the effects of certain public and private projects on the environment. Directive 2011/92/EU of the European Parliament and the Council Directive on Safety of Offshore Oil and Gas Operations (2013/30/EU).

70 Directive 2009/30/EC of 23 April 2009 amending Directive 98/70/EC as regards the specification of petrol, diesel and gas-oil and introducing a mechanism to monitor and reduce greenhouse gas emissions.

71 Council Directive 2004/67/EC of 26 April 2004 concerning measures to safeguard security of natural gas supply.

72 Directive 2001/80/EC of 23 October 2001 on the limitation of emissions of certain pollutants into the air from large combustion plants.

73 *Directive 2009/28/EC of 23 April 2009 on the promotion of the use of energy from renewable sources.*

74 European Commission (2011). Energy Efficiency Action Plan 2011. Communication. COM(2011) 109 final.

environmental research satellite launched in 2010 to measure sea ice thickness, and the Copernicus European Earth Observation Programme, which offers marine monitoring services and studies land and sea ice in the Arctic using data from European and Russian satellites.

## 9 Critical Factors for the EU Decision-Making

The analysis above reveals the complex relationship between EU policy-making and actual developments in Arctic offshore hydrocarbons extraction. The EU encounters numerous challenges in its interactions with Arctic partners in this policy area. Building on the input from stakeholders in the SADA consultation process, we have identified several issues that policy-makers should consider critical in assessing efforts taken so far and contemplating future actions relating to oil and gas developments in the Arctic.

First, local benefits of hydrocarbon extraction should be carefully considered. As highlighted during stakeholder consultation, all offshore activities are undertaken with essential onshore support. Moreover, they entail major changes in and challenges for the socio-economic landscape of neighbouring communities. Therefore, adequate facilities and competent capacity building in the communities should be addressed as a significant issue. In addition, social licence and corporate social responsibility should be considered as the basis upon which to build a responsible approach for any kind of planned oil and gas activities. It is also a question of ensuring the appropriate sharing of benefits on a broadly understood perspective and not just in economic terms. For instance, investment in technology advancement, research/education and healthcare services are important, since they can strengthen local communities facing opportunities and threats arising from the development of oil and gas offshore activities.

Secondly, tools for risk management and corresponding regulations constitute a key to responsible hydrocarbon extraction. Oil and gas exploration and development are considered high-risk activities (especially in terms of oil spills), so there is a clear need for effective legal frameworks and operational solutions (*e.g.* search and rescue capabilities). One of the responses to these challenges is the development of adequate and effective regulations targeted at the appropriate aspects of exploration, development and production of offshore oil and gas and its transportation to markets. Adopting and strengthening of cross-border regulations as well as sharing best practices and knowledge are recognised as opportunities to secure the interests, rights and responsibilities of different stakeholders.

Thirdly, without further and more in-depth research and improved understanding of the Arctic environment, the risks connected with offshore extractive and transport activities cannot be appropriately assessed. That is especially relevant for regions that could be considered for exploitation in the coming decades, but where typically Arctic challenges are already commonplace (such as the Kara Sea or west Greenland). Since the Arctic is largely composed of frontier regions in respect to offshore hydrocarbons, there is a clear need to gain more comprehensive knowledge that is required in all dimensions and phases of extraction activities. Research should be comprehensive and cover various dimensions of human activity in the Arctic, and not only those connected with oil and gas extraction.

## 10 Conclusion: The Way Forward for the EU

While interest in Arctic offshore hydrocarbon exploitation has increased in recent years, actual developments have been slow to follow, with major differences across the Arctic region. Advances in offshore technology and maritime transport as well as global markets are major drivers of Arctic oil and gas developments, while climate change plays a secondary role. Risk of long-lasting negative impacts from catastrophic events, huge distances and gaps in existing capabilities and infrastructure are among the key concerns.

The EU has limited but multi-faceted competencies regarding Arctic offshore hydrocarbon developments, such as through contacts with energy partners, climate and energy policies and research programmes. In the light of increasingly cautious approach of various actors to the prospect of Arctic hydrocarbon exploitation, this poses numerous challenges for the EU in regard to the energy resources component of the EU Arctic policy.

Development of the European Arctic offshore energy resources depends on many factors and is faced with numerous challenges. Navigating between these issues is for the EU as demanding a task as crossing the northern seas and adequate preparation is half the battle. Taking into consideration the specificity, diversity and scope of the Arctic offshore oil and gas developments, as well as their implications for Europe, there are several opportunities for new or enhanced forms of EU activities that correspond with its interests of the EU and its role in hydrocarbon developments. The following propositions have been developed by the authors, building on the ideas proposed by stakeholders in the consultation process as a point of departure.

- The EU should engage further in supporting innovative research and education in the areas of Arctic technology and the Arctic environment.

While further development of oil and gas offshore exploration and development should be focused on multi-dimensional risk reduction, broader and more advanced knowledge about the Arctic environment is required, as are advances in offshore technologies. In this respect, the key actions for EU support include ensuring long-term cross-disciplinary research programmes (*e.g.* Horizon 2020), development of the relevant capacities and infrastructure, as well as supporting more educational projects.

- The EU has little choice but to continue and strengthen energy dialogue with non-EU Arctic partners. Developments over the last three years on global energy markets underscore that the EU should continue to encourage transparent and competitive relations with energy suppliers, including those in the Arctic region. These dialogues could promote expanding the Northern Dimension to energy fields and engaging in new forms of co-operation with Norway. However, previous EU experiences in the nexus of energy security indicate that this could be a challenging task. Nevertheless, these efforts should be continued. The highest standards adopted (as was the aim upon the adoption the safety of offshore oil and gas operations directive) by the EU could serve as an example for neighboring jurisdictions.
- Enhancing funding and investment frameworks for environmentally and socially responsible Arctic hydrocarbon projects are clear areas for EU engagement. Successful offshore oil and gas developments (including construction of pipelines and transport of resources) can be achieved with improved funding and investment opportunities. Development of offshore oil and gas resources entails the obligation to pay strong attention to environmental and social risks, for instance by developing and demonstrating effective technological solutions and environmentally and socially responsible business models. International co-operation in this field would combine both political partnerships and long-term financial relationships. The EU has a strong position to participate in such initiatives. One idea would be to establish – in close collaboration with major partners, including bilateral, multilateral and local financial institutions – an international finance institution or financing framework to provide loans and make capital investments that would incorporate strong emphasis on environmental and social responsibility in Arctic hydrocarbon-related projects.

A few years ago, as some parts of the Arctic seas were presented as "almost open" for offshore hydrocarbon exploration and exploitation due to changes related to climate change and improved technologies, there was increased interest and expectations that development activities were on the verge of taking off. Today, equipped with better scientific understanding of the changes and more experience in the field, as well as shifts in the global oil markets, more caution is noted for near-term developments in the Arctic. This is also true in terms of the engagement of the EU involvement in the development of the Arctic offshore hydrocarbons.

CHAPTER 6

# Mining in the European Arctic

*Kim van Dam, Annette Scheepstra, Johan Gille, Adam Stępień and Timo Koivurova**

## Abstract

The European Arctic has been recently experiencing an upsurge in mining activities. This is reflected in an on-going interest from the industry, regulators and the public. However, current and future prospects are highly sensitive to mineral price fluctuations. The EU is a major consumer and importer of Arctic raw materials. As the EU is concerned about the security of supply, it attempts to encourage domestic mineral extraction.

Both Arctic communities and industry call for enhanced information flows, as well as improved and more inclusive decision-making frameworks. The EU should clearly articulate its interests related to mining in the European Arctic. The EU could further enhance its support for the collection and sharing of mining data and knowledge.

The EU regulatory framework could better contribute to harmonising environmental, economic and social assessments, paying special attention to local social issues and indigenous rights. The EU, as a major global actor, can also influence international governance, standard-setting and co-operation to facilitate increased responsibility in mining activities, including through dialogue with mining industry.

## 1 Introduction

The European Arctic contains vast amounts of mineral resources. Recently, interest in mining activity in the Arctic has been intensifying against the background of fluctuating prices of minerals. Global and international forces largely determine trends in mining development and mining is often significant for national economies. Nevertheless, it is largely in local Arctic communities that the environmental, economic, social and cultural impacts are felt. In these communities, the extractive resource industry may be viewed as an

* The authors would like to thank Kirsi Latola (Thule Institute, University of Oulu), Mikko Jokinen (Natural Resource Institute Finland), Outi Paadar (Sámi Education Institute), Marie-Theres von Schickfus (Ecorys; Ifo Institute) and Federica Gerber (Ecorys) for their comments and input.

 | DOI 10.1163/9789004303188_008

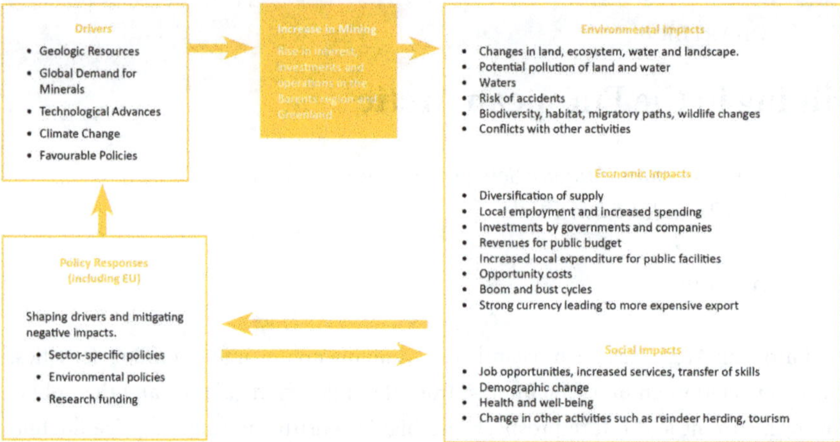


FIGURE 6.1 *Arctic mining activities: drivers and impacts*

opportunity for wealth creation but also as a threat to people's livelihoods, when mining activity interferes with other forms of land use such as reindeer herding.

Extracting minerals in the Arctic appears to be both challenging and expensive due to the extreme polar environment, remoteness and limited availability of (skilled) labour, although there are great differences between Arctic regions. Over the last 6–7 years, high market prices and improved technology had triggered interest and action by mining companies. The European Arctic is considered to be a region with political and economic stability, as well as high quality regulation. This makes the Arctic an attractive place to invest, although this is not without public debate in Arctic and non-Arctic states alike.

This chapter deals with the current increase in mining activity – with a focus on traditional metallic ores and rare earth elements – in the European Arctic, including Greenland and to a lesser extent Northwest Russia.[1] It provides a general overview of mining and its impacts on the environment, economy and society. In addition, the implications for the European Union (EU) are discussed through the identification of EU interests regarding extraction of minerals and by assessing relevant EU policies (see Figure 6.1).

1 The focus here is mainly on traditional metallic ores (base and precious) and rare earth elements (REEs). Industrial minerals and gemstone mines are generally excluded. The geographical coverage is the broad Arctic area as defined by the Arctic Human Development Report (2004). However, some examples and data from the Barents region are used. Some statistics refer to entire Nordic states.

## 2 Recent Upsurge in Mining Activity and Current Uncertainties

The states of physical infrastructure, regulatory and administrative frameworks, human resources and the societal awareness of mining vary from one country to another. There is a long history of mining in regions such as Fennoscandia, Svalbard and Northwest Russia. These regions have well-established social and physical infrastructure accompanied by regulatory frameworks to ensure that mining is a well-integrated part of the economy. In contrast, large-scale mining in Greenland is a relatively new activity, where there is little infrastructure and the technical challenges are sizable.[2]

In the beginning of 2000s, mining in Fennoscandia was thought to be in decline or stable at best. Recently, greater private sector interest and government attention have been giving signs of a modest increase in mining activity, primarily regarding exploration and early stages of mine planning. In the beginning of 2015, the mood has worsen following lower prices for some minerals (for instance iron, nickel, copper or molybdenum) and difficult financial situation of some companies active in the North (*e.g.*, Northland Resources).[3] At the end of 2014, there were altogether more than 40 active mines in Sweden, Finland and Norway, including mines that were reopened in the last decade and projects in the early phases of development (see Figure 6.2 and Picture 6.1).

Many Nordic communities are both excited and concerned by the planned developments, particularly in areas where traditional activities such as Sámi reindeer herding take place. The recent mine closures (*e.g.* in Pajala), decrease of jobs (*e.g.* in Svalbard) or salary cuts for staff (*e.g.* in Kirkenes) exacerbate the concerns of communities regarding dependence of employment and local economies on mining. Most Nordic countries recently revised their mining legislation or adopted strategies to stimulate mining development by focusing on economic opportunities. Moreover, in response to social concerns, there are numerous regulatory and research efforts (both by public authorities and the industry) to ensure responsibility in mining activities. For example, Sweden is investing considerably in infrastructure projects and in research and development. In 2011, the Finnish government issued a new Mining Act explicitly aimed at promoting mining in a socially, economically and ecologically sustainable

2 Haley, S., Klick, M., Szymoniak, N. & Crow, A. (2011). "Observing trends and assessing data for Arctic mining," *Polar Geography*, 34:1–2, 37–61.

3 The company running a mine in Pajala in Sweden (operations indefinitely suspended in October 2014) and developing Hannukainen project in Finland, has filed for bancrupcy in December 2014. Website of the Northland Resources at http://www.northland.eu/. Accessed 25 January 2015.

FIGURE 6.2 *Mining activities in Northern Fennoscandia and Greenland*
CARTOGRAPHER: RICARDO PREVETTONI, GRID-ARENDAL 2014

manner.[4] Nordic governments and agencies have also started initiatives focused on research and co-operation, such as the Finnish Funding Agency for Technology and Innovation's Green Mining programme;[5] the Norwegian state programme for gathering geophysical data; and the establishment of a

4 Koivurova, T. & Stepien, A. (eds.) (2008). *Reforming Mining Law in a Changing World, with Special Reference to Finland*, University of Lapland, Rovaniemi, Finland.

5 Green Mining Programme, TEKES, www.tekes.fi/en/programmes-and-services/tekes-programmes/green-mining/. Accessed 5 November 2013.

PICTURE 6.1 *Testing prior to the possible reopening of the Hannukainen mine, Finland*
SOURCE: YLE, *YLE.FI*

Nordic network on mining expertise – NordMin (with the participation of Greenland).[6]

Russia is among the world leaders in mineral production. In northwest Russia, the mining industry has a significant presence on the Kola Peninsula, the Komi Republic and the Republic of Karelia. However, the Russian mining industry has several obsolete plants, a comparatively slow rate of innovation and low labour productivity. Nevertheless, Russia is expected to invest in new exploration activities and strengthen business relations with neighbouring countries.[7]

Greenland has major potential for mining in the known geological occurrences along the coast.[8] In this typical frontier region with limited mining infrastructure and challenging physical circumstances, the number of mining licences issued increased from 39 in 2000 to 115 in 2013.[9] At the end

6 See: Nordic Council of Ministers, www.norden.org/en/nordic-council-of-ministers/council-of-ministers/nordic-council-of-ministers-for-business-energy-regional-policy-mr-ner/nordmin/project-description-nordmin. Accessed 13 February 2014.

7 Safirova, E. (2012). *US Geological Survey Minerals Yearbook 2010 – Russia, advance release.* U.S Department of the Interior, *U.S.* Geological Survey, http://minerals.usgs.gov. Accessed 10 July 2013.

8 What is under the ice sheet is largely unknown.

9 This includes both active prospecting and exploration licences. BMP, List of Mineral and Petroleum Licences, http://www.govmin.gl/images/stories/minerals/list_of_licences/list_of_licences.pdf. Accessed 16 March 2014.

of 2013, Greenland's only operating gold mine (Nalunaq Angel Mining) closed, but a number of projects are in advanced stages of development. However, so far none of them has entered into construction phase.[10] A recent report, however, suggests that eventually Greenland will have a small number of operating mines.[11] One of the most advanced is the rare earth oxides deposit at Kvanefjeld, which is second in size only to rare earth element (REE) deposits in China,[12] and which has received much attention in recent years. Another example of advanced project is ruby deposit in Aappaluttoq.[13] Mining is not well integrated into the overall economy: and thus, Greenland will be particularly sensitive to the boom and bust character of the industry and the risks of economic decoupling, that is, a situation in which economic benefits are exported to other regions.[14] Recent policy and regulatory changes instituted by the Greenland government favour mining development (see Figure 6.3), expecting that revenues will help finance expansion of its autonomy and possible independence. However, a recent study from the University of Copenhagen and the University of Greenland has suggested that Greenland would require 24 large-scale and profitable mines in order to cover the current budget transfer from Denmark.[15] In the final quarter of 2013, amid much controversy domestically, the Greenland government lifted its ban on uranium mining.[16]

---

10 In October 2013 exploitation permit was awarded for Isua iron ore mine to London Mining, but the operations have not commenced. The project has been now taken over by a Chinese company (Lucy Hornby (11 January 2015), "Chinese group General Nice takes over Greenland mine," Financial Times, http://www.ft.com/, accessed 25 January 2015). See: Geological Map http://www.geus.dk/minex/green-min-2010.pdf. Accessed 9 December 2013. Former prime minister of Greenland expected 3–4 mines to be operational by 2022 (Cecilia Jamasmie (6 March 2014), "Greenland embraces mining rush, but won't 'favour one country alone' – Prime Minister," Mining.com, accessed 25 January 2015), but the current prospects appear to be less positive.

11 True North Gems website at http://www.truenorthgems.com/, accessed 25 January 2015/.

12 Greenland Minerals and Energy Ltd, company's website at www.ggg.gl, accessed 25 January 2015.

13 Boersma, T. & Foley, K. (September 2014). "The Greenland Gold Rush: Promise and Pitfalls of Greenland's Energy and Mineral Resources," Brookings, www.brookings.edu, accessed 25 January 2015.

14 Duhaime, G. (2004). in Haley *et al.* (2011).

15 Committee for Greenlandic mineral resources to the benefit of society (2014). *To the Benefit of Greenland.* http://nyheder.ku.dk/groenlands-naturressourcer/rapportogbaggrundspapir/To_the_benefit_of_Greenland.pdf. Accessed 3 November 2013.

16 McGwin, K. (24 October 2013). Uranium ban overturned. Arctic Journal at http://arctic-journal.com/oil-minerals/uranium-ban-overturned. Accessed 20 November 2013.

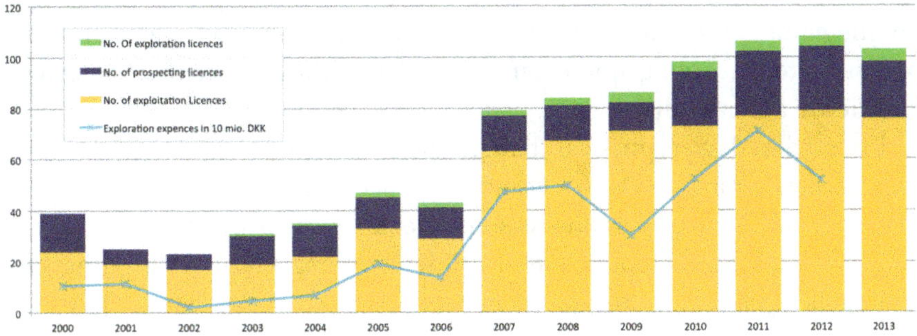


FIGURE 6.3 *Mineral licences in Greenland, 2000–2013*
Note: A prospecting licence is non-exclusive permission to explore in a given area, and thus permits more than one company to conduct exploration activities. An exploration licence has an exclusive character
SOURCE: BUREAU OF MINERALS AND PETROLEUM, GOVERNMENT OF GREENLAND, WWW.BMP.GL

## 3 Drivers

Having the **appropriate geology** is a condition for development. The European Arctic has significant mineral occurrences: the Fennoscandian Shield[17] contains minerals that are found in limited locations around the world and Greenland holds great potential for many minerals, including REEs and uranium. A number of drivers can be identified to explain the present trend. The main driver of the current upsurge is growing **global demand for mineral resources**, pushed by modernisation in emerging economies such as China and India, as well as by the deployment of advanced technologies such as wind turbine generators, mobile phones and hybrid cars, which require REEs and other critical minerals.

**Advances in technologies** that serve exploration, operation and transportation in mining are making Arctic resources more accessible and less expensive.[18] Examples include improved seismic exploration and mapping technologies and methods to mine in permafrost.

Further, the **legal, administrative and political landscape** supports development, although there is resistance from some stakeholders such as reindeer herders and tourism organisations. Of relevance is also the role of consulting companies conducting environmental impact assessments or economic feasibility analyses in terms of their competence and interaction with

17 Geologically, the Fennoscandian Shield is an exposed portion of the Baltic Shield and includes territories of Norway, Sweden, Finland, and Russian Kola Peninsula and Karelia.

18 Haley, S. *et al.* (2011), *op. cit.*, p. 55.

mining companies and administrations. The investments of states and the private sector, including junior companies, determine the extent of geological knowledge and new discoveries.

To a modest degree, physical changes due to **climate change** influence mining activities through easier (or cheaper) sea access to resources (in particular in Greenland), longer operating seasons, and possibly via lower transportation costs due to shorter shipping routes.[19] However, climate change also ushers in new challenges and hazards for the industry.

## 4 Impacts

The impacts of mining activities differ depending on the stage of mine development, the type of mining activity and the existing infrastructure. The decision on whether or not to explore and mine should ideally be based on an integrated assessment of the inter-related environmental, economic and social impacts. Importantly, exploration and exploitation result in different impacts and are usually regulated differently, also in terms of taxation or impact assessment requirements. Exploration, even if successful, is not always followed by extraction activities.

### 4.1 *Environmental Impacts*

Besides visible changes in the landscape, the environmental effects of mining can include the pollution of water, air and land. These impacts may continue long after the operative phase of the mine. Mining may alter the landscape, destroy reindeer grazing grounds, migratory routes and jeopardise fishing in rivers, lakes and seas. Sensitive Arctic ecosystems require long recovery times after environmental degradation. The nature of impacts varies depending on local conditions, type of resource and applied technology.

In particular, many communities have long-term concerns about what will happen after mine closure. As the boom-and-bust cycles of mining can turn active mines idle, there is concern about environmental management during periods of inactivity. A critical question is how to manage waste, decommissioning and rehabilitation when a mine ceases operation.[20] Nowadays, operators are legally required to have a mine closure and environmental restoration plan in

---

19 Rasmussen, R. *et al.* (2011). *Megatrends*. Nordic Council of Ministers, Copenhagen, p. 73. See also chapter by Sander *et al.* on changes in Arctic maritime transport, in this volume.

20 MMSD (2002). *Breaking new ground: the report of the Mining, Minerals, and Sustainable Development Project*, International Institute for Environment and Development and World Business Council for Sustainable Development, London.

place, but this is the most difficult phase to monitor.[21] Environmental impact assessments (EIAs) are intended to identify impacts and mitigation measures for the likely environmental and social impacts of the proposed mining activity, but they may not adequately address all the concerns of local and indigenous communities, tourist operators and environmental NGOs. Many stakeholders express particular apprehension regarding hazards and accidents during mine operations. For example, at the Talvivaara nickel mine in Finland, large quantities of contaminated water leaked into surrounding rivers and lakes in 2012 and 2013.[22]

Assessments of ecosystems and socioeconomic impacts must take account of other activities, such as wind power, infrastructure and other mine developments, and measure the cumulative impacts. Importantly, environmental performance is more and more connected to the economic feasibility of mining operations. Companies are required to uphold high environmental standards. These standards are increasingly an important factor in investment decisions as major environmental accidents put companies in a difficult financial situation and adversely affect the perception of the whole industry (as is the case with the Talvivaara mine).

### 4.2 *Economic Impacts*

Developing a mine involves investment flows, employment opportunities, trade and transport spending. Local employment can have positive impacts also at the national level. It generates multiplier effects as local consumption

PICTURE 6.2 *Abandoned mine in Pyramiden, Svalbard*
PHOTO BY FRITS STEENHUISEN, ARCTIC CENTRE, UNIVERSITY OF GRONINGEN

21 Kauppila, P., Räisänen, M.L. & Myllyoja, S. (eds.) (May 2013). (Best environmental practices in metal mining operations). The Finnish Environment 29en/2011 Finnish Environment Institute (SYKE).

22 Although Talvivaara lies outside of the boundaries of the Arctic as defined in this volume, the pollution case and subsequent bancruptcy in the Fall 2014 and criminal charges against company's leadership affected the perception of mining in the whole of Finland and certain extent Fennoscandia and affects regulatory developments.

increases and demand for goods and services boosts economic activity. Several mining companies now have stringent local content requirements, which may improve local employment.[23] These benefits should continue after a mine closes, in particular with regard to minimising the impact of job losses (see Picture 6.2). Many mining companies have adopted a Corporate Social Responsibility (CSR) agenda as part of their strategy to acquire their social licence to operate (trust, acceptance and support of communities). In addition, there are also general company and government investments, such as education, infrastructure and healthcare.[24] Royalties, fees or taxes can generate significant revenue for regional and national budgets. Royalties as such have not been introduced in Nordic countries and mining-specific fees or taxes are comparatively low (although Finland has been considering introducing a mining tax). As a result, the main budget income is from general tax systems or – as is for example the case with the LKAB in Sweden – profits generated by state-owned companies (Picture 6.3). However, the economic benefits from tax revenues depend on associated increases in government expenditure.

In order to be economically sustainable in the long term, some negative economic impacts must be mitigated. The costs and benefits of mining may be unfairly distributed between stakeholders, in particular where regulatory frameworks for equitable benefit, tax sharing and social and economic impact assessment provisions are insufficient. For some municipalities the costs of the increased needs for public services, such as health care, are not compensated by the local tax gains associated with mining. In addition, mining may contribute to an overall strategy of economic diversification in some regions and thereby complement the employment structure, with family members being able to work in various industries. However, it may also take away jobs from other local economic activities, such as reindeer herding or tourism.[25]

### 4.3 *Social Impacts*

Social impacts are both the positive and negative changes to many aspects of the culture and livelihoods of local and regional populations and communities,

23 Mining Association of British Columbia (October 2011). *Economic Impact Analysis*, http://www.mining.bc.ca/sites/default/files/resources/pwcmining-economicimpactanalysis_1.pdf. Accessed 1 July 2013.

24 International Council on Mining and Metals (2003), *10 Principles*, http://www.icmm.com/our-work/sustainable-development-framework/10-principles. Accessed 1 July 2013.

25 European Commission (May 2009), *All that Glitters is not Gold*, http://ec.europa.eu/research/sd/conference/2009/presentations/20/jakub_kronenberg_-_opportunity_costs_of_gold_mining.pdf. Accessed 1 July 2013.

and are closely related to the economic and environmental impacts. The social effects of new and existing mining activities occur mostly at the community level, potentially transforming the local economy, society and cultures, both indigenous and non-indigenous.[26] The fluctuating nature of extractive industries and their primary dependence on the mineral prices are one of the primary aspects for considering long-term social and economic impacts of mines. Recent indefinite suspension of operations in Pajala (just two years from the commencement of production)[27] left community in distress and many businesses and individuals with losses as they had made investments in a hope that the mine brings long-term developments for the community. The situation has also impact on the perception of socio-economic opportunities connected with mining in the whole region.

Mining activity potentially creates local jobs, infrastructure, services and businesses, and thus helps to address various social problems typically faced by remote small Arctic communities (see chapter by Stępień *et al.* in this volume). The associated development of transport infrastructure improves the accessibility of places that can benefit the local population and other economic sectors. In addition, local infrastructure and community services may be built or expanded to meet additional demand such as schools, administration, law enforcement, health care and emergency response. This includes the transfer of skills and technology to the local population. Some regions have adopted an active policy for local capacity building. The universities of Luleå (Sweden) and Oulu (Finland) initiated earlier cooperation in a format of a Nordic Mining School,[28] and Greenland has opened a mining school in Sisimiut,[29] both with EU support. In 2014, the University of Oulu has established Oulu Mining School as an independent faculty.[30] However, the interest of students in taking up the study programmes is largely dependent on the mid-term prospects for mining in their respective regions, and thus, fluctuates

26 *cf* Van Schooten, M., Vanclay, F. & Slootweg, R. (2003). "Conceptualizing social change processes and social impacts," in Becker, H.A. & Vanclay, F. (eds), *The International Handbook of Social Impact Assessment. Conceptual and Methodological Advances,* Cheltenham: Edward Elgar, 74–91; SDWG, Circumpolar Information Guide: 6.

27 Website of the Northland Resources at http://www.northland.eu/. Accessed 25 January 2015.

28 Nordic Mining School, http://nordicminingschool.eu/, Accessed 25 January 2015.

29 Website of the Sisimiut Technical School, http://kti.gl/. Accessed 25 January 2015.

30 Website of the Oulu Mining School, University of Oulu, http://www.oulu.fi/oms/. Accessed 04 February 2015. The developments are connected with defininng mining as one of the focus-areas of the University of Oulu.

from year to year. Therefore, the education of mining professionals often lags a few years behind the market cycles and public interest in mining.

In many communities, mining and associated activities interfere with other human activities and land uses such as reindeer herding, tourism, fishing and transport (see chapter by Latola *et al.* in this volume). Regions such as Lapland have had a history of out-migration and are now experiencing a localised influx of workers.[31] While this may bring new life to villages,[32] evidence indicates that many temporary newcomers develop only a utilitarian relation to the area, especially that majority of temporary migrant workers are present only during the construction phase of a mine.[33] This is often in sharp contrast to the relation that indigenous peoples have with their ecosystem. Mining can also impact the well-being and health of local populations. Impacts on leisure activities may be experienced directly, for example through noise, dust, vibrations, gaseous emissions, water effluents, or indirectly through the appearance of excavations and processing sites. Long-term impacts on the environment may also lead to health problems.

## 5 Implications of Arctic Mining for the European Union

The EU is a major consumer and importer of Arctic raw materials. The EU consumes about one-fifth of global metallic metals production, while its own production amounts to roughly 3%, and due to the limited number of new discoveries this reliance on imports is expected to rise in the coming decades.[34] Import dependence has made the security of the supply of raw materials a top policy priority, particularly for critical raw materials with deposits in the

---

31 Large scale law was approved by the Greenlandic Government approved a new law in 2012, allowing big scale mining operations (valued at at least USD 1 billion) to bring foreign workforce into the country. The law awaited long for approval of Danish parliament as it also dealt with uranium mining.

32 Smit, C.A. (2012). *Governance of oil, gas and mining development in Greenland and the Arctic*, Master thesis WUR, Netherlands; AFPA (2010).

33 Arctic Portal at http://portlets.arcticportal.org/mining-projects. Accessed 12 June 2013.

34 European Commission (2008, November 4). The raw materials initiative – meeting our critical needs for growth and jobs in Europe. Commission Communication. COM(2008)699final; European Commission (2008), Staff Working Document accompanying Communication: "The Raw Materials Initiative" SEC(2008) 2741. Weihed, P. (2012). The domestic metallic and mineral resources in Europe, Is the lack geological or political?, Presentation. Lulea University of Technology, http://www.industrialtechnologies2012.eu/sites/default/files/presentations_session/Par_Weihed.ppt. Accessed 10 February 2014.

PICTURE 6.3 *Kiruna town centre with the LKAB iron ore mine in the background, Sweden*
As mining activities are planned to be extended under the town's centre, the decision has been made to construct a new centre in a different location
PHOTO BY ADAM STĘPIEŃ, ARCTIC CENTRE, UNIVERSITY OF LAPLAND

Arctic.[35] The European Commission expects that the mining industry will account for as much as 20% of the EU's GDP (directly and indirectly) by 2020.[36] In general, it is estimated that over 30 million jobs in the EU are dependent on a stable supply of raw materials.[37]

A major (and potentially growing) part of the EU's domestic hard mineral supply comes from the Barents region (see Textbox 6.1). Further exploitation of European Arctic minerals may significantly influence EU supply by enhancing

35 Critical raw materials are important in the value chain but subject to high risk of supply interruption. The EU is fully dependent on imports of REEs from China, which are essential in manufacturing many modern technologies. In 2009 China accounted for 95% of the world's supply of REEs. See: Report of the Ad-hoc Working Group on defining critical raw materials (European Commission) http://ec.europa.eu/enterprise/policies/raw-materials/critical/index_en.htm. Accessed 16 March 2014.

36 European Innovation Partnership on Raw Materials, https://ec.europa.eu/eip/raw-materials/en. Accessed 15 December 2013.

37 European Commission (2008). Communication "The raw materials initiative – meeting our critical needs for growth and jobs in Europe," COM(2008) 699 final, 4 November 2008.

diversification and decreasing import dependence, especially from regions considered potentially unstable. Prospects for developing important REEs and raw materials further highlight the strategic significance of the Arctic in mineral policy and diplomacy. The European Arctic can therefore be seen as a fairly safe and stable supply region. A survey among mining companies conducted in 2013 by the Fraser Institute pointed to Finland and Sweden as the most promising mining territories in terms of public policies and potential.[38]

**TEXTBOX 6.1** *Importance of minerals production in Fennoscandia and the Russian North for the EU*

In general, a significant share of EU minerals production takes place in Arctic regions, though data for all minerals is not available. Sweden and Finland together are the principal mining and processing regions for the "EU35" – EU member states, EEA/EFTA and candidate countries including Turkey. In 2011, they accounted for 17.5% of EU35 silver production, 28% of gold, 10.5% of copper and 27% of zinc. In addition, the Russian North has significant mineral deposits and production, with the Murmansk Oblast (over 200 deposits of 40 types of minerals) contributing 80% of rare metals, and the Arkhangelsk Oblast housing the largest bauxite mine in Europe. With regard to the critical raw materials, Finland contributes 62% and Norway 18% of EU35 cobalt production.[39] Surveys in Greenland (primarily in west Greenland) indicate deposits of niobium, tantalum, graphite, platinum and other REEs.[40]

Mining is important for the EU's labour market (Picture 6.3). Notably, mining industries are international in terms of both their ownership structure and workforce. In the Barents region and Greenland, construction and operation of mines involves foreign labour, a noticeable portion of which comes from EU

38 Wilson, A., McMahon, F. & Cervantes, M. (2013). *Survey of Mining Companies 2012/2013*. Frasier Institute: Canada. http://www.fraserinstitute.org/research-news/display.aspx?id=19401. Accessed 10 March 2014.

39 British Geological Survey (2012). European Mineral Statistics 2007–2011. https://www.bgs.ac.uk/mineralsuk/statistics/europeanStatistics.html. Accessed 12 July 2013. See also ÅF-Infrastructure AB (2010). Supply of Raw Materials, Transport Needs and Economic Potential in Northern Europe. Final Report.

40 Bureau of Minerals and Petroleum Greenland website at http://www.govmin.gl/index.php/minerals/geology-of-greenland/mineral-occurrences. Accessed 15 July 2013.

member states, *e.g.* Poland. Greenland, with its small population of 56,000, is unable to provide the 4000 to 8000 skilled workers that are required during the construction phase.

Environmental protection is another key interest of the EU. Mines have significant local environmental impacts. Particular operations are noteworthy for the EU with regard to greenhouse gas emission targets (*e.g.* nickel) and mercury pollution (*e.g.* gold).

Sustainable development of the northern sparsely populated areas is an EU interest as defined in treaties and demonstrated by funding programmes.[41] Mining developments would add to economic diversity of these areas, but also increase their dependence on primary resource production. Moreover, the EU emphasises its commitment to the principles of cultural diversity and indigenous rights that may be affected by mining activities.[42]

## 6 Outlook to 2030

The global demand for mineral resources, in particular REEs, is likely to rise in the long-term, but the effect on prices of minerals is not straighforward.[43] Albeit with regional differences, mining in the Arctic is generally challenging, costly and uncertain, and the ongoing expansion of mining activity depends on the feasibility and willingness of investors to risk long-term investments. Technological advances will facilitate mining itself and contribute to increasing demand for certain minerals. The trend is expected to continue, including maintaining the boom-and-bust characteristics and uncertainty. Stricter regulations, for example on shipping, health and safety, and local and indigenous populations, are also expected. This should result in more attention being paid to social issues and social responsibility, and increase the importance of complying with international standards. The importance of Fennoscandia for

41 Treaty on the Functioning of the European Union, art. 174 "particular attention shall be paid to rural areas, areas affected by industrial transition, and regions which suffer from severe and permanent natural or demographic handicaps such as the northernmost regions with very low population density"; See the Northern Periphery Programme 2007–2013, http://www.northernperiphery.eu/en/home/ and chapter by Stępień *et al.* on social and cultural changes in the European Arctic, in this volume.

42 See: *e.g.* European Agenda for Culture, http://ec.europa.eu/culture/our-policy-development/european-agenda-for-culture_en.htm and EU External Action service, http://eeas.europa.eu/_human_rights/ip/index_en.htm. Accessed 13 November 2013.

43 See: *e.g.* Keramidas, K., Kitous, A. & Griffin, B. (2012). *Future availability and demand for oil gas and key minerals.* POLINARES working paper nr. 30.

European industry could potentially be growing due to EU and state policies that are favourable to domestic supply.

## 7 EU Influence on Arctic Mining: Assessing EU Policies

The EU influences the mining sector directly and indirectly through legislation and various policy measures. EU policy aims to create favourable conditions for mining in the European north. The Raw Materials Initiative, launched in 2008, identified measures to secure supplies of raw materials for the EU from domestic and international sources.[44] In addition, the EU published a communication aiming to tackle the challenges in commodity markets, specifically concerning raw materials.[45] Raw material supply (current and future) from EU domestic sources is fostered by promoting investment in extractive industries and enhancing knowledge. An EU working group produced a compendium of best practices, including social issues, stakeholder engagement and transparency, as well as considering the societal benefits of minerals extraction.[46] The Commission has encouraged member states to develop national minerals policies, set up comprehensive land-use planning policies for minerals, and to streamline permitting processes.[47] As the focus of the Raw Materials Initiative and its measures is on facilitating mining developments in Europe, surprisingly little attention is given to establishing a comprehensive environmental framework, participatory processes or the broader social dimension of mining.

The Barents region and Greenland can be viewed as secure source areas for minerals. So far, however, EU policy-makers have not given particular attention to the potential of the Barents region – the region with the most recent exploration discoveries. The European Innovation Partnership (EIP) for Raw Materials can be an important element in this respect, as it is intended to support the high-quality performance of the European mining industry. Nordic

---

44 European Commission COM(2008)699 final.

45 European Commission, Communication "Tackling The Challenges In Commodity Markets And On Raw Materials," COM(2011)25 final, 2 February 2011.

46 This report was produced by the working group on the exchange of best practices in land use planning, permits and geological knowledge sharing, http://ec.europa.eu/enterprise/policies/raw-materials/files/best-practices/sust-full-report_en.pdf. Accessed 4 March 2014.

47 See: European Commission Report on the implementation of the Raw Materials Initiative, COM(2013)442 final, http://register.consilium.europa.eu/doc/srv?l=EN&t=PDF&gc=true&sc=false&f=ST%2011876%202013%20INIT. Accessed 16 February 2014.

states already have a strong position – the Finnish Green Mining programme is a good example.[48] However, the EIP membership, which primarily consists of parties from the broader mining industry and academia, is limiting participation in the process.

Various EU regulations, many of which apply to EEA/EFTA countries, contribute to mitigating the environmental impacts of mining and setting limits to resource extraction. Examples include: Water Framework Directive and Groundwater Directive;[49] Mining Waste Directive and Landfill Waste Directive;[50] and more broadly, the Integrated Pollution Prevention and Control[51] and Seveso-III Directives.[52] The Mineral-Extracting Industries – Drilling Directive establishes the minimum requirements for improving the safety and health protection of workers related to drilling.[53] REACH Regulation 1907/2006/EC (Registration, Evaluation, Authorisation and Restriction of Chemicals)[54] applies to the mining industry both as a user of chemicals (mines have to report the use of chemicals to the supplier) as well as to mining products (ores and concentrates in the case of chemical alteration). While materials occurring in nature are exempted from REACH, they have to be registered under Classification, Labelling and Packaging Regulation.[55] An important framework is created by the Habitats and Birds Directives[56] and the Natura

48 Green Mining Programme, TEKES, www.tekes.fi/en/programmes-and-services/tekes-programmes/green-mining/. Accessed 5 February 2014.

49 Directive 2000/60/EC of 23 October 2000 establishing a framework for Community action in the field of water policy (extended later to the EEA) and Directive 2006/118/EC of 12 December 2006 on the protection of groundwater against pollution and deterioration.

50 Directive 2006/21/EC on the management of waste from the extractive industries and Directive 99/31EC.

51 Directive 2008/1/EC of 15 January 2008 concerning integrated pollution prevention and control (Codified version).

52 Directive 2012/18/EU on the control of major-accident hazards involving dangerous substances.

53 Council Directive 92/91/EEC of 3 November 1992 concerning the minimum requirements for improving the safety and health protection of workers in the mineral-extracting industries through drilling.

54 Regulation (EC) No 1907/2006 of 18 December 2006 concerning the Registration, Evaluation, Authorisation and Restriction of Chemicals (REACH).

55 Kauppila *et al.* (2013), *op. cit.*; Regulation (EC) No 1272/2008 on classification, labelling and packaging of substances and mixtures.

56 Council Directive 92/43/EEC of 21 May 1992 on the conservation of natural habitats and of wild fauna and flora; Directive 2009/147/EC of the European Parliament and of the Council of 30 November 2009 on the conservation of wild birds. Also; Regulation (EC) No 1221/2009 on the voluntary participation by organisations in a Community eco-management and

2000 network of protected areas. The European Commission issued guidance[57] dedicated to reconciling the environmental objectives with the desire to promote mineral extraction. The Commission has also encouraged the mining sector to undertake non-obligatory actions to enhance sustainable development and safe operations.

Since EIAs are critically important for mining projects, the minimum requirements established by the recently revised EIA Directive (EEA relevant) are of major significance for how mining projects are developed.[58]

EU policies regarding transport also influence mining activities in the Arctic. EU initiatives such as the trans-European transport network (TEN-T) play a vital role in enhancing capacity and multi-modality transport. The network has been recently updated in line with a new financial perspective. As the core EU transport network does not extend to the Barents region apart from the "Bothnian corridor" and Kiruna connection, the EU funding available for transport projects of importance for the Barents mining industry may be limited (see chapter by Stępień *et al.* in this volume).

The recent amendment to the EU Sulphur Directive[59] (following earlier MARPOL convention[60] amendments) limits the sulphur content in marine fuels after 2015, especially in the specified Emissions Control Areas such as the Baltic Sea. Some industry stakeholders fear that increased fuel costs could influence the economic conditions of mining operations in northern Sweden and Finland, thereby affecting their competitiveness. For example, Finnish industry estimated that the total increase in transport costs would amount to up to EUR 500 million per year.[61] On the other hand, the environmental gains, especially in the Baltic Sea, are appreciated by other stakeholders.

---

audit scheme (EMAS III) may be of relevance: although extractive industries are not identified as a priority sector; the directive deals also with waste management.

57 European Commission (July 2010). Guidance on undertaking non-energy extractive activities in accordance with Natura 2000 requirements.

58 Directive 2011/92/EU of 13 December 2011 on the assessment of the effects of certain public and private projects on the environment (codification).

59 Directive 2012/33/EU of 21 November 2012 amending Council Directive 1999/32/EC as regards the sulphur content of marine fuels.

60 International Convention for the Prevention of Pollution from Ships and 1978 Protocol (MARPOL 73/78), 1340 UNTS 184, 12 ILM 1319 (1973).

61 Nordström, K. (May 2013). "Sulfur directive impact on terminals in Baltic sea region, Some current reflections," ppt presentation, http://www.centrumbalticum.org/. Accessed 5 March 2014; European Commission, http://ec.europa.eu/environment/air/transport/ships.htm. Accessed 5 March 2014.

Through its research policies and actions, EU policy has supported Arctic research on innovation and sustainability in mining in the Framework Programme 7 (FP7) and EU regional funds.[62] Mining research projects (dealing with mining technologies, resources and sustainability) are also to be expected (first calls already published) in the Horizon 2020, where raw materials are identified as one of the key societal challenges.[63] The need for a rise in research and development funding for exploration technology will become evident over the coming decade. EIP is currently gathering "commitments" from industry partners that may constitute bases for networking and joint projects, and could support identification of specific research and development needs under Horizon 2020.

The EU has a special relationship with Greenland, which is underlined in the 2007–2013 EU-Greenland Partnership Agreement. Mineral resources were included as one of the six areas for co-operation, although the actual focus was rather limited. Recently, a Letter of Intent between the European Commission and the Government of Greenland enlisted co-operation in: geological knowledge; analysis of infrastructure and investment needs; capacity building; environmental impacts and social impacts.[64] There are expectations that minerals may be one of the key themes of the currently finalised partnership agreement for 2014–2020.[65] Greenland is seen as a potentially significant partner with the EU for REES. Apart from Greenland, the EU conducts raw materials dialogues and expert workshops with the United States and Russia, but so far with few specific outcomes, especially regarding Arctic issues. Free trade area agreements, *e.g.* with the United States and Canada, may come into effect in the near term, which may also influence the operations of international mining companies in the EU.

## 8 Critical Factors for EU Decision-Making

Critical factors for EU decision-making include uncertainties that should be taken fully into account. Drawing on stakeholder input in the consultation

62 See examples in Annex 2.

63 Horizon 2020, Work programme 2014–2015. *12. Climate action, environment, resource efficiency and raw materials. European Commission Decision C (2013) 8631 of 10 December 2013.*

64 European Commission – MEMO/12/428 13/06/2012 Greenland's raw materials potential and the EU's strategic needs. http://europa.eu/rapid/press-release_MEMO-12-428_en.htm. Accessed 4 March 2014.

65 The European Commission has commissioned a study on the significance of the mineral potential of Greenland for the EU economy and possible ideas for projects and co-operation.

process, several of the critical factors are highlighted below. Land-use conflicts, ranked high by the stakeholders, are covered in chapter by Latola *et al.*

### *Global and European Demand for Resources*

Mining activity remains highly sensitive to global demand for resources and commodity prices on the global market. This is particularly relevant in the Arctic, where mining is a comparatively highly capital-intensive activity. This causes a high degree of uncertainty, not only for the industry itself, but also for national economies and local communities that can be affected by the boom-and-bust character of mining.

### *Environmental Concerns and Uncertainty*

Stakeholders highlighted the importance of ecosystem services and land-use conflicts in relation to mining, in particular with reference to Sámi reindeer herding and nature-based tourism. EIAs are usually in place, but the effectiveness and degree of influence of EIAs varies in different countries and is generally not straightforward, since decisions are weighed in the context of other considerations. There is also concern over the increased risks of environmental disasters and the effects of permanent or temporary closures of mines.

### *Local Communities and Socioeconomic Impacts*

At the local level, there is often uncertainty and concern about the socioeconomic effects of new mine developments, in particular in relation to effects on the workforce and composition of the population. Social issues are usually considered as a part of an environmental assessment procedure (or a separate, albeit connected process, as in Greenland) or within the process leading to benefit agreements. Multinational companies are expected to adhere to the principles of Corporate Social Responsibility and to acquire an informal social licence to operate. Nevertheless, there are many unresolved issues, for instance in relation to land ownership and use.

### *Indigenous Peoples' Rights and Livelihoods*

Mining activities and their impacts on traditional livelihoods (especially reindeer herding) are of major concern for Arctic indigenous peoples. Reindeer herding requires vast areas for winter and summer pastures. Mining may lead to the reduction of reindeer grazing areas, resulting in land-use conflicts. There are various resource governance systems and arrangements connected with the distribution of benefits in the Arctic, and there are also a variety of co-management regimes. Issues of control over resources and property rights will evolve in the near future, partly due to international recognition and increasing awareness of the rights of indigenous peoples, manifested by the 2007 United Nations Declaration of Rights of Indigenous Peoples, which includes the concept of Free, Prior and Informed Consent (FPIC).[66]

### *Existing Decision-Making Structures and Policy*

This principle of using Free, Prior and Informed Consent for mining projects is related to the more general notion that there is a need for better and more inclusive decision-making structures and policies, where people are not only heard, but can also clearly influence decisions. On the one hand, many communities and stakeholders feel that the processes leading to decisions and the decision-making processes and structures themselves are inadequate for responding to challenges arising from mining projects. On the other hand, the industry finds itself faced with long permitting processes, administrative uncertainty and complex bureaucracy. Better and more inclusive processes are called for, including improved dialogue, communication and consultation throughout the entire project life-cycle. The existing decision-making structures need to be taken into account when policies are made at the EU level.

## 9 Conclusions: The Way Forward for the EU

The European Arctic regions have been recently experiencing an upsurge in mining activities, but both current and future developments are highly sensitive to minerals price fluctuations. The EU is a major consumer and importer of Arctic raw materials. Being concerned for the security of supply, it encourages domestic mineral extraction, among others, via its Raw Materials Initiative. The European Arctic is seen as a politically and economically stable region, characterised by high-quality regulation. However, so far the EU's role and interest in the European Arctic as a resource region has been limited. The EU does not have direct authority regarding some of the main critical issues (*e.g.* land use), but there are a number of key policy areas in which the EU plays a relevant role. Mining activities take place within a framework of EU regulations, including mitigation of environmental impacts. It appears that that while the EU may support mining developments in Greenland, the island will not constitute a major solution to Europe's demand for resources.[67] Within the

66 Hanna, F. & Vanclay, F. (2013). "Human Rights, Indigenous peoples and the concept of Free, Prior and Informed Consent," *Impact Assessment and Project Appraisal,* 31:2, 146–157.

67 Boersma and Foley (2014), *op. cit.*

SADA assessment process – with ideas coming from Arctic stakeholders taken a starting point – a number of ideas for further evolution of EU policies affecting mining developments in the region and EU approach to mining in general have been elaborated.

In order to ensure integrated assessments, monitoring and informed decisions, reliable and comparable data and information on mining activity in the European Arctic should be collected and updated frequently. Acquiring and sharing accurate information and best practices will benefit governments, businesses and communities. The EU also has a role to play in stimulating research, education and capacity building. The possible tools include communication and data platforms or research projects built on the needs of industry, national permitting authorities and communities. This process has already started with projects such as Promine or within the European Innovation Partnership (EIP) on Raw Materials, which aims to identify research needs and potentials. However, the present EIP lacks significant input from those both positively and negatively affected by mining activities, such as local communities or other land users.

Although there are many EU policies and regulations that have a connection with mining, there is no integrated comprehensive policy overview for the mining sector in the European Arctic. Current EU directives are detailed and prescriptive, whereas local conditions in the Arctic vary substantially. Therefore, more flexibility and local-level variation are required. There is a need for a greater focus on mining within the EU and the Arctic as an area with major potential, attention to social impacts, as well as more comprehensive and structured exchange of best practices between member states. Refinement of minerals within the Arctic regions could be supported, so that the regional economy gains greater benefits from the minerals extracted in the North.

EU policy should be directed towards ensuring that the current level of good practice in EIAs is maintained and improved where necessary. Improvements include addressing issues related to mine closure and safety, emergencies and hazards. Social and economic issues should be effectively addressed in assessment processes. For that, the EU needs a clear vision and policy to address the social and economic impacts in all phases of the mining lifecycle. There is a need for the inclusion of the general principles connected with social licence to operate into the EU regulatory framework covering mining activities, including EIAs. Harmonisation, basic standards (including the assessment of social impacts) and procedures may enable companies operating across national boundaries to perform more effectively.

For the EU in general, more efforts should be made to involve communities and indigenous populations in remote regions in relevant EU policies and directives. Particularly for mining activities, these efforts should be directed towards improving dialogue with and between stakeholders.

Eventually, various international environmental instruments may be relevant to mining operations, for example the Ramsar Convention on Wetlands. However, some relevant standards, like the Arctic EIA Guidelines adopted in 1997 under the Arctic Environmental Protection Strategy remain largely unknown to both regulators and companies. The Commission, in the development of its Arctic policy and its activities within the Arctic Council as an observer in principle, should focus attention on promoting and facilitating past and future Arctic Council work on environmental and social impact assessments. Co-operation within and across the mining industry may also influence mine operation norms and corporate standard setting. This can be done, for example, via the European Innovation Partnership or co-operation with the European Association for mining industries, metal ores and industrial minerals (Euromine). Also, EU dialogues on minerals with Arctic partners and suppliers of the EU market such as the United States, Russia, Canada, Norway and Greenland, may in the long term be used as a tool for promoting high standards in responsible mining. However, it is important to engage a broad spectrum of stakeholders, going beyond involving solely the industry.

To conclude, the times for mining industry are uncertain, especially taking into account the currently slower pace of growth in China, but the region – following the recent notion of boom – still experiences companies' interests and increased activity among national and local regulators and policy-makers designed to facilitate mining developments. If the EU, having at its disposal chiefly indirect and fairly weak instruments, wants to become a more active actor in European Arctic extractive industries, it has to take into account the current situation as well as the long-term prospects and a variety of scenarios. The fact that in the coming decade the interest in Arctic mining may subside should not discourage national and European policy-makers – working in harmonious cooperation – from introducing more responsible, participatory and socially conscious regulatory frameworks.

CHAPTER 7

# Activities Affecting Land Use in the European Arctic

*Kirsi Latola, Simo Sarkki, Adam Stępień and Mikko Jokinen**

**Abstract**

Globalisation and indirectly climate change have increased the pressures on developing new mining projects, transport routes and renewable energy in the European Arctic regions. At the same time, tourism and traditional livelihoods such as reindeer husbandry require large areas of pristine nature, which other activities may adversely affect.

The planning of new activities must respect the needs, culture and livelihoods of local and indigenous communities, including land rights. Proper assessment of social impacts is essential in order to mitigate conflicts between different values and interest groups. There is a need for enhanced information exchange between Arctic local and regional actors and EU institutions. Stronger inclusion of social aspects and challenges in the EU frameworks for impact assessment as well as in dialogue with Arctic partners including Russia is advised.

## 1 Introduction

This chapter focuses on various activities affecting land use in the European Arctic and especially in Fennoscandia, where European Union (EU) policies have large influence. In this context the Arctic refers to European Arctic as land use is discussed at the European level. The European Arctic is a resource-rich region with minerals, forests and hydrocarbons that attract domestic and international interest and investment. Northern communities often view

* Acknowledgments for input and comments: Timo Koivurova (Arctic Centre, University of Lapland), May-Britt Öhman (University of Uppsala, Sweden), Svein Lund (Norwegian Society for the Conservation of Nature), Jenni Laiti (student at University of Umeå, Sweden), Jonas Vannar (Sirges Sámi Community, Sweden), Kaisa Raitio (Swedish University of Agricultural Sciences), and Satu Luiro (Regional Council of Lapland, Finland).

 | DOI 10.1163/9789004303188_009

large-scale activities as a basis for economic sustainability.[1] Yet they may also have consequences such as losses of biodiversity, ecotourism and reindeer pastures. The culture and livelihoods of Arctic peoples – such as the Sámi – are tightly connected to the land they have occupied and used for centuries (Picture 7.1).

Based on the case of Finnish Lapland, Suopajärvi defines three distinct perspectives on the relationship between humans and nature: 1) traditional livelihoods such as reindeer husbandry and agriculture define nature as *lived space*; 2) industries such as mining, large-scale forestry and hydroelectric power generation see nature as a *resource*; and 3) tourism in the postmodern society sees nature as a place of *experience*.[2] The interactions among these three perspectives provide the key elements to understanding land-use conflicts in the European Arctic.

The objective of this chapter is to map multiple land uses, their interrelations, pressures on them and potential ways to manage contradictions between different land uses in the European Arctic. We do so by reviewing existing literature as well as policy documents, and identify key recommendations for enhancing sustainable land use. The recommendations are based on stakeholder consultations done within the "Strategic Environmental Impact Assessment of Development of the Arctic" project. We start by briefly outlining key drivers effecting on the Arctic land use after which we explore the interrelations between different land uses and identify social and environmental impacts of different land uses. Next, we discuss on governance of Arctic land uses including EU level policy making as well as local land use planning, and how such governance network could function to decrease contradictions. Then we make five recommendations on how Arctic land use could be made more sustainable. We conclude by identifying future challenges for sustainable land use in the Arctic.

## 2 Key Drivers of Land-Use Pressures

The most important factor putting significant pressure on the Arctic land use is economic globalisation. Global demand for resources is increasing the presence

1 Economic sustainability is the term used to identify various strategies that make it possible to use available resources to their best advantage. The idea is to promote the use of those resources in a way that is both efficient and responsible, and likely to provide long-term benefits. In the case of a business operation, it calls for using resources so that the business continues to function over a number of years, while consistently returning a profit.

2 Suopajärvi, L. (2003). Competing industries and contested nature in Finnish Lapland after World War II, in S. Moller, and S. Phonon (eds.), *Encountering the North. Cultural Geography, International Relations and Northern Landscapes*. (pp. 203–220). Ashgate, Aldershot.

PICTURE 7.1 *Arctic landscape – "empty" at first sight, but full of human activities*
PHOTO BY PAULA KANKAANPÄÄ, ARCTIC CENTRE, UNIVERSITY OF LAPLAND

of multinational companies, bringing with it investment, trade and technological innovation. For example, new Arctic mining developments and the reopening of old mines were stimulated primarily by global demand and attractive prices for minerals and metals (see chapter van Dam *et al.* in this volume).

Climate change is a critical driver of overall change in the Arctic biodiversity (see chapter by Strahlendorff *et al.* in this volume), but it also has indirect effects on land-use activities. Climate change is also a political driver as international climate agreements and climate policies aimed at reducing carbon dioxide emissions potentially increase the demand for renewable energy production.[3] An example of an indirect effect is the opening of the Northern Sea Route through which cargo would be transported to world markets. This would require new transportation infrastructure, such as roads, putting pressure on land previously used for tourism, reindeer herding, agriculture and other forms of livelihood, as well as for nature conservation. New roads and railways also provide new pathways for invasive species, which can

3 United Nations Framework Convention on Climate Change, UNFCCC, Kyoto Protocol.

affect species diversity and distribution. These additional impacts are often felt cumulatively, including other effects of climate change.

Preservation of the natural environment in order to protect biodiversity and avoid habitat fragmentation is an important driver affecting land use in the Arctic. The environment has an intrinsic value and is important for human well-being. A term often used in this context is "environmental / ecosystem services," which can be understood as benefits that the natural environment provides expressed in economic terms.

## 3 Main Land-Use Activities and their Interconnections

The land-use activities discussed here include mining, tourism, forestry, reindeer husbandry, renewable energy, transport, nature conservation and subsistence use of forests. Mining has a variety of impacts and interrelations with other human activities and is presented in chapter by van Dam *et al.* in this volume. Therefore, it is only discussed here from the perspective of its relationship (*e.g.* conflicts and synergies) with other land-use activities (Figure 7.1).

### 3.1 *Tourism*

Tourism is one of the largest sources of income in many northern areas; for example, in Finland some municipalities receive almost half of their revenue from tourism.[4] Tourism areas (*e.g.* ski resorts) are often connected to nature conservation areas. Nature conversation areas are also attractive for ecotourism. In some cases, parks have obtained sustainable tourism certifications, *e.g.* PAN Parks Certification.[5]

A variety of EU measures to facilitate transport connections and mobility, particularly for air transport (*e.g.*, low-cost airlines benefit from the liberalisation of EU air space and common EU rules for air passenger rights), have had a positive impact on the expansion of tourism in remote European Arctic locations.[6]

---

4 Satokangas, P. (2013). Matkailulla maakunta menestyy – Matkailun tulo- ja työllisyysvaikutukset 12 lappilaisessa kunnassa vuonna 2011. Lapin korkeakoulukonserni. Rovaniemi, p. 44. [County's profits come from tourism – the impacts of tourism on income and employment in 12 municipalities in Lapland in 2011].

5 The PAN Parks certificate is awarded to extensive wilderness-like protected areas that successfully combine nature conservation and sustainable nature tourism. www.panparks.org.

6 The number of European tourists has been rising since the 1990s with tourists coming primarily from Germany, France, the United Kingdom, Spain and the Netherlands. (Figures for Finnish Lapland).

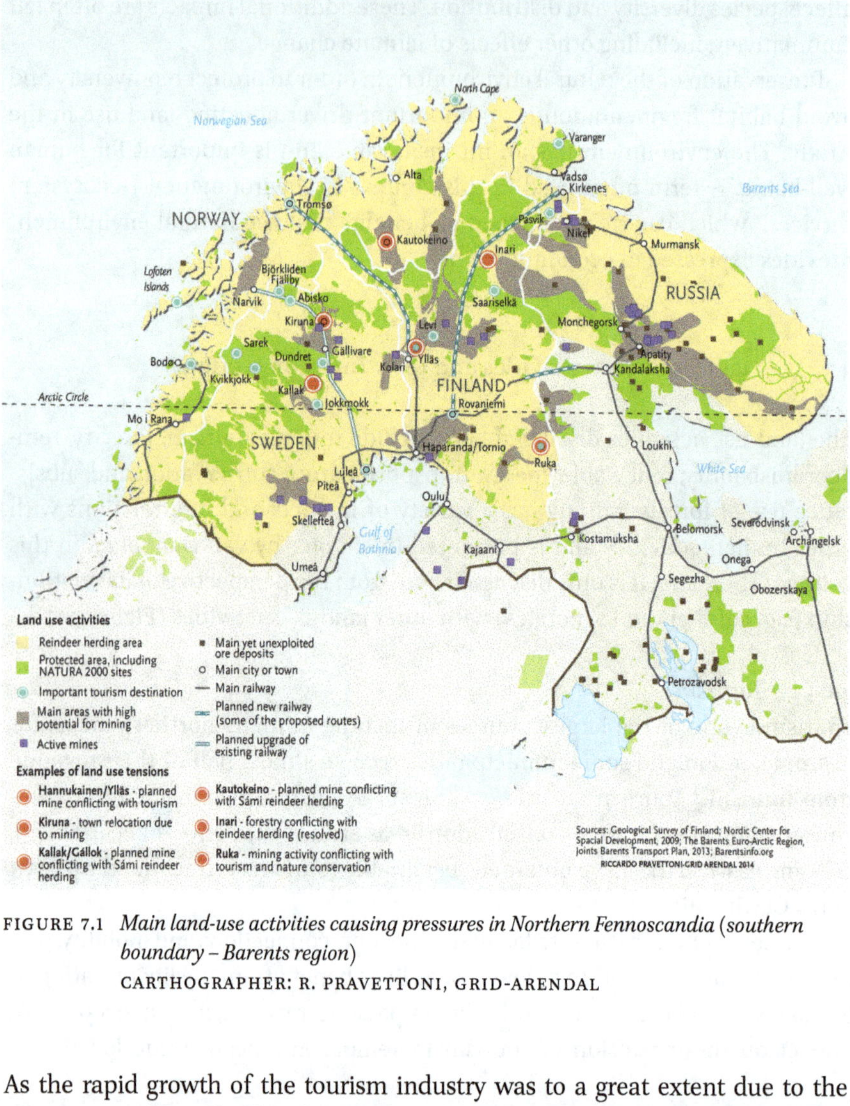


FIGURE 7.1 *Main land-use activities causing pressures in Northern Fennoscandia (southern boundary – Barents region)*
CARTHOGRAPHER: R. PRAVETTONI, GRID-ARENDAL

As the rapid growth of the tourism industry was to a great extent due to the Russian travellers (before the economic crisis in 2014–15),[7] the increasingly remote possibility of a visa-free regime between the EU/Schengen countries and Russia could lead to a significant growth in the number of Russian tourists in Fennoscandia and the development of the tourism infrastructure.

7 See: *e.g.* the Tourism Strategy of Lapland, Regional Council of Lapland website http://www.lappi.fi/lapinliitto/c/document_library/get_file?folderId=349619&name=DLFE-9598.pdf. Accessed 15 January 2014. Statistics of tourism in Finnish Lapland available at http://www.lappi.fi/lapinliitto/julkaisut_ja_tilastot/matkailu. Accessed 5 February 2014.

Mining development and operations are among the greatest threats to eco-tourism and have considerable impacts on the landscape. Open-pit mines adjacent to recreational areas such as national parks and ski resorts may decrease the number of visitors. A survey conducted in Finnish Lapland at the Ylläs ski resort next to the earlier planned Hannukainen mining project (Picture 7.2) and at the Levi ski resort next to Kittilä mine indicated that visitors come to Lapland for the pristine natural landscape and silence (Textbox 7.1). Tourists envisioned that mining would have more negative impacts on tourism than local people did.[8]

### TEXTBOX 7.1 *Can mining co-exist with tourism? – case of Hannukainen*

Studies were conducted about the Hannukainen project which was earlier planned in northern Finland to exploit iron ore deposits with re-opening of an open pit mine. The area has developed infrastructure with paved roads, rail and high voltage power lines. More importantly the mining site is located 8 kilometres from the Ylläs ski resort and the Pallas-Ylläs National Park, Finland's most popular park (see Picture 7.2).

The main concern arising from the Hannukainen mine development was that it could impair the image of the area as attractive for nature-based recreation. Tourists and especially tourism entrepreneurs saw it as a threat for the future. First problem was a plan to pipe treated process water from the mine to the Muonio River, one of the last major salmon rivers in Finland and an EU Natura 2000 protected area. Secondly the municipality of Kolari relies on tourism for 50% of its revenue and thirdly, reindeer herders were concerned about disruption from mining noise and activities, and the loss or fragmentation of grazing areas.

At the end of 2014 project Hannukainen was closed down and mining company Northland Mines bankrupted, mainly because of low iron market prices and problems in finding the financing.

After the project had been terminated, the tourism sector and reindeer herders were relieved. However, in 2015 a new company took over the sight and plans to open mine. Thus, the future prospects of the project can still significantly change. Also, the possible railway line to Tromsø could promote the

8 Jokinen, M. & Tyrväinen, L. (2013). Can We Predict with Tourist Opinions? http://www.metla.fi/hanke/7451/pdf/13052013-jokinen-ja-tyrvainen.pdf. Accessed 20 February 2014.

opening of the mine. Mines are examples of a high volume, a risky business where circumstances may change dramatically and large economic and social investments can vanish rapidly.

PICTURE 7.2 *Hannukainen old mine site near-by Ylläs ski resort*
PHOTO: NORTHLAND MINE LTD

## 3.2 *Forestry*

Forestry has traditionally been a large employer in Nordic countries, especially in Sweden and Finland (14% of EU/European Economic Area's [EEA] total forest area is located in northern Sweden, Norway and Finland). More recently the number of jobs has decreased due to heavy mechanisation and globalisation, for example as companies relocate pulp mills.[9,10] Forestry is still one of the key land-use forms in the Arctic, but the benefits from forestry are no longer distributed to local and regional actors as widely as before, and hence the position of forestry as self-evidently the most profitable form of land use is changing. Over the past two decades, both the number of tourists and the economic benefits of tourism have risen, while at the same time reindeer herding and nature conservation have gained more attention from policy-makers and the public. Sometimes this leads to conflicts between forestry and other activities, with forestry losing its earlier dominant position (*e.g.* the case of Inari, Figure 7.1). In Finland many forest disputes in the period 2000–2010 were

9 For example, in Finland this has led to the closing of the Kemijärvi pulp mill – a very important employer in the local area.

10 Sarkki, S. & Rönkä, A.R. (2012). "Neoliberalisations in Finnish Forestry," *Forest Policy and Economics* 15, 152–159.

resolved in favour of nature conservationists, reindeer herders and tourism entrepreneurs, resulting in a decline in the area of forest that can be used for industrialised forestry.[11,12]

Despite the absence of a common forest policy, the EU has attempted to facilitate sustainable forest management through policies or funding mechanisms focused on rural development, employment, climate change, energy, water and biodiversity.[13] In the latest EU Forest Strategy released in 2013,[14] the European Commission underlines the need for securing wood supplies, managing forests in a sustainable way and ensuring that forest-based ecosystem services are not adversely affected by climate change impacts. If implemented, this approach may be of importance for livelihoods dependent on the forests, in particular, the reindeer herding.[15] The European Commission has made efforts to advance negotiations on legally binding agreements on the management of forests in Europe, including on issues such as ecosystem services provided by forests, illegal logging, monitoring and reporting.[16] This agreement, especially if adopted by the Russian Federation, would be of major relevance to the forestry industry in the European Arctic.

### 3.3 *Renewable Energy*

Demand for wind power is anticipated to rise in the European Arctic due to above mentioned EU targets for renewable energy.[17] Wind power development plans often encounter resistance among local people due to the resulting

11 Sarkki, S. & Heikkinen, H. (2010). Social Movements' Pressure Strategies during Forest Disputes in Finland. *Journal of Natural Resources Policy Research* 2(3), 281–296.

12 Sarkki, S. & Karjalainen, T.P. (2012). Science and Issue Advocacy in a Forest Debate in Finland. *The Polar Journal* 2(1), 125–138.

13 European Commission (2013). Staff Working Document, SWD (2013) 342 final (for the document COM(2013) 659 final: A new EU Forest Strategy), Brussels, 20.9.2013. http://ec.europa.eu/agriculture/forest/strategy/staff-working-doc_en.pdf. Accessed 7 February 2014.

14 European Commission (2013). A new EU Forest Strategy: for forests and the forest-based sector. Commission Communication. COM(2013) 659 final. http://eur-lex.europa.eu/LexUriServ/LexUriServ.do?uri=COM:2013:0659:FIN:en:PDF. Accessed 7 February 2014.

15 This is the primary example, including the conflict over logging in Inari before 2010/2011. See the Sámi Council's position on the issue at: http://www.saamicouncil.net/files/20051116181056.pdf. Accessed 7 February 2014.

16 Ministerial Conference on the Protection of Forests in Europe, http://www.foresteurope.org/en/LBA. Accessed 7 February 2014.

17 In the European Arctic, especially in Finland and Norway, the amount of wind power produced annually is very low (Finland: 447 megawatts (MW) in 2013, Norway: 703 MW in 2012) compared to Sweden and Denmark (over 4 000 MW in 2013).

changes in the landscape and possible effects on eco-tourism. Wind power installations also disturb reindeer herding. The construction of hydroelectric power plants has changed the landscape and affected land use in the European Arctic. However, environmental policies (including Natura 2000) and a shift in public attitudes concerning hydropower (due to better understanding of the impacts in the 1970s and 1980s) have prevented construction of new hydropower plants and may even lead to a reduction in the current hydropower capacity.[18] The situation is different in Greenland where hydropower investments are key development priorities: as a way to provide power for isolated Greenlandic communities and reduce carbon dioxide emissions from diesel-fired power stations, but possibly also to encourage development of energy-intensive industries (as is for example the case with existing or planned aluminium smelters in Iceland and Greenland).

The EU has set the target of obtaining 20% of its energy from renewable sources by 2020 (Directive 2009/28/EC, which has EEA relevance) and 27% by 2030.[19] This goal facilitates renewable energy development as well as research. Given that Nordic states are close to reaching their national goals[20] and the 2030 EU target may not be translated into binding national targets,[21] the development of renewables could be facilitated by a variety of existing measures, established or encouraged by EU legislation,[22] rather than the EU

---

18 Energiateollisuus, http://energia.fi/energia-ja-ymparisto/energialahteet/vesivoima. Accessed 12 March 2014.

19 European Commission, http://ec.europa.eu/clima/policies/2030/index_en.htm. Accessed 29 January 2014.

20 Renewable energy in 2011 accounted for 31.8% of energy produced in Finland (90% of energy produced regionally in Lapland), Finland's 2020 national target is 38%; 46.8% in Sweden (2020 target – 49%); 65% in Norway (2020 target – 67.5%). See: Eurostat data on the share of energy from renewable resources, http://epp.eurostat.ec.europa.eu/portal/page/portal/energy/data/database; International Energy Agency (2013), Key World Energy Statistics 2012, http://www.iea.org/publications/freepublications/publication/kwes.pdf.

21 A final decision had not been taken as of time of publication of this report. European Commission, http://ec.europa.eu/clima/policies/2030/index_en.htm. Accessed 29 January 2014.

22 Such measures include: EU funding for research and development of renewable energy technologies and energy transport, investment in trans-European energy networks, energy market integration, instruments such as targeted private equity funds supported by the European Investment Bank, as well as projects (within cohesion policies) on renewable energy generation in remote communities or sharing experiences in

targets as such.[23] Due to the importance of forestry in Fennoscandia, regulations related to biomass energy are relevant for the European Arctic. Here, EU policies encourage the development of biofuels and biomass for primary energy consumption, heating and transport.[24]

### 3.4 *Transport*

Environmental regulations relevant to transport are expected to influence modes and patterns of transport in the north.[25] One example is the planned railway connecting Finnish Lapland with the Norwegian coast (Figure 7.1), which would be used as the main bulk cargo transport route, replacing the marine route from the Baltic Sea (which is an Emission Control Area for sulphur under MARPOL).[26] According to the industry, due to the lower limit for sulphur content in marine fuels (after 2015, 0.1% compared to 1% currently and 0.5% after 2015 outside of emission control areas, *e.g.* in the Barents Sea), transport will become too costly. The EU Directive 2012/33/EU[27] implements MARPOL limits within the EU (Finland refused to accept the MARPOL amendment but is bound by EU legislation).

EU transport policy promotes inter-modality and accessibility. By supporting the interconnectedness of remote regions with economic centres, the EU

wind power development with Russia. Northern Periphery Programme, http://www.northernperiphery.eu/en/projects/show/&tid=71. Accessed 27 January 2014. The project involves partners from Finland, Sweden, Iceland and the Faroe Islands. Projects Polar Wind and Polaris. Partnership Northwest Service Centre, http://www.fsc.net.ru/content4. Accessed 2 February 2014.

23 European Commission, Renewable Energy Progress Report, COM(2013) 175 final, http://eur-lex.europa.eu/LexUriServ/LexUriServ.do?uri=COM:2013:0175:FIN:EN:PDF. Accessed 30 January 2014.

24 Directive 2003/30/EC of 8 May 2003 on the promotion of the use of biofuels or other renewable fuels for transport, including progress reporting. See also European Commission, The Renewable Energy Progress Report, Communication, COM(2009) 192 final, Brussels, 24.4.2009; European Commission, Biomass Action Plan, Communication, COM (2005)628.

25 See: *Joint Barents Transport Plan* 2013 (September 2013). http://www.barentsinfo.fi/beac/docs/Joint_Barents_Transport_Plan_2013.pdf. Accessed 4 February 2014.

26 International Convention for the Prevention of Pollution from Ships and 1978 Protocol (MARPOL 73/78), 1340 UNTS 184, 12 ILM 1319 (1973). Entry into force: 1982 (Annexes 1 and 2).

27 Directive 2012/33/EU of 21 November 2012 amending Council Directive 1999/32/EC as regards the sulphur content of marine fuels.

may influence infrastructure developments resulting in direct impacts of supported projects as well as long-term trends in changes in land use driven by improved accessibility.

### 3.5 *Reindeer Husbandry*

Reindeer herding is believed to be a flexible activity that can co-exist with other land-use activities. In practice, however, this has usually meant that reindeer herders have had to move to other grazing sites. The landscape of northern Fennoscandia might appear to be empty at first glance, but in fact the land is divided between reindeer herding districts where the animals graze and migrate between winter and summer pastures. Mining, oil and gas extraction and large-scale forestry have reduced the size of available pasturelands for reindeer husbandry (Textbox 7.2). In Sweden and Norway reindeer herding is strongly connected to Sámi culture and practiced exclusively by the Sámi (in Finland it is practised by both Finns and the Sámi). Reindeer herders use traditional summer and (critically important) winter pastures that the family/village have used for generations (Picture 7.3). Land-use changes can result in the fragmentation of pastures or disturbance to calving and culling areas and reindeer migration corridors.

PICTURE 7.3 *Traditional Sámi reindeer herder summer camp, Skuolla, Sweden*
PHOTO BY CARL-JOHAN UTSI

## TEXTBOX 7.2 *Sámi perspective on mining – Case of Gállok*

A major political issue regarding the interaction between mining and land use in the Nordic countries concerns the rights of the Sámi. Gállok (Kallak), an area in Jokkmok municipality in northern Sweden, became globally known in 2013 and 2014 when Sámi and environmental activists demonstrated against iron ore mining (Picture 7.4). Due to the potential damages to natural and cultural values, especially Sámi reindeer herding, the governmental County Administrative Board of Norrbotten proposed in fall 2014 a rejection of the mining permission applied by the mining company Jokkmokk Iron Mines Ltd. In February 2015 the Government of Sweden – as a final administrative instance – decided to allow exploration activities.

The case of Gállok demonstrates the challenges of balancing mining, nature-based livelihoods and the rights of indigenous peoples. In Gállok, the environmental concerns include pollution caused by mining to ground and fresh water. The main issue, however, is the Sámi reindeer herding. The mining site is not vast, but combined with the infrastructure, transport vehicles, dust and noise it could have serious negative impacts on reindeer herding and Sámi culture. If the mine is opened, the migration route and utilisation of winter pastures will be endangered for three Sámi reindeer co-operatives (Sameby) and hundreds of families and households.

PICTURE 7.4 *Local people and Sámi demonstrating against the planned mining exploration activities at Gállok in summer 2013*
PHOTO BY CARL-JOHAN UTSI

Even when consultation among the local people and Sámi has been conducted, there have been differences in opinion on how open the dialogue has been and whether Sámi and their culture and livelihood have been taken into account by the municipality and other stakeholders in question. Open dialogue, collaborative learning and transparent governance are cornerstones of environmental conflict management and the reconciliation of mining and other land uses. Sometimes these procedures do not work and there is no true sustainable way to integrate different interests and land-use activities. Ore deposits and winter pastures are not transferable. In the case of Gállok, the socially and culturally sustainable co-existence of mining and reindeer herding might not be possible.

One commonly debated issue in all Nordic countries is predator management, regulatory protection and reindeer killed by wolves, wolverines, lynxes, golden eagles and brown bears. In the timeframe since Finland became a member of the EU, the number of large predators has increased.[28] Reindeer herders have adapted to climate change and EU policies (*e.g.* regulations on reindeer meat production and slaughtering), but they cannot adapt to the increasing numbers of reindeer killed by predators (in Finland, the number grew 2.5-fold between 1995 and 2007, with some cooperatives losing 60–70% of calves).[29] The government pays compensation for the killed reindeer, but that does not cover benefits for clothing and handicrafts and the additional time and costs incurred by herders when searching for reindeer carcasses. The management and policy regarding big predators varies between the countries, but still the reduced freedom of action resulting from loss of habitat, predation and legal constraints is having more negative impact on reindeer herding than the climate change.[30]

The concerns of the Sámi and reindeer herders highlight the need for the EU biodiversity and conservation framework to better take into account the reindeer

---

28 For example, a recent inventory of lynxes counted over 2700 individuals whereas in 1978 the number was about 100. LUKE. Natural Resources Institute Finland. http://www.luke.fi/en/. http://www.luke.fi/tiedote/ilvesten-maara-ennallaan/. Accessed 18 August 2015.

29 Vuojala-Magga, T. (2012). Adaptation of Sàmi Reindeer Herding: EU Regulation and Climate Change. In Tennberg, M. (Ed.), *Governing the Uncertain: Adaptation and Climate in Russia and Finland* (101–122), Springer Science + Business Media B.V.2012.

30 Tyler, N.J.C., Turi, J.M., Sundset, M.A., Strom Bull, K., Sara, M.N., Reinert, E., Oskal, N., Nellemann, C., McCarthy, J.J., Mathiesen, S.D., Martello, M.L., Magga, O.H., Hovelsrud, G.K., Hanssen-Bauer, I., Eira, N.I., Eira, I.M.G. & Corell, R.W. (2007). Sámi reindeer pastoralism under climate change: Applying a generalized framework for vulnerability studies to a sub-arctic socio-ecological system. *Global Environmental Change* 17, 191–206.

herding. Predators (protected within biodiversity frameworks) in addition to the large scale land-use activities such as mining and forestry are perceived as the main threats for the sustainability of the reindeer herding. Stakeholders representing reindeer herding emphasise that their livelihoods should be supported also within the EU framework (including indigenous rights). Several EU territorial co-operation projects already respond to this need. However, traditional livelihoods are not taken up strongly in environmental policies, transport frameworks or strategies referring to mining or forestry. Noticeably, some stakeholders (*e.g.* environmental non-governmental organisations driven by general environmental principles) are supportive of the EU biodiversity framework, including the protection of predators'.

### 3.6 *Nature Conservation*

Changing land use and the cumulative impacts of various activities are among the main threats to biodiversity.[31] The European Commission has adopted the EU Biodiversity Strategy to 2020, aimed at halting the loss of biodiversity and improving the state of Europe's species, habitats, ecosystems and the services they provide. A biodiversity strategy is being integrated into major EU policy frameworks.[32] So far the European Commission has had a limited presence in the Arctic Council's biodiversity work (*e.g.* Arctic Biodiversity Assessment). Although the Commission is a full member of the Barents Euro-Arctic Council, its representatives have not participated, for example, in the meetings of the Working Group on the Environment, which is in charge of the Barents Euro-Arctic Council's projects related to biodiversity, such as the Barents Protected Areas Network (BPAN) and the Green Belt of Fennoscandia.[33] However, both projects have been on the agenda of recent EU-Russia environmental dialogue meetings, which could lead to concrete outcomes if continued in the future.[34,35]

31 European Commission, http://ec.europa.eu/environment/international_issues/relations_russia_en.htm. Accessed 7 February 2014.

32 EU Biodiversity Strategy to 2020, European Commission, http://ec.europa.eu/environment/nature/biodiversity/comm2006/2020.htm. Accessed 29 January 2014.

33 Other relevant BEAC projects include: ecotourism and protected areas; conservation of the last pristine forests in the Barents Region; effects of climate change on biodiversity and ecosystem services in the Barents Region; and wetlands – conservation and ecosystem services, www.syke.fi.

34 European Commission, http://ec.europa.eu/environment/international_issues/relations_russia_en.htm. Accessed 7 February 2014.

35 See: Annual Report of the Working Group on Environment (Barents Euro-Arctic Council) (January 2014), http://www.barentsinfo.fi/beac/docs/WGE_Annual_Report_2012_2013.pdf. Accessed 6 February 2014.

The most important EU environmental regulations affecting the Arctic land use are the Natura 2000 network of protected sites and associated Habitats and Birds Directives (Council Directive 92/43/EEC and Directive 2009/147/EC).[36] This framework is also relevant for the indigenous rights of the Sámi in the north of Sweden and Finland, as it provides additional protection for many habitats that are also used for traditionally practiced nature-based livelihoods, such as reindeer herding and fishing. As these areas are considered to be important for the whole EU, possible and actual significant damages to designated sites can be addressed by the European Commission and EU courts. Consequently, major industrial developments may be limited in these areas. On the other hand, the same legislative framework protects predators, the numbers of which have grown significantly in the past few decades, resulting in increased loss of reindeer as discussed earlier (3.5. Reindeer Husbandry). However, national regulations in Finland and Sweden are critical and determining factors in Sámi people rights, as well as for other inhabitants practicing nature-based livelihoods.

Regulations such as the Waste Framework Directive (Directive 2008/98/EC) and the Water Framework Directive (Directive 2000/60/EC, WFD), which aim to improve the status of European water bodies by 2015, have direct implications for land use.[37] In the course of implementing the WFD, EU/EEA member states have adopted river basin management plans. The adopted basin-based approach may contribute to good governance of activities within river basins also in the European Arctic.[38]

Nature conservation does not as such put pressure on land use, but it significantly affects land use and all the activities discussed above. Arctic biodiversity is an irreplaceable cultural, scientific, ecological, economic and spiritual asset. However, climate change, industrial development, pollution, local disturbances and invasive species already affect the Arctic, and it is anticipated that the impacts from these stressors will be even greater in the future.[39] The challenges

---

36 Council Directive 92/43/EEC of 21 May 1992 on the conservation of natural habitats and of wild fauna and flora; Directive 2009/147/EC of the European Parliament and of the Council of 30 November 2009 on the conservation of wild birds (the codified version of Directive 79/409/EEC as amended).

37 European Commission, http://ec.europa.eu/environment/international_issues/relations_russia_en.htm. Accessed 7 February 2014.

38 See European Commission Report at http://ec.europa.eu/environment/water/water-framework/pdf/COM-2012-670_EN.pdf. Accessed 6 February 2014.

39 Conservation of Arctic Flora and Fauna (CAFF). 2013. Arctic Biodiversity Assessment: Report for Policy Makers. CAFF, Akureyri, Iceland.

for biodiversity are substantial, including habitat fragmentation and degradation. Construction of roads, railroads, pipelines, drilling and mine sites, and dams cause fragmentation of the landscapes and habitat losses, with major effects on biodiversity and hydrology. Habitat fragmentation can adversely affect species distribution and abundance, as well as nature-based livelihoods.

The expansion of industrial activity in the Arctic may also increase the local sources of pollution, waste, sewage and black carbon.[40] These risks to the environment affect human health as well as food and water security.[41] People (both indigenous and non-indigenous) in the Arctic have a unique relationship with nature, including the subsistence use of forests (*e.g.* berry and mushroom picking) and terrestrial and fresh water resources (*e.g.* hunting and fishing). A significant proportion of the local diet is derived from these traditional sources; thus, if land and water were to be contaminated, food safety would be at risk.

The drivers, land uses and their impacts are summarized in the Table 7.1.

## 4 Governance of the Land Use in the European Arctic

Governance affecting the land-use activities and their interactions is very broad, and only the most important aspects in relation to conflicts and cumulative impacts are discussed here. While various activities may be manageable individually, the cumulative effects might result in substantial environmental, social and economic changes or disruption, especially in the fragile and slowly recovering Arctic environment. Therefore, it is important to take into account the cumulative impacts from historical, ongoing and planned activities, as well as global factors such as climate change.

Environmental impact assessments (EIAs) are one of the key tools for understanding and communicating the implications of new developments, and for the possible creation of a dialogue between the various land users. EIAs include formal procedures for examining the impacts of a project as well as identifying alternatives and mitigation measures. However, the effectiveness of EIAs varies in different countries. Ideally, it should examine social aspects (as in Finland) or be accompanied by a separate social impact assessment (as in Greenland).

---

40 Conservation of Arctic Flora and Fauna (CAFF). 2013.

41 Nilsson, L.M., Berner, J., Dudarev, A.A., Mulvad, G., Odland, J.O., Parkinson, A., Rautio, A., Tikhonov, C. & Evengård, B. (2013). Indicators of food and water security in an Arctic Health context – results from an international workshop discussion. *Int. J Circumpolar Health 72*: 21530 – http://dx.doi.org/10.3402/ijch.v72i0.21530.

TABLE 7.1 *The land-use pressures, drivers and impacts in the European Arctic*

| Land-use pressure | Main drivers | Environmental impacts | Social impacts | Economic impacts |
|---|---|---|---|---|
| **Forestry and wood-based small and medium-sized industries:** A major land-use activity in the north. | Demand for timber, which is expected to increase in step with the demand for green energy. Northern regions of Finland, Sweden and Norway have 20 million hectares of forest. | Changes in landscape, decreased biodiversity, habitat destruction and fragmentation. Reduced nature values and impacts on water quality.<br>Increased monocultures. | Importance for local livelihoods and multi-use of wood.<br>Decrease in reindeer pasture areas and potential effects on reindeer husbandry culture.<br>Decrease in ecotourism areas and subsistence use of forests.<br>Negative impacts from clear-cutting on the mental well-being of local inhabitants. | More employment opportunities (including renewable wood-based products and handicrafts).<br>increased spending.<br>Increased tax revenues.<br>Increased infrastructure (*e.g.* roads).<br>This also has negative impacts, as a decrease in reindeer grazing lands leads to lower production in reindeer herding.<br>Also has negative impacts on ecotourism. |

| | | | | |
|---|---|---|---|---|
| **Nature Conservation:** Expansion of protected areas. Species protection. | Increased environmental awareness and NGO actions. Local, national and international policies and agreements. | Sustain biodiversity and habitats. Increase populations of big predators. | Increased human well-being of local people (cultural significance of land, subsistence use of forests such as berry and mushroom picking, which are "everyman's rights" in Finland and can be performed in protected areas as well). Increased nature-based tourism and recreational use of lands. Also has negative impacts, *e.g.* in Finland where the number of predators has increased so much that wolves and bears come to settlements and people are afraid to go outside of their homes. (The problem is not so great in other European Arctic countries.) | Loss of reindeer to predators, leading to lower economic growth. Decrease in areas used for forestry and wood-based industry. Increase in cultural ecosystem services (*e.g.* tourism) and economic ecosystem services.[42] |
| **Renewable Energy:** Development of wind and hydropower plants. | Environmental regulations. Local, national and international policies. Demand for sustainable energy. | Decreased biodiversity, habitat destruction and fragmentation. Disruption of migration paths. | Negative effects on reindeer husbandry and nature-based tourism. | Public costs of infrastructure. More employment opportunities. Increased tax revenues. |

TABLE 7.1 *The land-use pressures, drivers and impacts in the European Arctic* (*Cont.*)

| Land-use pressure | Main drivers | Environmental impacts | Social impacts | Economic impacts |
|---|---|---|---|---|
| **Tourism:** Expansion of tourism: more people, more places, more infrastructure. | Demand for winter and ecotourism in particular. Local economies are dependent on tourism (in some regions in Finland almost 50% of local income comes from tourism). | Increased air and land traffic and tracks (*e.g.* snowmobiles, mountain bikes), noise, land erosion, wastes, pollution.<br>Disturbance to reindeer and wildlife. | Demographic change: seasonal workers; shifts in social structure in rural communities, potentially leading to social problems. Job opportunities, increased services.<br>Decelerated migration of local people. | Increase in local employment and economy.<br>Increased use of public services (*e.g.* health care, airports). Investments by the government and private sector.<br>Increased tax revenues.<br>Increase in demand for local food products and wellness products. |
| **Mining:** Expansion of mining activities. | Global market demand for minerals.<br>Economic development policies. | Changes in the landscape, water and ecosystem.<br>Potential pollution.<br>Biodiversity, habitat, migratory route changes.<br>Reduced nature values and possible biodiversity losses. | Severe negative effects on reindeer herding and Sámi culture with loss of employment opportunities, especially in Sweden and Norway.<br>Potential negative effects on tourism.<br>Demographic change: influx of foreign workers; shifts in social structure in rural communities.<br>Job opportunities, skills transfer, increased services. Big differences between the regions. | Local employment and increased spending.<br>Investments by the government and private sector.<br>Increased tax revenues (note: this varies considerably among areas and mines).<br>Boom and bust cycles.<br>Decreased tourism and reindeer husbandry and other traditional livelihoods, leading to economic losses. |

| | | | | |
|---|---|---|---|---|
| **Reindeer Husbandry:** In Sámi regions in Sweden and Norway, only Sámi people can practice reindeer herding. In Finland, Finnish people can also practice reindeer herding. | Sustaining culture and traditional livelihoods in herding in Sámi areas as well in other areas where reindeer husbandry is practiced. | Changes in grazing areas, habitat losses and fragmentation. Increased land erosion via overgrazing and damage to land from all-terrain vehicles. Loss of biodiversity. | Traditional livelihoods support local, cultural and ethnic identity and keep remote communities alive. Threat of loss of traditional lifestyles affects cultural identity and peoples' well-being, especially in Sámi areas. | Household dependence on traditional livelihoods. Supports tourism. Subsistence costs of predator losses. |
| **Transport:** Development of new infrastructures and transport routes, railways (*e.g.* growth in land-based transportation due to increased cargo shipping on the Northern sea route). | Demand for new transport infrastructure for mining, tourism and other activities. | Biodiversity losses and habitat fragmentation. Increased noise. Increased accessibility to remote places. Reduced nature values. Search and rescue and disaster prevention in coastal and harbour areas. | Supports new settlements and migration, which affects needs for schools, housing, jobs, social life and well-being. | Economic stimulation. Public costs of infrastructure. More employment opportunities. Increased tax revenues. |
| **Agriculture** (excluding reindeer husbandry), sheep husbandry (especially in Iceland). | Maintaining the national heritage of sheep farming in Iceland. | Land and water pollution due to use of fertilisers, herbicides and pesticides. Land erosion and loss of biodiversity and habitat fragmentation caused by overgrazing by sheep. | | Income from exporting lamb meat and other agricultural products. |

TABLE 7.1 *The land-use pressures, drivers and impacts in the European Arctic* (Cont.)

| Land-use pressure | Main drivers | Environmental impacts | Social impacts | Economic impacts |
|---|---|---|---|---|
| **Freshwater fishing and fish farming** (in lakes in Finland and fjords in Norway). | Demand for fish due to overfishing of wild fisheries. | Nutrient pollution increased by fish farms, decreases in wild fish stocks (for example, salmon in Norway). | Mental well-being (recreational fishing and livelihood). | Increased economy and employment, but can also have the opposite effect, as fish farming can cause losses of wild fish stocks. |
| **Subsistence use of forests** (*e.g.* berry and mushroom picking). | Tradition. | Hunting and fishing may disturb population dynamics. | Increased health and well-being, both mental health and healthy food consumption. | Increased income for local people and foreign workers (companies import workforce from countries with "cheap labour") and local companies producing berry products and exporting mushrooms (For instance, *Boletus edulis* mushrooms are exported from Finland to Italy). |

Social impacts are also cumulative and should be assessed for each new project, both within EIAs and in spatial and land-use planning. Strategic environmental or integrated (including social and economic aspects) assessments serve this purpose. Broader frameworks for impact assessments include instruments such as the Espoo Convention[42] (for transboundary impact assessment) or the much less known Arctic Environmental Protection Strategy's (AEPS) Arctic EIA Guidelines.[43]

Recently, voluntary governance mechanisms exceeding legal requirements have been emerged. In the mining industry, much attention has been given to the notion of a "social licence," which is often acquired by companies exceeding the legal requirements regarding matters such as stakeholder participation. Similarly the tourism and forestry companies develop industry standards or eco-labels.

Governance tools for interaction between the various land-use forms include local land-use planning, participatory resource planning and compensation schemes. International mechanisms for protection of Arctic biodiversity include the Barents Protected Areas Network (BPAN) project,[44] an ongoing process under the Convention of Biological Diversity to facilitate the description of ecologically and biologically significant areas in the Arctic.

The EU has no direct authority regarding land-use planning in the Arctic. However, EU policies and regulations have influence on the discussed activities relevant for Arctic land use and can at least potentially manage conflicts between the land uses. Some of the EU policies which may fulfil this function include the EU framework for environmental and strategic impact assessment (Directive 85/337/EEC [2011/92/EU] and Directive 2001/42/EC) creates an important framework for common standards, applicable throughout Fennoscandia, such as by ensuring that certain projects are obliged to undergo an environmental impact assessment (EIA). It also protects culturally-significant landscapes. The EIA framework in the EU has been recently amended. Some stakeholders have expressed concerns that the scope of its applicability might be too broad and it could place an additional bureaucratic burden on private actors. The EU's dialogue with the Russian Federation

42 Convention on Environmental Impact Assessment in a Transboundary Context (Espoo, 1991) – the "Espoo Convention."

43 Arctic Environmental Protection Strategy (AEPS, predecessor of Arctic Council), Guidelines for Environmental Impact Assessment in the Arctic. Finnish Ministry of Environment, 1997.

44 Barents Protected Areas Network project, http://www.bpan.fi/. Accessed 23 February 2014.

regarding Russian ratification of the Espoo Convention[45] (and its Kiev SEA Protocol) is of significance for the Barents region, as it would create a common binding framework for trans-boundary impact assessments.

In the case of spatial planning the EU has some initiatives, such as the European Spatial Development Perspective (1999) for promoting the exchange of regional experiences. More practically, the INSPIRE Directive establishes an infrastructure for spatial information in Europe to support environmental policies and policies/activities having environmental impacts.[46]

Although the European Union supports indigenous (and in particular Sámi) rights on a declaratory level, there are virtually no Arctic-relevant provisions addressing the issue of land rights in the above-listed EU policies affecting the land use. For example, land-use rights within the framework for renewable energy and indigenous rights violations in forestry management are primarily applicable to biofuels and timber imported from developing states.[47]

## 5 Critical Factors for the EU Decision-Making

The critical factors for the EU decision-making and recommendations were developed by the authors based on the comments and ideas given at the stakeholder workshop which brought together the representatives from the governmental organizations, entrepreneurs, reindeer herders, Sámi and research organizations. Additional feedback was collected via online questionnaire.[48] The critical factors highlight the importance of taking into account the opinions of the local people and the socio-economic impacts of various existing and planned activities.

### 5.1 *Human Well-Being and Social Sustainability*

The concept of human health and well-being is a combination of physical and mental health, in which efforts to sustain the culture, language and traditional

45 Convention on Environmental Impact Assessment in a Transboundary Context (Espoo, 1991) – the Espoo Convention.

46 More at http://inspire.ec.europa.eu/. Accessed 17 February 2014.

47 European Commission. Staff Working Document for Renewable Energy Progress Report. SWD(2013) 102 final, http://eur-lex.europa.eu/LexUriServ/LexUriServ.do?uri=COM:2013:0175:FIN:EN:PDF. Accessed 3 February 2014; European Commission, Staff Working Document SWD (2013) 342 final.

48 See Annex 1.1 and Annex 1.2 in the *Strategic Assessment of Development of the Arctic* Report, available at www.arcticinfo.eu/sada.

way of life are indispensable elements. Therefore, any action that disrupts normal daily life can have effects on health and well-being. Food and water supplies are fundamental to life and can be altered by climate change or human activities (*e.g.* pollution, contaminants and access to food supplies).[49] Land-use activities should not risk human health and well-being and therefore social sustainability should be taken into account in policy-making.

### 5.2 *Public Participation*

The role of stakeholders in the environmental planning process as well as their opportunities to influence decisions relevant to land use has expanded in recent years. Participatory management planning for national parks is a good example, with a greater role being played by local tourist enterprises and reindeer herders. Yet, critics question whether the existing participatory processes provide genuine possibilities for influencing decision-making. Various stakeholders emphasise different values: while non-governmental organisations (NGOs) advocate for environmental values, locals underline the community's economic development.[50]

Addressing cumulative impacts and the possibility of social conflicts requires open, inclusive and democratic conflict – and a problem-solving mechanisms and partnerships. Social and environmental assessments alone are not sufficient. Participation from the public, private and voluntary sectors based on mutual respect is necessary if ecologically balanced and economically and socially sustainable developments are to be achieved.

Challenges include the power relations between various stakeholders; the human and resource capacity of social actors for taking part in to the consultation process; the clarity of the interconnection between consultation/participation, decision-making and the possible participation overload as it is sometimes the case with the Sámi parliaments in Fennoscandia.[51]

49 Nilsson, L.M. & Evengård, B. (2013). Food and water security indicators in an Arctic health context. *A report by the* AHHEG/SDWG, *and the* AMAP/HHAG *during the Swedish chairmanship of the Arctic Council 2011–2013.* Publications from Arctic Research Centre no. 1. Umeå University.

50 Sarkki, S. (2011). *The Site Strikes Back: Multi-level forest governance and participation in northern Finland.* PhD thesis. Thule Institute & Discipline of Anthropology, University of Oulu, Finland. Acta Universitatis Ouluensis B 102.

51 Stepien, A., Koivurova, T., Gremsperger A. & Niemi, H. (2014). Arctic Indigenous Peoples and the Challenge of Climate Change, in Tedsen, E., Cavalieri, S. & Kraemer, R. (eds.), *Arctic Marine Governance: Opportunities for Transatlantic Cooperation.* Dordrecht: Springer.

### 5.3 *Indigenous Peoples' Rights*

Decision-makers need to acknowledge the indigenous people's connection to the traditional lands as activities affecting land use can have adverse effects on their culture and identity. Cultural pressures can create negative social impacts, such as increased school drop-outs, substance abuse and suicides, all of which are major challenges among the indigenous youth.[52]

Finland and Sweden have not ratified the 1989 ILO Convention No. 169[53] yet, as in both countries there is an ongoing discussion about Sámi rights to land. The issue of access to land and waters and land ownership is important for all traditional livelihoods, but it is perhaps most clearly evident in the case of reindeer herding. International indigenous legal instruments may be helpful in decisions on land rights and in setting up participatory processes.[54] For example, the provisions of the ILO Convention put obligations on states in this regard.

## 6 Conclusion: The Way Forward for the EU

Future holds numerous challenges and uncertainties connected with the Arctic land use. Globalisation and indirectly climate change have increased multiple pressures. The activities requiring the large areas of pristine nature such as tourism and reindeer husbandry are often affected negatively by the activities such as mining, forestry, transport or building of a renewable energy.

Given that mining activities are expected to increase in the Arctic region it is anticipated that new conflicts will emerge and eventually policymakers will have to address these challenges. Incidents like the Gállok mine conflict have highlighted the issue of the Sámi land rights and indigenous rights. This might lead to a decrease in mining activities in Sámi areas in the future. If not, the future of Sámi reindeer herding is uncertain. In the light of the multiplicity of pressures from the large-scale activities and policies within and especially the policies regarding the big predators, the reindeer husbandry, the subsistence use of forests and water supplies, and the Sámi culture could be degraded or

52 Arctic Council, SDWG Highlights Open Discussion Session in Gällivare, Sweden, 2012.

53 International Labour Organization (ILO) Convention no 169 concerning Indigenous and Tribal Peoples in Independent Countries (Geneva, 76th ILC session (27 Jun 1989); Entry into force: 5 Sep 1991).

54 Raitio, K. (2008). *"You Can't Please Everyone" – Conflict Management Practices, Frames and Institutions in Finnish State Forests.* PhD thesis. University of Joensuu.

lost. On the other hand, the future of the Sámi reindeer husbandry is also dependent on the overall change of the Sámi culture itself (see Chapter 9). If the traditional way of life is not found attractive by the young Sámi who have more other options for their future than ever before, maintaining the traditional Sámi reindeer culture can be challenging even without the pressures from the land-use activities.

Globalisation is expected to either keep the tourism stable or increase it. However, the economic recession and climate change can also cause the negative trends. The dominant tourism activities are difficult to predict, whether it will be mass tourism, *e.g.* in ski resorts, or more expensive and specifically tailored nature-based tourism, or both. As an Arctic tourism is heavily dependent on snow and ice conditions, the unpredictable conditions caused by climate change may adversely affect the industry's growth potential. On the other hand, the impacts of climate change to the competitive locations in Europe may be much more severe than in the North.

In the forestry sector uncertainties are related to increased pressures for nature protection, an increased demand for bio-economy including renewable energy and biofuels, the relocation of pulp production, the development of certification systems for forestry, and the views of the local and regional actors concerning the benefits gained from the sector.

Due to the challenges and uncertainties, the numerous land-use conflicts might be expected to continue and become increasingly difficult to resolve if the indigenous and local people's rights are not acknowledged and participatory processes are not implemented. The planning of new activities must respect the needs, culture and livelihoods of local and indigenous communities, including their land rights. Proper assessment of social impacts is essential in order to mitigate conflicts between different values and interest groups. When European Arctic land-use issues are considered, EU policy-makers should pay particular attention to the aspects of human well-being and social sustainability, public participation and indigenous rights. This is especially important when these elements differ from the needs and values typical for the more densely populated areas in the south. Increasing social aspects in land use planning could take place by stronger inclusion of Social Impact Assessment in EIA.

The EU plays a varying policy role in the European Arctic depending on the locality and the issue. Therefore, both in general and in the context of EU policy-making, there is a need for more knowledge on local issues, culture and livelihoods. Facilitating knowledge exchange between regions, providing tools for collaborative research and developing formal and stakeholder engagement tools would increase knowledge sharing and the quality of decision-making, including cohesion between policies at different levels of the governance. Without knowledge on how people use the land, including reindeer herding, subsistence use of forests, hunting and all aspects of daily life, it is impossible to assess the impacts of new initiatives. Thus, new governance structures should be developed and implemented for connecting stakeholders, European and national policy-makers, thereby allowing Arctic stakeholders to participate more effectively in the decision-making and consultation processes.

Finally, a stronger inclusion of social aspects and challenges in the EU frameworks for impact assessment as well as in dialogue with Arctic partners including the Russian Federation is advised. In northern Finland a recent survey showed that local tourism entrepreneurs had little trust in the EIA conducted for planned mining activities in the region. The main reason for this mistrust is that the EIA is carried out by companies or by consultants hired by companies.[55] Social impact assessments are not often conducted or their role in the EIA process and reports is minor.[56] Therefore, in order to carry out a reliable social impact assessment, international principles and guidelines should be followed in EIA processes throughout Europe. Here, the EU could take leadership, or, to a limited extent, a regulatory role. The EU has recently amended its EIA directive,[57] putting greater emphasis on participatory elements such as clarity and transparency of documents and decisions for the general public. The change from "human beings" to "population and human health" among factors for which impacts are to be assessed could invite the possibility of better assessment of social issues, but the practical effect of such a relatively minor adjustment is dependent on the national implementation. Internationally, the European Commission should continue to encourage the Russian authorities to ratify the Espoo Convention. Strategic environmental or integrated (including social and economic aspects) assessments are crucial governance tools, especially for sparsely populated areas and for addressing the cumulative impacts of activities that require large land areas.

---

55 Jokinen, M. (2014). Hannukaisen kaivos ja matkailu (Hannukainen mine and tourism). http://www.metla.fi/hanke/7451/pdf/Matkailun-kehitysnakymat_seminaari_17.2.2014.pdf. Accessed 26 February 2014.

56 Suopajärvi. L. (2013). Social impact assessment in mining projects in Northern Finland: Comparing practice to theory, Environmental Impact Assessment Review, 42, 25–30.

57 Directive 2014/52/EU of the European Parliament and of the Council of 16 April 2014 amending Directive 2011/92/EU on the assessment of the effects of certain public and private projects on the environment.

CHAPTER 8

# Socioeconomic and Cultural Changes in the European Arctic

*Adam Stępień, Karolina Banul, Annette Scheepstra, Kim van Dam, Kirsi Latola and Timo Koivurova**

## Abstract

The chapter provides overview of the Arctic sociocultural landscape, highlighting innovative and growing Arctic cities, thinning-out rural areas, demographic challenges, and dependence on extractive and primary industries. Indigenous peoples often experience these elements in distinct manners.

The EU has a number of programmes that support socioeconomic development and co-operation in the North, as well as relevant transport policies and environmental regulations. When designing and carrying out actions affecting socioeconomic and cultural development, the EU decision-makers should take into account: the region's intra-regional and core-periphery connectivity; power structures, social conflicts and cultural diversity; human-nature interactions; as well as the state of innovation, entrepreneurship and education.

The EU's focus on entrepreneurship and innovation within co-operation and cohesion programmes is likely to continue in the future, although greater attention to gender issues and indigenous peoples is recommended. Intra-regional accessibility and connectivity must not be neglected. The special characteristics and needs of Arctic cities need to be taken into account in EU policies and programmes.

## 1 Introduction

This chapter discusses selected social and cultural trends in the European Arctic (see Figure 8.1). Arctic cultures are characterised by high resilience and

* The authors would like to thank stakeholders who participated in the consultations and other contributors, especially Birgitta Evengård (University of Umeå), Janika Luukinen (East and North Finland Office in Brussels), Mikael Janson and North Sweden Office in Brussels, North Norway European Office, Mid Sweden EU Office, Päivi Ekdahl (Regional Council of Lapland) and Ole Damsgaard (Northern Periphery Programme Secretariat), for their inputs, comments and suggestions (including written input and statements).

 | DOI 10.1163/9789004303188_010

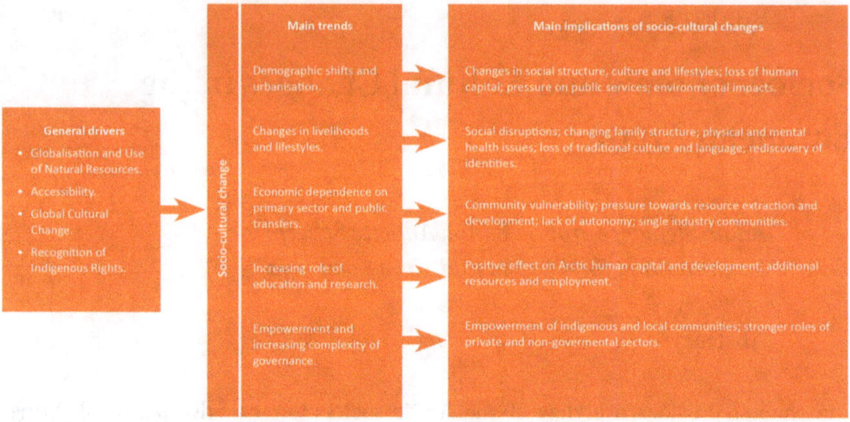


FIGURE 8.1 *Overview of the main sociocultural drivers and trends and their implications in the European Arctic*
SOURCE: ADAM STĘPIEŃ; PRODUCED BY ARCTIC PORTAL

adaptive capacity, but some aspects of social change have been challenging.[1] The main issues discussed include changing demographics and urbanization, on-going dependence on public transfers and primary industries, on-going changes in lifestyle and livelihood, rising role of education and research and shifts in governance. Peripherality is an important feature of the region. Also, the presence of indigenous peoples distinguishes the North from the rest of Europe. As societies and cultures are by definition very complex and dynamic, the choice of issues and perspectives in this chapter is to certain degree arbitrary, but is believed to reflect the current emphases in debates on the sociocultural development of the European Arctic.

## 2 Key Sociocultural Trends in the European Arctic

### 2.1 *Complex Demographic Trends and Urbanisation*

The *Arctic Human Development Report* (AHDR) (2004) estimated that there are four million people living in the Arctic, of whom 10% are indigenous, ***e.g.*** Inuit, Sámi and Nenets (Figure 8.2). Since 2000, there is 1.4% less people living in the Arctic, primarily due to continued population decline in the Russian Arctic

1 Larsen, J.N. & Fondahl, G. (Eds.), (2014). Arctic Human Development Report: Regional Processes and Global Linkages, Nordic Council of Ministers, TemaNord 2014:567, doi:10.6027/TN2014-567, see also 2004 report, Arctic Human Development Report (AHDR) 2004. Arctic Stefansson Institute, Akureyri, Iceland; ArcticStat, 2010 Census for Russian Federation, at http://www.arcticstat.org. Accessed 10 January 2014.

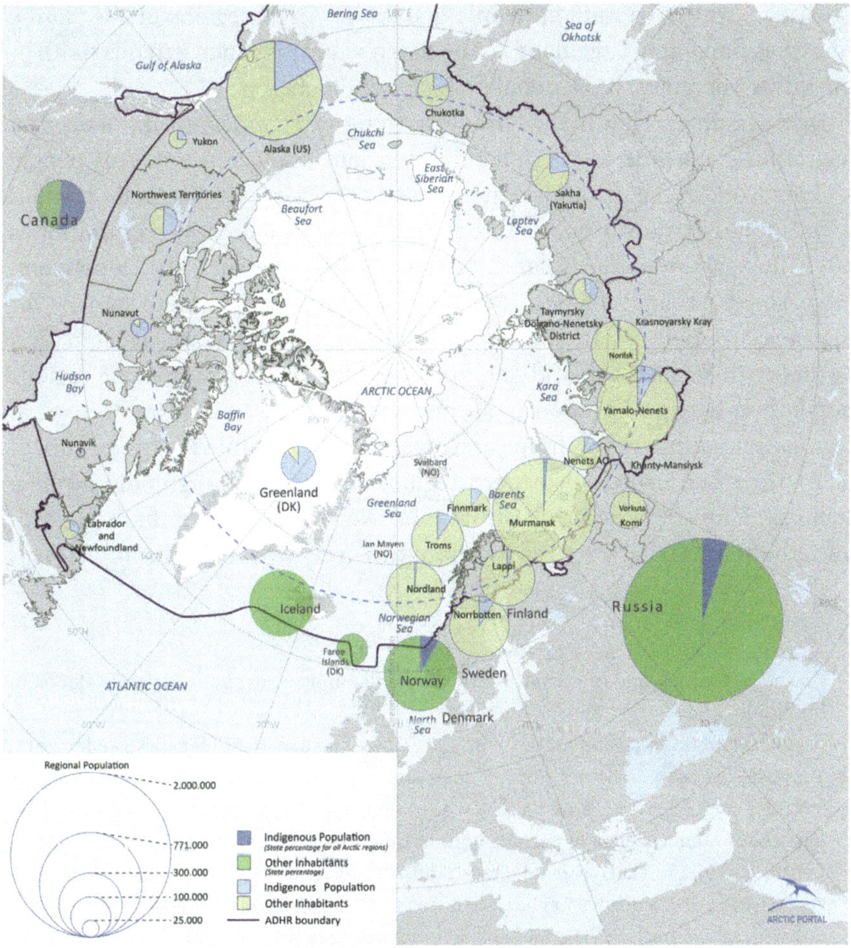


FIGURE 8.2 *Arctic indigenous and non-indigenous population*
SOURCE: ARCTIC PORTAL AND ARCTIC CENTRE, UNIVERSITY OF LAPLAND, 2014, BASED ON STATISTICAL DATA[2]

2 Note: The *Arctic Human Development Report* (AHDR) (2004) estimated that there are four million people living in the Arctic, of whom 10% are indigenous, e.g. Inuit, Sámi and Nenets. 1.3 million people live in the Arctic regions of the Nordic countries (including Greenland). According to the AHDR boundary: the three northernmost counties of Norway, Norrbotten county in Sweden, Lappi (Lapland) in Finland, whole territory of Iceland, the Faroe Islands and Greenland). The Barents region (which extends south of the AHDR boundary) has a population of six million. Arctic areas in Russia, according to AHDR (2004) include: the Murmansk Oblast, the Nenets, Yamalo-Nenets, Taimyr, and Chukotka autonomus okrugs, Vorkuta City in the Komi Republic, Norilsk and Igarka in

(ADHR II, 2015).[3] 1.3 million people live in the Arctic regions of the Nordic countries (including Greenland).[4] The Barents region (which extends south of the AHDR boundary) has a population of six million.

Demographic trends in the European Arctic are significantly influenced by migration – north-to-south and rural-to-urban – and the influx of people seeking work in the resource extraction and services sectors. Arctic populations undergo transformation from traditional small, rural communities often living in remote, isolated conditions into modern, ICT-dependent, increasingly urban societies. The patterns differ across the region – for instance, the population is growing in northern Norway and Iceland, and declining in Finnish Lapland and northwest Russia (where in some regions population decline between 1990s and 2010s reached 20–30%[5]).[6] In most regions net out-migration from rural areas has been coupled with the growth of Arctic urban centres. Northern regions that defy demographic decline, such as Finnish Northern Ostrobotnia, Norwegian Troms and Swedish Västerbotten, are characterized by strong urban centres, high education levels,

---

Krasnoyarsky Kray, and those parts of the Sakha Republic whose boundaries lie closest to the Arctic Circle.

Source: Arctic Portal and Arctic Centre, 2014, based on data from: Statistics Sweden 2011, Tilastokeskus 2013, Statistics Norway 2013 and Sámi Statistics 2014 (Statistics Norway), Statistics Iceland 2012, Faroe Statistics 2013, Statistics Greenland 2013 (for Greenland indigenous number refers to persons born in Greenland), Barents Euro-Arctic Council, US Census 2010, (Russian) Federal State Statistics Service 2013–2014, Census (Russian Federation) 2010, Statistics Canada 2006–2011, US Census Bureau 2010, Statistics Alaska 2012, Arctic Centre, University of Lapland estimates (data based on estimates with discrepancies between available sources). Numbers for Sakha Republic (municipalities on or above the Arctic Circle) based on estimates only. All numbers, although based on statistics, are illustrative, estimate and approximate, often due to difficulty of specifying exact number of indigenous peoples living in the particular region.

3 Heleniak T. (lead), "Arctic Populations and Migration", in Larsen and Fondahl, G. (Eds.) (2014).

4 According to the AHDR boundary: the three northernmost counties of Norway, Norrbotten county in Sweden, Lappi (Lapland) in Finland, whole territory of Iceland, the Faroe Islands and Greenland.

5 Population census from 1989 and 2011 shows population decline in almost all northern regions of Russia – from –18% in Karelia Republic, up to –31% in Murmansk Oblast. The reason is higher mortality level and out-migration primarily from urban areas. The only region with positive population change is Yamal-Nenets Aut. Okrug (6%). See, Heleniak, T. (2013). "Boom and bust: Population change in Russia's Arctic cities". Arctic Urban Sustainability Conference 30–31 May 2013, George Washington University (pp. 1–8).

6 Rasmussen, R. *et al.* (2011). *Megatrends*. Nordic Council of Ministers; AHDR (2004).

and presence of stronger service- and knowledge-based economy, including existence of vibrant research and academic centres or hubs for innovation and new technologies. However, positive developments are often limited to larger urban areas.

Urbanisation is a global trend connected with modernisation. Urban areas offer economic opportunities, education, culture and social networks. In the Arctic, urbanisation has been driven by an increase in regional trade and establishment of administration centres, industrialisation, the expansion of the welfare state, resource extraction or military facilities.[7] Each Arctic region has its own characteristics, partly connected to specific national industrialization and modernization processes. Arctic Russia, with the history of forced labour, development strongly supported by the state and Soviet legacies, is here a good example.[8] The emergence of knowledge-based economy may lead to strengthening the process of urbanisation. At the same time, conditions for viable economic and social activities are becoming limited in thinning-out rural areas.[9] Urbanisation entails a complex set of processes, changes in lifestyle and complex relation between people and places. It is important not only where people live and what they produce, but who they are, how they live in terms of economic well-being, political organisation and the distribution of power, demographic structure (*e.g.* family size), as well as social and family relations. Increased accessibility (transport networks) and development of information and communication technologies constitute key factors. Therefore, many aspects of urbanisation may nowadays occur in the areas previously not considered "urban".[10] Indigenous people living in cities face

7 Rasmussen *et al.* (2012); AHDR (2004); Berman, M. & How, L. (2013). Remoteness, Transportation Infrastructure, and Urban rural Population Movements in the Arctic, in Hansen, K.G. *et al.* (Eds.), *Proceedings from the first international conference on urbanisation of the Arctic* (pp. 109–121), Nordregio, Stockholm; Dubois, A. & Roto, J. (2012). Making the best of Europe's Sparsely Populated Areas. On making geographic specificity a driver for territorial development in Europe. Nordregio Working Paper 2012:15, pp. 18–19.

8 Dubois and Roto 2012, op. cit., pp. 18–19; Nuykina, E. (2011). Resettlement from the Russian North: an analysis of state-induced relocation policy. Arctic Centre Report No. 55. Rovaniemi: University of Lapland.

9 Northern Periphery Programme (NPP) (2013). Programme Area Analysis (for consultation on the Northern Periphery and Arctic Programme 2014–2020), www.northernperiphery.eu. Accessed 10 February 2014. See: e.g. Staalesen, A. (15 January 2014), Hi-Tech regions are Arctic population winners. BarentsObserver,http://barentsobserver.com/en/society/2014/01/hi-tech-regions-are-arctic-population-winners-15-01. Accessed 15 February 2014.

10 Dybbroe, S., Dahl, J. & Müller-Wille, L. (Eds.). (2010). *Acta Borealia* 27(2), Special Issue: History Matter: Dynamics of Arctic Urbanization.

particular challenges, as their connection to traditional livelihoods and access to language education may be limited.[11] Consequently, they often find it difficult to maintain their cultural identity.[12]

Young people, especially women, are increasingly moving to Arctic urban centres and cities in the south, attracted by economic and educational opportunities. This has raised the share of the elderly population in some areas, resulting in gender and age imbalances, and threatening the fabric of social services (*e.g.* workforce shortages and limited resources in the health, education and elderly care sectors).[13]

Historically, in-migration has significantly influenced the Arctic social landscape. People migrating to northern regions are often attracted by employment opportunities in extractive industries or the quality of life connected to landscape/nature values. Moreover, an influx of migrants and urban expansion result in the need for improved services and facilities (housing, utility services, health care, education and transport). The migration from the new EU member states (especially Poland) and countries such as Thailand is increasing.[14]

Arctic gender issues have recently received more attention.[15] Challenges include male-dominated rural areas and low female participation in traditional and resource-based industries. However, women have a comparatively strong position in northern governance structures.[16] Women are more

---

11 In Finland, over 70% of Sámi children live outside of the Sámi Homeland Area in the north of Lapland, where the Sámi enjoy access to Sámi-language schooling.

12 Kishigami, N. (2002). "Inuit identities in Montreal, Canada", *Études/Inuit/Studies,* 26(1), 183–191; Reid, C. (2002). "Aboriginal urban communities in Canada", *Indigenous Affairs* 3–4, 49–53. Pedersen P. and Nyseth T. (2012). "Urban Sámi and the City as a frame for the development of a new Sámi cultural form in Scandinavia", in Hansen, K.G., Rasmussen, R.O., & Weber, R. (Eds.). (2012). First International Conference on Urbanisation in the Arctic. Conference 28–30 August 2012 Ilimmarfik, Nuuk, Greenland: NORDREGIO.

13 Rasmussen *et al.* (2011); AHDR (2004); NPP (2013); Janson, M. (2012). Northern Sparsely Populated Areas. Working Uniquely Together. Presentation at the Committee of Regions, 19 January 2012.

14 Rasmussen *et al.* (2011), *op.cit.*

15 For example, the Arctic Council is currently implementing an action on gender equality in the region, www.arctic-council.org. Accessed 5 February 2014.

16 Women account for 56% of the Swedish County of Västerbotten's Council (compared to 43% in Finnmark and 35% in Finnish Lapland, with Russian regions falling significantly behind). The Sámi Parliament in Norway had 50–50 gender composition after the 2005 elections and companies such as LKAB (a state-owned company operating, *inter alia*, the

interested in obtaining higher education, but the availability of matching jobs in the rural areas is limited, resulting often in migration. Researchers from the Nordic Centre for Spatial Development (Nordregio) believe that areas that manage to attract women will be the "winners of the future".[17] Major problem when discussing gender issues remains lack of gender-disaggregated data specific to the Arctic regions, although some progress in this area has been made in the last years.

### 2.2 *Changing Livelihoods and Lifestyles*

The Arctic economy is characterised by the co-existence and interdependence of a formal and informal economy.[18] The major components of the formal "cash" economy include tourism, fisheries, large-scale mineral and energy development, forestry and reindeer husbandry. The informal economy consists of small-scale subsistence use of forests (*e.g.* berry and mushroom picking), hunting, reindeer herding, fishing and trapping, and is also important for cultural practices and identities (see Picture 8.1). In the European Arctic the relative role of traditional activities as a source of livelihood has been declining over the last century.

Tourism in the Arctic often utilizes traditional activities and local cultural heritage, constituting a crucial supplementary or the main source of income for those engaged in traditional livelihoods. Projected increases in tourism may offer potential economic benefits for local communities. How Arctic communities allow their natural and cultural resources to be used by visitors and how they benefit from tourism depends on local attitudes, management and resources.

Changes in lifestyle bring about a cultural transformation, including alterations in family structure, values and cultural forms of expression. These can lead to positive developments, *e.g.* the increasing role of women in society, and negative ones, *e.g.* barriers to inter-generational knowledge transmission or loss of indigenous languages.[19]

---

Kiruna iron mine) highlight the position of women in traditionally male-dominated extractive industries. See: *e.g.* Staalesen, A. (4 February 2014) "Best on Women and Democracy", Barents Observer at http://barentsobserver.com/en/society/2014/02/best-women-and-democracy-04-02. Accessed 13 February 2014.

17 Dubois and Roto (2012), *op.cit.*

18 ACIA (2005). Arctic Climate Impact Assessment. Cambridge University Press.

19 Aesaether, N. & Baerenholdt, J.O. (Eds.). (1998). *Coping strategies in the North. Local Practices in the Content of Global Restructuring.* Copenhagen: Nordic Council of Ministers.

PICTURE 8.1 *Inuit hunters with snowmobiles*
PHOTO BY PAULA KANKAANPÄÄ, ARCTIC CENTRE, UNIVERSITY OF LAPLAND

Lifestyle changes, combined with climate change, have had an impact on human health and well-being (although Fennoscandia has been less affected than other Arctic regions). Due to changes in climate, flora and fauna, humans in the North could be exposed to new micro-organisms, causing vector-borne infections. Contaminants such as pollen, persistent organic pollutants or mercury are also a threat to health. Dietary changes have increased obesity rates, Type 2 diabetes and cardiovascular diseases.[20] Many Arctic communities are also afflicted with domestic violence, substance abuse and high suicide rates.

### 2.3 *Ongoing Dependence on the Primary Sector and Public Transfers*[21]

Substantial hydrocarbon and mineral resource developments in the Arctic region are important contributors to national economies, especially in Russia and Fennoscandia. In addition, fisheries and forestry remain vital industries.

20 Parkinson, A.J. & Evengård, B. (2009). Climate change, its impact on human health in the Arctic and the public health response to threats of emerging infectious diseases. *Global Health Action* 2, doi: 10.3402/gha.v2i0.2075.

21 Rasmussen *et al.* (2011), *op.cit.*

Exploitation of natural resources accounted for about 31% of (whole) Arctic GDP in 2003[22] (higher levels in some Russian and North American areas, as well as in Greenland and Faroe Islands due to importance of fisheries) and 5 to 10% of the work force in the European Arctic. Hydrocarbon and mineral resource developments make Arctic regions important contributors to national economies, especially in Russia and Fennoscandia.[23] Primary industries and resource extraction strongly link Arctic regions to the global economy and provide resources for social development, but they also expose these regions to market and price fluctuations.[24] Single-industry communities are particularly vulnerable to boom-and-bust cycles. The recent closure of a mine in Pajala, Sweden or concerns over future of coal mining around Longyearbyen in Svalbard are among the latest examples. Moreover, primary industries tend to often create islands of economic activity, rather than serving as engines of development for entire regions.

The public sector and transfers include government employment, welfare payments, pensions, as well as development policies and infrastructure maintenance. The public sector is responsible for 20–50% of economic activity in most Arctic regions, and dominates the expanding service sector (*e.g.* education, health care and administration). The share of public sector employment in the European Arctic (30–55%) is higher than the average for developed states (5–28%) (Figure 8.3). The manufacturing sector is in general unrepresented compared to the EU average.[25]

As regional authorities in the European Arctic attempt to reduce dependence on government transfers, there is greater interest in developing natural resources. Simultaneously, governments are increasing support for activities that offer alternatives to resource-based economies, such as tourism, creative industries, research and innovation or aquaculture.

### 2.4 *Rising Role of Education and Research*

The education level in the European Arctic is generally high (although comparatively lower in Greenland) and lays a solid foundation for enhancing Arctic human capital and empowering Arctic communities. On the other hand, centralised educational systems have often had adverse implications for

22 New figures are not available but for the whole Arctic region the general share of the primary industries has not changed significantly during the past decade.

23 Rasmussen et al. (2011), *op.cit.*; Glomsrød and Aslaksen (2008), *op.cit.*

24 Dubois and Roto (2012), *op.cit.*; NPP (2013), *op.cit.*

25 NPP (2013), Programme Area Analysis, *op.cit.*

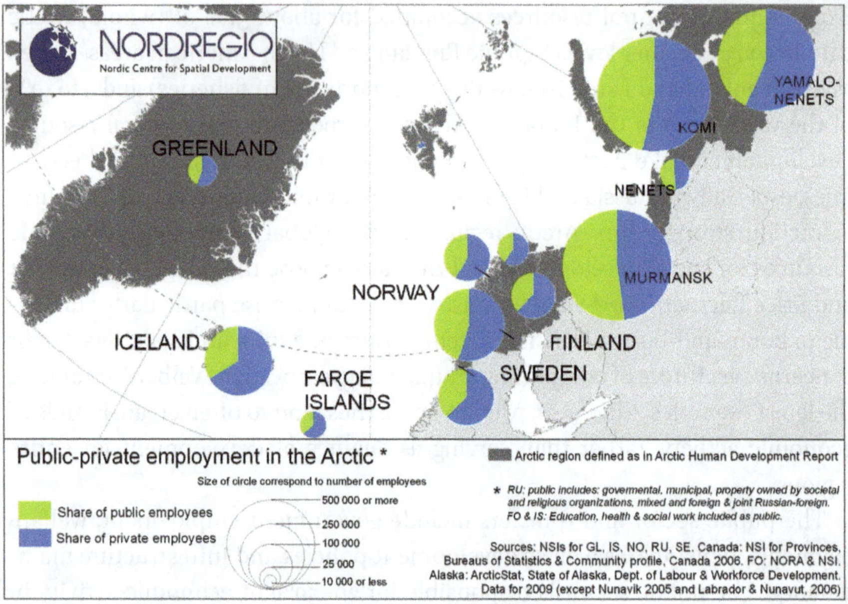


FIGURE 8.3 *Public and private employment in the European Arctic, 2010*
SOURCE: JOHANNA ROTO, NORDREGIO, 2010, MODIFIED

indigenous cultures. Education and research also create jobs and bring resources into communities. International co-operation constitutes an important element of Arctic research, based on organisations such as the International Arctic Science Committee and the University of the Arctic.

Human capital is critical for economic and social development in the Arctic. Although human capital in the Arctic is seen as underdeveloped, this overlooks the diversity of creativity among Arctic residents, based on informal and traditional knowledge.[26] Education allows people to both benefit from and develop alternatives to primary industries. At the same time, high levels of education may stimulate greater out-migration from rural areas. Importantly, women dominate the realm of education in most of the Arctic.

## 2.5 *Increasing Inclusiveness and Complexity of Governance*

Governance has a crucial role in boosting resilience and adaptive capacity to changes in the Arctic. Globalisation and increasing international attention to climate change are transforming the way the Arctic is governed. Faster and

26 Rasmussen *et al.* (2011), *op.cit.*

more extensive networks of communication make for greater awareness and engagement at all levels.

The sharing of power and responsibilities between national governments and regional/municipal authorities has become increasingly complex. Because of demographic changes, the balance between the need for democratic representation at regional/local level and the capacity to provide basic services is not satisfactory. As a result, local authorities depend more heavily on national government support and municipalities and regions are merged into bigger administrative units (as in Greenland, Finland and Russia).

Various intergovernmental and regional forms of co-operation between Arctic nations and other stakeholders (especially indigenous organisations) have emerged over the last 20 years, such as the Arctic Council, the Barents Euro-Arctic Council (with the associated council grouping regional authorities) and the Northern Forum (cooperation between northern regions).

Non-state actors have become increasingly active in advocating interests and values of various groups, including environmental organisations and industry associations. The role of indigenous peoples has changed throughout the Arctic, due to reasons such as the establishment of Sámi Parliaments in Fennoscandia and self-government in Greenland, coinciding with the evolution and adoption of international norms. In Russia, the indigenous influence on decision-making is comparatively less visible. Most legal systems currently include safeguards for indigenous land rights, with the degree of protection for these rights differing between jurisdictions.

## 3 What Is Driving Social and Cultural Changes in the European Arctic?

Putting a finger on what is pushing social and cultural shifts is not an exact science. Nevertheless, here we touch on four drivers that are influencing transformation: globalization and resource demand, accessibility, global cultural change and the recognition of indigenous rights.

### 3.1 *Globalisation and Demand for Natural Resources*

Global economic shifts shape social and cultural development around the world and the Arctic is no exception, especially in light of the privatisation and commercialisation of Arctic industries.[27] Robust economic growth in

27 UN Industrial Development Organization (UNIDO) (2010). *Structural Change in Global Economy: Main Features and Trends*. UNIDO website at www.unido.org/. Accessed 4 July 2013; AHDR (2004).

emerging economies shapes demand for Arctic natural resources and influences Arctic migration, urbanisation, politics, governance and global connections. Globalisation results in competition between regions for companies, skilled workers, tourists and public investments (also within the EU context).[28] Resource exploitation and resistance to certain large-scale developments have been key factors in the emergence of indigenous activism and indigenous rights.

### 3.2 *Accessibility*

The Nordic northern peripheries are among the least accessible regions in Europe (measured by ground accessibility) (see also Textbox 8.1). Insularity, one-directional linkages, proportionally high dependence on air and maritime transport, the dominance of north–south connections and high costs are features of all modes of Arctic transport. Initiatives to facilitate Arctic-Arctic (east–west) transport connections have so far had limited success.[29]

In remote regions, communication technologies provide crucial opportunities for people and services, including education, entertainment, health, administration, as well as social and political life or identity building. While coverage and digital competence appear to be strong in the European Arctic, the costs, quality and capacity of the networks may pose significant limitations in locations such as Greenland.

For northern companies, ICT allows access to global niche markets, although conversely information technologies may primarily promote the greater integration of local markets.[30] Intra-regional connections are crucial, in terms of both infrastructure and spaces for co-operation, as actors functioning in the same economic, social and physical environment are better positioned to build networks necessary for the emergence of a knowledge-based economy.

Although improved transport and ICT infrastructure is hoped to encourage people to remain in rural areas, better accessibility coupled with higher levels of education often facilitates migration to urban areas.[31]

---

28 Dubois and Roto (2012), *op.cit.*

29 See: *e.g.* NPP 2013, Programme Area Analysis; Gløersen, E., Dubois, A., Copus., A. & Schürmann, C. (2005). *Northern peripheral, sparsely populated regions in the European Union.* Report. Nordregio; Dubois and Roto (2012), *op.cit.*, pp. 65–66.

30 Dubois and Roto (2012), *op.cit.*, pp. 65–66.

31 Rasmussen *et al.* (2011), *op.cit.*

TEXTBOX 8.1 *Remote and peripheral – northern sparsely populated areas*[32]

The northern peripheries of Nordic states have been recognised within the EU's cohesion policy as "regions which suffer from severe and permanent natural or demographic handicaps such as the northernmost regions with very low population density" (Treaty of the Functioning of the European Union, TFEU, Art. 174). Peripherality should be understood as a political, socioeconomic and cultural construct (*e.g.* meaning remote, rural, fragile or less-favoured), rather than only a demographic or geographic one. Limited access to advantages inherent to agglomerations has implications for social interactions, the availability of public services and economic activity (including the small size of the local economy, limited local demand, high transaction, transport and logistics costs, lack of specialised services, the dominance of traditional industries and dependence on extractive industries). Importantly, peripherality is dynamic, changing due to economic shifts or infrastructural investments (or the degradation of existing infrastructure).[33]

### 3.3 *Global Cultural Change (Cultural Globalization)*

Arctic social and cultural changes reflect global, particularly western, cultural trends. At a general level, these include: declining respect for authority; increasing emphasis on freedom of expression and equality of opportunities; growing social and political tolerance; emancipative orientation towards the role of women; wider political protests; and an increasing emphasis on democratic principles combined with dissatisfaction with the democratic process.[34] These trends are coupled with the spread of popular culture, information technology, virtual networks and the culture of innovation. In the increasingly globalised world, notwithstanding developments within the region, Arctic societies will undergo a transformation that mirrors these global cultural developments.

32 See: Gløersen *et al.* (2005), *op.cit.*

33 Dubois and Roto (2012), *op.cit.*; Copus, A. (2001). From core-periphery to polycentric development: concepts of spatial and aspatial peripherality, *European Planning Studies* 9, 4, 539–552, p. 540.

34 Dalton, R. & Welzel, C. (2011). "Mapping and Tracking Global Cultural Change", www.democracy.uci.edu/node/6151. Accessed 20 June 2013.

PICTURE 8.2 *Sámi Parliament in Norway in session, Karasjok*
PHOTO BY DENIS CAVIGLIA, 2013

### 3.4 *Indigenous Activism and Recognition of Indigenous Rights*

Over the last four decades, indigenous peoples have become more active in international forums, with a focus on human rights. Their key demands include self-determination, land rights, cultural development, and participation in decision-making. The International Labour Organization (ILO) Convention No. 169 concerning Indigenous and Tribal Peoples (1989),[35] the UN Declaration of the Rights of Indigenous Peoples (2007) and the establishment of the UN Permanent Forum for Indigenous Issues are the main achievements of the global movement. The influence of international indigenous law in the European Arctic varies: from major significance in Norway (see Picture 8.2) and Denmark/Greenland, moderate acknowledgment in Finland and Sweden (land rights issue being the most problematic) and a fairly complex situation in Russia.

35 International Labour Organization (ILO) Convention no 169 concerning Indigenous and Tribal Peoples in Independent Countries (Geneva, 76th ILC session (27 June 1989); Entry into force: 5 September 1991).

## 4 Outlook to 2030

The Arctic regions will very likely remain highly dependent on resource extraction as well as public transfers from national budgets over the next twenty years. This socioeconomic dependence will continue to drive public policy and priorities as well as social attitudes. Communities and authorities will continue to attempt to attract more extractive industries and at the same time diversify local economies, primarily towards tourism, services, and the elements of knowledge-based economy. The recent economic crisis (2008 onwards) has increased pressure on the public sector, and this is experienced more strongly in remote areas due to their financial and employment dependence on national budgets. Consequently, key uncertainties for the future include volatile resource prices and regional development policies implemented by Arctic states.

Economic and social life will likely increasingly concentrate in major urban centres, resulting in the increasing importance of Arctic cities.[36] Current demographic challenges may be expected to remain a problem throughout the region (including implications for governance and service delivery) with population growth in major towns and resource extraction areas and decline/thinning-out in rural areas. The rising importance of Arctic cities and the developments in industrial primary sector will likely create pockets of positive demographic and socio-economic trends.

The continued presence and expansion of academic and research institutions in the North (assuming sustained ongoing political focus on the Arctic issues in the decades to come) will contribute to economic and social diversification. Nevertheless, the development of a knowledge-based economy will be limited to the major Arctic urban centres. Indigenous rights are likely to gain increasing attention, but land rights will probably remain a challenging issue throughout Northern Fennoscandia.

## 5 How Does the EU Influence Social and Cultural Changes in the Arctic?

The role of the European Union in shaping the direction of sociocultural changes in the region is limited, with the greatest influence in EU Arctic regions

36 Gløersen *et al.* (2005), *op.cit.*

and through various cohesion and regional co-operation instruments. However, as all economic activities have a social dimension, a broad range of EU policies, *e.g.* environmental legislation, may contribute to changes in the sociocultural landscape. Policies designed for the development of the entire EU may not always be effective in the peripheral Arctic context.[37] In many policies, that has been acknowledged; for example, the EU/EEA State Aid Guidelines allow for additional support for regions with special characteristics.[38]

### 5.1 *EU Funding for Regional Co-operation and Cohesion*

The European Commission estimated that EUR 1.14 bn has been dedicated to regional development in the EU and neighbouring Arctic regions in 2007–2013.[39] A number of EU programmes cover the European Arctic: cohesion funding in North Finland and Sweden, Bothnia-Atlantica, InterregIVA/North, Kolarctic ENPI (European Neighbourhood and Partnership Instrument) and the Northern Periphery Programme (NPP) 2007–2013.

The NPP – part of a territorial co-operation objective within EU's cohesion policy – is a good example of the EU engagement together with its post-2013 continuation, the Northern Periphery and Arctic Programme (NPA). The NPP aimed at developing the economic, social and environmental potential of peripheral and remote communities by promoting innovation and competitiveness as well as the sustainable development of natural and community resources. Stakeholders have had a generally positive view of the NPP. The programme has had a visible impact in developing innovative solutions in public service provision (including ICT and self-organisation), creative industries and aquaculture. However, the major shortcoming of the NPP was the lack of involvement of the private sector (due to state aid constraints).

The current financial perspective does not significantly increase the funding for northern development but programmes' priorities have undergone evolution in line with general transition in the EU funding frameworks. The design of programmes within the new 2014–2020 financial perspective is finalized or in the final stages. That includes the new Northern Periphery and Arctic Programme (NPA) (Figure 8.4), which has been approved by the European Commission in December 2014 and the first main call within the programme

37 Dubois and Roto (2012), *op.cit.*, p. 11.

38 Guidelines on national regional aid for 2007–2013. Official Journal C 54 of 4.3.2006.

39 EU (2012). *Developing a European Union Policy towards the Arctic Region: progress since 2008 and next steps*, JOIN (2012) 19 final.

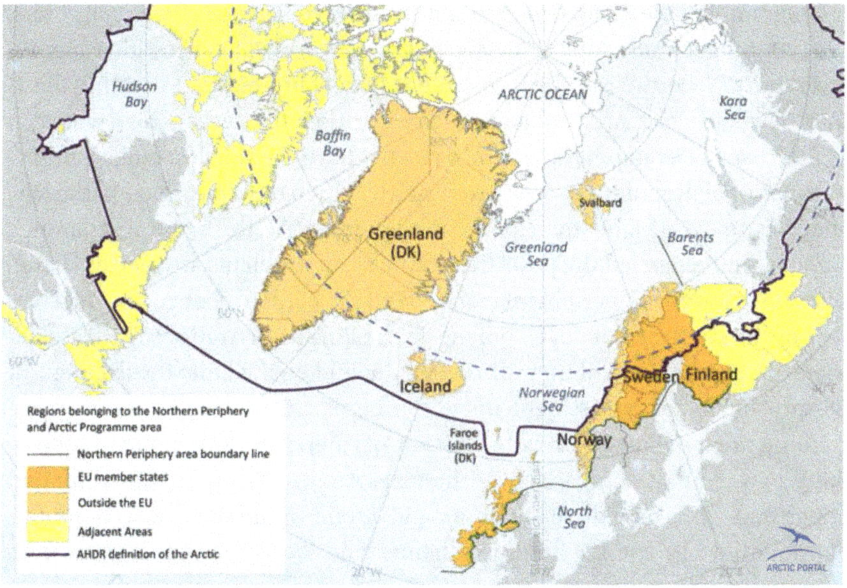


FIGURE 8.4 *EU Northern Periphery and Arctic Programme 2014–2020 area*
SOURCE: ARCTIC PORTAL, BASED ON NORTHERN PERIPHERY PROGRAMME AND NORDREGIO, 2013

has been opened.[40] The new programme builds on key priorities of the NPP, focusing on small and medium-sized enterprises, innovation, and sustainable resource and energy developments.[41] There is a concern that the new structure of cohesion funding has limited the choice of priorities within the NPA and will lead to support for fewer themes, in ways that do not always fit the specific needs in the region.

40 Northern Periphery and Arctic Programme (2015), Second Call Announcement, programme's website, http://www.northernperiphery.eu/files/archive/Downloads//Programming_process_2014-2020/Second_Call/Second_Call_Announcement.pdf. Accessed 26 January 2015. The NPA operates under the European Regional Development Fund.

41 Currently, four priorities have been identified: innovation to maintain and develop robust and competitive communities, promoting entrepreneurship to realise the area's competitive advantage, fostering energy-secure communities through promotion of renewable energy and energy efficiency, protecting, promoting and developing cultural and natural heritage, with a focus on transfer of knowledge and technology, sustainable use of resources and demographic development (NPA programme overview 2014).

Programme objectives, owing to the strong involvement of regional actors, correspond generally to the key social and cultural challenges identified in this report. Nevertheless, the NPA's role is largely limited to promoting desirable developments and enhancing co-operation between actors who can facilitate such developments, as the NPP/NPA have the smallest budget among transnational programmes (approximately EUR 100 million, although the NPA budget is 20–30% higher than for the NPP). Adding "Arctic" to the programme's name has not changed the priorities, as the main problems are seen as shared with other European peripheral regions, and the climate change not currently seen as the key driver of developments in the European Arctic.[42] The key challenges in the implementation of the NPA will likely include: involvement of the private sector; assessment of results based on the impact on the programme area; co-operation with Russian partners; and the limited scope of the programme in comparison to the NPP. A more substantial involvement of partners from outside of the European Arctic would have been desirable, but is limited by the EU funding schemes and lack of strong interest from other partners.

The priorities of cohesion programmes covering northern Sweden and Finland are also generally in line with the challenges identified in this chapter.[43] The notion of "smart specialisation" in the post-2013 cohesion framework is generally commendable, but decision-makers must ensure that this does not mean that Arctic regions are in practice limited to the role of a European resource base. Following this new EU framework, for example Finnish Lapland has adopted "Lapland's Arctic Specialisation Programme", incorporating the increased interest in the Arctic into identification of region's strong sides.[44]

42 Based on programming documents. Northern Periphery Programme, www.northernperiphery.eu. Accessed 14 February 2014.

43 Sparsely populated areas receive an extra allocation within the cohesion policy. Although it has been decreased (from EUR 35 to 30 per inhabitant, constituting, for instance, 38% of cohesion funding assigned for east and north Finland, thus representing a fairly significant component of the programmes' budget), the overall funding in northern Sweden is similar to that in previous funding periods and 13% lower for east and north Finland (but only 2% lower for Lapland). Although there is currently one operational programme for mainland Finland, a separate implementation plan for east and north Finland has been drawn up (Personal communication with the Brussels offices of north Sweden and east and north Finland and with regional authorities.)

44 Regional Council of Lapland (2013), Lapland's Arctic Specialisation Programme, Summary, http://www.lappi.fi/lapinliitto/c/document_library/get_file?folderId=1483089&name=DLFE-21423.pdf. Accessed 25 January 2015.

Overall, projects within the EU-funded programmes[45] have promoted and encouraged the diversification of the northern economy through supporting youth entrepreneurship, creative industries and media, combining traditional livelihoods and business, including assistance for Sámi entrepreneurs, and developing tourism. Similarly, various projects address Arctic demographic challenges: promoting local development; strengthening urban and rural services; as well as promoting cultural heritage and projects dedicated to social well-being, including elderly and physically challenged persons. Such projects are limited in scope and resources, but they have important inspirational leverage, *e.g.* by promoting the exchange of experience.

Owing to the crucial role that local and regional actors play in deciding on the priorities of the cohesion and co-operation programmes, the objectives of the EU funding schemes are in line with the key needs and they respond to the main challenges in the region. The gradual evolution of EU's funding frameworks towards increased focus on innovation, research and development could in principle be beneficial for the European Arctic regions, as they belong to the richer regions of the EU. That is especially true for regional centres of innovation, but the relevance of these developments may be limited to main towns in northern Fennoscandia. Moreover, there is also a risk that emphasis in the future EU programmes on the main Europe's economic engines may pull away funding towards major centres in the south. In the coming years much effort on the side of northern regions is likely to be devoted to avoid the realization of such a scenario in the post-2020 EU funding schemes.

A shortcoming of the EU funding structure is the lack of co-operation between programmes, the cohesion framework and EU policies covering sectors such as transport, agriculture or fisheries. The so-called "Bodø Process" (initiated by Norway), which brings together programmes and funding frameworks in the European Arctic (including Barents co-operation, the Nordic Council of Ministers and EU programmes), is a step in the right direction.

A major challenge connected with the programmes implemented in the region is co-operation with Russian partners. This co-operation is affected by the overall – currently tense – political situation as well as internal regulatory frameworks in Russia regarding, for example, the operation of non-governmental

45 A compilation of the relevant projects and actions can be found in Dahlbäck B., van der Watt, L.-M., Jagodziński, K., & Kankaanpää, P. (2014). European Arctic Initiatives Compendium. Preparatory Action, Strategic Environmental Impact Assessment of development of the Arctic. Arctic Centre, University of Lapland, http://www.arcticinfo.eu/images/pdf/Compendium.pdf. Accessed 26 January 2015.

organisations. There is a concern among local stakeholders[46] that funding for programmes such as Kolarctic ENPI (EPI in 2014–2020 financial perspective) would be limited in the future.

### 5.2 *Accessibility*

The long-standing criticism that Trans-European Transport Networks neglect the special needs of remote regions to a certain extent can be upheld for the upcoming financial perspective.[47] Until 2020, major support (80 to 85% of transport networks expenditure) will be dedicated to the core network linking key EU centres, which in Northern Fennoscandia includes only the "Bothnian corridor" and the link to Narvik in Norway.[48] A broader "comprehensive network" is to allow all regions to access the core transport nodes. However, the social and economic development of peripheral regions depends greatly on intra-regional connectivity and the emergence of local clusters capable of generating critical mass, not only on core-periphery connections.[49]

Various projects within EU-funded cohesion and regional co-operation programmes are directed towards developing transport connections and mitigating the adverse effects of remoteness (through concrete investments, transport subsidies for ports in the Gulf of Bothnia, feasibility studies and innovations). The impact of these projects is difficult to assess as the key challenges – deficit in east–west connections, high costs of transport and the disadvantaged position of certain localities – have remained largely unchanged over the last decade, or have even become more pronounced due to the thinning-out of the rural areas. Enhancing ICT services in remote communities, including e-medicine and e-learning, appears to have more tangible impacts.

Stakeholders from the private sector and local administration have underlined that various EU actions directed at lowering GHG emissions and air pollution, although commendable at the European level, may have a proportionally higher impact on transport costs in the northern periphery than in the lower latitudes. One example is the directive limiting the sulphur content in marine

---

46 Input from the EU office of East and North Finland. Personal communication, 24 March 2014.

47 See, *e.g.* Spiekermanfl, K. & Wegener, M. (1996). Trans-European networks and unequal accessibility in Europe. *European Journal of Regional Development* (EUREG), 35(4), 4196; Dubois and Roto (2012), *op.cit.*, p. 64.

48 Railway connections encircling the Gulf of Bothnia.

49 Dubois and Roto (2012), *op.cit.*

fuels (discussed in the chapter by Latola *et al.*),[50] as some companies are reconsidering their investment plans due to the expectations of higher transport costs in the Baltic Sea.[51] Another example is the possibility of future stricter standards for heavy-duty vehicles (trucks and buses, which constitute the basis for cargo and passenger transport in remote areas), as the European Commission is currently developing a strategy to reduce $CO_2$ emissions from such vehicles (constituting 6% of total EU emissions).[52]

### 5.3 *Research, Education and Cross-border Co-operation*

EU programmes for student and teacher exchanges and professional training have become an important element of the educational framework in the region. The EU's Seventh Framework Programme (2007–2013) funded Arctic research at about EUR 20 million a year,[53] and Horizon 2020 is expected to have even greater and more focused expenditure on Arctic research. Stakeholders clearly see Arctic research as an area where the EU's role is most visible, although they note that there is a deficit in funding for Arctic social sciences.

The EU-Greenland Agreement supports education, vocational training and the development of human resources. Progress in these areas since 2007 has been recorded.[54] As still only 11% of the population in Greenland has a university degree and many educated Greenlanders live outside of the island, primarily in Denmark, the ongoing focus on education and training, in line with the priorities of the Greenlandic government, is vital.[55] In 2007–2013, Greenland received EUR 175 million, which will rise to over EUR 217 million in 2014–2020.

50 Directive 2012/33/EU of 21 November 2012 amending Council Directive 1999/32/EC as regards the sulphur content of marine fuels.

51 There are estimates that peg the decrease in sea transport at 10–21%, mirrored by an increase of 5–11% in rail transport and 5–6% in road transport. (Personal communication, Mid Sweden EU Office [Jämtland and Västernorrland counties], 10 March 2014).

52 The European Commission is currently developing a strategy to reduce $CO_2$ emissions from such vehicles. See: "Road transport: Reducing $CO_2$ emissions from vehicles", http://ec.europa.eu/clima/policies/transport/vehicles/index_en.htm. Accessed 10 January 2014.

53 European Union (2012). Developing a European Union Policy towards the Arctic Region: progress since 2008 and next steps. Joint Communication of the European Commission and the High Representative of the European Union for Foreign Affairs and Security Policy to the European Parliament and the Council. Brussels, 26.6.2012. JOIN(2012) 19 final.

54 Mid-term Review of the EU/Greenland Partnership 2007–2013 (2006/526/EC), 8 May 2012, http://ec.europa.eu/europeaid/where/octs_and_greenland/documents/mtr_grl-eu_partnership_2007-2013_en.pdf. Accessed 20 February 2014.

55 Particip (September 2013). Report: Study to evaluate the performance of higher education in Greenland. European Commission. http://naalakkersuisut.gl/. Accessed 10 February 2014.

In addition, Greenland may participate in other programmes funded from the EU budget, including research, education or innovation (*e.g.* within NPP/NPA programmes) as well as receives financial contributions (around EUR 18 million for 2013–2015) within the Fisheries Partnership Agreement.

Support for international co-operation in the Arctic is one of the EU's Arctic policy objectives. EU funding for cross-border co-operation includes research platforms, co-operation between companies, NGOs (Arctic NGO Forum), joint public services and development of information channels.

### 5.4 *Traditional Livelihoods and Indigenous Peoples*

Exclusive Sámi rights to traditional livelihoods, primarily reindeer husbandry, are safeguarded in a Protocol to Finland's and Sweden's Accession Treaty (Protocol 3).[56] Also various EU environmental regulations are of relevance for indigenous livelihoods (see chapter by Latola *et al.* in this volume).

EU-funded programmes acknowledge the dynamic nature of indigenous culture and many projects aim to develop creative industries and facilitate cultural co-operation, events and network-building, rather than focusing on the protection of heritage. The 2007–2013 sub-programme InterregIVA/North/Sápmi focused on developing Sámi languages and language resources.[57] The existence of a separate "Sápmi" sub-programme was seen as a positive development. Its creation allowed many Sámi actors to conduct activities vital for cultural development and contributed to strengthening Sámi cross-border co-operation. There are concerns that Sámi objectives would be lost among other programme activities after 2014, as the Interreg programme for 2014–2020 does not include a separate "Sápmi" sub-programme but rather specifies Sápmi as a second (next to "Nord") programme area. Sámi-specific objectives are visible throughout the new programme activities, but whether indigenous projects receive as much support as in the previous financial perspective depends on particular calls and project proposals.[58]

56 The protocol provides Finland and Sweden with the right to grant the Sámi people exclusive right to reindeer husbandry (as well as to other rights). To this day Finland has not exercised this right regarding reindeer husbandry.

57 InterregIVA/North, http://www.interregnord.com/en/about-the-programme/goals-and-strategies.aspx. Accessed 15 February 2014.

58 Draft document on Interreg North 2014–2020 (in Finnish). InterregIVA/North, http://www.interregnord.com/media/64197/program%204%200%20-%20fin.pdf. Accessed 10 February 2014.

In a pan-Arctic context, EU policy statements support enhancing EU-indigenous dialogue in the Arctic. There are, however, problematic issues, as the Inuit in Greenland and Canada are concerned about the EU ban on placing seal products on the EU market.[59] Despite an exemption granted to indigenous peoples, the Inuit claim that – due to the collapse in the global market for seal products following the ban – their traditional practices and culture have been adversely affected.[60] Beyond the European Arctic, commercial (or non-indigenous) seal hunters in Canada argue that the ban has been designed with the goal of extinguishing their sealing traditions dating back hundreds of years.[61] In addition, the EU position regarding the aboriginal quota within the International Whaling Commission is of relevance to Greenlandic whaling.[62]

Largely in connection with the overspill of the seal ban, the European Commission engaged in a more structured interaction with indigenous peoples. Three meetings in the format of "Arctic Dialogue" were organized (in 2010, 2013 and 2014 in Brussels, and in addition, a side-event during a conference in Tromsø in January 2011). During the 2011 meeting, a number of possible ways to make the contacts between the EU and Arctic indigenous peoples more effective were proposed, including the possibility of creating an indigenous office in Brussels. The downside of the meetings was that the participation of the indigenous representatives was rather incidental and lacking continuity. The meetings were focused more on the format of dialogue than specific EU policies and consisted to a great extent of the presentation of various EU projects relevant for Arctic indigenous peoples. These discrepancies are currently being addressed, reflecting the general learning process within the EU. The 2013 meeting was opened by Commissioner Damanaki, which could be seen as a

59 Regulation (EC) No 1007/2009 of 16 September 2009 on trade in seal products, Official Journal 31 October 2009.

60 Cambou, D. (2013). The Impact of the Ban on Seal Products on the Rights of Indigenous Peoples: A European Issue, *Yearbook of Polar Law* 5, 389–415. Hossain, K. (2012). The EU ban on the import of seal products and the WTO regulations: neglected human rights of the Arctic indigenous peoples? *Polar Record,* 49(2), 154–166; European Bureau for Conservation and Development (2012). The Impact of the EU Seal Ban on the Inuit Population in Greenland. Report from a seminar in the European Parliament. 7 February 2013. Brussels.

61 Sellheim, N. (2013). The Neglected Tradition? – The Genesis of the EU Seal Products Trade Ban and Commercial Sealing, *Yearbook of Polar Law* 5, 417–450.

62 Koivurova, T., Kokko, K., Duyck, S., Sellheim, N., & Stepien, A. (2012). The present and future competence of the European Union in the Arctic. *Polar Record* 48 (4), 361–371.

symbolic gesture towards indigenous representatives. The event was also fairly well followed-up, which constituted a clear shortcoming of earlier meetings. With the October 2014 meeting, the Arctic Dialogue format is becoming regular and more focused. As there is greater continuity in indigenous participation, it becomes possible to have a more in-depth discussion especially on the issues critical for the Sámi, for example mining developments in Fennoscandia where the EU is one of the regulators.[63] The EU representatives also try to involve the Sámi on a more systematic basis, including discussions on establishing the Sámi presence in Brussels.[64]

## 6 Critical Factors for EU Decision-making

The landscape of Arctic social and cultural change is diverse, and even if we focus on the European part of the Circumpolar North, there are major differences between particular regions. Therefore, considering socio-cultural dimensions in policy-making poses a major challenge. Basing on the SADA workshops and online consultations, four critical factors for decision-making – or rather clusters of these factors – have been identified. These factors are issues of importance but also uncertainty – they constitute the likely key socio-cultural challenges for the coming decades and at the same time issues that may be easily overlooked in the larger, general policy-making processes. Consequently, these are the areas which need to be taken into account when decisions that have bearing on socio-cultural development of European Arctic regions are taken, especially if such decisions are made for much broader constituency, whether at the national or the European level.

### 6.1 *Intra-regional and Core-periphery Accessibility and Connectivity*

Actions facilitating or jeopardising accessibility and connectivity should be carefully considered, as their consequences may be far-reaching. Physical accessibility, including transport networks and ICT-based connectivity, is of

63 Personal communication with the European Commission staff (September 2014) and indigenous leaders (Sámi Council) (Brussels, 14 October 2014).

64 European Commission, "Summary of 'Arctic Dialogue' Workshop – 9 March 2010 – Brussels" MARE.C1/EH/ZB/2010; Personal communication with the European Commission DG Mare officer, Brussels, May 2013; Observations from Arctic Dialogue meeting in October 2013, Brussels; Personal communication with a Sámi and Inuit leaders attending the October 2013 meeting, October–December 2013.

major importance in sparsely populated remote regions. Accessibility and connectivity expand the scope of opportunities and options for employment, social and cultural life and are vital for knowledge- and innovation-based economic development and contemporary lifestyles. Traditionally, the development of peripheries has been seen as dependent on connectivity with the main economic, social and political centres. However, intra-regional connectivity is equally important as it leads to inter-regional synergies and the critical mass needed for innovation, dynamism and competition within the global market and which is vital for regional cultural development.[65]

### 6.2 *Power Structures, Social Conflicts and Cultural Diversity*

Despite being sparsely populated, the European Arctic is characterised by power structures within and between communities including urban–rural interactions and relations with the national and global political and economic centres. Many important decisions are taken at the global or national level, where the peripheral regions have little influence on decisions.[66] Various social conflicts are not uncommon and their mitigation and resolution often constitutes a major challenge. Tensions between economic, social and environmental interests may occur, especially in light of new resource developments. The rich cultural diversity of the European Arctic regions needs to be taken into account as a part of the social landscape of the region, as an element of the power networks and as background for social conflicts. Policymakers need to understand these power-conflict-culture frameworks when considering actions affecting the region (e.g. in the realm of environmental conservation, resource extraction or transport infrastructure), in order to not add to existing or create new social conflicts and avoid endangering cultural diversity of the region.

### 6.3 *Human-nature Interactions*

Each society and its natural environment are interconnected on a number of levels. This is particularly important for northern, including indigenous, communities, whose livelihoods, economy, culture, identity and leisure-time activities depend directly on the natural environment. The understanding of resilience – a popular concept in current discussion on the future of Arctic regions – is based specifically on the analysis of social-environmental

65 See also Dubois and Roto (2012), *op.cit.*

66 NPP (2013), *op.cit.*, p. 5.

interactions. Nature or "wilderness" is often seen as a resource by the tourist industry and is part of the image of the Arctic.

### 6.4 *Innovation, Entrepreneurship and Education*

The level of innovation and entrepreneurship within Northern communities as well as the level of education provide an important frame of reference for policy-making. This should be taken into account when making decisions concerning extractive industries or programmes aimed at supporting local development. Education, research, entrepreneurship and innovation are closely linked, forming a basis for a knowledge-based economy and driving bottom-up development. Arctic local knowledge and non-technological innovativeness are important elements of this framework. More diverse regional economies are "more conducive to the creation of innovation" and inter-sectoral dynamics may foster innovation spillovers from one sector to the other.[67] Although Nordic states are characterized by high degree of entrepreneurship and innovation, in peripheral, rural regions the levels are usually lower than the national average.

## 7 Conclusion: The Way Forward for the EU

The presented picture of social-cultural changes in European Arctic regions is necessarily diverse and complex. Social development in the region is characterised by generally growing, often highly innovative Arctic cities and thinning-out rural areas that face demographic and resource challenges. At the same time, regional economies and societies are strongly dependent on extractive/primary industries and support from national budgets. Accessibility and connectivity, especially intra-regional and cross-border, are among the key concerns. Indigenous peoples experience the challenges faced by all Arctic inhabitants in a distinct manner. Therefore, these challenges should be addressed in the light of indigenous peoples' rights.

The EU has a number of programmes that support socioeconomic development and co-operation in the North, as well as relevant transport policies and environmental regulations. Various EU programmes in the North are well-aligned with the needs identified by regional actors, primarily because decision-making takes place at the local/regional level. When designing and

67 Dubois and Roto (2012), *op.cit.*, p. 50; Simmie and Martin (2010), *op.cit.*, p. 30; Lundmark (2006), *op.cit.*, p. 10.

carrying out relevant policies, the EU decision-makers should take into account: the region's intra-regional and core-periphery connectivity; power structures, social conflicts and cultural diversity; human-nature interactions; as well as the state of innovation, entrepreneurship and education. Building on the outcomes of the interaction with stakeholders within the SADA assessment process, a possible ways forward for enhancing EU's presence in the region can be proposed.

First, the EU needs to strengthen and broaden in scope its current efforts to give voice to Arctic communities in policy developments that may affect them. The European Arctic is a very diverse region, with each area having unique challenges. Local specifics require locally designed strategies, which the EU could then support.[68] EU policy priorities should be adjusted to changing circumstances, perceptions and social needs. That requires dialogue with Arctic stakeholders. Social issues should be taken into account, for example in EU environmental policies, especially when the interests and values of vulnerable groups are at stake.

Arctic stakeholders, especially indigenous peoples, often lack the capacity to engage in consultation processes or follow various policy or regulatory developments. The EU should be proactive in reaching out to these Arctic actors. Forums such as Arctic Dialogue are steps in the right direction. However, there is a clear need for institutional solutions supplementing existing EU structures (e.g. the Committee of Regions or consultations within impact assessments) and for incorporation of Arctic, including indigenous, actors from outside the EU. In the near future, a strong involvement of various stakeholders may be needed in regard to the EU Seal Regulation and the examination of its impacts, especially that the issue has been recently raised by the European Parliament.[69] In line with the recent agreement with Canada regarding the seal ban,[70] the EU may undertake more efforts to inform the European public on the Inuit seal hunt and facilitate marketing of seal products in line with the indigenous exemption.[71]

68 Dubois and Roto (2012), *op.cit.*

69 European Parliament. (2014). Joint Motion for a Resolution on the EU strategy for the Arctic (2013/2595(RSP)), http://www.europarl.europa.eu/sides/getDoc.do?pubRef=-//EP//TEXT+MOTION+P7-RC-2014-0229+0+DOC+XML+V0//EN. Accessed 15 March 2014.

70 CBC News North (14 October 2014). "Canada, EU edge toward agreement on Inuit sealskin products", http://www.cbc.ca/news/canada/north/canada-eu-edge-toward-agreement-on-inuit-sealskin-products-1.2798211. Accessed 20 January 2015.

71 See also the report by the WWF, Gerde, E. (December 2013). "Seals in Greenland. The important component of culture and economy", The Last Ice Area Project. WWF.

Second, the EU should continue to focus on supporting entrepreneurship and innovation (including social innovations[72]) in the region.[73] That has to be done in alignment with northern values and lifestyles and with increasing emphasis and sensitivity to indigenous youth and gender issues. As external investments triggering the emergence of a knowledge-based economy are limited, long-term development can originate primarily from inside the region.[74] Areas of innovation where EU support may have comparatively greater added value include creative industries, e-services, leisure-time activities, innovations in traditional industries or cold climate technologies.

Youth (especially women) who are learning, living and working in the Arctic should be seen as the cornerstone of local entrepreneurship and innovation.[75] Moreover, programmes designed over the next 10–20 years could more actively engage migrants, who, if given an opportunity, may greatly contribute to regional development.[76]

Emphasis on indigenous entrepreneurship (including social entrepreneurship) should be continued. The potential of the young indigenous generation (which is very active socially and politically) could be better addressed in the EU programmes. Separate funding lines for projects addressing indigenous-specific challenges are needed, as these may be less visible within general funding schemes.

The focus on innovations and entrepreneurship can be better incorporated in research funding, exchange programmes and regional programmes supporting

---

72 *Social innovations are new ideas (e.g. products, services and models) that simultaneously meet social needs (more effectively than alternatives) and create new social relationships or collaborations.* (*Open Book of Social Innovation,* Murray, R., Calulier-Grice, J. & Mulgan, G., March 2010). For the European Commission, "such solutions are both social in their ends and in their means. They can take the form of genuine innovations or improved solutions." (European Commission Social Innovation, http://ec.europa.eu/enterprise/policies/innovation/policy/social-innovation/index_en.htm. Accessed 10 December 2013.)

73 Focus on innovation, research and education is clearly supported, for example in the Kirkenes II Declaration (Declaration on the 20th Anniversary of the Barents Euro-Arctic Cooperation, Kirkenes, Norway, 3–4 June 2013).

74 Dubois and Roto (2012), *op.cit.*, p. 50; Simmie, J. & R. Martin (2010). The economic resilience of regions: towards an evolutionary approach. *Cambridge Journal of Regions, Economy and Society* 3, 27–43, p. 30; Lundmark, L. (2006). Restructuring and employment change in Sparsely Populated Areas: Examples from Northern Sweden and Finland, Doctoral dissertation, Umea University, GERUM 2, p. 10.

75 Dubois and Roto (2012), *op.cit.*

76 Yeasmin, N. (2013) "Implementation of the EU Immigration Policy in the Barents Euro-Arctic Region: Towards a Framework for Policy Analysis", *Yearbook of Polar Law*, Vol. 5.

educational or research institutions. The EU could also support the establishment of networks dedicated to research and innovation, which could promote co-operation between various research programmes and funding schemes (e.g. EU/EEA programmes, Barents co-operation and even taskforces in the Arctic Council).

Thirdly, the investments in entrepreneurship, innovation and cultural development may miss their targets if intra-regional accessibility and connectivity is insufficient. The EU is in a comparatively (to others policy-areas discussed in this volume) good position to influence accessibility and connectivity in the Arctic. There is a need for a holistic and comprehensive approach to accessibility including transport infrastructure, information flows, ease of crossing borders, and opportunities/spaces for dialogue and interaction. Some experts consider intra-regional connectivity a "sounder alternative to upgrading the transport system than direct core-periphery linkages".[77]

In terms of physical infrastructure, a comprehensive network within the Trans-European Transport Network should not be neglected. Cross-border co-operation and venues such as Barents co-operation may provide support in the planning phase, but over the longer period, after 2020, there is a need for more targeted and substantial support for intra-regional connections.

Cross-border co-operation, especially between Nordic states and northwest Russia, is an area where the EU can play a major role. Additional projects that support economic connectivity and people-to-people connections are needed.[78] Moreover, in the light of currently tense relations between the EU and Russia, focusing on practical co-operation undertakings, may serve upholding channels of collaboration and trust in the North.

Eventually, special needs of Arctic cities should be better considered in relevant EU policies and programmes. Arctic urban areas are small in comparison to large cities in southern latitudes but perform a variety of functions normally associated with larger centres (see Picture 8.3). For Arctic cities, strategies and supportive tools that are tailor-made to their needs may be more appropriate than policies designed for urban, rural or sparsely populated areas. Arctic cities and their unique challenges should be included to a greater degree in initiatives directed at urban development. Examples include the EU's Smart Cities and Communities Initiative, CONCERTO initiative or EIB's JESSICA Urban

77 Dubois and Roto (2012), *op.cit.*, p. 64.

78 In fact, some stakeholders during the SADA consultations pointed out that such programmes are currently less visible than in the 1990s and early 2000s.

PICTURE 8.3 *Tromsø, Norway, one of the main urban centres in the European Arctic*
SOURCE: GETTY IMAGES

Development Funds.[79] An urgent issue is to support indigenous identities and cultures in urban environments.

The EU should take advantage of expertise existing in the North and facilitate production of knowledge regarding Arctic urban development. That includes the exchange of experiences, also with Greenland and Russia.[80]

The European Union is already visible in the sphere of socio-cultural development in the European Arctic regions and with the new 2014–2020 financial perspective its activities can indeed make a difference. However, EU actions need to be aligned with the developmental strategies of Nordic states and coupled with a better understanding of EU's regulatory impact on the region. Such knowledge can be acquired only through an ongoing engagement with a broad array of Arctic stakeholders.

79 Concerto, http://concerto.eu/; DG-Regio, http://ec.europa.eu/regional_policy/thefunds/instruments/jessica_en.cfm. All accessed 18 February 2014.

80 See the Northern Sparsely Populated Areas (NSPA) network position on the European Commission's Smart Cities and Communities Initiative of the Horizon 2020 programme, http://www.nspa-network.eu/. Accessed 13 February 2014.

CHAPTER 9

# European Arctic Initiatives: Capacities, Gaps and Future Opportunities

*Lize-Marié van der Watt, Arne Riedel, Björn Dahlbäck, Elizabeth Tedsen, Kamil Jagodziński and Paula Kankaanpää**

## Abstract

This chapter has a different format than other parts of this volume as it primarily provides an inventory of various existing European Arctic initiatives as well as the overview of identified gaps in information and communication regarding the region. These serve as a factual support for discussion in previous chapters. It is not possible to understand the EU's position in the Arctic governance or analyse the actions of the EU institutions without bearing in mind the complex landscape of structures, institutions, programmes and actions that constitute the EU-Arctic nexus.

The beginning sections provide an overview of Arctic initiatives undertaken by the EU and of their relevance to the EU by outlining the nodes of knowledge-producing initiatives, for example through industrial, coordination or development programmes. This chapter draws upon the inventory, as well as additional stakeholder consultation to identify knowledge strengths as well as ascertain opportunities to build capacity and address potential information and communication gaps. Further, the chapter provides an overview of the *Gap Analysis Report* (GAR), which aimed to show remaining information needs for Arctic stakeholders and policy-makers that are unmet by existing initiatives and activities. In addition, this chapter highlights remaining challenges in the Arctic perceived by the stakeholders as well as potential communication and dissemination instruments to address the

* The authors would like to acknowledge all the members of the project network who contributed to compilation of information and executing the gap analysis survey, in particular: Roberto Azzolini (European Polar Board, European Science Foundation), Nicole Biebow (Alfred Wegener Institute, Germany), Georgina Cronin (Scott Polar Research Institute), Frederic Guillon (European Polar Board, European Science Foundation), Heather Lane (Scott Polar Research Institute), Simona Longo (National Research Council of Italy), Anastasia Leonenko (Tromsø Centre for Remote Sensing, UiT), Corrado Leone (National Research Council of Italy), Outi Paadar (Sámi Education Institute, Finland), Katherine Weingartner (Ecologic Institute), Irina Zhilina (Arctic Centre, University of Lapland; UiT The Arctic University of Norway).

 | DOI 10.1163/9789004303188_011

identified information needs. The chapter concludes with an outline of the potential of a future EU Arctic Information Centre in serving as a hub for information users and providers alike.

## 1 Introduction

The European Union invests heavily in research that addresses a changing European Arctic. This research ranges from curiosity-driven science projects that seek to describe and explain changes in the physical and social environment to more applied research, addressing, for example, mitigation or governance issues.[1] Besides research and other knowledge production initiatives, like carrying out assessments of different kinds, the EU is making substantial investments in promoting the sustainable development of Arctic resources through a variety of instruments (*e.g.*, regional funding and cross-border cooperation programmes), contributions that are easy to overlook since they often do not contain the keyword "Arctic".

The following description of Arctic initiatives – both undertaken by the EU and of relevance to the EU – outlines nodes of knowledge-producing initiatives, for example through industrial, coordination or development programmes. Indeed, it is not possible to understand the EU's position in the Arctic governance or analyse the actions of the EU institutions without bearing in mind this complex landscape of structures, institutions, programmes and actions that constitute the EU-Arctic nexus. This overview of the broad range of Arctic initiatives and shedding light on existing gaps complements the discussion in other chapters in this book and is in itself an exhaustive source of factual information regarding the EU-Arctic nexus.

This can be drawn upon to identify knowledge strengths as well as ascertain opportunities to build capacity and address potential information and knowledge gaps.[2] The EU Arctic Information Centre Preparatory

---

1 These are readily available through the Community Research and Development Information Service (CORDIS) searchable database which details research output from EU-funded projects, including individual projects as well as major multi-institution projects, such as activities funded by the Seventh Framework Programme (FP 7).

2 For a detailed version the reader is directed to the complete compendium: Dahlbäck B., van der Watt, L.-M., Jagodziński, K. & Kankaanpää, P. (2014). European Arctic Initiatives Compendium. Preparatory Action, Strategic Environmental Impact Assessment of development of the Arctic. Arctic Centre, University of Lapland, http://www.arcticinfo.eu/en/ .Accessed 20 February 2015.

Action[3] created a compendium to aid in the identification of recent and current Arctic initiatives on a cross-sectorial basis, to be used by European institutions.

Taking a step further from the *Compendium* and utilizing a survey of Arctic stakeholders and information users, the Preparatory Action next assessed and grouped gaps in Arctic information needs. The resulting *Gap Analysis Report* (GAR), aimed to show remaining information needs for Arctic stakeholders and policy-makers that were unmet by existing initiatives and activities.[4]

The first sections of this chapter highlights select cross-sectoral Arctic initiatives, starting from an inventory of international and regional processes, EU programmes and actions, initiatives undertaken by EU member states as well as other actors such as the private industry. The latter sections move to analysing gaps, by providing an overview of the methodology of GAR, and then presenting some of its major findings, and also recommendations towards better exchange of information from the Arctic to the EU and from the EU to the Arctic.

## 2 European Union Initiatives in the Framework of Developing the EU Arctic Policy

Initiatives can take the form of self-contained programmes or projects. However, there are initiatives in the framework of developing a EU Arctic policy which can be identified as strategic processes followed by institutions within the EU that inform and shape its Arctic activities. This includes leadership, regulation and adaptive co-management strategies, such as taking part in consultative workshops or having delegates present at policy-shaping meetings such as those internationally coordinating governance strategies or lobbying initiatives. Following are *examples* of key initiatives that are helping to shape the EU's Arctic Policy.

3 See the project ("Strategic Environmental Impact Assessment of development of the Arctic") website at www.arcticinfo.eu.

4 For a full version of the findings and their discussions according to human needs in the Arctic, Arctic stakeholders and Arctic regions, the authors refer to the complete GAR: Tedsen, E., Riedel, A., Weingartner, K., Azzolini, R., Guillon, F., Longo, S., Leone, C., Paadar, O., Leonenko, A. (2014). "Gap Analysis Report," Preparatory Action, Strategic Environmental Impact Assessment of development of the Arctic. Arctic Centre, University of Lapland, http://www.arcticinfo.eu/en/. Accessed 20 February 2015.

### 2.1 *The EU in the Arctic-specific International and Intergovernmental Agreements and Regulatory Bodies*

Arctic Council[5]

The Ottawa Declaration of 1996 formally established the Arctic Council as a high level intergovernmental forum to provide a means for promoting cooperation, coordination and interaction among the eight Arctic States, with the involvement of the Arctic Indigenous communities (represented by six organizations as permanent participants) and other Arctic inhabitants. The forum works on common Arctic issues, in particular issues of sustainable development and environmental protection in the Arctic. The EU applied for observer status to the Arctic Council in 2008. In 2013, the Arctic Council received the EU's application affirmatively, deferring the final decision but inviting the EU to observe Council proceedings (see chapter by Stępień and Koivurova in this volume). The EU actively engages in several working groups of the Council, including the Arctic Monitoring and Assessment Programme (AMAP); Protection of the Arctic Marine Environment (PAME); and the Emergency Prevention, Preparedness and Response (EPPR), and was involved for instance in the *Arctic Ocean Review*.

Barents-Euro Arctic Council[6] and the Northern Dimension

The European Commission has been a member of the Barents Euro-Arctic Council since its establishment, although its engagement over the last two decades has been rather limited. The facilitation of cooperation in the Barents Euro-Arctic Region is routed through two cooperative councils, coordinated by the International Barents Secretariat. The intergovernmental Barents-Euro Arctic Council[7] members include Denmark, Finland, Iceland, Norway, Russia, Sweden and the European Commission. The Interregional Barents Regional Council[8] consists of thirteen counties of sub-national entities. The Working Group of Indigenous Peoples,[9] with representatives from the Sámi, Nenets and Vepsians has an advisory role to both the councils.

The EU primarily engages in the work of the BEAC through the Northern Dimension, which since 2006 has been a common policy of the EU, Iceland, Norway and Russia. It has been conceived as a common platform for promoting

5 http://www.arctic-council.org/index.php/en/. All links re-accessed on 20 March 2015.

6 http://www.beac.st/in-English/Barents-Euro-Arctic-Council.

7 www.beac.st/in-English/Barents-Euro-Arctic-Council/Introduction.

8 www.beac.st/in-English/Barents-Euro-Arctic-Council/Barents-Regional-Council.

9 www.beac.st/in-English/Barents-Euro-Arctic-Council/Working-Groups/Working-Group-of-Indigenous-Peoples.

dialogue and concrete cooperation as well as strengthening stability and promoting economic integration, competitiveness and sustainable development in Northern Europe.

Sustained Arctic Observing Network (SAON)[10]

SAON is a process to support and strengthen the development of multinational engagement for sustained a coordinated pan-Arctic observing and data sharing systems that serve societal needs, particularly related to environmental, social, economic and cultural issues. It was established by the Arctic Council and the International Arctic Science Committee (IASC) in 2007.[11] The European Environmental Agency (EEAgency) is represented on the SAON Board. The EEAgency is an EU agency, tasked with providing sound, independent information on the environment.[12]

### 2.2 *International, Regional and Intergovernmental Agreements and Regulatory Bodies of Relevance for the Arctic*

Climate and Clean Air Coalition to Reduce Short-Lived Climate Pollutants[13]

The EC joined the coalition that aims to reduce short-lived climate pollutants in 2012. This initiative should complement UN efforts to reduce global greenhouse gas emissions, including those affecting the Arctic.

The Conference of the Parties (COP) to the United Nations Framework Convention on Climate Change (UNFCCC)[14]

The convention and the conferences forge a legally-binding global regime and is a core international strategy of the EU. Negotiation roadmap initiatives also address climate change in the Arctic.

The Convention for the Protection of the marine Environment of the North-East Atlantic (OSPAR Convention)[15]

OSPAR is the mechanism by which fifteen governments of the western coasts and catchments of Europe, together with the European Union, cooperate to

10 http://www.arcticobserving.org/.
11 http://www.iasc.info/.
12 http://www.eea.europa.eu/.
13 http://www.unep.org/ccac/.
14 http://unfccc.int/2860.php.
15 http://www.ospar.org/.

protect the marine environment of the North-East Atlantic, including parts of Arctic waters.

Espoo Convention on Environmental Impact Assessment[16]

The convention sets out the obligations of Parties to assess the environmental impact of certain activities at an early stage of planning. It also lays down the general obligation of States to notify and consult each other on all major projects under consideration that are likely to have a significant adverse environmental impact across boundaries. Since 2011, the EU has collaborated closely with the Russian Federation, as the latter intensified internal procedures towards the ratification of the convention, which would that way become of key importance in the European Arctic.[17]

International Whaling Commission (IWC)[18]

The International Whaling Commission (IWC) is the global intergovernmental body charged with the conservation of whales and the management of whaling based on the 1946 International Convention for the Regulation of Whaling. The European Union is a member. Whaling regulations has an impact on the human and non-human Arctic environment (see more in a chapter by Stępień et al. in this volume).

The International Maritime Organisation (IMO)[19]

The EU is involved on a number of IMO committees with Arctic relevant mandates, for example the Maritime Environment Protection Committee and the Maritime Safety Committee, to which the sub-committee designing the Polar Code reports. The Polar Code[20] will regulate safety for ships operating in polar waters, covering the full range of design, construction, equipment, operational, training, search and rescue and environmental protection matters relevant to ships operating in the inhospitable waters surrounding the two poles. The part of the Polar Code dedicated to safety has been adopted in November 2014 and the environmental measures are expected to be adopted in 2015 (see more in a chapter by Sander et al. in this volume).

16 http://www.unece.org/env/eia/eia.html.

17 The Russian Federaction has already applied Espoo Convantion for example in the NorthStream gas pipaline project.

18 http://iwc.int/home.

19 http://www.imo.org/Pages/home.aspx.

20 http://www.imo.org/MediaCentre/HotTopics/polar/Pages/default.aspx.

### Minamata Convention on Mercury[21]

The EU was one of the drivers of the negotiations leading up to the Minamata Convention on Mercury. The treaty, signed in 2013, is designed to protect human health and the environment from anthropogenic emissions and releases of mercury and mercury compounds. Several Arctic Council (Arctic Monitoring and Assessment Programme) reports have contributed to the global understanding of mercury and its effects in the Arctic in particular.[22]

### Regional Fisheries Management Organisations (RFMO)[23]

RFMOs are international organisations formed by countries with fishing interests in an area. RFMOs with an Arctic dimension that the EU is a partner of includes the North East Atlantic Fisheries Commission (NEAFC); North Atlantic Salmon Conservation Organization (NASCO) and bilateral agreements with Greenland, Faroe Islands, Iceland and Norway.

### Stockholm Convention[24] and the Protocol of the United Nations Economic Commission for Europe Convention on Long-Range Transboundary Air Pollution (UNECE LRTAP)[25]

The Stockholm Convention on Persistent Organic Pollutants (2004) is a global treaty to protect human health and the environment from persistent organic pollutants (POPs) to which the EU is a signatory. There is an ongoing process of adding new pollutants to the so-far modest list of substances. The EU contributed to Arctic related initiatives under UNECE LRTAP as well as to the Arctic Council's Task Force on short lived climate forces and tipping points, whose regulation are sought by these protocols and conventions.

### United Nations Declaration on the Rights of Indigenous Peoples[26]

The 2007 United Nations Declaration on the Rights of Indigenous Peoples has been strongly supported by the EU and frames the international legal context of EU engagement with indigenous peoples in the Arctic.

---

21 http://www.mercuryconvention.org/.

22 Arctic Council, "Statement to the Diplomatic Conference on the Minamata Convention on Mercury" 9–11 October 2013. Available at http://www.arctic-council.org/index.php/en/document-archive/category/407-statements?download=1898:minamata-convention-on-mercury-october-2013.

23 http://ec.europa.eu/fisheries/cfp/international/rfmo/.

24 http://www.unido.org/index.php?id=5279.

25 http://www.unece.org/env/lrtap.

26 http://www.un.org/esa/socdev/unpfii/documents/DRIPS_en.pdf.

United Nations Law of the Sea (UNCLOS)[27]

The EU, a party to UNCLOS, is fully compliant to the Convention, including any EU's activities referring to the Arctic. The EU also sponsored relevant studies, *e.g. Legal Aspects of Arctic Shipping* (2010).[28] The EU is following developments in the Northern Sea Route and Northwest Passage in context of UNCLOS and shipping regulations.

### 2.3 *Research and Research Related Agreements*

Galway Statement on Atlantic Ocean Cooperation[29]

The "Galway Statement on Atlantic Ocean Cooperation" was signed by the representatives of the European Union, the United States and Canada in 2013. The partners agreed to join forces on Atlantic Ocean Research. The goal is to better understand the Atlantic Ocean and promote the sustainable management of its resources and connect the ocean observation efforts of the three partners. The work will also study the interplay of the Atlantic Ocean with the Arctic Ocean, particularly in relation to climate change.

European Environment—State and Outlook[30]

The latest European Environment State and Outlook Report was published in 2015. The report, produced by the European Environment Agency, addressed a number of Arctic issues, in particular climate change, as was already the case in the 2010 edition.

Soil Atlas of the Northern Circumpolar Region.[31]

The EC Joint Research Centre (JRC) with partners from northern EU countries, as well as Norway, Iceland, Greenland, Canada, the USA and Russia produced a soil atlas in 2010 as part of their contribution to the International Polar Year (2010). The project included science communication to a broad group of stakeholders on the characteristics of northern soil, its environmental importance and global significance.

---

27 http://www.un.org/depts/los/convention_agreements/convention_overview_convention.htm.

28 http://ec.europa.eu/maritimeaffairs/documentation/studies/documents/legal_aspects_arctic_shipping_summary_en.pdf.

29 http://ec.europa.eu/research/iscp/pdf/galway_statement_atlantic_ocean_cooperation.pdf.

30 http://www.eea.europa.eu/soer.

31 http://eusoils.jrc.ec.europa.eu/library/maps/Circumpolar/.

Black Carbon Research

The JRC[32] in cooperation with the United Nations Environment Programme (UNEP), World Meteorological Organization (WMO) and several other partners conducted research on black carbon, with Arctic implications. This resulted in publication of an article in 2012, titled "Simultaneously mitigating near-term climate change and improving human health and food security",[33] which had drawn on the 2011 UNEP led *Integrated Assessment of Black Carbon and Tropospheric Ozone*.[34]

## 2.4 *EU-supported Infrastructures of Significance to the Arctic*

The EU contributes substantially to infrastructure that supports research and monitoring of the Arctic region, on different scales, including from space.

Infrastructure for Spatial Information in Europe (INSPIRE) Directive[35]

The INSPIRE directive aims to create a EU spatial data infrastructure. This will enable the sharing of environmental spatial information among public sector organisations and better facilitate public access to spatial information across Europe. A European Spatial Data Infrastructure will assist in policy-making across boundaries, including the Arctic (see more in the chapter by Latola et al. in this volume).

Copernicus[36]

Copernicus, previously known as GMES (Global Monitoring for Environment and Security), is the European Programme for the establishment of a European capacity for Earth Observation. This initiative is headed by the European Commission in partnership with the European Space Agency (ESA) and the EEAgency (also see Table 2.2). The ESA is developing five families of Sentinel missions specifically for Copernicus, the first of which has been scheduled to launch in 2013. The Sentinels will provide a unique set of observations, starting with the all-weather, day and night radar images from Sentinel-1 to be used for land and ocean services. Sentinel-2 will deliver high-resolution optical images for land services and Sentinel-3 will provide data for services relevant

32 https://ec.europa.eu/jrc/.

33 http://ec.europa.eu/dgs/jrc/index.cfm?id=1410&obj_id=14370&dt_code=NWS&lang=en#iabcto.

34 http://www.unep.org/dewa/Portals/67/pdf/BlackCarbon_report.pdf.

35 http://inspire.jrc.ec.europa.eu/index.cfm.

36 http://www.copernicus.eu/.

to the ocean and land. Sentinel-4 and Sentinel-5 will provide data for atmospheric composition monitoring from geostationary and polar orbits, respectively. Sentinels 1–3 will contribute to environment, economic development and sovereignty and security policy priorities in the Arctic, providing data for monitoring changes in land cover, pollution monitoring, northern shipping and disaster response. Copernicus aims to provide reliable and up-to-date information on planetary and climate change to decision makers, businesses and citizens. The Copernicus land monitoring service provides geographical information on land cover and on variables related, for instance, to the vegetation state or the water cycle. It supports applications in a variety of domains such as spatial planning, forest management, water management, agriculture and food security, etc. (see more in chapters by Strahlendorff et al. and Sander et al. in this volume).

Group on Earth Observation System of Systems (GEOSS)[37]

The EU supports the GEOSS initiative. This "system of systems" aims to link together existing and planned observing systems around the world and support the development of new systems where gaps currently exist. It seeks to promote common technical standards so that data from the thousands of different instruments can be combined into coherent data sets. This includes the Arctic Observing System.

Galileo[38]

The Galileo programme is Europe's initiative for a state-of-the-art global satellite navigation system, providing a highly accurate, guaranteed global positioning service under civilian control. The fully deployed system will consist of 30 satellites and the associated ground infrastructure. Galileo will be interoperable with GPS and GLONASS (Russian Global Navigation Satellite System), the two other global satellite navigation systems. It has Arctic implication in terms of, for example, navigation in the Arctic Ocean. The first rudimentary services have been provided since November 2014 (see more in Sander et al. in this volume).

Marine Knowledge 2020[39]

Recently initiated, Marine Knowledge 2020 brings together marine data from different sources with the aim of helping industry, public authorities and

---

37 http://www.earthobservations.org/geoss.shtml.

38 http://ec.europa.eu/enterprise/policies/satnav/galileo/index_en.htm.

39 http://ec.europa.eu/maritimeaffairs/policy/marine_knowledge_2020/.

researchers find the data and make more effective use of them to develop new products and services, as well as improving the understanding of how the seas behave. This includes data on the Arctic basin.

## 2.5 *European Environmental Agency Initiatives in Monitoring and E-infrastructures*

Shared Environmental Information System (SEIS)[40]

SEIS was established to improve the collection, exchange and use of environmental data and information across Europe. SEIS aims to create an integrated web-enabled, EU-wide environmental information system, by simplifying and modernizing existing information systems and processes. SEIS includes environmental monitoring data from the Arctic Region.

Eye on Earth Platform[41]

Eye on Earth is the result of a public-private partnership bringing together expertise from industry and public organisations. The EEAgency, Esri and Microsoft Corporation collaborated to launch the Eye on Earth Network, the online community for sharing and discovering data about environment. This new cloud computing-based network promotes the principles of public data access and citizen science. It includes Arctic data.

## 2.6 *EU Instruments, Institutions and Policy Areas with Arctic Applications*

Framework Programmes for Research[42]

The Arctic was important in the sixth and seventh framework programmes, the major research funding instrument of the EU. This was especially visible in calls focussing on environmental analyses and climate change research. Horizon 2020, the framework programme for 2014–2020, focusses on coupling research and innovation to enhance smart, sustainable and inclusive growth and jobs in the EU. It seeks achieve this with its emphasis on excellent science, industrial leadership and tackling societal challenges, and Arctic related research plays here a role. Key FP 6 and FP 7 grants are highlighted in the thematic section of this chapter.

---

40 http://www.eea.europa.eu/about-us/what/shared-environmental-information-system-1.

41 http://www.eyeonearth.org/en-us/Pages/Home.aspx.

42 http://ec.europa.eu/research/index.cfm.

#### EU-PolarNet[43]

One of the actions implemented in the framework of Horizon 2020 is research coordination. A newly established network of EU research institutes and institutions operating until 2020 is to enhance better use and sharing of research infrastructures, facilitate science cooperation and develop – in the process of co-design with relevant stakeholders – the European Polar Research Programme. The project covers both poles as well as both natural and social sciences.

#### Northern Dimension[44]

The Northern Dimension is a joint policy between EU, Russia, Norway and Iceland. The ND Policy was initiated in 1999 and renewed in 2006. The policy aims at providing a framework to:

- promote dialogue and concrete cooperation;
- strengthen stability, well-being and intensified economic cooperation;
- promote economic integration, competitiveness and sustainable development in Northern Europe.

In addition to the four ND Partners namely EU, Russia, Norway and Iceland, also participating are:

- EU Members States in national capacity;
- Regional Councils, *e.g.* the Arctic Council, the Barents Euro-Arctic Council (BEAC), the Council of the Baltic Sea States (CBSS) and the Nordic Council of Ministers (NCM);
- International Financial Institutions (IFIs), *e.g.* European Bank for Reconstruction and Development (EBRD), the European Investment Bank (EIB), the Nordic Investment Bank (NIB) and the Nordic Environment Finance Corporation (NEFCO) as well as other financial institutions;
- universities and research centres and business community;
- Canada and the United States as observers;
- Belarus participates in practical co-operation.

To facilitate ND project implementation, four Partnerships have been established to deal with the following thematic issues:

---

43 http://www.eu-polarnet.eu/.

44 http://eeas.europa.eu/north_dim/index_en.htm.

- environment (NDEP),
- public health and social well-being (NDPHS),
- transport and logistics (NDPTL),
- culture (NDPC).

An ND Institute (NDI) and ND Business Council (NDBC) have been established to involve academia and business community into ND cooperation.

### European Instrument for Democracy and Human Rights[45]

The European Instrument for Democracy and Human Rights provides, *inter alia,* direct support to civil society organisations working on indigenous issues. Its largest Arctic and sub-Arctic contribution is capacity building to pursue traditional livelihoods in the Russian Federation, earlier it was engaged in the support for indigenous organizational development.

### European Union Regional Policy: European Regional Development Fund (ERDF)[46]

The ERDF financed the European Territorial Co-operation objective (ETC), which covered three types of programmes in the period 2007–2013: cross-border programmes;[47] transnational co-operation programmes[48] and interregional co-operation programmes.[49] Through these programmes, several projects in the northernmost regions of the European Arctic have been funded. Summaries of the major programmes funded by each type of programme are given here. Additionally, individual projects are highlighted under the thematic section of this chapter

### Transnational Co-operation Programmes

The Northern Periphery Programme 2007–2013 involved community support for some of the northernmost, sparsely populated regions within the European Territorial Co-operation Objective framework, incorporation regions in Ireland, Finland, Sweden and the United Kingdom, with the participation of the Faeroe Islands, Greenland, Iceland and Norway. The programme aimed to help peripheral and remote communities in the northern margins of Europe to develop their economic, social and environmental potential. This was achieved

45 http://www.eidhr.eu/.
46 http://ec.europa.eu/regional_policy/cooperate/cooperation/index_en.cfm.
47 http://ec.europa.eu/regional_policy/cooperate/cooperation/crossborder/index_en.cfm.
48 http://ec.europa.eu/regional_policy/cooperate/cooperation/transnational/index_en.cfm.
49 http://ec.europa.eu/regional_policy/cooperate/cooperation/interregional/index_en.cfm.

through transnational collaboration in the fields of innovation, business competitiveness, accessibility, sustainable development, natural resources and cultural heritage. In the 2014–2020 framework, the Northern Periphery Programme is succeed by the Northern Periphery and Arctic Programme[50] (see more in Stępień et al. in this volume).

### Interregional Co-operation Programmes

INTERREG IVC has provided funding for interregional cooperation across Europe. It is implemented under the European Community's territorial co-operation objective and financed through the ERDF. The overall objective of the INTERREG IVC Programme has been to improve the effectiveness of regional policies and instruments. Projects typically built on the exchange of experiences among partners who are ideally responsible for the development of their local and regional policies. INTERREG IVC funded projects in Northern Sweden and Finland.[51] The programme is being continued for 2014–2020 as INTERREG EUROPE and includes Sápmi as a distinct geographical area.[52]

The Operational Programme "North"[53] between Finland, Sweden and Norway run for the period 2007–2013. The geographical location, cold climate and long distances make heavy demands on infrastructure and communications, while the vast labour market regions result in additional costs in terms of maintaining a good level of service. The overall objective of the Programme was to strengthen the competitiveness and cohesion of the region. For the Sápmi sub-Programme, the aim was to develop Sámi cultural life and industry by making use of their resources in an ecological and sustainable way. The Programme strategy addressed the needs and common challenges identified in the cross-border region by developing methods and structures that facilitate cooperation between the regions (see also Stępień et al. in this volume).

### European Neighbourhood and Partnership Instrument[54]

The European Neighbourhood and Partnership Instrument (ENPI) supports the European Neighbourhood Policy (ENP).[55] It was operational since 1 January

50 http://www.northernperiphery.eu/en/content/show/&tid=237.

51 http://www.interreg4c.eu/programme/.

52 http://www.interreg4c.eu/fileadmin/User_Upload/PDFs/INTERREG_EUROPE_Cooperation_Programme_summary.pdf.

53 http://ec.europa.eu/regional_policy/country/prordn/details_new.cfm?gv_PAY=FI&gv_reg=ALL&gv_PGM=1287&gv_defL=7&LAN=7.

54 http://ec.europa.eu/europeaid/how/finance/enpi_en.htm.

55 http://eeas.europa.eu/enp/index_en.htm.

2007 and has been replaced by European Partnership Instrument, which covers also collaboration with partners in developing states worldwide. Together with the ERDF it co-funds programmes such as Kolarctic,[56] a development programme in which the northern regions of Finland, Sweden, Norway and the Russian Federation participates. The 2007–2013 budget for Kolarctic has amounted to €70.48 million, of which €28.4 million was EU funding. Due to current tensed relations between the EU and Russia the future of the Kolarctic programme for 2014–2020 is uncertain.

### 2.7 *Arctic Inter-Service Group* (*AISG*)

The Arctic Inter-Service Group is a channel for regular and continuous information exchange between the European Commission (and between its various DGs), the European External Action Service (EEAS) and the agencies (EEAgency and the EMSA).

## 3 Infrastructural Initiatives of European Union Member States

Individual EU member states undertake many Arctic initiatives and it is crucial in the context of developing an EU Arctic policy, and EU Arctic initiatives, to have an overview of these. These initiatives, however, differ vastly in scale and type. The following set of characteristics was identified as relevant to for the purposes of this volume.

- **Initiatives that are taking place on a country level, whether on national, bilateral, multi-lateral or non-governmental scale.** In other words, this does not exclude initiatives mandated by other actors than *national governments*. This makes it possible to include major industrial or business initiatives and initiatives taken by, for example, lobbying groups.
- **Initiatives that are long-term, currently on-going and high level (in the relevant context).** The compendium seeks to describe major initiatives undertaken in the respective countries. Given the diversity of European countries in terms of, for example, how their Research and Development sectors are structured, this approach allows for the mention of comparatively major or influential initiatives undertaken in countries with different resource allocations.
- **Initiatives that self-identify as Arctic, or have the Arctic region at its core.**
- **Initiatives that fall within the framework of *development* of the Arctic.**

56 http://www.kolarcticenpi.info/en.

This section on the EU member states' initiatives is divided into two parts. The first is descriptive of **processes**, namely on-going activities and procedures to deliver products that may impact sustainable development in the Arctic. One of the more manifest ways in which countries take Arctic initiatives is through the articulation of an Arctic strategy or position (see Table 9.1). The second part mostly focusses on initiatives to establish underlying systems for activities in the Arctic, or **infrastructures**. "Infrastructures" entail physical infrastructural initiatives that is necessary for operations in the Arctic. Institutions are administrative or organizing initiatives, virtual or actual, that facilitates activities in the Arctic. These systems also enable processes – for example the research programmes or commercial development.

TABLE 9.1 *List of European Union countries' Arctic policy documents and statements*

| Country | Authority releasing document | Title of *latest* document | Date of release |
|---|---|---|---|
| Kingdom of Denmark | Ministry of Foreign Affairs | Denmark, Greenland and the Faroe Islands: Kingdom of Denmark Strategy for the Arctic 2011–2020 | 2011 |
| Finland | Prime Minister's Office | Finland's Arctic Strategy | 2013 |
| Sweden | Ministry of Foreign Affairs | Sweden's Strategy for the Arctic Region | 2011 |
| France | The National Center for Scientific Research* | Prospective recherches polaires | 2012 |
| Germany | Federal Ministry of Education and Research | Rapid Climate Change in the Arctic: Polar Research as a Global Responsibility | 2012 |
| The Netherlands | Ministry of Foreign Affairs | Policy Framework: The Netherlands and the Polar Regions, 2011–2015 (Summary of Dutch document) | 2012 |
| Poland | Ministry of Foreign Affairs | Statement of Minister M. Szpunar to Swedish Presidency of the Arctic Council | 2012 |
| United Kingdom | Foreign and Commonwealth Office | UK Policy Towards the Arctic | 2013 |
| Norway (EEA) | Ministry of Foreign Affairs | The High North: Visions and strategies | 2011 |
| Iceland (EEA) | Parliament (Althingi) | A Parliamentary Resolution on Iceland's Arctic Policy | 2011 |

Only listing traditional research infrastructures and institutions could exclude important systems that underlie the knowledge production process. For example, industries and cultural institutions (whether indigenous or not), are also influential sources of information and knowledge production. For this reason, also a short section on industry has been here included.

## 3.1 *European Union Arctic Countries*

Kingdom of Denmark

Greenland is outside of the EU but is one of the Overseas Countries and Territories with association arrangements with the EU. Greenland is part of the Danish Realm. The Faroe Islands have negligible Arctic infrastructural or institutional initiatives, but has an active Arctic strategy, especially in the context of fisheries and climate change.[57] The Faroes are also not part of the European Union.

*Research and Education*

The Greenland Institute of Natural Resources, is a major research institution, owned by the Government of Greenland.[58] Located in Nuuk, the Institute is also responsible for the field station at Kobbefjord and the research vessels R/V Sanna and R/V Pâmiut. Initiatives undertaken by and through the Institute are intended to provide the scientific basis for an assessment of sustainable use of the living resources in and around Greenland as well as to protect the environment and secure biological diversity. The Kangerlussuaq International Science Support (KISS) facility, a subsidiary of Mittarfeqarfiit/Greenland Airports,[59] at Kangerlussuaq, western Greenland, serves as an important logistical hub to the inland ice cap.

Research infrastructures operated from Denmark are mostly maintained by universities. The University of Copenhagen maintains the year-round Arctic Station[60] located on the south coast of the Disko Island in central west Greenland. The University of Copenhagen also maintains the Sermilik[61]

57 www.mfa.fo/Files/Filer/fragreidingar/kunningarfaldari-eng8.pdf.

58 www.natur.gl/en/.

59 www.mit.gl/ (sciencesupport@glv.gl).

60 arktiskstation.ku.dk/english/about/.

61 geo.ku.dk/english/research/field_station/.

summer station in South East Greenland. Aarhus University operates Zackenberg Research Station,[62] located in North-East Greenland and owned by the Government of Greenland. In early 2013, Aarhus University received a grant for the substantial extension of Station North in northernmost Greenland.[63]

Aarhus University also hosts the Arctic Research Centre (ARC),[64] an institutional initiative launched in 2012. The ARC has a partnership agreement with the Greenland Institute of Natural Resources and the University of Manitoba (Canada) in an Arctic Science Partnership and the Centre focusses on joint, interdisciplinary research campaigns. Although funding for the institution is currently time-limited, the possibility has been articulated that the Centre may turn into a department in the long run.

From 2015 also a web portal "ISAAFFIK Arctic Gateway" will be operational. It is dedicated to sharing information within scientific community and beyond referring to the Arctic and particularly Greenland, Faroese and Danish initiatives and infrastructures.

#### *State*

Danish state-run institutions which include the Arctic as a distinct focus area include the Danish Meteorological Institute,[65] the Geological Survey of Denmark and Greenland[66] and the Danish Geodata Agency.[67]

#### *Industry*

Founded in 1992, the Royal Arctic Line A/S[68] is an example of a non-research specific infrastructure. It has an exclusive concession for the transportation of all sea cargo to and from Greenland and between Greenlandic settlements. As such, it provides essential infrastructural support to oil and mineral exploration, one of the key industries that also generate knowledge affecting – and effecting – developments in the Arctic.

---

62 www.zackenberg.dk/.

63 scitech.au.dk/en/current-affairs/news/show/artikel/aarhus-universitet-bygger-forskningsstation-i-nordgroenland/.

64 arctic.au.dk/.

65 www.dmi.dk/en/about-the-dmi/profile/introduction-to-dmi/.

66 www.geus.dk/.

67 www.gst.dk/English/.

68 www.royalarcticline.com/.

### Finland

#### *Research and Education*

Several Finnish universities have focus areas on research and development related to the Arctic. At Aalto University's School of Engineering, Arctic technology is a priority. Arctic maritime technology and winter navigation, key research areas, are both important to Finland as it offers major business opportunities for companies engaged in international trade. Aalto University also operates the Aalto Ice Tank, a multipurpose ice testing tank, which enables the study of a wide range of hydrodynamic phenomena in ice-free conditions.[69] The universities of Helsinki,[70] Lapland,[71] Oulu[72] and Turku[73] operate research units in northern Finland. The University of Helsinki accounts for a considerable percentage of Finnish Arctic research, for example in the fields of geology, geography, physics and geophysics.

The University of Lapland is the northernmost university in the European Union. It conducts research on Arctic populations, communities, the environment, art and design and their interaction. Additionally, it is assigned nationwide responsibility for social and legal research related to the Sámi people. The Arctic Centre,[74] based at the University of Lapland, is concerned with global change, sustainable development and environmental and minority law in the region. Its nationwide role includes the dissemination of scientific information, exhibition activities and expert duties related to the Arctic and Barents Euro-Arctic Council.[75] The Arctic Centre is seeking to establish itself as a hub for the EU Arctic Information Centre. The University of Lapland also houses the University of the Arctic International Secretariat,[76] which is responsible for the administration of the cooperation network between the universities, polytechnics and other educational institutions of the Arctic countries. The universities belonging to the network promote the exchange of researchers, students and teachers in the northern regions. The Lapland University of Applied Sciences[77]

69 appmech.aalto.fi/en/department/facilities_and_equipment/infras/.

70 www.helsinki.fi/university/.

71 www.ulapland.fi/InEnglish.

72 www.oulu.fi/english/.

73 www.utu.fi/en/Pages/home.aspx.

74 www.arcticcentre.org/InEnglish.

75 www.beac.st/in-English/Barents-Euro-Arctic-Council.

76 www.uarctic.org/organizations2.aspx?group=AdmUArcticDirectorAndInternationalSecretariat&title=UArctic%20President%20and%20International%20Secretariat.

77 www.ramk.fi/en.

specialises in research, training and development of sustainable forest use; the coordination of the use of natural resources; and the management of low-temperature conditions. The University of Lapland, the Lapland University of Applied Sciences and the Lapland tourism college jointly runs the Multidimensional Tourism Institute,[78] an expert in the Arctic tourism industry.

The University of Oulu is an international science university engaged in research into northern and Arctic issues in several fields of science. The university's Giellagas Institute[79] has the mandate to provide education in the Sámi language and culture. The Thule Institute,[80] based at the university, is engaged in research into the environment, natural resources and northern fields of activity. For this purpose, it operates a Centre for Arctic Medicine and the NorNet network coordinating environmental and natural resources research. The Oulu Mining School[81] and the Nordic Mining School,[82] established in collaboration with the Luleå University of Technology[83] in Sweden respond to the growing needs of the mining industry. The Sodankylä Geophysical Observatory is a national institute subordinated to the University of Oulu.

The Sámi Education Institute (Sámi oahpahusguovddáš),[84] is a multidisciplinary institute of education providing instruction in the Sámi language and culture as well as offering a wide range of vocational training.

Arctic research is one of the Finnish Meteorological Institute's (FMI)[85] strategic priorities. The FMI Arctic Research Division studies the various layers of the polar atmosphere, biosphere and the surface of the earth, generating accurate data on the atmosphere, climate and the environment. The FMI also operates the Arctic Research Centre located in Sodankylä, Lapland.[86] In addition to its expertise in the fields of marine ecology, ice research, shipping and the northern environments, the Finnish Environment Institute (SYKE)[87] is in involved in a range of Arctic Council projects to gather data on environmental toxins, climate change and short-lived climate forcers (SLCF).

78 matkailu.luc.fi/In-English/Institute.

79 www.oulu.fi/giellagasinstitute/.

80 www.oulu.fi/thuleinstitute/.

81 www.oulumining.fi/.

82 nordicminingschool.eu/.

83 www.ltu.se/.

84 www.sogsakk.fi/index.php?option=com_content&view=article&id=56&Itemid=1&lang=en.

85 en.ilmatieteenlaitos.fi/.

86 en.ilmatieteenlaitos.fi/arctic-research.

87 www.syke.fi/en-US.

The Finnish Institute of Occupational Health Oulu unit[88] initiated research into the evaluation and management of the detrimental impacts of low temperatures. The Technical Research Centre of Finland (VTT), a non-profit organisation, carries out low-temperature research, low-temperature technology.[89]

Tekes – the Finnish Funding Agency for Innovation has launched 100 million Euro Arctic sea program.[90] The Academy of Finland, which represents Finland at international polar science bodies, has an Arctic specific funding call.[91]

*State*

Agrifood Research Finland,[92] the Finnish Forest Research Institute[93] and the Finnish Game and Fisheries Research Institute[94] have been operating in their respective fields in the north. In the beginning of 2015, the three institutes came together to form a Natural Resources Institute.[95] Another state agency with a northern regions mandate is the Geological Survey of Finland[96] which carries out geological, geochemical and geophysical research and natural resources exploration in northern regions. The institute's expertise ranges from the preparation of control schemes and the evaluation of effectiveness and risks to the assessment of the lifecycle impacts of consumption and production. The governmental Radiation and Nuclear Safety Authority (STUK)'s[97] regional laboratory in northern Finland is the northernmost laboratory in the European Union to monitor radioactivity. It is also part of the environmental monitoring and assessment network for Arctic areas.

*Industry*

The Lapland Chamber of Commerce[98] has created the Arctic Business Forum,[99] with the view of bringing together leading international companies

88 www.ttl.fi/en/contact/oulu/Pages/default.aspx.

89 www.vtt.fi/?lang=en.

90 www.tekes.fi/en/whats-going-on/news/finland-sets-its-sights-on-growth-in-arctic-seas/.

91 www.aka.fi/en-GB/A/Academy-of-Finland/Media-services/Releases1/April-2014-call-Academy-funding-for-Arctic-research-energy-research-societal-security-ICT-and-research-infrastructures/.

92 portal.mtt.fi/portal/page/portal/mtt_en.

93 www.metla.fi/index-en.html.

94 www.rktl.fi/english/.

95 https://www.luke.fi/english.

96 en.gtk.fi/.

97 www.stuk.fi/en_GB/.

98 www.lapland.chamber.fi/index.php/in-english.

99 www.arcticbusinessforum.com/.

with business interests in the European High North. The Chamber has been one of the key actors involved in creation of the Arctic Economic Council.[100] The new body, formed in 2014, brings together industries (including indigenous industries) from around the Circumpolar North in order to enhance cooperation and provide views and inputs from business community into the work of the Arctic Council, while remaining independent from the Arctic Council.

Arctech Helsinki Shipyard[101] is a joint venture owned with equal shares by STX Finland and Russian United Shipbuilding Corporation (USC). They specialized in Arctic shipbuilding technology and innovation. Apart from the infrastructural importance of Arctic shipbuilding, a company like Arctech also fosters cooperation between the marine industry clusters of Russia and Finland. In addition to model and full scale testing services, Aker Arctic,[102] for example, offers sundry types of consulting, design and engineering services, field expeditions, training and other technology services associated with technologies and operations in icy or severely cold conditions. Arctia Shipping Oy[103] owns and operates the Finnish icebreaker fleet. During the cold seasons they ensure that maritime traffic to and from Finnish ports runs smoothly. During the summer season, their multipurpose icebreakers work in the Arctic waters to ensure safe operations in the offshore oil- and gas fields.

### Sweden

#### *Research and Education*

The Tarfala Research Station, member of INTERACT network and operated by Stockholm University, is situated in the high alpine Kebnekaise Mountains, northern Sweden and close to Storglaciären, one of the best studied glaciers in the world.[104] Polar research in Sweden runs the gamut of disciplines and both basic and applied research is done. The Stockholm,[105] Lund,[106] Umeå[107] and Uppsala[108] Universities are amongst the universities that provide institutional

---

100 http://arcticeconomiccouncil.com/.
101 arctech.fi/.
102 www.akerarctic.fi/company.htm.
103 www.arctia.fi/services.
104 www.ink.su.se/english/tarfala-research-station.
105 www.su.se/english/.
106 www.lunduniversity.lu.se/.
107 www.umu.se/english.
108 www.uu.se/en/.

support for Arctic research, as does the Royal Institute of Technology, KTH[109] the Swedish University of Agricultural Sciences[110] and the University of Gothenburg.[111] Research institutions like the Stockholm Environmental Institute,[112] the Stockholm Resilience Centre[113] and the Stockholm Peace Research Institute[114] also have long-term Arctic programmes. Similarly, the FOI (Swedish Defence Research Agency),[115] which conducts security and defence research mainly – but not exclusively – for the Swedish Defence Force, is also conducting research into Arctic security issues.

A recent institutional initiative with a very specific Arctic focus is the establishment of the Arctic Research Centre at Umeå University (Arcum).[116] Arcum is rooted in the Northern Studies research focus of the University of Umeå more generally. Research within the framework of Arcum is a response to the demand for research-based knowledge. It provides a multi-disciplinary response to present and future demands of research-based knowledge for the responsible development in the North.

The Swedish Institute of Space Physics (IRF)[117] is a governmental research institute which runs the Polar Atmospheric Research Programme, comprising of studies of the dynamics, electrodynamics, chemistry and aeronomy of the troposphere, stratosphere and mesosphere. The Swedish National Space Board[118] in cooperation with the European Space Agency and specifically Canada, Finland, and France also operates the Odin satellite, which has an Arctic specific mission in its study of ozone depletion. Launched in 2001, the Odin was designed to combine two scientific disciplines on a single spacecraft in studies of star formation/early solar system (astronomy) and of the mechanisms behind the depletion of the ozone layer in the earth's atmosphere and the effects of global warming (aeronomy).

The European Incoherent Scatter Scientific Association (EISCAT)[119] has its headquarters in Kiruna, Sweden. The experimental sites of EISCAT are located in the Scandinavian sector north of the Arctic Circle. Investments and

---

109 www.kth.se/.
110 www.slu.se/en/.
111 http://www.gu.se/english.
112 www.sei-international.org/.
113 www.stockholmresilience.org/.
114 www.sipri.org/.
115 foi.se/en/.
116 www.arcum.umu.se/english/.
117 www.irf.se/.
118 www.snsb.se/en/Home/Space-Activities-in-Sweden/Satellites/Odin/.
119 www.eiscat.se/.

operational costs are shared between the China (PRC) Research Institute of Radiowave Propagation, National Institute of Polar Research, Japan, the Research Council of Norway, Science and Technology Facilities Council, United Kingdom, Solar-Terrestrial Environment Laboratory, Nagoya University, Japan, the Finnish Academy, and the Swedish Research Council. It was established to conduct research on the lower, middle and upper atmosphere and ionosphere using the incoherent scatter radar technique.

*State*

The Swedish Polar Research Secretariat[120] is a government agency under the Ministry of Education and Research that promotes and co-ordinates Swedish polar research and development, as well as monitor, promote and assist in international negotiations, collaborations and cooperation with the EU. The Secretariat follows and plans research and development, as well as organises and leads research expeditions to the Arctic and Antarctic regions. The Secretariat actively works to improve environmental protection in the polar regions. The Swedish Polar Research Secretariat has a long time agreement with the Swedish Maritime Authority to use the research vessel and icebreaker *Oden* for research purposes.[121] The Secretariat also operates Abisko Scientific Research Station, an INTERACT member about 200 km north of the Arctic Circle in Sweden.[122]

Other state institutions with Arctic or Northern specific tasks include the Swedish Maritime Administration,[123] which apart from *Oden*, is also responsible for Sweden's icebreaker fleet, providing crucial infrastructural support in the Baltic and the Gulf of Bothnia. The Swedish Agency for Marine and Water Management[124] is responsible for fishing and environmental monitoring and research activities and their international unit is also responsible for the relevant international agreements that concerns the Arctic. The Swedish Environmental Protection Agency[125] provides the institutional base for Swedish initiatives relating to environmental protection of the Arctic and the Swedish Forest Agency. It also has a section focussing specifically on northern forestry.[126]

120 www.polar.se/.

121 www.sjofartsverket.se/en/Maritime-services/Winter-Navigation/Our-Icebreakers/Research-VesselIcebreaker-Oden/.

122 www.polar.se/en/abisko.

123 www.sjofartsverket.se/en/.

124 www.havochvatten.se/.

125 www.swedishepa.se/.

126 www.skogsstyrelsen.se/en/.

Environment Climate Data Sweden (ECDS) is an infrastructural initiative facilitating the searching, publication and long-term storage of data for research in the fields of environment and climate. The ECDS consists of a clearinghouse mechanism, allowing for the searching and publication of relevant data; and a service infrastructure, providing additional support to scientists throughout the whole research process. It contains Sweden's IPY data and is a repository of past and current data from Swedish polar research expeditions.[127] ECDS is hosted by the Swedish Meteorological and Hydrological Institute (SMHI), a government agency that manages and develops information on weather, water and climate that provides knowledge and advanced decision-making data for public services, the private sector and the general public. SMHI also conducts Arctic research.[128]

*Industry*

The Swedish state-owned mining company, Luossavaara-Kiirunavaara AB (LKAB)[129] has subsidiaries and operations in a number of countries around the world. Their major assets are the iron ore mines in Sweden's far north, including Kiruna. Other than building and maintaining rail and port infrastructures, the company is undertaking the major task of moving a sector of Kiruna town itself – including most of the town centre – in order to facilitate the expansion of mining operations.

### 3.2 *EU State Observers at the Arctic Council*

France

The French Polar Institute Paul Emile Victor (IPEV) is a public interest group formed by nine public and parastatal bodies – a consortium of leading French research bodies and agencies. IPEV is an agency of resources and expertise to support scientific research in the Arctic.[130] IPEV, launched in 2013, is a partner of the French Arctic Initiative.[131] It runs highly interdisciplinary programmes for research on key scientific issues in the Arctic. It also runs a national database of Arctic researchers. Together with the German Alfred Wegner Institute: Helmholtz Centre for Polar and Marine Research (AWI),[132] IPEV runs the AWIPEV Arctic Research base at Ny-Ålesund on Svalbard.[133]

127 www.smhi.se/ecds.

128 www.smhi.se/en/Research/satellite-data-provide-insight-into-melting-arctic-ice-1.29845.

129 www.lkab.com/.

130 www.institut-polaire.fr/ipev/l_institut.

131 www.chantier-arctique.fr/en/index.php.

132 www.awi.de/en/institute/.

133 www.awi.de/en/infrastructure/stations/awipev_arctic_research_base/.

An important research infrastructure enabling scientific initiatives is the privately run and publically supported Tara Expeditions, which operates the Tara, a sailing research vessel which operates in polar areas.[134] It has been used in EU-funded projects, such as DAMOCLES.

Germany

The Alfred Wegner Institute: Helmholtz Centre for Polar and Marine Research (AWI) is the central German research facility for the polar regions.[135] It is the national manager and implementation agency of the National German Arctic and Antarctic Programme. It also has a mandate to advise the German government in all matters concerning the polar regions. It operates the R/V *Polarstern*, a high class ice breaking research vessel and floating large scale laboratory to support research in the Arctic and Antarctic. Recently, an initiative was launched to create an Arctic Research Icebreaker Consortium for Europe (ARICE), which aims to implement a joint European / International Consortium for the operation of the European heavy icebreakers *Oden* (Sweden) and *Polarstern.* This initiative is supported by several European countries, as well as Canada and some international institutions.[136] AWI also undertook the initiative to host the International Arctic Science Committee, IASC,[137] a non-governmental, international scientific organization. The IASC mission is to encourage and facilitate cooperation in all aspects of Arctic research, in all countries engaged in Arctic research and in all areas of the Arctic region. The Helmoltz Centre for Ocean Research in Kiel also conducts marine research in Arctic areas.[138]

Apart from the research station AWIPEV on Svalbard, which is jointly run with the French, AWI also operates the Research Station Samoylov in the Lena Delta with the Russian Lena Delta Reserve.[139] Another German-Russian research infrastructure initiative is the Otto Schmidt Laboratory for Polar and Marine Research (OSL),[140] located in St Petersburg. The OSL provides a basis for coordination and development of the research projects carried out within the framework of the Bilateral Agreement on Cooperation in Polar and Marine

134 oceans.taraexpeditions.org/en/a-2-5-years-marine-and-scientific-expedition.php?id_page=1.

135 www.awi.de/en/institute/.

136 faro-arctic.org/fileadmin/Resources/DMU/GEM/faro/2013_Nicole__ARICE_for_FARO.pdf.

137 www.iasc.info/.

138 http://www.geomar.de/en/research/expeditionen/exp/completed/0/0/.

139 www.awi.de/en/infrastructure/stations/samoylov_station/.

140 www.otto-schmidt-laboratory.de/?Home.

Research between the Russian Federation and Germany. The OSL focusses especially on the support of young scientists in Russia and Germany and together with other research institutions jointly runs Arctic specific programmes such as the Master Program for Polar and Marine Research (POMOR).[141]

### Italy

Italy's institutional and infrastructural Arctic initiatives are mainly undertaken by the National Research Council.[142] It has a dedicated Polar Support Unit, which is also responsible for the Italian Arctic Station Dirigible *Italia*,[143] a multidisciplinary research facility located in Ny-Ålesund, Svalbard. The National Institute of Oceanography and Experimental Geophysics (OGS),[144] an internationally oriented public research institution, has polar areas as a dedicated pillar of research activity and the OGS represents Italy on a number of international polar research management and research infrastructure committees.

### The Netherlands

The Willem Barentz Polar Institute[145] is a conglomeration of institutes which actively contributes to Dutch polar activities. It includes the major institutions with Arctic research initiatives, including the Royal Netherlands Institute for Sea Research,[146] the Royal Netherlands Meteorological Institute,[147] the Free University of Amsterdam,[148] and Wageningen University.[149] The Arctic Centre,[150] based at the University of Groningen, is also part of the Willem Barentz Polar Institute and its current host. The Arctic Centre is largely involved in social science and humanities related research in the Arctic. The Netherlands' national research council has a funding instrument for polar research initiatives, the Netherlands Polar Program.[151] The Netherlands Arctic Station is a government supported infrastructural initiative and operates during summer months in Ny-Ålesund, Svalbard.[152] It is an INTERACT observer.

141 pomor.spbu.ru/.
142 www.cnr.it/sitocnr/Englishversion/Englishversion.html.
143 www.polarnet.cnr.it/content/view/162/58/lang,en/.
144 www.ogs.trieste.it/en.
145 wbpi.webhosting.rug.nl/index.php?nr=89.
146 www.nioz.nl/.
147 www.knmi.nl/index_en.html.
148 www.falw.vu.nl/en/.
149 www.wageningenur.nl/en/Research-Results/Projects-and-programmes/Arctic.htm.
150 www.rug.nl/research/arctisch-centrum/.
151 www.nwo.nl/en/research-and-results/programmes/Netherlands+Polar+Programme.
152 www.arcticstation.nl/.

### Poland

The Committee on Polar Research of the Polish Academy of Sciences provides the organizational infrastructure for Polish polar research. The members of PRC represent all scientific disciplines and come from more than 24 scientific institutions in Poland. It is also responsible for the scientific patronage and development of Polish polar research infrastructures.[153] This includes five research stations on Spitsbergen, Svalbard, namely the Stanisław Siedlecki Polish Polar Station in Hornsund,[154] the Stanisław Baranowksi Polar Station of Wrocław University,[155] the Nicolaus Copernicus University Polar Station, Kaffioyra,[156] the Calypsobyen Polar Station of Maria Curie-Skłodowska University[157] and the "Skottehytta" – expedition base of Adam Mickiewicz University in Poznań.[158] The Polish Polar Station, Hornsund is an observer to INTERACT. The Polish Academy of Sciences also owns the tall ship, RV *Oceania*. The training and research vessel *Horyzont* II, which is also used for Arctic research, is owned by the Gdynia Maritime University.[159]

### Spain

The national polar authority of Spain is the Spanish Polar Committee,[160] which includes a technical secretariat. Spain's Navy administers its polar research vessel, R/V *Hesperides* and the support vessel *Las Palmas*. The National Polar Data Centre is an infrastructural initiative that ensures long term archiving of data.[161] More than fifteen Spanish research institutes research groups with Arctic projects currently running.[162]

### United Kingdom

Arctic research support and coordination in the UK is the task of the NERC Arctic Office.[163] The Arctic Office is funded by the Natural Environmental Research

153 www.kbp.pan.pl/index.php?lang=en.
154 hornsund.igf.edu.pl/index.php.
155 polar.geom.uni.wroc.pl/.
156 www.home.umk.pl/~geopolar/stacja/STACJA.HTML.
157 geografia.umcs.lublin.pl/wyprawy/.
158 www.staff.amu.edu.pl/~svalbard/.
159 www.am.gdynia.pl/en/.
160 www.idi.mineco.gob.es/portal/site/MICINN/menuitem.7eeac5cd345b4f34f09dfd1001432ea0/?vgnextoid=9b6fefb8b7c0f210VgnVCM1000001d04140aRCRD.
161 //hielo.igme.es/index.php/en/.
162 www.arctic-council.org/index.php/en/document-archive/category/50-information-day-of-the-arctic-council-in-copenhagen-28-may-2010?download=183:spain.
163 www.arctic.ac.uk/.

Council (NERC)[164] and hosted by the British Antarctic Survey (BAS).[165] BAS manages the UK Arctic Research Station[166] at Ny-Ålesund on Svalbard, the station is an INTERACT observer. NERC also operates the four polar research vessels, the *James Clark Ross, Ernest Shackleton, RRS Discovery* and *RRS James Cook.* The James Clark Ross operates primarily in the eastern Arctic Ocean.[167] It also operates several research aircraft.[168]

Another institution which provides a springboard for Arctic initiatives, and runs several themselves, is the Scott Polar Research Institute, a centre for research into both polar regions at the University of Cambridge.[169] A large number of universities in the UK have Arctic research projects, including most in the Russell Group (umbrella association for 24 UK's universities).[170] Some universities have research themes focussing on Arctic and sub-Arctic research, such as the University of Aberdeen[171] and the University of Southampton, Ocean and Earth Science, National Oceanography Centre Southampton (NOCS).[172]

### 3.3 *Other European Union Countries*

The EU/EEA and affiliated countries represented on the European Polar Board[173] (which covers both the boreal and austral poles), but who are not observers at the Arctic Council, include Austria, Belgium, Bulgaria, the Czech Republic, Estonia, Luxembourg, Portugal and Switzerland. Besides time-limited research projects located within the various countries, there are also Arctic and polar specific institutes in some of these countries (the institute are not all necessarily members of the European Polar Board). This includes, for example, the Austrian Polar Research Institute is a research consortium that promotes and coordinates research and education in the area of polar sciences, including social sciences, at the participating organisations.[174]

164 www.nerc.ac.uk/index.asp?cookieConsent=A.

165 www.antarctica.ac.uk/.

166 www.arctic.ac.uk/infrastructure/research-station/.

167 www.arctic.ac.uk/infrastructure/research-vessels/.

168 www.arctic.ac.uk/infrastructure/aircraft/.

169 www.spri.cam.ac.uk/.

170 www.russellgroup.ac.uk/our-universities/.

171 www.abdn.ac.uk/the-north/.

172 www.southampton.ac.uk/oes/index.page?.

173 www.esf.org/hosting-experts/expert-boards-and-committees/polar-sciences/about/membership.html.

174 www.polarresearch.at/.

In Belgium, the International Polar Foundation (IPF)[175] provides an interface between polar science and society. The IPF's Arctic initiatives include promoting polar education and exploration, as well as running the annual Arctic Futures symposium, promoting high-level policymaker – stakeholder interaction.

## 4 Other European Initiatives

### 4.1 *Non-Governmental Initiatives*

A number of high-profile organisations and networks operating at national or intergovernmental level within European countries have launched initiatives that aim to inform Arctic leadership and management strategies. Many, but not all, of them are observers to the Arctic Council.[176]

On the non-governmental front, the groups involved range from independent conservation foundations to activist groups. For example, the WWF, a conservation foundation with national offices in all the European Arctic countries except Iceland, since 1992 has been running the WWF Arctic Programme.[177] The programme entails a variety of scientific research and advocacy projects. The WWF is an observer to the Arctic Council. On the other side of the spectrum the activist group Greenpeace has been running a highly visible "Save the Arctic"[178] campaign.

### 4.2 *Intergovernmental*

On an intergovernmental level, involving the majority of European countries, the United Nations Environment Programme (UNEP)[179] has also recently initiated a process planning well-coordinated Arctic activities, utilizing its global environmental mandate and convening authority to contribute to sustainable development in the Arctic. The United Nations Development Program (UNDP)[180] and the United Nations Economic Commission for Europe (UN-ECE)[181] also have observer status at the Arctic Council. The International Work Group for Indigenous Affairs (IWGIA),[182]

175 www.polarfoundation.org/.

176 www.arctic-council.org/index.php/en/about-us/arctic-council/observers.

177 wwf.panda.org/what_we_do/where_we_work/arctic/.

178 www.greenpeace.org/international/en/campaigns/climate-change/arctic-impacts/.

179 www.unep.org/regionalseas/programmes/independent/arctic/.

180 www.undp.org/content/undp/en/home.html.

181 www.unece.org/#.

182 www.iwgia.org/regions/arctic.

headquartered in Denmark, is an international, non-governmental human rights organization supporting indigenous peoples' rights with observer status at the Arctic Council. For decades the IWGIA conducted studies and promoted rights of Arctic indigenous peoples.

### 4.3 *European International Indigenous Organisations*

More regionally focused bodies in Europe include the Sámi Council,[183] an NGO and permanent participant to the Arctic Council with Sámi member organizations in Finland, Russia, Norway and Sweden. The Council works in collaboration with the UN and EU. The primary aim of the Sámi Council is the promotion of Sámi rights and interests in the four countries where the Sámi are living. Inuit in Greenland are represented by the Inuit Circumpolar Council (ICC),[184] an NGO that is also a permanent participant in the Arctic Council. The ICC has been participating in several of the Council's working groups.

### 4.4 *Nordic Initiatives*

The International Centre for Reindeer Husbandry,[185] funded by the Norwegian government, hosts the Secretariat of the Association of World Reindeer Herders (WRH) – which promotes professional, commercial, and cultural contact between the different reindeer peoples of the world, and disseminates information about reindeer husbandry. WRH has observer status to the Arctic Council.

Other Nordic specific organizations with observer status at the Arctic Council, and running Arctic focused programmes as part of their broader mandate, include the Nordic Council of Ministers (NCM),[186] a forum for Nordic governmental co-operation and the Nordic Environment Finance Corporation (NEFCO),[187] an international finance institution. NordForsk,[188] an organisation under the NCM, has launched a major initiative to establish a cross-cutting Nordic co-funding programme, Noria-Net Arctic,[189] in response to the multiple societal challenges and new opportunities in the Arctic region.

183 www.saamicouncil.net.
184 www.inuit.org/.
185 reindeerherding.org/about-us/.
186 www.norden.org/en/nordic-council-of-ministers.
187 www.nefco.org/.
188 www.nordforsk.org/en.
189 www.nordforsk.org/en/programs/noria-net-arctic.

Norway, Iceland, Greenland and the Faroe Islands are the founding signatories of the North Atlantic Marine Mammal Commission (NAMMCO), an international body for cooperation on the conservation, management and study of marine mammals in the North Atlantic.[190]

Country specific initiatives to facilitate international collaboration include, for example the Arctic Society in Finland[191] established in 2012 aims to support and monitor Finland's activities in the Arctic region and to coordination of Finnish policy in relation to its activities. In addition, the Advisory Board is responsible for raising awareness about Arctic issues and for forging connections with corresponding bodies in other countries.

The Norwegian Barents Secretariat is owned by the three northernmost counties of Norway: Nordland, Troms and Finnmark. There are three Russian offices: Murmansk, Archangelsk and Nenets office. The Norwegian Barents Secretariat aims at developing the Norwegian-Russian relations in the north by promoting and funding Norwegian-Russian cooperation projects. The Secretariat is also a centre of competence on Norwegian-Russian relations and, in broad strokes, supports Barents Euro-Arctic cooperation.

Initiated by the Icelandic president, the Arctic Circle[192] is a forum with a mission to facilitate dialogue and strengthen the decision-making process through involving a range of decision-makers across all sectors. Participants include a cross section of funding bodies, universities, companies, NGOs and media partners. Arctic Frontiers,[193] an independent Norwegian network organising an annual summit in Tromsø, Norway, provides a platform for all Arctic stakeholders to define priorities for development and research.

### 4.5 *Circumpolar Initiatives: University of the Arctic*

The University of the Arctic[194] is a cooperative network of more than 130 institutions, including a large contingent of European universities, colleges, and other organisations committed to higher education and research in the North. It is a decentralized organization, with offices, programs and other functions hosted at member institutions in the Circumpolar North.

190 www.nammco.no/Nammco/Mainpage/.

191 arktinenseura.yhdistysavain.fi/.

192 www.arcticcircle.org/.

193 www.arctic-frontiers.com.

194 www.uarctic.org/Frontpage.aspx?m=3.

## 5 Monitoring and Assessment Initiatives

The SAON process was initiated by the Arctic Council and has been underway since early 2007.[195] Its purpose is to support and strengthen the development of multinational engagement for sustained and coordinated pan-Arctic observing and data sharing systems that serve societal needs, particularly related to environmental, social, economic and cultural issues. SAON promotes the vision of well-defined observing networks that enable users to have access to free, open and high quality data that will realize pan-Arctic and global value-added services and provide societal benefits. Its goal is to enhance Arctic-wide observing activities by facilitating partnerships and synergies among existing observing and data networks ("building blocks"), and promoting sharing and synthesis of data and information. SAON is also committed to facilitating the inclusion of Arctic indigenous peoples in observing activities, in particular by promoting community-based monitoring (CBM) efforts. Reports on country and organisation specific observing activities can be found on the SAON website.[196]

BarentsWatch (BW)[197] is an initiative by 27 central Norwegian state agencies and research institutes. The aim is to expand the number of recognised partners in the future as part of the continuous development of BarentsWatch. It is a comprehensive monitoring and information system for sea and coastal areas from Denmark in the south, to Greenland in the west, the North Pole in the north and Novaya Zemlya in the east. The ambition is to be able to share information internationally in the future.

Polar View (PV)[198] was initiated by the ESA and the European Commission, with participation from the Canadian Space Agency, under the Copernicus programme. PV has participants and team members from Australia, Belgium, Canada, Denmark, Estonia, Finland, France, Germany, Italy, Norway, Sweden, and the UK. It aims to build a cohesive international network that meets the following objectives: engages a wide spectrum of end users who are convinced of the value of the services and products; provides a suite of desirable Environmental Observation (EO)-related services and products to public users; provides additional EO-related services and products to private users; and

195 www.arcticobserving.org/.

196 www.arcticobserving.org/index.php?option=com_content&view=article&id=66&Itemid=100017.

197 www.barentswatch.no/.

198 www.polarview.org/.

interfaces in a mutually beneficial way with the cryospheric science and climate change community. Current PV service lines include: Sea Ice Monitoring and Forecasting; Iceberg Monitoring; Ice Edge Monitoring; Ice Drift Trajectories; River Ice Monitoring; Lake Ice Monitoring; Glacier Monitoring; Snow Monitoring.

ANISTIAMO: Addressing New Challenges in Satellite Based Maritime Surveillance and Arctic Monitoring[199] is an initiative of Kongsberg Satellite Services in Norway with participation by organisations in Ireland and Finland. ANISTIAMO builds on previous research that focused on satellite derived information for maritime surveillance, and seeks to continue working with maritime agencies (*e.g.* naval organisations, coast guards) that are potential users of satellite-based products and services. With this in mind, the primary objectives of the initiative are to: validate the capability to provide products and services responding to requirements for information expressed by end users in the maritime security and Arctic Environmental Monitoring community; demonstrate benefits and utility for a defined set of products and services to a representative group of end users under operational conditions; obtain clear, credible statements from participating end users on the utility of the products and services delivered; as well as compile convincing evidence on the viability of a future operational case for the products and services considered within the target demand sectors.

International Arctic Systems for Observing the Atmosphere (IASOA)[200] is an on-going initiative to advance coordinated research objectives from independent pan-Arctic atmospheric observatories through (1) strategically developing comprehensive observational capacity, (2) facilitating data access and usability through a single gateway, and (3) mobilizing contributions to synergistic science and socially-relevant services derived from IASOA assets and expertise. Partner observatories are located in the USA (Barrow, Alaska), Canada (Alert and Eureka), Kingdom of Denmark (Summit in Greenland), Norway (Ny-Ålesund on Svalbard), Sweden (Abisko), Finland (Sodankylä) and Russia (Tiksi and Cherskii).

The ESA,[201] (with 20 member states in Europe and cooperation agreements with other countries and agencies), manages two major research infrastructure initiatives: Copernicus (see in Section 2.3.) and Cryosat-2.

199 www.cmrc.ie/projects/addressing-new-challenges-in-satellite-based-maritime-surveillance-and-arctic-monitoring-%28anistiamo%29.html.

200 iasoa.org/iasoa/index.php?option=com_frontpage&Itemid=1.

201 www.esa.int/ESA.

The Cryosat-2[202] infrastructure initiative also falls under the ESA. CryoSat-2's mission is to study the Earth's polar ice caps, and is dedicated to precise monitoring of the changes in the thickness of marine ice floating in the polar oceans and variations in the thickness of the vast ice sheets that overlie Greenland and Antarctica. CryoSat-2 will primarily: determine regional trends in Arctic perennial sea-ice thickness and mass; and determine the contribution that the Antarctic and Greenland ice sheets are making to mean global rise in sea level.

26 European states participate in the European Organization for the Exploitation of Meteorological Satellites or EUMETSAT Polar System (EPS) Metop.[203] This organisation's prime objective is to provide continuous, long-term data sets, in support of operational meteorological and environmental forecasting and global climate monitoring, in which the Arctic plays an important role.

Arktika, an initiative by Russian Federal Space Agency (ROSCOSMOS), indications of interest from Italy among others. The Arktika system, estimated to be worth around 70 billion roubles ($2.5 billion US), will monitor climatic changes, survey energy resources in the Arctic region as well as provide high-speed communications services. The system has been recently approved by the Russian Economic Development Agency and according to ROSCOSMOS has also received support from the World Meteorological Organization. The new Arctic satellite cluster will be based on already operational remote-sensing weather and telecommunication satellites and will also receive radio signals from the COSPAS-SARSAT international search and rescue (SAR) system.

Nuuk Basic[204] is an extensive cross-disciplinary ecological monitoring programme in low Arctic West Greenland. Its partners include the Department of Bioscience, Aarhus University,[205] the Greenland Institute of Natural Resources,[206] the Greenland Climate Research Centre,[207] the University of Copenhagen[208] and Asiaq – Greenland Survey[209] and receives both private and public funding.

202 www.esa.int/Our_Activities/Observing_the_Earth/CryoSat.

203 www.eumetsat.int/website/home/Satellites/index.html.

204 nuuk-basic.dk.

205 bios.au.dk/en/.

206 www.natur.gl/en/.

207 www.natur.gl/index.php?id=663&L=3.

208 www.ku.dk/english/.

209 www.asiaq.gl/.

## 6 Commercial Development in the European Arctic

Commercial development initiatives not only co-produce knowledge, but have a tangible effect on the Arctic environment. Given the European Free Trade Area and other trade agreements, tax revenue companies create for nations, and the potential importance of Arctic resources for the European economy, a perusal of commercial initiatives is included in this inventory of Arctic initiatives. Some companies are majority-owned by nation states, others are headquartered or closely associated with specific nation states and yet others are regional or multinational. *Examples* of initiatives are given based for each of the four areas covered by the EU 2012 inventory: Hydrocarbons and minerals, fisheries, transport and tourism.

Initiatives to exploit ***hydrocarbons and minerals*** in the Arctic are often in the media spotlight. Several Europe-based oil and gas companies have initiated the process of exploring or exploiting Arctic resources, for example the Arctic Liquefied Natural Gas (LNG) activities of the French oil and gas company, Total,[210] or the investments in Arctic drilling by the Italian-based multinational Eni.[211] Royal Dutch Shell, an Anglo-Dutch company, has several projects and exploration initiatives in Arctic conditions, including in the European Arctic.[212] Danish Maersk Oil[213] has licenses off the Greenland coast in Baffin Bay.

Hydrocarbons and mineral extraction initiatives is not restricted to major oil, gas and mining companies and several other initiatives are linked to it. Nunaoil,[214] for example, is fully owned by the Government of Greenland and represents all public interests in all exploration licenses in Greenland. Finnish industries with initiatives with an Arctic edge include companies researching and developing oil spill recovery equipment adapted to Arctic, such as Lamor (Larsen Marine Oil Recovery)[215] which has its headquarters in Finland and works closely with several Arctic countries, including Finland, Canada and the United States on oil spill response and recovery in the Arctic. Tekes,[216] the Finnish Funding Agency for Technology and Innovation, launched a Green

210 total.com/en/energies-expertise/oil-gas/exploration-production/strategic-sectors/lng/innovations/lng-arctic.

211 www.eni.com/en_IT/attachments/investor-relations/presentation/2012/eni-in-the-arctic/Eni-in-the-Arctic.pdf.

212 www.shell.com/global/future-energy/arctic.html.

213 www.maerskoil.com/pages/default.aspx.

214 nunaoil.gl/en/about-nunaoil/nunaoil.html.

215 www.lamor.com/.

216 www.tekes.fi/en/community/Home/351/Home/473.

Mining Programme[217] initiative (2011–2016), the main objective of which is to make Finland a global leader of the sustainable mineral industry.

The two countries with the largest ***Arctic fisheries*** in Europe are not members of the EU, namely Norway and Iceland. Nevertheless, the EU is the major export market for Arctic fish (especially from the North Atlantic) and fisheries has played an important role in EU environmental politics.

The Iceland Responsible Fisheries Foundation[218] is an initiative funded by the Icelandic government and operates the Iceland Responsible Fisheries logo. This logo indicates the Icelandic origin of fish catches in Icelandic waters and responsible fisheries management. Major Icelandic fisheries companies such as HB Grandi,[219] ISI Seafood[220] and Samherji[221] uses the logo. The Norwegian Seafood Council[222] is an initiative with another angle – it markets Norwegian Seafood and does reputational risk management and communication for the Norwegian Seafood industry. Havfisk[223] (previously Aker Seafoods) is Norway's largest white fish company, trawls along the Norwegian coast, the Barents Sea and around Svalbard. It is endorsed by, amongst others, the Marine Stewardship Council,[224] which sets standards for sustainable fisheries, and is currently running an assessment of fisheries in the Arctic Ocean.[225] However, most northern fisheries are not necessarily identified as Arctic, but rather as North Atlantic or North-East Atlantic.

Major European ***transport*** initiatives in the Arctic are usually related to rail transport and shipping. Discussions are on-going (September 2013) within the Barents region to initiate public-corporate partnerships to expand the railway transport system in the Barents-Arctic region, especially for the export of ore mined in the far North. Several infrastructural initiatives, especially taken by companies in Finland have been discussed in the previous section. In terms of governance processes at least two major initiatives are underway. The International Maritime Organisation,[226] to which all EU and Arctic countries are members, is busy developing a polar for shipping operations in polar waters.

217 www.tekes.fi/programmes/GreenMining.

218 www.responsiblefisheries.is/.

219 www.hbgrandi.com/Home.

220 www.is.is/.

221 www.samherji.is/en.

222 en.seafood.no/.

223 www.havfisk.no/en.

224 www.msc.org/.

225 www.msc.org/track-a-fishery/fisheries-in-the-program/in-assessment/arctic-ocean/.

226 www.imo.org/MediaCentre/HotTopics/polar/Pages/default.aspx.

This dovetails several other agreements already in place under the IMO umbrella that affects shipping in some Arctic regions, for example mandatory ship reporting in the Barents Area. Another, voluntary industry-led initiative is the Arctic Marine Best Practice Declaration document, which is supported by international bodies such as the International Union of Marine Insurance[227] and the Nordic Association of Marine Insurers.[228] The initiative was partly driven by Arctic Marine Solutions, a Swedish company that specializes in quantification and operation of ice management for Arctic operations.[229]

The Norway- based Association of Arctic Expedition Cruise Operators (AECO),[230] to which many major European tour operators belong, is a major initiative in ***tourism*** industry to regulate and represent the views of Arctic expedition cruise operators and related industries. It has mandatory guidelines for its member tour operators, as well as visitor guidelines for tourists. Tourism in the Arctic areas of European countries is usually regulated regionally by counties and municipalities.

## 7 Other European States

### Norway

One of the major institutional Arctic initiatives in Norway is FRAM, the High North Research Centre for Climate and the Environment,[231] a constellation of institutions contributing to maintaining Norway's prominent status in the management of environment and natural resources in the North. The Norwegian Polar Institute (NPI),[232] a member of FRAM, represents Norway on several international forums. The NPI is active within the fields of scientific research, mapping and environmental monitoring in the Arctic and Antarctica. The Institute advises Norwegian authorities in strategic and thematic matters relating to the Polar Regions, represents Norway internationally on various occasions and is Norway's competent environmental authority in Antarctica. The Institute equips and organises major expeditions and owns the research

227 www.iumi.com/images/gillian/Clippings/IUMI%20Arctic%20Declaration%20Release%2023%204%2013.pdf.

228 www.cefor.no/Industry-Policy/News/Arctic-Best-Practice-Declaration/.

229 arcticmarinesolutions.se/index.php.

230 www.aeco.no/about-aeco/.

231 www.framsenteret.no/.

232 www.npolar.no/en/about-us/.

vessel *Lance* as well as the Sverdrup Research Station in Ny-Ålesund. The FRAM centre also hosts the Arctic Council Secretariat.[233]

UiT The Arctic University of Norway[234] located in Tromsø, is another prominent FRAM member. UiT's key research focuses on the polar environment, climate research, indigenous people, peace and conflict transformation, telemedicine, medical biology, space physics, fishery science, marine bioprospecting, linguistics and computational chemistry. The university also has several other Arctic related initiatives, including the establishment of national research groups. It is a majority owner of the Northern Research Institute (Norut),[235] which carries out public sector and industry research commissions, with special expertise in the Northern regions, and UiT is an initiating partner of the National Centre for Petroleum Activities in the Arctic. The latter centre, to be seated in Tromsø, received seed money from the Norwegian state in 2012 and brings several institutions together to focus on petroleum extraction-related research in an Arctic context.

The Institute of Marine Research,[236] also a member of FRAM, is Norway's largest centre of marine science. Its main task is to provide advice to Norwegian authorities on aquaculture and the ecosystems of the Barents Sea, the Norwegian Sea, the North Sea and the Norwegian coastal zone. About 50% of Institute's activities are financed by the Ministry of Fisheries and Coastal Affairs. The Institute owns several research vessels.[237]

The NPI, the Institute for Marine Research, and UiT have commissioned (at a cost of NOK 1.4 bln) the construction of research vessel *Kronprins Haakon*, an ice-class Polar 10 (PC 3) Icebreaker which should be ready for delivery in 2017.

The University Centre in Svalbard (UNIS), also a member of FRAM, is a share-holding company, owned by the Norwegian Ministry of Education and Research. UNIS's goals are to provide university level education in Arctic studies, to carry out high quality research, and to contribute to the development of Svalbard as an international research platform. It is an important clearing house for research on Svalbard. UNIS is also in charge of the Svalbard Integrated

233 www.arctic-council.org/index.php/en/contact.

234 uit.no/startsida.

235 www.norut.no/en/Norut/About-us.

236 www.imr.no/en.

237 www.imr.no/filarkiv/2003/12/Our_Ships_And_The_Men_Whose_Names_They_Bear.pdf/en.

Arctic Earth Observing System (SIOS).[238] The overall goal of SIOS is to establish an Arctic Earth Observing System in and around Svalbard that integrates the studies of geophysical, chemical and biological processes from all research and monitoring platforms.

In terms of research stations, two Norwegian stations are part of the EU-INTERACT initiative. Finse Alpine Research Centre[239] is located in the northwestern part of the Hardangervidda mountain plateau. Even though the University of Oslo is the official owner, state funding for building the station was provided on the condition that the Universities of Bergen and Oslo have equal rights to the use of the station for research and education. Bioforsk Svanhovd[240] belongs to the Norwegian Institute for Agricultural and Environmental Research (Bioforsk). It is located in the Pasvik area in North-East Norway.

The Centre for High North Logistics (CHNL)[241] was established as an international knowledge hub for businesses, research institutions and authorities so that they can develop effective and sustainable logistics solutions for northern sea areas. One of their initiatives is the creation of an online database, Arctic Resources and Transportation Information System (ARCTIS), a knowledge hub to provide the best available information on non-living resources, shipping and logistics in the Arctic.[242]

Since much of its activities take place in the Arctic, Statoil,[243] the Norwegian oil and gas extraction company in which the Norwegian government holds a majority share, has a dedicated Arctic unit and a specific focus on the far north of the Norwegian continental shelf. Besides infrastructural development in the north, Statoil has taken an institutional corporate initiative in conducting research and development programs tailored to meet the challenges of oil and gas extraction in the north.

### Iceland

The Stefansson Arctic Institute,[244] located in Akureyri, operates under the auspices of the Icelandic Ministry for the Environment and Natural Resources. It has

238 www.sios-svalbard.org/servlet/Satellite?c=Page&pagename=sios/Hovedside mal&cid=1234130481072.

239 www.finse.uio.no/.

240 www.bioforsk.no/ikbViewer/page/prosjekt/hovedtema?p_dimension_id=19512&p_menu_id=19528%20%20%20&p_sub_id=19513&p_dim2=19514.

241 www.chnl.no/.

242 www.arctis-search.com/ARCTIS+Database+%28Arctic+Resources+and+Transportation+Information+System%29.

243 www.statoil.com/en/OurOperations/FarNorth/Pages/default.aspx.

244 www.svs.is/english/about.htm.

a mandate to facilitate and coordinate Arctic research in Iceland and to advise the government on Arctic research matters. It is located in the same building as two Arctic Council secretariats hosted by Iceland, Conservation of Arctic Fauna and Flora (CAFF)[245] and Protection of the Arctic Marine Environment (PAME).[246] Also located in Akureyri is the Arctic Portal, which aims to provide the institutional infrastructure for a comprehensive gateway to Arctic information and data on the internet. It hosts a number of Arctic-related websites.[247] The Icelandic Arctic Cooperation Network is to facilitate cooperation amongst Icelandic public and private organizations, institutions, businesses and bodies involved in Arctic issues – among other things in research, education, innovation and monitoring, or other activities relevant to the Arctic region.[248]

In terms of other research infrastructures, Litla-Skard, an Icelandic INTERACT member is not a typical research station but a bio-monitoring site. The site is operated jointly by the Agricultural University of Iceland,[249] the Icelandic Institute of Natural History,[250] the Icelandic Meteorological Office,[251] the Environmental and Food Agency of Iceland,[252] and the Iceland Forest Service.[253]

## 8 Understanding Arctic Information Needs: A Lot Is Going On, So What Is Still Missing?

As the previous sections show, a wide range of "Arctic" initiatives already exists on a number of levels. However, Arctic stakeholders and policy-makers still see the need for improvements of the knowledge base in a variety of human needs and thematic areas.

The *Gap Analysis Report* (GAR) within the "Strategic Environmental Impact Assessment of development of the Arctic" project thus pursues two major goals. First, it aims to identify and analyse the Arctic information needs of stakeholders and policy-makers, as well as the wider public, where applicable. Second, the GAR endeavours to offer recommendations on ways to improve knowledge (reducing information gaps) and to improve two-way communication between

245 www.caff.is/.

246 www.pame.is/.

247 arcticportal.org/.

248 nordurslodanetid.is/index.php/en/.

249 landbunadur2.lbhi.is/index.aspx?GroupId=410&TabId=416.

250 en.ni.is/.

251 en.vedur.is/.

252 www.ust.is/the-environment-agency-of-iceland/.

253 www.skogur.is/english.

information providers and users (reducing communication gaps). The identified gaps also reflect the potential role of an EU Arctic Information Centre. This section offers a short overview of the methodology used for the GAR, the stakeholder survey results and analysis and the report's recommendations. For more information, please refer to the original GAR.[254]

## 9 The Gap Analysis Methodology

The GAR, and consequently this chapter, has focused primarily on the European Arctic, defined as including Finland, Sweden, Norway, Iceland, Denmark, Greenland and the Faroe Islands.[255] The non-European Arctic (*i.e.*, Russia, Canada, and the United States) has been also considered where relevant for the information needs of European Arctic stakeholders and policy-makers and in order to better evaluate existing information, but was not the primary focus of analysis. The focus on the European Arctic is appropriate as this is where the influence of the EU is the most prominent.[256]

A "gap" usually refers to a (empty) space between (existing) things – a missing part.[257] "Information" is an organized set of knowledge that is used to produce added value in human activities, reduce uncertainty and assist in decision-making.[258]

---

254 Elizabeth, T., Riedel, A., Weingartner, K., Azzolini, R., Guillon, F., Longo, S., Leone, C., Paadar, O., Leonenko, A. (2014). "Gap Analysis Report," Preparatory Action, Strategic Environmental Impact Assessment of development of the Arctic. Arctic Centre, University of Lapland.

255 Denmark, Finland, and Sweden are Member States of the EU and Iceland and Norway are EEA/EFTA member states. Greenland and the Faroe Islands are not a part of the EU or EEA/EFTA (although Greenland is a member of the Overseas Countries and Territories Association), but are considered here as part of the Danish Realm.

256 See *e.g.*, Timo Koivurova et al., "EU Competencies Affecting the Arctic" (DG for External Policies, Oktober 2010); Sandra Cavalieri et al., "EU Arctic Footprint and Policy Assessment – Final Report," Dezember 2010, http://arctic-footprint.eu/sites/default/files/AFPA_Final_Report.pdf.

257 See, *e.g.*, Merriam-Webster, "Gap," accessed March 6, 2015, http://www.merriam-webster.com/dictionary/gap.: "a space between two people or things; a hole or space where something is missing; a missing part."

258 Sylvia G. Faibisoff, S.G. & Ely D.P. (1974). "Information and Information Needs," ERIC Document Reproduction Service, 2; Prasad, H.N. (2012) *Information Needs and Users*, B.R. Publishing Corporation; Rice Knowledge Bank, "Concept 10: Information Gaps," accessed October 8, 2013, http://www.knowledgebank.irri.org/ipm/concept-10-information-gaps.html.

The terms "needs" and "gaps" are used here synonymously, with the understanding that a gap represents an unfulfilled need of an information user. This section focuses on two sides of these gaps or "information needs": information gaps and communication gaps.

1. First, we look at "information gaps", information needs defined within the framework of existing knowledge where there is a lack of existing information to fill an information user's need.
2. In other cases, information needs can be traced back to insufficient knowledge transfer and failures to successfully exchange or transfer information from providers to users. These failures to convey existing information are addressed in this report as "communication gaps."

The main part of the input into GAR has been gathered from stakeholders and policy-makers, which appear in the roles of information providers and information users alike, and in some cases can be both. Stakeholders are defined as actors who have interests in Arctic developments or who are affected by Arctic policies. Different occupations may lead to distinct Arctic information needs. For instance, policy-makers also have interests in Arctic developments or may be affected by EU policies, but are distinguished by having particular needs that pertain to Arctic governance.

For the analysis of information needs, gaps were first categorized based upon identified human needs with relevance for Arctic stakeholders: (1) *Living in the Arctic*, (2) *Investing in the Arctic*, (3) *Working in the Arctic*; (4) *Travelling in the Arctic*, (5) *Governing the Arctic*; and (6) *Understanding the Arctic*. Human needs are understood within the context of information.

In a second step, information gaps and communication gaps are examined according to thematic areas which are based on seven key Arctic overarching themes identified in the *Strategic Assessment of Development of the Arctic*[259]: (1) climate change in the Arctic; (2) changes in Arctic maritime transport, (3) development of oil/gas exploitation in the Arctic; (4) development of mining in the European Arctic; (5) changing nature of Arctic fisheries; (6) modernization of societies and cultures in the European Arctic; and (7) European Arctic landscape under increase pressure from various forms of land use. The combination of the human needs with the thematic areas resulted in the matrix as shown in Table 9.2.

259 Stępień, A., Koivurova. T. & Kankaanpää, P. (eds.), *Strategic Assessment of Development of the Arctic: Assessment Conducted for the European Union*, Arctic Centre, University of Lapland, commissioned by the European Commission, at www.arcticinfo.eu/sada.

TABLE 9.2 *Arctic human needs and mega-trends*

| Human need | Thematic area | | | | | | | |
|---|---|---|---|---|---|---|---|---|
| | **Climate change** | **Fisheries** | **Land use** | **Maritime transport** | **Mining** | **Oil and gas** | **Society and culture** | **Other** |
| Living in the Arctic<br>Investing in the Arctic<br>Working in the Arctic<br>Travelling in the Arctic<br>Governing the Arctic<br>Understanding the Arctic | | | | | | | | |

The primary information source was a questionnaire, developed basing on the above methodology and used to assess information and communication gaps. The questionnaire was shared with an extensive – non-representative – list of stakeholders and policy-makers based upon input from project partners. As such, stakeholders were not selected with equal representation across various geographic locations, sectors and interest groups and the survey does not represent a statistically valid sample across Arctic stakeholders, although this was sought to the extent possible within the limited scope of the GAR. An English-language questionnaire was sent out to a total of 898 individuals. In addition, a second version of the questionnaire in Russian was sent out to another 122 individuals. These results were gathered in separate databases so as to enable an easier distinction between regional information needs. For further details to the questionnaire, its structure and potential limitations, please refer to the original Gap Analysis Report.[260]

260 Tedsen et al. (2014), *op.cit.*, p. 21.

## 10 Stakeholder Survey Results and Main Findings

The survey results show a diverse picture of information needs and gaps within the group of participating stakeholders. As mentioned above, the representation of stakeholders is not representative. Thus, results should be read broadly: to draw conclusions on information and communication needs, to reveal certain trends, to support recommendations for filling information needs and to define the role of a prospective EU Arctic Information Centre.

A few respondents found that the pre-selected options were not a suitable fit for their identified information needs, while others pointed to needs that clearly intersected across multiple trends. For example, climate change is related to expanding human activities and trends in maritime transport or oil and gas extraction. Needs may cover more than one category, too; *e.g.*, where more information in the natural sciences is ultimately used for governance purposes. These linkages were evidenced from the responses, which exhibited cross-over between categories. On the whole, the (qualitative) analysis of the content of the individual free text responses on specific gaps was given greater weight in analysis than the (quantitative) analysis of selected sub-needs and thematic areas, which did not always clearly correlate or may have covered multiple areas.[261]

### 10.1 *Information Gaps and Communication Gaps*

Overall, the division between identified information gaps (50.4%) and communication gaps (49.6%) was evenly split.[262] In general, the information gaps showed a lack of knowledge on and understanding of the widespread changes happening in the Arctic region. Climate change was a predominant theme, although all of the thematic areas – climate change, maritime transport, oil and gas exploitation, mining, changes to societies and cultures, and land use – were repeated themes in both information and communication gaps and the identification of major challenges for the Arctic. Social and cultural changes,

261 The response rate of the survey was far higher within the English speaking group of stakeholders. The main (English) survey received a 16.5% response rate, while the Russian language survey received a response rate of 5.7%. Nonetheless, the response rate does not invalidate the survey's responses since they are assessed qualitatively and anecdotally.

262 A number of respondents, however, did not seem to understand or follow the distinction between information gaps and communication gaps. Another important aspect to consider is that respondents' might not have had sufficient information to evaluate whether gaps were information or communication-related. In other words, by not having access to information, one could be led to believe that it does not exist.

too, were leading issues. For information gaps, other common themes in respondents' answers included:

- a need for integrated and cumulative assessments of impacts,
- monitoring efforts and baseline studies,
- impacts of resource extraction,
- sustainable development alternatives,
- maritime transport,
- northern and indigenous cultures and lifestyles,
- demographic changes,
- land use,
- investment and employment opportunities,
- policy gaps.

Communication gaps described in the survey generally illustrated inefficiencies or confusion in gathering information from multiple sources, failures to communicate between stakeholders or governments, and a perceived lack of understanding about the Arctic region and its people. Themes within these responses included:

- a need for more centralized information,
- sharing information on indigenous peoples and Arctic cultures,
- discourse on the Arctic that fails to recognize regional variations and differences,
- failures to transmit information on training and preparedness,
- communication gaps between different stakeholders,
- failure to communicate information between governments or government levels.

Many needs and gaps were found to be overlapping, but in general, the breakdown by human need enabled a useful perspective on what information is needed and for what, as well as to categorize types of needs for subsequent discussion. Similarly, the division of information needs according to stakeholder groups and regions helped to examine the needs of different users, as well as help assess the reach of the survey and existing network. Not surprisingly, the types of responses from many stakeholder groups mirrored the backgrounds of the survey respondents. The human need of "Understanding the Arctic" received the largest number of responses, with a relatively even split between the sub-needs of natural sciences and social sciences. This is particularly interesting given the multi-purposed nature of the "need". However, the weight given to different needs or uses could be expected to change with a more comprehensive stakeholder network and alternative methods of engagement and communication, which may be seen as next steps for research.[263]

## 10.2 *Problems and Challenges in the Arctic*

The main challenges identified by respondents offered insight on and further context for the analysis of information needs. To begin with, the thematic areas used in analysis of information and communication gaps were also reflected in the main challenges, although with certain distinctions. All of the thematic areas arose in the responses on Arctic challenges, particularly climate change and society and culture.

Many respondents highlighted challenges related to information and communication gaps in their responses.[264] This shows that some respondents saw information generation and provision as the principle concerns for the Arctic. Regarding a lack of information, about half of responses mentioned a general lack of knowledge on the Arctic or Arctic issues, while a nearly equal amount addressed challenges regarding knowledge about the changing environment on all stages of observation and management. Communication-related challenges were about information flow and reliability. Information and communication gaps were perhaps most prominent in challenges for respondents who also identified needs for "Investing in the Arctic", who considered these gaps as key challenges for future investments in the region.

In looking at other challenges identified by respondents in relation to the information needs they named, there was overlap in some cases, and divergences in others. In the case of the latter, this may indicate that for some respondents, information is not what is seen as needed to meet major Arctic challenges.

For the human need of "Living in the Arctic", challenges and needs showed significant overlap regarding social and environmental changes on local communities. Likewise, information needs and main challenges identified according to "Understanding the Arctic" and natural sciences focused on climate change impacts and processes.

263 For a full overview of the information and communication gaps, structured by Activities in the Arctic, Arctic stakeholder groups, and Arctic regions, see the discussion of the replies in sections 2, 3, and 4 in the GAR.

264 Survey respondents' answers identifying major Arctic challenges were not required (nor intended) to be based on the information needs. However, because participants were first asked questions of the survey on perceived information gaps or communication gaps, this likely inadvertently influenced responses.

Respondents with "Governing needs" identified a range of Arctic-specific issues that went beyond the information and communication gaps mentioned for "Governing the Arctic". Challenges focused primarily on climate change and local and indigenous issues. Climate change – the information need with the most responses overall – was listed repeatedly as a main challenge. The discrepancy between the information and communication gaps and the main Arctic challenges here could be read to mean that while fundamental problems are relatively well-understood, more particularized information needs are priorities for governance purposes. An alternative interpretation could be that certain global issues (*i.e.*, climate change) present challenges at the local, regional, or national level, but not necessarily direct information needs. For respondents identifying needs on "Understanding the Arctic" and social sciences, there was also some discrepancy, with respondents focusing more on cooperation and governance, climate change, and oil and gas in the main challenges, and less on society and culture, which were focuses of information needs, perhaps indicating greater threats at the international level than at the local.

When looking at the relationship between answers from various stakeholder groups, stronger correlations could be observed. Thus, for the most part, it appeared that certain groups of self-identified stakeholders saw information gaps and communication gaps for the same issues that they viewed as posting the greatest challenges to the Arctic.

### 10.3 *Communication and Dissemination*[265]

Information and communication gaps may not only impair decision-making, but can ultimately block effective governance and pose hurdles in the growth of people, organizations, and communities. As described above, a communication gap refers to a state where information is not communicated to users completely or properly. In order for communication to be efficacious and reach a significant or desired number of recipients, it is necessary to:

- Define the target: The starting point for any communication action is the definition of the intended objective. This will subsequently determine how, when, by what means, and how often to communicate.
- Identify the interests of the different parties: This can be done, for example, through results obtained from targeted surveys of information users, as was done for this report and to inform the suggestions herein.

265 A complete overview of the recommendations and the potential methods of dissemination are provided in Section 7 of the GAR.

- Identify the interactions between the various types of targets: There may be differing interactions and responses between audiences and targets. For example, the scientific community may be primarily interested in the study of climatic changes, while Arctic communities may be more interested in how climate change affects quality of life.
- Identify means of communication: Different modes of communication are useful for different targets. For example, stakeholders such as policy-makers, the general public, indigenous communities, and scientific researchers may all respond to (and require) different types of information products.

The survey highlighted the need to use web tools in promoting new or additional information, or rather, to improve the flow of information and communication. More than 50% of respondents indicated that they consulted websites to enhance knowledge and fill information needs. Respondents from European Arctic and non-Arctic countries indicated that they both used and had a general preference for (non-EU) internet web sites.

When splitting replies along the stakeholder groups, clear preferences arose as well. For the scientific community, there was a prevalence (more than 30%) for receiving information from scientific journals. Some of the most commonly cited scientific journals included *Nature, Science, Polar Journal,* and *Arctic.* Respondents from governance, NGO, and industry backgrounds cited general preferences for receiving information through websites and newspapers.

In addition to more traditional dissemination methods, it can be useful to use less traditional strategies. For example, workshops, conferences, or online discussion lists can yield a higher level of engagement from stakeholders. A high number of respondents noted an interest in these types of information exchange activities.

### 10.4 *How a Future EU Arctic Information Centre Could Help Meet Arctic Information Needs*

The EU Arctic Information Centre is an initiative proposed in the Communication of the European Commission in 2008[266] and reiterated in the consecutive policy statements from the European Parliament, Council of the European Union, European Commission and the High Representative for Foreign and Security Policy. The initiative is conceived as a network of leading European institutions and organizations with Arctic knowledge and expertise

266 European Commission (2008). "The European Union and the Arctic Region," Communication COM(2008)763final.

in communication, under the leadership of the Arctic Centre of the University of Lapland in Rovaniemi (see the introductory chapter in this volume).[267]

The gap analysis makes clear that Arctic issues and challenges are marked by numerous information and communication gaps. Respondents to the survey felt that a great deal of needed information either did not exist, or that existing information was not accessible or synthesized well enough. In light of these deficiencies, there are clear functions for an EU Arctic Information Centre to perform in helping to fill information needs and to meet the EU's Arctic objectives of promoting engagement and dialogue with Arctic states, indigenous peoples, local inhabitants and other partners.[268] Although a more prominent role for the Centre is evident for filling communication gaps, there are also ample opportunities for supporting the elimination of information gaps.

### Filling Information Gaps

To help fill gaps in information, where existing knowledge either does not exist or is inadequate, the EUAIC as a network could facilitate information sharing and research collaboration between institutes. Institutionalized international collaboration could help to develop long-range plans for data collection and sharing, particularly for monitoring and observations, facilitating improved knowledge creation. Serving as an information hub or clearinghouse could potentially help guide researchers towards available data (*e.g.*, through collection of metadata) and support enhanced research efforts. Coordinated research could also aid integrated analyses and regional impact assessments, which were named as gaps in survey responses. These functions would support the EU's Arctic objectives of facilitate research and channelling knowledge, as well as international cooperation.[269]

Apart from serving as one of the nodes in the frameworks facilitating research collaboration, the EUAIC could help inform and support EU research agendas for the Arctic region, ultimately leading to the creation of new, essential knowledge for filling unmet Arctic information needs. Support in filling

267 See also the project website at www.arcticinfo.eu.

268 European Commission and High Representative (2012). "Developing a European Union Policy towards the Arctic Region: progress since 2008 and next steps," EU Commission and High Representative of the European Union for Foreign Affairs and Security Policy, Joint Communication to the European Parliament and the Council, JOIN(2012)19 final, p. 4.

269 European Commission and high representative (2012), "Developing a European Union Policy towards the Arctic Region...," pp. 6f. and 17f.

information gaps is not only relevant for stakeholders in Arctic research but also for governments, as can be seen in the replies from government stakeholders, where a large number of the information gaps hinted towards the need of a better science-policy interface.

Filling Communication and "Access to Information" Gaps

As described, many respondents experienced challenges in either accessing existing information or in synthesizing reports, data, and research from multiple and scattered sources. The EUAIC as a hub based on the network of institutions with Arctic expertize could help to improve the flow of information and reduce or eliminate communication gaps by connecting information users and providers.

A large number of respondents felt there was a need for centralized information. The Arctic region spans eight countries and includes very diverse subregions and Arctic information needs – and sources – stretch far beyond, as demonstrated in the survey results. Moreover, important Arctic issues and trends span (and link between) disciplinary areas. The Centre could serve as an intermediary by being a central point of information exchange, where information users could find sources and connect with providers.

The EUAIC could help to better distribute information and improving the flow of information. First, the Centre could serve as a conduit through which to exchange information between policy-makers and Arctic communities. Multiple respondents noted that it was challenging for Arctic communities and local-level interests to be included in national, regional, European, or international decision-making processes. Second, the network could also help to improve information sharing from Arctic communities and transfers of meaning to non-Arctic groups. Third, other respondents commented on a need for better communication between industry and communities, or between government and industry. Fourth, it can help various stakeholder to better understand values and culturally-sensitive narratives. Many of the gaps identified by respondents described misunderstandings regarding the Arctic region and its peoples, particularly from the side of non-Arctic publics and interest groups. Overall, this would contribute to stronger foundations for Arctic cooperation and sustainable development.

## 11 Conclusion

Even when just skimming the surface, it is clear that a large number of initiatives are being undertaken, and that capacity is being built to launch these initiatives. It is also clear that Arctic initiatives do not necessarily operate exclusively in the Arctic, and that not all initiatives undertaken in the Arctic self-identify as *Arctic*. What is clear though is that not all knowledge about the Arctic is produced by research projects. Although scientific research remains a central tenet in understanding the Arctic, there are many other, sometimes nebulous, sometimes targeted, initiatives that affect how the Arctic is known.

Categorising initiatives for the compendium has not been a formulaic task, as the drivers behind initiatives often make them incommensurable. Every nation state, for example, has different constellations of institutions tasked with managing and conducting polar research, and even more complex are commercial initiatives as are the ways in which they are associated with countries differ vastly. This can lead to questions as to what extent a commercial initiative can really be tied to a country. The Norwegian government, for example, is a majority shareholder of Statoil, whereas the French government has very few shares in Total – even though it is known as a French multinational. A continuously updated searchable electronic database with proper meta-data could prove of great use for those trying to find their way through a variety of multifaceted actions carried out by different actors. The tractability and longevity of recently started initiatives are hard to judge, and the information presented will necessarily become quickly outdated. It is extremely important that entities supplying information about their Arctic initiatives understand how the information is to be used and what value it may have for them. Furthermore, due to the sheer heterogeneity of the EU and EEA/EFTA members, it would be difficult to capture a birds-eye view of initiatives in the Arctic without access to information being facilitated by the partners forming the EUAIC initiative network. A broad, continuous initiative thus enhances the accessibility of Arctic knowledge.

Continuity is also a key factor when looking at the main source of input for the *Gap Analysis Report* that is the point of view of Arctic experts and stakeholders. The GAR offers a useful illustration of Arctic information needs as seen through the eyes of Arctic stakeholders – at this point in time. The results are not statistically representative, but serve to highlight certain types of information and communication gaps and trends regarding Arctic issues. Although the scope of the GAR in the context of a preparatory action was limited, it can also be seen as a building block for further research, such as performing targeted assessments of information and communication gaps for specific issues and users that allows a more detailed examination and analysis. It will also enable the utilization of the growing stakeholder networks being developed. Finally, the GAR can help to assess gaps better (whether "truly" information or "just" communication gaps) via the *Arctic Initiatives Compendium* – if it is updated and expanded in the future – and/or other databases.

However, most importantly, for its purposes, the GAR provides a look at how an EU Arctic Information Centre and network could be used within the context of existing Arctic information and communication gaps. Generally, these potentials are stronger in the area of communication, but the Centre could also facilitate the reduction of information gaps.

CHAPTER 10

# Role and Effectiveness of Assessments in Policy-making: On the Importance of the Process

*Małgorzata Śmieszek, Karolina Banul, Paula Kankaanpää, Timo Koivurova, Pamela Lesser and Adam Stępień*

## Abstract

Global and regional assessments have become increasingly common elements in international, national and local policy-making. They can be understood as organized efforts to harness scientific information to inform policy makers both from private and public sectors at all stages of decision-making. Growing use of assessments stems from a view that more widely shared information can add to a more effective management of complex interactions between humans and nature. At the same time, it presupposes that an enhanced understanding of impacts of human actions, presented with options for alleviation of these impacts, can provide incentives for decision-makers to carry out policies in a more sustainable way.

Assessments are often identified with the final products they deliver, *i.e.* reports. However, they can be better understood as social processes embedded within particular institutional settings where expert knowledge related to a policy problem is framed, integrated, interpreted, and eventually presented in final documents. It is also in the process of the conduct of assessment, and the design features of this process, where roots of assessment's potential effectiveness lie. Next to defining main concepts related to assessments, this chapter explains the background for their influence in decision-making.

## 1 Introduction

Global and regional assessments, primarily environmental, have become increasingly common elements in international, national and even local policy and decision-making.[1] As large-scale environmental problems and their

1 Clark, W.C., Mitchell, R.B., & Cash, D.W. (2006). "Evaluating the Influence of Global Environmental Assessments" In R.B. Mitchell, W.C. Clark, D.W. Cash, & N.M. Dickson (Eds.), *Global Environmental Assessments. Information and Influence* (pp. 1–28). Cambridge, Massachusetts: MIT Press.

 | DOI 10.1163/9789004303188_012

consequences cross borders and know no jurisdictional limits, addressing them requires cooperation among countries, interaction between scientists and policy makers, and inclusion of actors from all levels of the scale, from the local to the global.[2] Part of the response to these challenges have become assessments, understood as organized efforts to harness scientific information to inform policy makers both from private and public sectors at all stages of decision-making. The increasing role of assessments has had its roots in a view that better and more widely shared information can add to more effective management of complex, transnational interactions between humans and nature.[3] As examples from the environmental domain have proven, actors from all sides of the stage have an interest in the effective conduct of assessments, from scientists and practitioners willing to contribute their efforts to increase knowledge and improvement of existing policies[4] to decision makers in business and governments looking for scientific data and analysis as a basis for their decisions and pursuit of their policies.[5] In addition, the reasoning behind assessments supposes that a better understanding of impacts of human actions, decisions and behaviours, presented with options for alleviation of these impacts, can provide incentives for political, social and economic decision makers to carry out their policies in a more sustainable way.[6] The number and importance of assessments is expected to increase even further in the future along with greater pressures on natural resources by the growing population and effects of industrialization and globalization, thus calling for concerted actions based on sound and scientifically grounded information to mitigate negative effects of these developments.

The assessments are often viewed through products they deliver, frequently in the form of a report or publication. However, they can be better understood as social processes, embedded in particular institutional settings, within which expert knowledge related to a policy problem is framed,

2 Ostrom, E. (1990). *Governing the Commons: The Evolution of Institutions for Collective Action.* Cambridge: Cambridge University Press; Young, O.R. (2002). *The Institutional Dimensions of Environmental Change: Fit, Interplay, and Scale.* Cambridge, Massachusetts: MIT Press.

3 Clark et al. (2006).

4 Bolin, B. (1994), "Science and Policy Making," *Ambio*, 32(1), 25–29.

5 Bronk, D.W. (1994). "Science Advice in the White House," *Science*, 186(11), 116–121, http://www.sciencemag.org/content/186/4159/116.citation. Accessed 20 February 2015; Carnegie Commission on Science (Ed.). (1994), *Science, Technology and Congress: Expert Advice and the Decision-Making Process.* New York: Carnegie Commission on Science, Technology, and Government. http://www.ccstg.org/pdfs/OrganizationalReforms0294.pdf. Accessed 20 February 2015.

6 Clark et al. (2006).

integrated, interpreted, and presented in documents to inform decision-making.[7] Assessments constitute communication channels to bridge the gap between scientists and policy makers and are a key interface between science and policy.[8] As such they may influence the formulation, implementation and evaluation of public policy; hence, they are also of interest to business, nongovernmental organizations, regulatory offices, etc.[9] Yet, assessments may vary to a great extent in what type of influence they exert and the degree to which they affect the policy sphere. Therefore it is not enough to look at the scientific output of an assessment – to evaluate its effectiveness one has to look at the entire process which led to production/collection of research results, both the scientific and political context in which it was carried out, and understand which design features of the process can inhibit or strengthen an assessment's influence.

The aim of this chapter is to shed light on the influence of assessments in policy-making. The chapter first defines the main concepts related to assessments and distinguishes between their various types. It outlines their characteristics and frameworks for their evaluation, continues with the assessments' potential contributions to decision-making and concludes with conditions increasing their effectiveness. As the majority of chapters in this book are based on the assessment conducted for the European Union, this contribution is vital to understand why carrying out of such an undertaking was considered beneficial. To this end it provides conceptual and theoretical background for various methodological choices made in designing the *Strategic Assessment of Development of the Arctic* process. The chapter is based on the report *Assessments in Policy-making: Case Studies from the Arctic Council* prepared within the framework of the project "Strategic Environmental Impact Assessment of development of the Arctic" funded by the European Commission.[10]

---

7 Farrell, A.E., & Jäger, J. (Eds.) (2006). *Assessments of Regional and Global Environmental Risks. Designing Processes for the Effective Use of Science in Decisionmaking*. Washington, DC: RFF Press; Farrell, A., VanDeveer, S.D., & Jäger, J. (2001). "Environmental assessments: four under-appreciated elements of design." *Global Environmental Change*, 11, 311–333.

8 National Research Council. (2007), *Analysis of Global Change Assessments: Lessons Learned.* Washington, DC: The National Academies Press. http://www.nap.edu/catalog.php?record_id=11868. Accessed 20 February 2015.

9 Miller, C.A. (2006). "The Design nad Management of International Scientific Assessments. Lessons from Climate Regime," In Farrell, A.E., & Jäger, J. (Eds.). *Assessments of Regional and Global Environmental Risks. Designing Processes for the Effective Use of Science in Decisionmaking* (pp. 187–205). Washington, DC: RFF Press.mitche.

10 The report can be downloaded from the project website at http://www.arcticinfo.eu/en/assessment-in-policy-making.

## 2 Defining Assessments

The number of global assessments has been steadily growing in recent years, in part because many existing international agreements and national mandates require regular assessments to support their execution and revision. Due to the amount and variety of their types it is difficult to clearly distinguish elements that correctly define and apply to all assessments. In the literature[11] the term "assessment" is generally explained as a collective process that assembles scientific knowledge for the use of decision-makers to address key questions, decisions, or uncertainties.

International organizations carrying out global environmental assessments (UN, UNESCO, EEAgency) follow the definition of Mitchell *et al.* and interpret *assessments* as "formal efforts to assemble selected knowledge with a view toward making it publicly available in a form intended to be useful for decision making".[12] To fully understand the scope of the definition, the authors further clarify the meaning of its components. Formality of the process refers to its sufficient organization in a way that elements like product, participants and issuing authority can be easily recognized. Selected knowledge recognizes that assessments can vary in respect to what issues are included, how knowledge about the issue is collected for the purpose of assessment and whether new data is to be produced or the existing information is to be selected, summarized and analysed. In addition, the term "knowledge" is interpreted rather broadly, so the information included in an assessment is more empirical than definitional. In the majority of cases it comes from the scientific research, but it may also be combined with local, traditional practitioners' or indigenous knowledge. Finally, an assessment's decision-making support function has a public character and encompasses a broad list of actors – governments, private corporations, research laboratories, NGOs, and civil society. In that sense, assessments differ from expertise prepared for decision-makers, the latter having a smaller scope of users and not always being available to the public.[13]

11 Farrell and Jäger (2006), *op.cit.*; Mitchell, R.B., Clark, W.C., & Cash, D.W. (2006). "Information and Influence." In R.B. Mitchell, W.C. Clark, D.W. Cash, & N.M. Dickson (Eds.), *Global Environmental Assessments. Information and Influence* (pp. 307–338). Cambridge, Massachusetts: The MIT Press; National Research Council (2007).

12 Mitchell et al. (2006), *op.cit.*, 3.

13 Clark, W.C., Mitchell, R.B., & Cash, D.W. (2006). "Evaluating the Influence of Global Environmental Assessments." In Mitchell, R.B., Clark, W.C., Cash, D.W. & Dickson, N.M. (Eds.), *Global Environmental Assessments. Information and Influence* (pp. 1–28). Cambridge, Massachusetts: MIT Press; UNEP and IOC-UNESCO. (2009), *An Assessment of Assessments Findings of the Group of Experts. Start-up Phase of a Regular Process for*

Regardless of their scope, topic or discipline, assessments share some common features. These include assessments' ability to connect the domain of science and policy, often through public and deliberative processes that interact with social needs to receive decision-relevant information. Usually assessments are completed in a form of a report and are often viewed primarily through the products they deliver, frequently in the form of such a final publication. However, a report is not necessarily needed to effectively influence the decision-making process.[14] In fact, it is the interface between science and policy that is the key factor that contributes to the importance of assessments as a method to inform and consequently potentially influence decision-making. Therefore, an assessment should be considered more as both the product (report) and the process which led to its creation. The report (or any other form of delivery of results chosen to inform policy-makers) presents a synthesis of experts' knowledge and the underlying data and information used in the analysis. The process encompasses institutional settings founded to guide and carry out the assessment, including their mandate, composition and procedures to be followed during the endeavour. There is a consensus in literature that while the product of an assessment has a clear value as a presentation of scientific findings, it is the process behind the product that builds an assessment's influence capacity and effectiveness.[15]

### 2.1 *Types of Assessments*

The variety of assessments is an effect of diverse internal design elements, such as: applied data and knowledge, geographic coverage, thematic scope, methodologies, and regularity in the conduct of assessment. For example, the scale may range from local through national to global, while the scope may be defined on the level of broad themes, current situation status, threats, impacts or response measures.[16] However, these elements of assessments'

---

*Global Reporting and Assessment of the State of the Marine Environment including Socio-economic Aspects*. http://www.unep.org/regionalseas/globalmeetings/12/wp04-assessment-of-assessments.pdf. Accessed 20 February 2015.

14 National Research Council (2007), *op.cit.*

15 Farrell, A.E., Jäger, J., & VanDeveer, S.D. (2006). "Overview: Understanding Design Choices," In A.E. Farrell & J. Jäger (Eds.), *Assessments of Regional and Global Environmental Risks. Designing Processes for the Effective Use of Science in Decisionmaking* (pp. 1–24). Washington, DC: RFF Press; UNEP and IOC-UNESCO (2009).

16 United Nations Environment Programme (UNEP). (2007), *Global Marine Assessments: A survey of global and regional assessments and related activities of the marine environment.* http://www.unep-wcmc.org/medialibrary/2010/09/10/66977c19/GlobalMarineAssessments.pdf. Accessed 20 February 2015.

processes and products as well as the general type of assessment that is to be undertaken are defined early during its inception stage, which in turn depends on factors external to the assessment, namely the scientific, policy, and political context.[17]

The state of scientific knowledge and relevant policy debates create a particular context for an assessment, which is conducted in order to inform certain decisions. The scientific context is comprised of, among others, maturity of the field and the amount of data available on the topic, which consequently play a crucial role in the type of assessment that can be undertaken. The political context to the assessment answers the question of what kind of contribution the assessment can deliver, which goals it should accomplish and which decisions it can inform. Furthermore, depending on whether the issue at stake is already a part of the policy agenda or not, the assessment in the former case is contingent upon whose agenda it is and how much attention the issue has gained, whereas in the latter case assessment's goal is to establish the importance of an issue.[18]

Based on mandate and goals, four types of assessments can be distinguished:[19]

1. *Process assessments* summarize and synthetize scientific knowledge in order to describe the current status and past trends in relevant processes, as well as characterize the extent and the drivers of the change.
2. *Impact assessments* characterize, diagnose, and project the risks or impacts of human activities, or natural pressures (*e.g.* climate change, pollution) on the social, economic and natural environment. The analysis of impacts is usually focused on some particular sectors or regions and it includes identifying key vulnerabilities and potential strategies to enhance resilience. Impact assessments often draw on results from process assessments, yet they are far more complex as they consider not only impacts themselves, but also interactions among them.
3. *Response assessments* identify and evaluate potential responses and adaptations that could reduce human contributions or vulnerabilities to the change at issue. They may evaluate current policy measures as well as recognize new alternative options and assess their feasibility, state of development, and potential contribution to solve the problem.
4. *Integrated assessments* examine the links among systems scrutinized in the above forms of assessments. They may involve sequencing activities – process, impact, and response assessments conducted as an

17 National Research Council (2007), *op.cit.*

18 *Ibid.*

19 *Ibid.*

iterative cycle. Their integrative aspect is based on taking into account interactions and cumulative effects of all pressures (social, economic, environmental), sectors and ecosystem components.

In theory, the categories of assessments presented above aim at answering different sets of questions and vary in their levels of analytical complexity, applied data and analysis methods, as well as their potential contribution to decision-making. In reality however, most of the conducted assessments are hybrids of these presented ideal types.[20]

Additionally, depending on the scope, sectoral or thematic assessments may be distinguished:

1. *Sectoral assessment* is focused on a specific sector of human activities, such as fishing, tourism, energy, etc.
2. *Thematic assessment* covers at least one ecosystem component (*e.g.* permafrost) or theme (*e.g.* marine pollution). It can explore impacts of various sectors over that theme and assess how changes in that theme consequently may, in turn, have an effect on the included sectors.

In case of sectoral and thematic assessments it is possible to evaluate processes, impacts and responses within one assessment.[21]

Eventually, *impact assessments* (IAs) constitute a type of assessments that is the most often carried out, thoroughly researched and, consequently, accompanied by an impressive assemblage of standards and guidelines. There are many different kinds of impact assessments (IAs), from which the oldest and probably best-known are Environmental Impact Assessments (EIAs). Yet, they are all in a continual state of evolution. Once dominated by a sectoral approach (*i.e.* focusing only on environmental issues, health effects, etc.), impact assessments have been moving away from this and toward an integrated approach based on the synergies between the three pillars of sustainability (environment, society, and economy). Perhaps the best example of this integrated approach is the advent of the already-mentioned global environmental assessments that have arisen in response to urgent, worldwide issues such as climate change. Therefore, various elements and questions deliberated in the scholarship dedicated to impact assessments (especially EIAs) have had influence on and remain relevant for the general discussion on the effectiveness of all assessments.

---

20 *Ibid.*

21 UNEP and IOC-UNESCO (2009).

A number of types of impact assessments can be distinguished. *Environmental Impact Assessment* (*EIA*) – referring to individual development projects – and *Strategic Environmental Assessment* (*SEA*) – focused on evaluation of the effects of plans and programmes – are legal and governance procedures intended to ensure that the environmental effects are taken into account. Consultation with the public and relevant stakeholders is usually a vital feature of EIAs and SEAs. *Sustainability Impact Assessment* (*SIA*) can be defined (following the European Sustainable Development Network) as a "systematic and iterative process of the likely economic, social and environmental impacts of policies, plans, programs and strategies enabling stakeholders concerned to participate proactively".[22] *Human Rights Impact Assessment* (*HRIA*) which has emerged recently is a tool for systematically identifying, predicting and responding to the potential human rights impacts of a business operation, capital project, government policy or trade agreement.[23] *Social Impact Assessment* is best understood as "an umbrella or overarching framework that embodies the evaluation of all impacts on humans and on all the ways in which people and communities interact with their socio-cultural, economic and biophysical surroundings".[24] Eventually, *Global Environmental Assessments* (*GEA*) represent highly complex processes of assessing the influence of human activities on the ecosystem and vice versa. The end result should be an assessment of either past or future stress factors (chemical contaminants, anthropogenic interventions or natural disasters), their influence on ecosystems and their components.[25]

## 2.2 *Assessment of Assessments*

An *Assessment of Assessments* (AoA) can be distinguished as a special category that seeks to evaluate assessments themselves in order to improve their functioning as well as increase their support to decision making. The AoA analyses both the efficiency of the assessment's production (particularly in light of numerous assessments conducted at the same time and including the same actors or organizations) as well as the effectiveness of its results

22 Berger, G. (2007), *Sustainability Impact Assessment: Approaches and applications in Europe*. ESDN Quarterly Report, (June), http://www.sd-network.eu/quarterlyreports/reportfiles/pdf/2007-June-Sustainability_Impact_Assessment.pdf. Accessed 20 February 2015.

23 NOMOGAIA website, nomogaia.org. Accessed 20 February 2015.

24 International Association for Impact Assessment (IAIA) website, http://www.iaia.org/. Accessed 20 February 2015.

25 Mitchell, Clark and Cash (2006), *op.cit.*

(whether the increasing number of assessments being carried out actually strengthens the underpinning of policy with knowledge). As such, the AoA consists of two dimensions: (1) concerns related to methodology and applied information, and (2) concerns regarding the importance of the assessed issue at stake.

Global and regional assessments have progressively become an easily accessible source of information about human and natural ecosystems. Due to an increasing number of international agreements and national mandates that require or promote the employment of assessments as a policy-making tool, their number has been steadily growing. Whereas representation and involvement of different interest groups and knowledge holders in the process remains undisputable, such situations when multiple assessments are being carried out without proper coordination can bring about contending demands, lead to redundancies and omissions, and risk lowering the quality of conducted assessment projects. Seeing the number of people involved and resources being spent on assessments, it is reasonable to ask about their usefulness to policy processes. Do assessments matter? How can they affect decision-makers and policy choices? Finally, what elements condition their influence? Answers to these questions are far from straightforward, and measuring of the impact of assessments remains a challenge. Yet, there are elements and features that literature illuminates as critical to the effectiveness of assessments.

## 3 Assessments' Contribution to and Influence on Policy-making

As has been already defined, the assessment is the collective, deliberative process of summarizing, reviewing and evaluating scientific and local knowledge for the use of decision-making to address key problems, issues or uncertainties. The main aim of the assessments is to inform decisions. In other words, ***being influential*** in this context means for the assessment to have an ability to affect the issue domain including not only the actors participating in the process, but also their interests, resources, beliefs and applied strategies; the institutional settings; and the behaviours of involved actors such of decisions, agreements and policies, and impacts of these behaviours on the outside world. In evaluation of an assessment's effectiveness, one should not look only at the policy outcomes, that is, adopted formal legislative or regulatory practices. Change in the issue domain (*e.g.* environmental policy) is a continuous process that starts primarily by changing the understanding of the issue at stake and the beliefs of process participants. With the course of time that may lead to changes in other elements of the issue domain like interests and goals related to problems addressed by the assessment.[26]

Still, different types of assessments have different abilities to affect policy-making. Their diversity comes from the variety of scientific and policy contexts in which they are carried out, the range of goals they aim to achieve, and the scope of their mandates. These differences also depend upon the stage of the issue development within the policy-making process, ranging from identification of the problem to debating it. On the one hand, when the issue is in the early stage of policy-making, previously not being discussed on the policy agenda, the assessment can help to introduce the problem to the political debate rather than change policy immediately and directly. This happened for instance for persistent organic pollutants through assessments conducted under the auspices of the Arctic Environmental Protection Strategy and the Arctic Council.[27] On the other hand, once the problem is in the mature stage, already debated within the policy-making process, the way in which various actors and audiences perceive the issue is unlikely to change fundamentally.

In spite of these differences, an assessment's potential contributions to policy debate can be identified as follows. First, the assessment may *establish the significance of an issue* and elevate it onto the decision-making agenda, especially when the political context for the issue is immature. Second, when already an on-going political debate involves some conflicting claims about scientific questions that are seen as important for taking a decision and proceeding with action, the assessment may *provide an authoritative resolution to the issue*. However, the conditions for this contribution are related to sufficient scientific knowledge and the political body already dealing with the issue. Third, when the political debate considers alternative options for the issue, the assessment can *link alternative actions to consequences* and help to reach an agreement on the consequences of these choices. However, such a scientifically funded statement linking decisions with their consequences depends on the willingness of the actors involved to consider the results of the assessment. Fourth, when members of a decision-making body find themselves sharing a specific technical problem, the assessment may *recommend common technology alternatives and solutions*. Fifth, in case of conflicting instruments and answers to policy-relevant questions, the assessment *helps to identify and*

26 UNEP and IOC-UNESCO (2009), *op.cit.*; A.E. Farrell et al. (2006), *op.cit.*

27 Downie, D.L. & Fenge, T. (eds) (2003). *Northern Lights Against POPs: Combatting Toxic Threats in the Arctic,* McGil-Queen's University Press; Koivurova, T., Kankaanpää, P. & Stepien A. (2015), "Innovative Environmental Protection: Lessons from the Arctic," Journal of Environmental Law, Advance Access: doi:10.1093/jel/equ037.

*clarify research priorities* on key matters at stake. Finally, it has a potential to *demonstrate that policy is providing environmental benefits*.[28]

## 4 Effectiveness of Assessments

Defining the effectiveness of assessments is by no means a straightforward task. The problem of agreeing on a single definition of assessments' success stems from the variety of contexts in which the assessments are carried out, the time scale on which the success of assessments is being evaluated (some effects can become visible only in the long-term perspective), the diversity of their goals, applied strategies and potential contributions, and, perhaps most importantly, from a number of different actors who evaluate assessments from their distinct perspectives and interests. In addition, the influence of assessments depends to a large extent on how well they fit within a given scientific and political context.[29]

This chapter follows a simple definition of effectiveness proposed by researchers working within the Global Environmental Assessment Project, so that "more effective assessments are more likely to have significant influences on the corresponding issue domain and its development".[30] Still, it is important to keep in mind the relational character of assessments. It means that one can evaluate their effectiveness only in relation to particular targeted audiences. As concerns, perspectives, knowledge, data and assumptions differ significantly among actors, the assessment's results can be accepted or not depending on political, social, economic and other factors beyond the scope of the assessment process and control. Consequently, when evaluating the effectiveness of assessments, one has to ask: Effective according to whom? Effective in achieving which goals over what time?[31]

### 4.1 *Determinants for Assessments' Effectiveness*

Regardless of the intended type of contribution of assessments to policy-making, research conducted on a number of regional and global assessments related to complex environmental problems has shown that only some assessments managed to significantly affect decisions or behaviours of policy-makers, while others had little, if any, impact on their actions. As such the

28 National Research Council (2007), *op.cit.*

29 National Research Council (2007), *op.cit.*, 5.

30 Farrell et al. (2006), *op.cit.*, 7.

31 National Research Council (2007), *op.cit.*

identification of criteria for effective assessment and answering the question of why some assessments have more influence than others have become of crucial importance.[32] The review of literature leads to a conclusion that even though assessments vary in a way they influence the issue/policy domain, general sources of their effectiveness can be found within their attributes of salience, credibility and legitimacy.[33] In other words, an assessment viewed by its audience as more salient, more credible and more legitimate is more likely to induce change in this audience's beliefs, thus be more influential and effective.

*Salience* of the assessment is a measure of its perceived relevance to the potential users, whether it addresses their needs and concerns, and provides information in a form and at a time it can be used. The attribute of salience is determined to a large extent during the framing stage so that the problem, its impacts and potential solutions to it are defined and linked to issues over which decision-makers have control and are interested in. Secondly, the geographic scale and timing must meet the needs of the information users. The assessment findings ought to be reframed in a way that is applicable for national and local conditions. In addition, the information has to be delivered at the right time, that is, before decision is made. On the contrary, an assessment will most likely be ignored by the audience if it does not address a problem relevant for the users or if in discussion of its impacts it fails to identify responses or actions that audiences can undertake to mitigate or adapt to the identified problem. Thirdly, on-going and explicit processes that encourage participation by and are responsive to decision-makers are particularly important to fostering salience. Finally, salience often depends on factors and conditions that go beyond the assessment process – its relevance may be contingent upon external events resulting in the rise or fall of salience of a particular issue over time.[34]

*Credibility* of the assessment relates to scientific believability and the quality of data, methods and approaches applied in that assessment. The audience has to be convinced that the scientific content of the assessment is "true" or at least better than competing information. The attribute of credibility should address an assessment's technical and local components. Whereas the former one is often based on credentials of process and participants of the assessment, if they are experts in their field, are trustworthy and provided accurate

32 Clark et al. (2006), *op.cit.*; Farrell and Jäger (2006), *op.cit.*; Farrell et al. (2001), *op.cit.*; Mitchell, Clark, and Cash (2006), *op.cit.*

33 Mitchell, Clark and Cash (2006), *op.cit.*; UNEP and IOC-UNESCO (2009), *op.cit.*

34 Mitchell, Clark and Cash (2006), *op.cit.*

information in the past; the latter one stems from taking into account local conditions and knowledge, and fitting the higher-scale results into the local context by well-established networks between information providers and users.[35] Furthermore, credibility is a property developed slowly and steadily over time, which confirms the importance of the assessment process during which relevant stakeholders bring in local data and expertise, while gaining a better understanding of the assessment's methods and results. Finally, credibility may depend on a degree of consensus on the debated issue and consistency of new information with already existing knowledge and well-established facts – the more consistent it is, the more credible it may be viewed.

*Legitimacy* refers to the perceived fairness and impartiality of the assessment process, having considered values, concerns, and perspectives of the relevant audience. Legitimacy is linked to questions of who participated and who was excluded from the process; which causes, impacts and policy options were taken into account; and how information was produced and disseminated. Due to the complexity of human-environmental interactions, the assessment producers have to make choices regarding what to focus on and analyse, and what to leave aside. Such selection is inherently, if often implicitly, linked with the promotion of certain goals and values over others.[36] To ensure that results of the assessment are viewed as fair, relevant stakeholders (so those affected by the policy supported by the assessment) or at least their representatives whom stakeholders believe voice their goals and concerns, should be involved in the process. Otherwise, excluded relevant actors may consequently question the assessment's legitimacy. Yet, even assessments whose results do not correspond with interests of a particular group, can be perceived as fair if views of that group were accurately represented in the assessment process.[37]

Salience, credibility and legitimacy are considered three essential properties of an influential assessment process. However, it should be stressed that these attributions are ascribed to assessments by their users, they are not themselves factors inherent to the process. In other words, they are a matter of subjective judgement and not of an independent reality. Therefore, the

---

35 Jasanoff, S., & Martello, M.L. (Eds.). (2004). *Earthly Politics: Local and Global in Environmental Governance*. Cambridge, MA: MIT Press; Moser, S.C. (2006). "Climate Change and Sea-Level Rise in Maine and Hawai'i: The Changing Tides of an Issue Domain." In R.B. Mitchell, W.C. Clark, D.W. Cash, & N.M. Dickson (Eds.), *Global Environmental Assessments. Information and Influence* (pp. 201–240). Cambridge, Massachusetts: MIT Press.

36 Farrell et al. (2006), *op.cit.*

37 Farrell et al. (2006), *op.cit.*; Mitchell, Clark and Cash (2006), *op.cit.*

goal of assessment producers and designers should be to increase the number of stakeholders who find and consider the assessment as salient, credible and legitimate.

Whereas salience is this attribute of assessment which is closely linked to effective communication with its targeted audience, both credibility and legitimacy are fundamentally related to a question of trust, that is, whether people judge that an assessment can be trusted. It is, however, important not to confuse these two kinds of trust (credibility and legitimacy) since they both are required in the assessment process, but reaching them may come through different design choices and means, often characterized by trade-offs. While credibility is attributed to the assessment by scientific experts on the basis of indicators similar to ones they use to gauge the trustworthiness of other scientific outcomes, legitimacy is attributed to assessment by its stakeholders on the basis of perceived fairness, balance in representation, transparency of process and other criteria similar to those they use to evaluate any other political or administrative practices. In other words, legitimacy answers the question of who has interests at stake in the assessment, while credibility responds to what kind of expertise is demanded to understand the debated issue. It is important to keep this difference in mind since both types of trust may be required in the process, but their earning may come through different means and design choices.[38]

One of the challenges associated with a conduct of effective assessment is that the relation between attributes of salience, legitimacy and credibility is characterized by a trade-off, meaning that efforts to maximize one of these aspects tend to decrease the others. For example, actions taken to increase the credibility of an assessment process, like isolating scientists from the policy domain, may result in decreasing its salience, and, consequently, lowering chances for the assessment to be influential. Similarly, enhancing the legitimacy of assessments by inclusion of scientists who represent views of groups that the assessment seeks to influence may risk the credibility of the process in the eyes of the other decision-makers and observers. Methods and factors aiming at resolution of this and other challenges are presented in the next part.

### 4.2 *Design Features for Successful Assessments*

As outlined earlier, for the assessment to be effective, its audience have to view it as salient, credible and legitimate. Yet there are certain challenges in the conduct of assessments that may inhibit their influence on the targeted audience and decision-making processes. Effectiveness of assessments can be lost in many ways: from insufficient control or disagreements over scientific data; through

38 National Research Council (2007), *op.cit.*

addressing questions relevant only from the perspective of the research community, but not from the viewpoint of the end-users of the produced information; to adopting a "one-size-fits-all" policy, without localizing synthesized knowledge and tailoring it to local needs and concerns. To avoid such flaws, the assessment producers during the design phase should focus on several factors that are of great importance in fostering influence of both process and product of the assessment. These elements encompass, *inter alia,* framing of the assessment process, the science-policy interface, engaging stakeholders, connecting science with decision-making, the review process, consensus building, characterizing uncertainty and providing a strategic communication plan. Addressing them adequately increases the likelihood that the given assessment will be perceived as salient, credible and legitimate by its intended audience.

Firstly, framing is next to engaging stakeholders and managing science-policy interface one of the key elements in the design of successful assessment. On the basis of underlying worldviews and beliefs, within particular institutional settings and among diversity of goals of different participants, framing of the assessment determines the problem under examination. It resolves which of its elements will be analysed and which will be left outside the scope of investigation, and how different ideas will be used and interpreted. Framing not only guides the everyday activities of practitioners involved in the assessment, but it also defines the selection of people who will be included in the assessment and the design of the entire process. As such, framing is crucial in shaping assessment's credibility and legitimacy, ensuring whether those whose interests are at stake and who will be affected by decisions resulting from the process are involved in it. Moreover, framing is likely to determine whether those who have knowledge on the issue participate in the process in ways that allow their knowledge to influence the debate.

Secondly, science-policy interface is another element of fundamental importance in achieving credibility, legitimacy and salience of the assessment. Forms of interactions between scientists and policy-makers within the process may range from complete isolation of the scientific community from decision-makers, to institutionalized collaboration and deliberative process between two groups. Yet, regardless of the undertaken approach and preferred type of interaction, both groups have to maintain their respective identities, which are based on completely different goals: finding the truth in the case of scientists, and responsible use of power in the case of policy-makers,[39] otherwise they

39 Farrell et al. (2006), *op.cit.*; Lee, K.N., quoted in Farrell, A., VanDeveer, S.D., & Jäger, J. (2001). "Environmental assessments: four under-appreciated elements of design," *Global Environmental Change*, 11, 311–333.

will lose sources of their credibility and legitimacy. Therefore, clearly articulated boundaries are necessary, particularly between those ordering the assessment and those carrying it out. The regulatory body and expert group negotiate boundaries of their interactions and decide upon the issues that each will deal with separately and issues which will be shared between them.[40] The assessment in this context can be understood as a boundary organization between two entities where maintaining an explicit boundary is crucial for results of the entire assessment process, including its review stage and acceptance of scientific results by the authorizing body.

Thirdly, broader stakeholder participation, going beyond established science-policy nexus, is at present considered a basis for assessment's credibility, legitimacy and salience. Stakeholders include all those who are interested in and affected by the assessment process, and benefits from their engagement are twofold. First, for the immediate assessment outcome, participation contributes to the opening of an assessment to different types of knowledge and information coming from outside of science, as well as raises the interests of various groups in the assessment, the understanding of the process and trust in the balanced character of the final product. Second, in the long-term perspective – primarily in connection with the assessment process itself – stakeholder engagement builds trust and a shared knowledge base as well as enhances general awareness of the existence of multiple perspectives on the issues in question. Participation in assessments can be seen as a capacity-building and empowering process (equipping participants with new knowledge in assessment methodology and tools), as well as, in general terms, contributing to democratic society and responsible decision-making. Properly conducted consultations augment the development of long-lasting partnerships between researchers, decision-makers and stakeholders, which is vital in future cooperation.[41]

In a broader sense stakeholder engagement should lead to the actual co-production of knowledge, allowing especially those commissioning the assessment and those who are using its results to influence the assessment process and its outcome. Consequently, the assessment can be better aligned with

40 Guston, D.H. quoted in Farrell et al. (2001), *op.cit.*; National Research Council (2007), *op.cit.*

41 Arctic Environmental Protection Strategy (AEPS). (1997), *Guidelines for Environmental Impact Assessment (EIA) in the Arctic*. Finland: Sustainable Development and Utilization. Finnish Ministry of the Environment. http://arcticcentre.ulapland.fi/aria/procedures/eiaguide.pdf. Accessed 20 February 2015; National Research Council (2007), *op.cit.*; Therivel, R. (2010). *Strategic Environmental Assessment in Action*. London: Earthscan.

decision-making processes and have a structure adjusted to decision-makers' ways of thinking and needs. This concerns the accurate timing of delivering relevant information, their format and scope as well as determines the need for broader public participation. At the same time the main difficulty connected with stakeholder engagement lies in balancing between acquiring meaningful involvement of stakeholders (especially including decision-makers) and the type of stakeholders' influence over the process, which may skew the scientific outcomes. Whereas the former one ensures assessment's salience, the latter may undermine its credibility.

Fourth, connecting science with decision-making also goes beyond negotiating and maintaining a clear boundary between scientists and policy-makers. It addresses a frequently occurring mismatch in scale and timing between information delivered by assessment producers and information needs of policy-makers. Therefore, the ability to connect science with decision-making requires the assessment to be acquainted with given institutional, political and economic contexts and the capacity to develop decision support tools that produce salient, context-specific information, available at right time and scale. For example, on the one hand, tailoring of integrated models to a particular region or decision-making context may enhance the ability of these assessments to be utilized by decision-makers. On the other hand, it also shows how regional assessment can be included, or nested, in a broader framework of national or global assessments – to draw from them, but also enrich them with local knowledge and expertise.

Fifth, transparency, quality control and a review process play a very significant role in establishing legitimacy and credibility of the assessment process. In general terms, transparency means that individuals interested in the assessment can look into its process and evaluate for themselves data, applied methods and taken decisions. In practical terms, the literature highlights two points to increase assessment's transparency and via them its credibility and legitimacy. To address the different information needs of different interested parties (*e.g.* experts and laymen) the assessment should make available both a summary and its basic data. Moreover, the best way to achieve transparency is the standardization and institutionalization of procedures for availability of necessary information.[42] Quality control describes the process of ensuring that material contained in the assessment report is consistent with the underlying data and analysis, which makes it crucial to the credibility of the assessment. Whether material in the report and underlying data match each other is a

42 Farrell et al. (2006), *op.cit.*

matter of experts' agreement. In light of debates on what makes up an expert opinion and to further ensure unbiased presentation of assessments' results, the report goes often through a review process. The review process has a potential to increase both credibility and legitimacy of the assessment thanks to many individuals from a larger range of stakeholders involved in its evaluation. As such, the risk that experts or policy-makers will promote their own agenda can be minimized with the inclusion of a balanced group of reviewers with various viewpoints and multidisciplinary expertise, often outside the field being assessed.

Still, the existence of dissent views raises an issue of consensus building between an assessment's participants in order to be able to provide clear guidelines for decision-makers, necessary for fostering the effectiveness of assessment. There are many definitions of consensus in the realm of assessments. One way to achieve the agreement is to explain differing opinions as inherent uncertainties of the state of knowledge or as alternative interpretations of available information. Another is inclusion, though it is rather rare, of "minority reports" of those with dissenting views. Furthermore, to incorporate differing perspectives of participants, some assessments widen their parameters of uncertainty, while others, most often perhaps, simply avoid areas where the greatest discords prevail, like in the case of extremities of possible outcomes (for consequences of such choices see below). Finally, from the perspective of achieving greater assessment legitimacy, it is not only a question of how differing opinions are included in the report, but also how the consensus itself is defined and on the basis of which rules it has been reached. Consensus can mean a majority of votes or the lowest common denominator, but also that "nobody spoke loudly enough against a point" or powerful actors did not oppose the issue. In addition, consensus often reflects agreement only of those present and participating, with the exclusion of opinions of those who were unable or not invited to join the process.[43] Instead of reaching the consensus by all means, the assessment report could, for example, provide for fair presentation of all sides of the argument, with clear explanation of how each conclusion has been drawn, and to allow information users to evaluate it on their own.[44] Regardless of the preferred solution, addressing the above points at the outset of the assessment process is important to enhance its legitimacy, thus its impact and influence.

The seventh design feature is the treatment of uncertainty. Assessments are often meant to inform decision-makers about matters that are to them

43 Farrell et al. (2001), *op.cit.*

44 National Research Council (2007), *op.cit.*

either new or controversial for reasons of their policy implications. Yet, research synthesized for the purpose of assessments is frequently characterized by uncertainty that cannot be reduced or eliminated in the short-term and even in a longer time perspective. To differentiate it from undesired ambiguity about research results, the effective assessment should describe the level and sources of such uncertainty in order to deliver more confident and reliable results of the analysis to decision-makers, to help them understand the present state of knowledge and assess the potential effectiveness and risk associated with certain policy decisions. The uncertainty can be treated both through quantitative and qualitative methods, with the latter ones applied often in cases where an objective measurement of uncertainty is not possible due to the complexity of the issue at stake (like in the case of climate change). In such situations the characterization of uncertainty is based on experts' opinions and qualitative metrics such as "likely" or "highly probable" to which experts agree in the assessment process.

In case of assessments whose primary goal lies in reporting on the scientific consensus of a particular issue, the experts representing a broad spectrum of stakeholders and disciplines gathered in a panel must reach an agreement on what to include in the assessment and how to present its results. This type of consensus-seeking assessment is more prone to ignore the occurrence of extreme events and exclude them from the scope of analysis. However, attention should be paid to the fact that purposeful omission of extremities may not be serving the long-term interests of the policy-community as it risks the mischaracterization of a problem as a whole, and can in the long-term undermine credibility and salience. To avoid such a situation, the literature recommends stressing the participatory side of assessments, instead of reliance only on the final product for delivery of the assessment's results. Engagement of decision-makers in the stages of the assessment process where consensus on uncertainty is being discussed can improve their understanding of presented outcomes and contribute to the design of more sustainable policies.[45]

Finally, to understand scientific findings by the targeted audience, a strategic communication plan is necessary. The objective of the plan is to stimulate individuals to think about problems, risks, solutions, and consequently influence policies, decisions, and behaviour. To reach this goal, it should recognize and respond to interests, motivations, and values of an assessment's

---

45 Patt, A. (2006). "Dealing with Uncertainty. How Do You Assess the Impossible?" In Farrell, A.E. & Jäger, J. (Eds.), *Assessments of Regional and Global Environmental Risks. Designing Processes for the Effective Use of Science in Decisionmaking* (pp. 119–137). Washington, DC: RFF Press.

audiences, and address their knowledge base, barriers and possible resistance. The effective communication plan is based on frequent consultations with stakeholders, media outreach, engaged dialogues and meetings with key audiences, and, finally, diversity of publications tailored to meet multiple audiences. The successful outreach strategy should be characterized by flexibility – so it can vary with objectives and audiences and deliver products differing in complexity, policy relevance, geographical scope, and technical emphasis.

## 5 Conclusions

The increasing interest in global and regional assessments of different kinds stems primarily from concerns for better-informed, more effective, more efficient and more transparent policy-making.[46] Due to their fundamental role in bridging the gap between scientists and policy-makers, the assessments, understood not merely as their final products or reports, but more as social processes and communication channels, can influence the formulation, implementation and/or evaluation of public policies, though in different forms and to various extent. Regardless of the given context and particular issue at stake, three major properties of salience, legitimacy and credibility were identified as critical in raising the likelihood that the knowledge contained in the assessment can prove to induce change in the policy domain. Yet, salience, legitimacy and credibility are not factors *per se*, but attributions made by the information-users often on the basis of the process that led to the information or knowledge creation. In order to encourage recipients to label the assessment as relevant, legitimate and credible, those designing and carrying it out should pay attention to features like framing, science-policy interface, stakeholder participation, transparency, consensus building, treatment of uncertainty and a comprehensive communication plan. In addition to already-mentioned elements, very practical (therefore perhaps sometimes underestimated) are also time constraints for completion of the project vs. timeline consistent with the state of underlying knowledge base, as well as the scope of planned works and human resources dedicated to the project.[47]

46 Berger, G. (2007). *Sustainability Impact Assessment: Approaches and applications in Europe*. ESDN Quarterly Report, (June). http://www.sd-network.eu/quarterlyreports/report files/pdf/2007-June-Sustainability_Impact_Assessment.pdf. Accessed 20 February 2015.

47 Farrell et al. (2006).

As a part of an adequate framing, the assessment should include a well-articulated mandate with clearly defined and realistic goals and objectives corresponding with needs of policy-makers. The mandate should encompass a detailed implementation plan, guidance on what decisions the assessment is meant to inform, and material on how progress towards prescribed goals will be gauged.[48] Furthermore, an appropriate framework ought to be developed to ensure that the assessment will be able to deliver answers to posed questions, feed the information needs of its target users and safeguard that the scope and scale of the assessment will match the scope and scale of the choices made on its basis. Last, but definitely not least, resources and funding dedicated to the assessment should correspond with its mandate and defined goals. That should also include often overlooked means to support proper stakeholder participation and communication activities.[49]

All elements discussed in this chapter are of fundamental importance in the conduct of assessments and they have been identified in literature on the basis of analysis of both global and regional assessments, conducted in many parts of the world and in many environments, focused on various elements and including representatives of numerous disciplines. They provide lessons for the conduct of future assessments and offer potential for raising their effectiveness, and consequently, their greater impact and contribution to better-informed policy-making.

---

48 National Research Council (2005) as quoted in: National Research Council (2007), *op.cit.*

49 National Research Council (2007), *op.cit.*

CONCLUSION

# The Region of Uncertainty – Arctic Change and Possible Pathways for the EU

*Adam Stępień, Timo Koivurova and Paula Kankaanpää**


## Abstract

The concluding chapter brings together the key messages of the thematic studies both regarding the status of Arctic developments and the EU's role in the Arctic change. An attempt is made to draw a balanced and complex picture and underline uncertainties. The discrepancy between the impacts of climate change on environment and on the socioeconomic developments is highlighted and the moderate pace of these socioeconomic developments is discussed. A number of suggestions for the EU overarching policy-making in the region are given, focusing on the Union's role in the European Arctic, mechanisms for dialogue and engagement and the production and use of knowledge.


## 1 Introduction: Aiming at a Balanced Assessment

The picture of the Arctic in change and the EU's role in that transformation drawn by the contributions to this book is that of uncertainty and complexity. There is a growing acknowledgment that developments in the Arctic are far from both the overly-optimistic and overly-pessimistic visions still prevalent three-four years ago. That means we need to abandon the already tattered notions of the Arctic economic boom, the inter-state conflicts originating in the Arctic or the scramble for Arctic resources. At the same time, studies dedicated to the EU-Arctic nexus are moving from general discussion on the position, actorness and credibility of the EU in the plane of Arctic affairs towards an increasing focus on practical and specific questions, such as EU funding, the EU's concrete contributions to Arctic research or the activities of the European parties within Arctic-relevant international decision-making processes. This volume serves to further a more balanced view of the transformation the region is undergoing as well as to concretize

* Although the concluding chapter was drafted by the editors of this volume, all report authors are acknowledged for participating in bringing together the ideas that are presented.

 | DOI 10.1163/9789004303188_013

the role of the EU in this transformation. Therefore, the assessment process leading to the *Strategic Assessment of Development of the Arctic* report, and consequently, to this book, had as one of its primary goals to shed light on the current status of Arctic change and trends in the region. The focus has been on real, although often not attention-grasping, challenges and problems faced by various Arctic actors. To a great extent, arriving to a more balanced overview was possible owing to the interaction with Arctic stakeholders. As a result, one of the key terms in this book is "uncertainty", as the future of Arctic environmental change, economic development and socio-cultural transformation, as well as the role of the EU in this future transformation are as yet connected with ambiguities.

In the realm of environmental change much is already understood. However, our collective capacity to account for the multiplicity of factors and to model the future change is still far from satisfactory. This is visible in the scarcity of data needed for the implementation of adaptation policies at a local level. The region still lacks sustained monitoring and observation. On the other hand, it should be underlined that the understanding of the state and trends pertaining to natural world appears to be at least sufficient for general decision-making (*e.g.*, climate change mitigation), as various studies and recommendations coming from the Arctic Council or IPCC have shown.[1]

In a somewhat sharp contrast with the natural world, the comprehension of the future economic, social and cultural developments – on which this volume largely focuses – leaves even more space for improvement. This is in spite of significant research efforts and noticeable progress within Arctic social sciences in the last two decades. Future outlooks are based on foundations composed largely of uncertainties. It is not to say that little can be said about the socio-economic future of the Arctic, but the picture is necessarily complex and we can trust that those delivering simple and straightforward answers are likely to be wrong.

Consequently, the analysis of the Arctic change requires embracing the complexity of the region and the integration of the environmental, economic, social, cultural and political aspects. One needs to find equilibrium between generating a straightforward outlook of Arctic change for the benefit of a reader or a decision-maker and avoiding presenting an over-simplified vision of the regional transformation.

1 See, Kankaanpää, P. & Śmieszek, M. (eds.) (2014). *Assessments in Policy-Making: Case Studies from the Arctic Council. Preparatory Action,* Strategic Environmental Impact Assessment of development of the Arctic. Arctic Centre, University of Lapland.

Part of this complexity is enormous diversity between the Arctic regions, even within the European Arctic, where the geographical focus of this book lies. There are many commonalities between Arctic regions, but even common characteristics are manifested differently across the Circumpolar North. There are numerous examples: the Barents Sea entails less or different risks connected with shipping, tourism or hydrocarbon extraction in comparison to other, heavily ice-infested Arctic waters (chapters by Sander *et al.* and Łuszczuk *et al.*); mining in Northern Fennoscandia is connected with a different set of problems than in Greenland (van Dam *et al.*); and the implementation of international indigenous rights depends greatly on the specific local context (Latola *et al.* and Stępień *et al.*). The acknowledgment of this diversity should be self-understood and obvious, but all too often analyses and policy documents discuss "the Arctic" in abstract and general terms. The EU is but one of many actors present in the Arctic and interested in enhancing its activities in the region. Each of these actors, the EU included, also adds to the diversity of Arctic regions through its regulatory frameworks and actions.

Bearing in mind this diversity, this concluding chapter presents a few general messages regarding the development of the Arctic, the nature of EU-Arctic nexus, as well as suggests the overall frames in which the EU Arctic policy could be further developed. The focus here is on the overarching EU strategy rather than specific actions as they are discussed in the thematic chapters.

One of the questions is whether the augmented engagement of external (or "southern") actors in the Arctic will continue in the light of slower than expected expansion of economic activities. Correspondingly, would there be enough pressure for the development of needed regulatory frameworks as the sense of urgency is departing Arctic policy agendas.

## 2 The Environmental Impacts of Climate Change and Globalization Contrast with the Moderate Pace of Socio-economic Developments

The discussion throughout this book shows that the global economy and climate change remain key drivers of changes in the European Arctic. Neither climate change impacts nor the implications of economic developments can be analysed independently; instead, they should always be examined holistically and in the light of existing governance frameworks.

Globalisation in all its forms is the main driver of current socioeconomic trends in the European Arctic. Global prices of minerals and hydrocarbons are key determinants of extractive resource developments. Both the upsurge in Arctic mineral exploration and exploitation over the past five years, and current industry concerns regarding the profitability of many operating and planned mines reflect global markets and the outlook for demand in emerging economies (van Dam *et al.*). Lower natural gas prices have put some investment decisions on hold (*e.g.* Shtokman field project), while high oil prices have earlier encouraged companies to invest in expensive exploration projects (*e.g.* off the coast of Greenland or in the Barents Sea). The continuation of these exploration activities is now put into question by the falling price of oil in the global markets, at least for the time-being (Łuszczuk *et al.*). As destinational shipping is expected to be the most important element of maritime transport, the transport needs of Arctic extractive industries are among the critical determinants of Arctic maritime traffic (Sander *et al.*). Demand for the products of fisheries and aquaculture, together with the management systems in place, significantly influence these industries and the communities that depend on them (Arnarsson and Justus).

As the Arctic warms two times faster than the global average,[2] climate change presents a major challenge for the region, given the dependence of human-natural systems on the cryosphere and the fragility of Arctic ecosystems. The decrease in the sea ice extent and thickness in the Arctic Ocean as well as the melting of the Greenlandic ice sheet, thawing permafrost and coastal erosion are the clearest impacts. However, in Northern Fennoscandia, changes in snow cover or lake/river ice conditions are the most pronounced effects.

The resulting changes in Arctic biodiversity and landscape also impact on human societies. Arctic communities are already affected by a broad variety of economic, social, cultural or political changes. Climate change is an additional pressure, testing the adaptive capacities and resilience of peoples and communities and augmenting existing uncertainties. The resilience and adaptive capacity of environmental-social systems may not be sufficient to withstand

2 IPCC (2013). Climate Change 2013: The Physical Science Basis. Contribution of Working Group I to the Fifth Assessment Report of the Intergovernmental Panel on Climate Change [Stocker, T.F., Qin, D., Plattner, G.-K., Tignor, M., Allen, S.K., Boschung, J., Nauels, A., Xia, Y., Bex, V. & Midgley, P.M. (eds.)]; CAFF. (2013): Arctic Biodiversity Report. Synthesis. Conservation of Arctic Flora and Fauna. Arctic Council; ACIA (2005). Arctic Climate Impact Assessment. Arctic Council.

the accumulation of the multiple pressures discussed in this book.[3] Consequently, while mitigation of global change (both environmental change and globalization, including cultural transformation) and ongoing knowledge-building are still seen as primary responses, the implementation of more concrete adaptation actions increasingly needs to be considered.

There is a widespread belief that climate change itself will lead to increased economic opportunities in terms of Arctic maritime transport, fisheries or resource extraction, and that these opportunities might balance out or even outweigh the negative impacts of climate change in the Arctic. This is far from certain, as while climate change already adversely impacts Arctic ecosystems and nature-based livelihoods, it has so far had a limited role in triggering Arctic economic development, in particular in the European part of the region.

Climate change affects economic activities in the Arctic both positively and negatively. The current and future influence of different types of drivers cannot be thoroughly quantified, but the majority of the researchers and stakeholders involved in this assessment share the same general view of the currently limited role of climate change in socioeconomic development, which contrasts with its profound impact on Arctic environment. This holds not only for extractive industries, but also for tourism, forestry, fisheries and even reindeer herding. Relative to other activities discussed in this report, Arctic maritime transport is likely to be the most affected by the consequences of climate change, even though a variety of constraints and uncertainties exist.

In the longer-term perspective climate change is likely to become an increasingly important factor in shaping the Arctic economic and social landscape through physical and environmental changes. Moreover, the recent IPCC Fifth Assessment Report highlights the severity of likely impacts around the globe.[4] Global developments associated with climate change have an indirect influence on the Arctic: via changes occurring in other regions (*e.g.*, by shaping global economic growth) and via the consequences of climate change mitigation policies, for example by shaping the demand for Arctic hydrocarbons or facilitating the development of renewable energy in the region.

3 The resilience and adaptive capacity receives nowadays much attention in the discussion on the Arctic human-environmental systems, as is visible for instance from the Arctic Resilience Report. See, Nilsson, Annika. E. (ed.), Stockholm Environment Institute and Stockholm Resilience Centre (2013). Arctic Resilience Interim Report 2013. Arctic Council. www.arctic-council.org. Accessed 10 January 2014.

4 See: Intergovernmental Panel on Climate Change (IPCC) (2014). Climate Change 2014: Impacts, Adaptation and Vulnerability. Summary for Policy-makers. Fifth Assessment Report. See http://ipcc-wg2.gov/AR5/images/uploads/IPCC_WG2AR5_SPM_Approved.pdf. Accessed 31 March 2014.

While we highlight the influence of markets and climate change impacts, the Arctic is not a "wild west" where the changing nature and economic forces solely determine the future. The role of regulatory frameworks and administrative or political decisions remains crucial. This is, for instance, the case with the opening of new areas for oil and gas exploration and legislation pertaining to reindeer herding or nature protection. Local dynamics, social challenges and conflicts, environmental concerns, indigenous rights, as well as local perceptions of needs, risks and opportunities may facilitate, enhance or hinder particular projects or developments. Moreover, various elements of cultural globalisation or the IT revolution have a major imprint on social transformation throughout the region (Stępień *et al.*). The Arctic is distinct but certainly not disconnected from global changes.

So far, the pace of socioeconomic developments is in general moderate. This is in contradiction to the dominant media coverage portraying climate change as ushering in a race among states and businesses for the region's plentiful hydrocarbon resources, minerals and navigational highways. This image of the region has been fuelled by events such as the 2007 and 2012 Arctic Ocean September sea ice minima, planting of the Russian flag at the North Pole, increased number of Arctic transit voyages (even though the increase was rather moderate), and the interest of Asian states and companies. However, these dramatic narratives do not find support among expert circles or local actors.[5]

Instead, economic developments and social changes occur mostly gradually and unevenly across the Arctic. In the coming decades, there might be sectors (*e.g.* minerals mining, van Dam *et al.*) that stagnate or even bust. Therefore, it is not guaranteed that economic affluence resolves the social challenges troubling today many remote Arctic locations.

The Arctic Ocean proper (compared to adjacent waters such as the Barents or Beaufort seas) is an area that receives particularly much attention from environmental NGOs, media, policy-makers and the public. However, the developments in fisheries, shipping and hydrocarbon extraction in this area are predicted to be either very limited or decades away (Sander *et al.*; Arnarsson and Justus; Łuszczuk *et al.*).

In terms of international relations, the Arctic remains a zone of co-operation and no major tensions originating from within the region are expected. However,

5 Koivurova, T. (2013). The Dialectic of Understanding Progress in Arctic Governance, *Michigan State International Law Review*, 22, 1–21; Arbo, P., Iversen, A., Knool, M., Ringholm, T. & Sander, G. (2013). "Arctic Futures. Conceptualisations and images of a changing Arctic," *Polar Geography*, 36(3), 163–182.

conflicts outside the Arctic – especially, the current situation between the Western powers and Russia due to the conflict in Ukraine and the Russian annexation of Crimea – may affect regional governance, even if likely to a comparatively lesser degree than other areas of international co-operation between Russia and the West.

Consequently, policies and strategies risk being misguided if they are based on such notions as "Arctic boom". This does not mean that current and expected economic and social developments do not require enhancement of policies and governance systems as well as investments in research and infrastructure. Owing to the characteristics of the Arctic environmental and social landscape, even activities that are moderate in scale may be connected with major impacts. There is a need to monitor change and adapt policies to shifting social, economic and environmental conditions. Furthermore, it is always possible that unexpected political and economic events (*e.g.* energy or political crises) will trigger or restrict economic developments.

There is a risk that as the expected rapid developments are unlikely to materialize in the near-term perspective, the political attention to the Arctic affairs decreases. Consequently, the pressure on addressing real challenges in the region could subside, leading to regulatory, monitoring or funding gaps. While we should appreciate that at least in regard to large-scale human activities there seems to be more time to design appropriate regulatory and technological solutions, the challenges do not disappear. The involvement of regional actors is necessary to understand actual challenges and develop effective, tailor-made responses.

Industries may complement one another to contribute to a more diversified economic structure. Infrastructures created for one activity may beneficially serve other industries. The availability of viable Arctic transport may serve as an enabler of various activities (tourism, extractive activities, mining, forestry, etc.) and may in the long run serve economic development outside the Arctic as well. However, conflicts also emerge. If fisheries and hydrocarbon extraction or tourism and mining are developed in the same region, tensions or local conflicts could occur (Arnarsson and Justus; Łuszczuk *et al.*; Latola *et al.*). The impacts are particularly pronounced when multiple activities result in cumulative impacts. Some livelihoods, like reindeer herding, are more vulnerable to pressures and there may be limits to the cumulative impacts they can withstand. In addition, Arctic hydrocarbon extraction in the long term involves a dilemma: climate change that plays a role in opening the Arctic – mainly through transport accessibility – to offshore hydrocarbon extraction is partly caused by the combustion of fossil fuels, and bringing a new hydrocarbon province into production will exacerbate the effects.

## 3 The EU and the Arctic: Taking the Relationship Forward

The EU's role differs depending on the sector as well as geographically: in the EU Arctic, EEA, broader European Arctic, whole circumpolar North or the Arctic Ocean proper. It is important that EU policy-makers and other European actors (such as media, NGOs, national decision-makers) perceive the European Arctic's biological and cultural diversity, social and economic development and the rights of its indigenous peoples as a "European issue", just as is the case with any other EU region.

The EU not only influences the Arctic via its environmental and economic footprint,[6] but is itself also affected by changes in the region, as shown in the chapters within this volume. Of critical consequence for Europe are Arctic amplification effects within the changing global climate, including the rise in the sea level, and the significance of the Arctic for shaping Europe's weather patterns (chapter by Strahlendorff *et al.*). Gradual opening of Arctic sea routes will be important for European transport. Arctic shipping will require construction of ice-classed vessels, many of them likely to be designed and constructed in the EU (Sander *et al.*). Arctic fisheries are an important source of food for Europe (Arnarsson and Justus). The EU is a major importer of Arctic oil and gas (Łuszczuk *et al.*). Northern Fennoscandia is one of the main regions for EU domestic minerals production (van Dam *et al.*). European tourists increasingly take advantage of the North's recreational potential and its rich biodiversity (Latola *et al.*). Northern cities are innovation centres of importance at the European level. Arctic cultures – including the culture of the Sámi, the EU's only recognised indigenous people (within the European continent[7]) – are an indispensable part of Europe's cultural diversity (Stępień *et al.*).

Over the last decade, the European Union has made much progress in clarifying its approach to the Arctic, moving towards more nuanced and cautious approaches (Stępień and Koivurova in this volume). The currently upheld overall aim is to ensure that the EU policy is responsible, based on knowledge and engagement.[8] Future evolution of EU strategic thinking should also be

6 See Cavalieri, S. et al. (Ecologic Institute and others) (2010). "EU Arctic Footprint and Policy Assessment Report." http://arctic-footprint.eu/. Accessed 10 January 2014.

7 For instance, French Guiana is fully a part of the European Union, with the indigenous population of the region holding EU citizenship.

8 Developing a European Union Policy towards the Arctic Region: progress since 2008 and next steps. Joint Communication of the European Commission and the High Representative of the European Union for Foreign Affairs and Security Policy to the European Parliament and the Council. Brussels, 26.6.2012. JOIN(2012) 19 final.

realistic, focused on areas where the EU has the greatest influence, aligned with Arctic governance frameworks, and aimed at addressing genuine environmental, social and economic challenges faced by the region. The areas where the EU has the greatest credibility as a policy actor certainly include climate change, research, technological expertise, and high safety and environmental standards.

Policy-making processes addressing Arctic issues or affecting Arctic regions have to take diversity of the Arctic into account. Stakeholder engagement may help to understand specific local concerns. EU policy-makers and other EU stakeholders need to act with care when discussing "the Arctic" in an abstract manner. Statements true for the European Arctic or for the EU Arctic may lead to misunderstandings when applied to other parts of the Circumpolar North.

In the light of region's diversity, the complexity and fragmentation should not be necessarily seen as disadvantages of Arctic governance.[9] Even within the fragmented governance landscape, the EU can positively contribute to gradual integration and enhancement within some sectors of Arctic governance, such as shipping or biodiversity. This can be achieved primarily owing to the EU's influence on the relevant international frameworks and participation in the venues of Arctic regional governance.

In order to strike the balance between consistence and flexibility of the EU's Arctic policy and to focus on areas where it can make the greatest positive difference, the future EU Arctic policy could more clearly accentuate the EU's role and priorities in the European Arctic (not necessarily only the EU Arctic). In this way the EU would improve its image in the region and underline its status as an Arctic actor. Although the main global trends and pan-Arctic environmental priorities should not be overlooked, such a more focused approach could result in EU institutions gaining Europe-specific Arctic expertise, leading also to greater influence at the circumpolar level. Because of the European Arctic, the EU is in a different position in regard to Arctic affairs than actors like China or India. There appears to be a rising recognition of such positioning of the EU in the region, as the need to strengthen the European Arctic dimension in the overall EU's Arctic policy has been emphasized also in the recent EU policy documents, especially in the European Parliament's resolution on the EU strategy for the Arctic from March 2014.[10]

9 Young, O.R. (2011). "If an Arctic Ocean Treaty is Not the Solution, What is the Alternative?" *Polar Record* 47, 327–334.

10 European Parliament. (2014). Joint Motion for a Resolution on the EU strategy for the Arctic (2013/2595(RSP)), http://www.europarl.europa.eu/sides/getDoc.do?pubRef=-//EP//TEXT+MOTION+P7-RC-2014-0229+0+DOC+XML+V0//EN. Accessed 15 March 2014.

However, challenges particular to the European Arctic – as a region distinct within the broader, circumpolar context – as well as goals and priorities specific for that region are not clearly elaborated in the EU Arctic statements. The policy documents should identify which aims and actions refer to the Circumpolar Arctic and which to the European and the EU Arctic realms. In this context, various EU cohesion and regional co-operation funding instruments are among the most important tools at the EU's disposal. It could prove advantageous to bring a variety of EU programmes, initiatives and actions in the European Arctic under a common framework. That may be beneficial both for long-term policy performance and for enhancing perception of the EU within the region. And indeed, the Council in its Conclusions from May 2014 encouraged the Commission "to ensure effective synergies between the various EU funding instruments in the Arctic region",[11] to which call the Commission responded later in 2014 with opening a consultation process on the "streamlining [of the] EU funding in the European Arctic".[12]

In the previous European Commission college, the "Arctic voice" was largely shared between the European External Action Service and the DG Maritime Affairs and Fisheries, with coordinative meetings between officers dealing with Arctic issues within different services. Such arrangement encouraged focus on Arctic affairs as primarily external and maritime, while the EU Arctic was to certain extent left at the margin. So far, balancing between the European – Circumpolar Arctic or external-internal dimensions in the Jean-Claude Juncker's Commission would need to be done within the framework of the previous arrangements. However, bringing together environment and maritime affairs portfolios in the hand of one commissioner could be seen as potentially strengthening the terrestrial dimension of the EU Arctic policy. Additionally, the network members of the "Strategic Environmental Impact Assessment of development of the Arctic" project indicated that there is a need for an intergovernmental panel for the EU Member States and EU institutions. Established by the EU and ideally supported by the network of Arctic expertise institutions, the panel could facilitate discussions about EU policies regarding the Arctic region, EU Arctic strategy, and Arctic initiatives in the EU and its Member States. Thus, vertical coherence within the EU could be enhanced.

11 Council of the European Union, Council conclusions on developing a European Union Policy towards the Arctic Region, Foreign Affairs Council meeting, Brussels, 12 May 2014.

12 European Commission, Public consultation on streamlining EU funding in the European Arctic, http://ec.europa.eu/dgs/maritimeaffairs_fisheries/consultations/arctic-eu-funding/doc/consultation-paper_en.pdf. Accessed 14 February 2015.

## 4 Practical Steps for the EU: Enhanced Understanding of and Response to Arctic Change in Cooperation with Arctic Partners and Stakeholders

Numerous uncertainties and the dynamic nature of Arctic change require an in-depth understanding of the physical, biological and social processes. Thus, enhancing Arctic knowledge, at least partly through involvement of Arctic partners and stakeholders, and taking part in regional cooperation remain the key concrete contributions of the EU.

The EU is an important sponsor of Arctic research, and plays a key role in the development of technologies and innovations necessary to address Arctic challenges. However, the findings of EU-funded research could be better communicated to EU decision-makers, Arctic stakeholders and the EU public at large in formats adjusted to the needs and capacities of particular audiences. The role of science communication is indispensable. Moreover, other forms of knowledge (for instance, coming from stakeholders) need to be taken into account in decision-making.

One of the key means towards a more comprehensive understanding of Arctic change is assessment work. Assessments are particularly important as tools bridging science and policy in the Arctic context, where a number of actors external to the region are present and where some local actors lack capacities to conduct their own knowledge-building activities. Assessments bring together available knowledge and information in formats that could contribute to forging a common understanding among researchers, sectors of the public and policy-makers. Thus, assessments enhance knowledge- and participation-based decision-making.[13] There is a particular need for integrated assessments, which should be characterised by greater attention to social and socioeconomic problems than is currently paid. Such integration should occur at all levels of assessment work: from environmental impact assessments and strategic integrated assessments to regional environmental assessments. Some important issues recur across the chapters and could be taken up in greater detail in further assessment work in regard to the relationship between the EU and the Arctic, including: biodiversity, short-lived climate forcers, community viability, indigenous peoples' rights, participation, and research.

A more effective and meaningful participation of Arctic stakeholders in decision-making processes is a vital component of a response to social and environmental changes and to the rising complexity of Arctic governance. It is

13 See also, Kankaanpää and Śmieszek (2014), *op.cit.*

crucial to enhance two-way communication between Arctic stakeholders and EU decision-makers as well as to facilitate space for stakeholders to enter into dialogue with each other. Arctic inhabitants, communities, businesses, local governments and organisations lack information on the EU's role, interests and relevant activities in the region. Enhanced participation enables understanding of values and livelihoods that might be neglected from the perspective of densely populated European economic centres, where the human-environment relation (*e.g.* subsistence use of forests) may not be as vital for culture and identity as in the North (chapters by Latola *et al.* and Stępień *et al.*). However, at the same time, the EU institutions need to take into account limited capacities of many Arctic actors[14] and better coordinate various stakeholder consultations mechanisms. Currently, a number of processes – *e.g.*, "Strategic Environmental Impact Assessment of Development of the Arctic" commissioned by the DG Environment, operation of the Arctic NGO Forum, the DG Mare consultations on streamlining Arctic funding and the work with stakeholders within the EU-Polarnet process leading to the European Polar Research Programme, supervised by the DG Research – engages in fact the same group of actors. Better coordination would allow avoiding stretching the capacities and patience of Arctic academic, NGO, policy-making, local and indigenous communities.

EU policies designed for a broad European constituency may also need to be assessed in the context of Arctic-specific challenges. That is because particular measures may entail outcomes in the North that diverge from those anticipated in Europe's more southern latitudes, including environmental and transport regulations (chapters by van Dam *et al.*; Latola *et al.;* and Stępień *et al.*). Where relevant, the European Commission's impact assessments of proposed policies or regulations could incorporate a special focus on how such new policy or legislative proposals influence the region.[15] Due to the complexity of both Arctic realities and EU policy frameworks, the identification of policies that have consequences in the Arctic constitutes a major challenge and requires stakeholder engagement. EU cohesion and co-operation programmes

14 Stepien, A., Koivurova, T., Gremsperger A. & Niemi, H. (2014). "Arctic Indigenous Peoples and the Challenge of Climate Change," in Tedsen, E., Cavalieri, S. & Kraemer, R. (eds.), Arctic Marine Governance: Opportunities for Transatlantic Cooperation. Dordrecht: Springer.

15 As was already partly suggested (regarding environmental impacts) in the Commission's 2008 Arctic Communication. See European Commission (2008). Communication COM/2008/0763 from the Commission to the European Parliament and the Council – The European Union and the Arctic Region.

in the North are an example of the added value provided by stakeholder involvement. There, the key role of local actors in setting objectives has resulted in the alignment of local perceptions of needs and challenges and the goals of EU-funded programmes.[16]

In the context of participation and stakeholder engagement it must be remembered that indigenous peoples underline that they are also rights-holders. The participation of indigenous peoples (in particular the Sámi) in decision-making should be addressed in the light of evolving international indigenous rights (including land rights and the principle of free, prior and informed consent), primarily the UN Declaration of the Rights of Indigenous Peoples.[17] Responsible decision-making with regard to EU policies that may affect Arctic indigenous communities requires their meaningful participation. The concept of establishing a more permanent presence of the Arctic indigenous peoples or the Sámi in Brussels remains relevant (see Stępień and Koivurova; as well as Stępień *et al.* in this volume).[18] Such representation has to be independent from state and regional authorities and would need to address the constraints of indigenous organisations' human and financial capacities.

The EU institutions should build on their experience and enhance already existing engagement mechanisms. This refers in particular to the (EU – Indigenous) Arctic dialogue format, by continuing the path taken in the 2013 and 2014 meetings and making the dialogue more regular, including continued long-term participation of indigenous leaders. The discussions should be more focused and specific, including practical, pressing matters and EU strategic interests in the Arctic (for example, by discussing the EU's strategic interest in developing EU-domestic resource extraction).

In order to enhance its legitimacy, presence and influence in the region, the EU has to co-operate closely with Arctic states and local actors.[19] That includes substantial contributions to the work of the Arctic Council in the EU's capacity as an *observer in principle,* and perhaps a full observer in the coming years. Support for and participation in Arctic Council knowledge-building and standard-setting activities regarding maritime shipping, climate change adaptation, black carbon, oil spills, and biodiversity are particularly

16 At least according to feedback received in the stakeholder consultations.

17 United Nations Declaration on the Rights of Indigenous Peoples (2007), General Assembly Resolution 61/295, New York, 13 September 2007.

18 Already suggested at the 2010 "Arctic Dialogue" meeting. See the website of the European Commission's DG Maritime Affairs and Fisheries at https://webgate.ec.europa.eu/maritimeforum/content/1831. Accessed 4 March 2014.

19 As has been clearly acknowledged in consequent EU Arctic policy documents.

relevant. Emphasis should be given to the involvement at the level of the Arctic Council's working groups.

Within the area of greatest EU influence – the European Arctic – the European Commission should engage in more active and substance-oriented participation in Barents co-operation, including encouraging and supporting long-term actions and coming forth with its own proposals.

As strongly highlighted by stakeholders, although very challenging (especially after March 2014), collaboration with Russian partners in the region is a necessary element of EU Arctic policy and regional governance in the European Arctic. Since the early 1990s, Arctic cooperation has been largely a trust-building project and the primary result of the tensions connected with the crisis in Ukraine is the collapse of trust between the West and Russia. Without this trust, the cooperation may continue, but could deteriorate to technical issues and purely formal communication lacking any real content. There appears to be a broad consensus – also within the EU institutions – that an effort should be made for the current tensions between Russia and the West to have minimal impact on the practical and people-to-people aspects of Arctic cooperation.[20] The Arctic cooperation cannot be completely detached from the global events. Technical cooperation in the Arctic Council or in the Barents Euro-Arctic Region appears so far to withhold the storm, although not without problems.[21] We are yet to see the effects of the conflict in Ukraine on the new post-2014 EU programmes or developing more ambitious projects with Russian partners, including research cooperation. However, in the light of the international crisis, Arctic regional cooperation could be seen as one of the areas where the EU can productively engage Russia and maintain it as one of the policy spaces from which the future post-crisis EU-Russia relationship could be revitalized. While the participation of the EU in the circumpolar Arctic cooperation meets with difficulties and anxiety of the Arctic actors (Stępień and Koivurova in this volume), it is in the European Arctic that such ties can be maintained and even strengthened.

---

20 Discussion during the seminar "EU in the Arctic, Arctic in the EU" on 11 September 2014 in Brussels (final seminar of the "Strategic Environmental Impact Assessment of Development of the Arctic" project).

21 Some aspects of people-to-people cooperation appear to be more affected by the weak ruble than the tensed international situation.

# Index

www.ingramcontent.com/pod-product-compliance
Lightning Source LLC
LaVergne TN
LVHW011110300926
849160LV00008B/336
* 9 7 8 9 0 0 4 3 0 3 1 7 1 *